T0397603

Advance Praise for *Beyond Collective Action Problems*

"Nobel prize–winning Elinor Ostrom's study of farmer-managed irrigation systems in Nepal was the foundation of her famous theory of governance of the commons. With Ostrom's blessings and data, Atul Pokharel, whose own family played a pivotal role in these successful community-managed irrigation systems, returns to them to compare how they have fared three decades later. What emerges is a gem of a book, a rare large-scale, temporal study of shared resource management, as painstakingly researched as it is powerfully argued. A magisterial multimethods research design allows Pokharel to develop a sophisticated theoretical framework that centers on a novel factor—farmers' perceptions of fairness. Pokharel's remarkable work is essential, accessible reading for scholars and practitioners of development alike."—Prerna Singh, Mahatma Gandhi Associate Professor of Political Science and International and Public Affairs, Brown University

"Atul Pokharel has shown once again that irrigation management is an ideal arena in which to study and understand collective action as a generic problem. The costs and benefits are very tangible, as is their distribution. His analysis with a time perspective of more than 30 years, combining quantitative and qualitative data, shows that sustained cooperation is a more significant phenomenon than just 'collective action,' which formal game theory has usually framed as a one-off decision. Pokharel's focus on perceived fairness as a determining factor is consistent with my own experience introducing participatory irrigation management in Sri Lanka, Nepal, and other countries. He elaborates usefully on Elinor Ostrom's consideration of equity, something that social scientists have mostly paid little attention to."—Norman Uphoff, Professor Emeritus of Government and International Agriculture, Cornell University

"For scholars, as well as practitioners, who care about community management of physical infrastructure, this book demonstrates, conclusively, that a sense of fairness in the way organizations operate is the key to their performance. This book takes forward the research by Elinor Ostrom, a Nobel Laureate in Economics, to a new height by showing that only community-based organizations that distribute work load and resources fairly are sustainable in the long run. A must read for Political Economists and development planners who seek institutional understanding of success in developmental outcomes."—Bishwapriya Sanyal, Ford International Professor of Urban Development and Planning, MIT

Atul Pokharel has given us a fresh approach to a bundle of vexing societal problems: cooperation, fairness, and governmental roles in promoting the public interest. The prose is engaging, the insights are profound, and the implications will ripple across a wide variety of communities of scholars and practitioners, from irrigation and farming to cities and digital infrastructure.—Andrew L. Russell, Professor of History, SUNY Polytechnic Institute

Beyond Collective Action Problems

Perceived Fairness and Sustained Cooperation in Farmer Managed Irrigation Systems in Nepal

ATUL POKHAREL

OXFORD
UNIVERSITY PRESS

Oxford University Press is a department of the University of Oxford. It furthers the University's objective of excellence in research, scholarship, and education by publishing worldwide. Oxford is a registered trade mark of Oxford University Press in the UK and certain other countries.

Published in the United States of America by Oxford University Press 198 Madison Avenue, New York, NY 10016, United States of America.

CIP data is on file at the Library of Congress

ISBN 978–0–19–775579–2

DOI: 10.1093/oso/9780197755792.001.0001

Printed by Integrated Books International, United States of America

MIX
Paper
FSC   FSC® C183721

This book is dedicated to Iva, Ira, and Sritika.
You were patient beyond reason.

CONTENTS

PREFACE

The book is based on fieldwork for my doctoral dissertation at MIT, completed in 2014. However, the origin story begins before that. Some years before, Elinor Ostrom gave me a data set that her team used decades earlier to formulate their celebrated frameworks for governing the commons: 233 farmer-managed irrigation canals in Nepal. I went on to repeat this study using the same methods and instruments. This resulted in the first of its kind large-N data set of commons governance institutions over time. What set it apart was its strong internal validity, two observations per system, and recorded interviews with irrigators. This allowed me to, for the first time, directly examine the dynamics of cooperation and the factors affecting it in these types of situations in situ over decades. I found that the same set of cases that had informed Ostrom's dominant understanding of cooperation showed, on follow-up, that the key factor in sustained cooperation was perceived fairness. The myriad other factors that had been predicted by theory to affect individual incentives to cooperate mattered less than expected.

From the novel data set, the insights emerged gradually. They suggest that we begin to develop a new understanding of robust cooperation that is centered on avoiding patent unfairness. However, the evidence also showed that such an understanding would need to begin from a different conception of human beings, and a different philosophical framework. Instead of primarily reasoning as though they were instrumentally rational, many farmers reasoned as though they were motivated by perceptions of unfairness. What is more, these perceptions had common elements across cases—they were not entirely unique to each person. This led to the eventual realization that if the central challenge to initial cooperation is the well-studied collective action problem, the primary challenge to cooperation over time is a new type of problem: the problem of remaining fair (or fairness problems). I develop these ideas in this book, supported by relevant findings, and examine some of their implications for local governance of shared infrastructure.

The key insight that led to this formulation arose not from the new data set, but from the over 1,200 hours of interviews with 827 irrigators. This type and volume of qualitative data is not something that my predecessors had access to. An analysis of these interviews revealed that rather than behaving as though they were primarily boundedly rational actors seeking self-benefit in situations of uncertainty, a significant number appeared to behave as individuals attempting to avoid patent unfairness. The challenge in writing this book was understanding this unfairness aversion, describing it systematically and grasping how perceived fairness is a necessary condition for robust cooperation.

This journey began in the Autumn of 2010 when Elinor Ostrom gave a presentation about farmer-managed irrigation systems in Nepal at the Lincoln Land Institute. From the audience, I saw names that I recognized. My family, dependent on agriculture until one generation before mine, had relied on one of the farmer-managed irrigation systems in that presentation. The lecture derived three claims from these systems—they were more efficient, better maintained, and more equitable than comparable government-managed systems. Why? Because they were primarily managed by farmers. This was in line with the stories I had heard about the dysfunctional government that I had grown up under in Nepal. It reaffirmed my belief that even geographically isolated locations could do it on their own. It was reassuring because it seemed to confirm prevalent understandings—groups of farmers can do a lot and the government gets in the way.

However, I was curious about three things that weren't mentioned in the presentation: in my experience, some locals often sought out government assistance and involvement particularly in financial, technical and conflict matters; and the relationships with government agents were often far more ingrained than the image of isolated farmers in remote parts of Nepal conveys. There had been a ten-year civil war since these systems had been studied, and it remained a mystery how they fared.

So, I traveled to various parts of Nepal with several guides including non-governmental organizations (NGOs), Maoist cadres, and government extension agents. I lived with them, visited local drinking holes with them, walked hundreds of hours with them, and visited irrigation systems with them. And when I got back, I wrote an email to E. Ostrom with some things that I could not explain based on that presentation. With the intention of doing something small but more systematic to see what I misunderstood, I asked for the names of the systems in their study. Her reply surprised me. She not only encouraged me but handed me their data set (The Nepal Irrigation Institutions and Systems Database) and coding forms with the blessing that if I could figure out how to use it, "you are free to do what you want with it." This started a conversation that would unfortunately be cut short with her passing.

The journey that began there would end up connecting me to my roots. As I scrutinized the studies of irrigation systems, I encountered something unexpected. In his 1989 description of one of these cases, the Sange Patyeni Kulo, Dr. Prachanda Pradhan, noted how the villagers were particularly active and one farmer stood out as adept at working with the government. His initiative, it seemed, was responsible for significant improvements to this system in the decades prior. It would turn out that this farmer was my grandfather. When I visited this system later during fieldwork, I offended many by not approaching them personally. They only heard about me after I had left. I was unable to eat at their homes when I was doing fieldwork and I have not forgotten how some had been brought to tears with disappointment. "I could not feed Gobardhan's grandson when he came to our village," one older gentleman lamented. I hope that their generosity has made it into this work.

My first order of thanks, therefore, goes to Elinor Ostrom. Inspired by the thoroughness of her team's work, and boosted by her help, I set out to extend that important work in a different direction in order to add to the database. The work here was done in the rigorous spirit of Ostrom herself, with her blessings and crucial support. She blessed my ambitious (and we thought, impossible) goal of repeating and extending the entire study thirty years later and encouraged me to pursue this line of inquiry. Indeed, the findings address weaknesses that Ostrom (and others) had already suspected needed attention. Several people have asked me what she would have thought of this work. I suspect she would have found something interesting in my observations and would have appreciated the methodological honesty that I have tried to practice.

In many places, I have framed my arguments as criticisms of views suggested by Ostrom. This is only because Ostrom provides the most empirically supported, clearest, and most compelling arguments I have encountered in support of that community's school of thought as applied to shared resource governance. Although I am no longer in complete agreement with that view, it is not due to the lack of clarity of Ostrom's formulation.

In the same breath, I would like to thank five others who influenced this work beyond description. Bish Sanyal consistently encouraged me to push through to the conclusion while giving me the freedom to actually do so. The final words of this work are therefore based on his question upon hearing the raw findings from my fieldwork: "Are you saying that sustainability is a consequence of fairness?" Richard Locke gave me everything I needed to get started and provided me moral, financial, and academic support throughout the journey. It was a decisive turning point when Rick asked me after I presented the modest small-N study I was contemplating, "What do you think it would take to redo the whole thing?" Amartya Sen alerted me to fairness, urged me to turn away from reading the literature and toward listening carefully to the 827 interviews, guided me in my readings of relevant philosophy texts, and gave me a clear goal by alerting me, "The road from fairness to Ostrom is a long one." I took building it as a challenge, and have made it this far because of his steady hand. Judith Tendler's influence also pervades this work. She led me to ask Ostrom for the data set in the first place and guided my thinking very carefully thereafter. Finally, John F. Nash Jr., my mentor and friend, constantly encouraged me to complete the "expedition" that I started with him as a research assistant roaming n-dimensional space looking for solutions to three-person cooperative games. Neither of us could have known that beyond our topological explorations lay the formidable dragons of human perception.

Many have read the manuscript in parts, at various stages and in different forms. They have all provided valuable suggestions for which I offer thanks. Usha Pokharel, Jagadish C. Pokharel, Norman Uphoff, Robert Bates, Prachanda Pradhan, Ganesh Shivakoti, Robert Yoder, Ulrich Frey, Jonathan Morduch, and John Forrester were invaluable. Shruti Punjabi and Julie Elliott provided excellent research assistance. Without the steady help and friendship of Eleni Manis, my philosophical explorations would have taken far longer and moved much slower. Ajaya Budhathoki, Sujana Dhital, Uday Ale, and all of my enumerators were instrumental in helping with the data collection. Ajaya's care in transcribing interviews was unmatched, and his dedication to the project was essential. The companionship of friends who walked with me throughout this journey, in particular Omprakash Gnawali, Andre Kurs, Aaron Silberstein, Rajesh Veeraraghavan, and Monica Belevan, helped me endure. There are many more to thank for discussions and encouragement: [Anu, Amul, and Ayush] Pokharel, Prerna Singh, Andrew Russell, Natasha Iskandar, Paul Smoke, Mike Piore, Annette Kim, Alice Amsden, Lawrence Susskind, Deborah Stone, Jinhua Zhao, Gabriella Carolini, Jason Jackson, Abby Spinak, Meenu Tewari, Charlie Hoch, Balakrishnan Rajagopal, Nicholas Marantz, Tijs Van Maasakkers, Yuan Xiao, Amit Prothi, Jeffrey Hammer, Arun Agrawal, Tony Levitas, Andrew Scrank, Patrick Heller, Zairo Cheibub, Elicia Ratajczyk, Nirupama Rao, Bernadette Baird-Zars, Ingrid Gould Ellen, Harry Blair, and everyone else I have missed.

My daughters Iva and Ira and my wife Sritika patiently allowed the project to mature and take on the better developed form that it now has. Without Sritika's encouragement and support, this work would have remained merely a shadow of what it has become. Ira's uncompromising demand for attention proved perfect for turning away from the project and turning back when the mind was better rested. Her impositions were critical for steady forward progress. Iva's irresistible "Hey!" carried me across the finish line. All of them patiently, and sometimes unknowingly, endured the personal demands of this project.

I am deeply indebted to the farmers, officials, scholars, and others who made time for me. Some sheltered me when I was stranded in the middle of a jungle at midnight and jackals wailed on all sides. Others sat and talked for hours. Others warned me of dangers, intellectual and political, that lie ahead. I have tried to honor your memory by listening closely to your words, again and again, while trying to carefully understand your reasons, and faithfully sharing them with the wider world. None of this will be new to you, and I hope that I have been a worthy scribe.

Finally, my editor at Oxford University Press, David McBride, and the series editor Ashutosh Varshney, deserve much credit for taking on a project that many others felt was too challenging. Thank you. What you are about to read was also made far more accessible by two thoughtful reviewers they selected. Shortcomings in this book are of my own doing.

Sustained Cooperation, Fairness Problems, and Irrigation Systems

Why do some groups successfully sustain cooperation to use and maintain shared resources while others don't? In a world in which a majority of people live in cities and depend on shared physical infrastructure, where the shared digital infrastructure of open source software undergirds the internet, where water and other natural resources are increasingly scarce, understanding the conditions under which community governance can be both equitable and sustainable is of critical importance to scholars and policy makers alike. This book aims to improve our understanding of this fundamental phenomenon of sustained cooperation around shared resources through the study of 233 long-running community-managed irrigation systems in Nepal—a rare, large scale, study over time of common governance institutions. It does so by revisiting and expanding upon, three decades later, the famous set of successful irrigation systems in Nepal that Elinor Ostrom cited in her Nobel Prize speech (Nobel Media AB, 2014) as inspiring the development of the widely influential framework of *Governing the Commons* (Ostrom, 1990) and associated work.

These community-managed irrigation systems in Nepal show the hallmarks of long-enduring community resources: the right institutions, high social capital, relative autonomy and a robust ability to solve collective action problems. Yet decades later some continue to perform well, conceptualized in terms of physical condition and ability to adequately and reliably deliver water, while others have declined. Why? What lies beyond collective action problems?

The answer to this puzzle of sustaining cooperation, I argue, lies in understanding how communities address what I call the fairness problem. Across these cases, the longer individuals cooperate the more they become aware of how far their cooperative arrangement has diverged from the initial promise of fairness. This perception of fairness affects their commitment to maintaining the shared resource and participating in the institutions for governing it.

Variations in perceptions of fairness, reflected in how willing each individual is to continue to cooperate, are hypothesized to make these systems more or less robust to shocks, which together generate divergences in the performance of the shared infrastructure. I construct this argument using a mixed methods approach—using ethnographic observations and over eight hundred interviews with individual farmers to build the fairness argument and using a statistical analysis of a novel data set of these irrigation systems between 1976 and 2013 to support it.

The ability to devise institutions to help solve collective action problems is widely believed to be one of the most significant determinants of sustained cooperation in groups (Ostrom, 1990). While there is, in general, a positive relationship between the condition of community infrastructure and robust local institutions for collective action, there are some exceptions (Meinzen-Dick, 2007). Drawing on a combination of 827 structured, open-ended farmer interviews,[1] 30 focus group interviews, an examination of formal documents of Water User Associations, participant observation at community meetings and ethnographic observations from two villages, I trace the variations in performance of these systems to differences in how fair the users perceive their institutions to be. I show how these individuals behave as though they are unfairness averse.

In order to explore the determinants of sustained cooperation that are not accounted for by differences in the institutions for solving collective action problems, I first compare the reasons users reduce their cooperation with their reasons for sustaining it. The reasons for those who stopped cooperating are particularly interesting: they appear to be related to fairness, and unrelated to the reasons for previously continuing to cooperate. Following the comparison across these two types of individuals, I analyze the different reasons for stopping or reducing one's cooperation to identify seven common fairness-related reasons across individuals for reducing cooperation.

I then use cross-sectional and longitudinal statistical analyses to examine the plausibility of this fairness argument across all 272 irrigation systems in a first-of-its-kind data set, including nearly all subnational districts in Nepal. Addressing a range of alternative explanations including external shocks such as civil war, weather events, assistance from government agencies, and outside actors, group heterogeneity—including gender, ethnicity, language and political affiliation, trust, and prior cooperation—I show that perceived fairness, measured through the seven indicators of fairness derived from interviews, is a more reliable indicator of the performance of these systems over time.

---

[1] See Appendix 1: Methods, which tabulates the characteristics of the respondents as well as interview protocols.

I generalize this argument beyond these irrigation systems in Nepal in two main ways. First, by developing the concept of unfairness aversion, I show how the conceptual framework underlying the collective action focused approach to cooperation—itself based on modern game theory—can only incorporate a special case of the fairness problem. Second, I trace the framework for governing the commons from Elinor Ostrom (McGinnis, 2011), a framework which the cases in this book were used to develop, to its philosophical underpinnings in social contract theory to argue that adopting a more inclusive moral conception of human behavior is necessary to understand the relationship between fairness and cooperation.

Beyond adding to the large corpus of studies on irrigation governance in South Asia by authors such as Norman Uphoff (1991), Robert Wade (1979), Robert Chambers (1988), Elinor Ostrom (Ostrom et al., 2011), Arun Agrawal (2001), Ulrich Frey (2020), and many others, this book promises to push forward the scholarship on the determinants of sustained cooperation in the provision of public goods in two key ways. The dominant paradigm in the scholarship on the collective provision of public goods has been that of collective action problems. A number of influential studies on commons governance, public goods provision, and taxation have established a positive relationship between perceived fairness and collective action problems in public service provision. Classic studies by Mancur Olson Jr. (1965), Robert Axelrod (2006), Robert Williamson (1975), Elinor Ostrom (1990), and Margaret Levi (1989) have all sought to explain the provision of public goods and services with respect to credibly preventing free riding, shirking, and otherwise opportunistic behavior. Recent studies by Samuel Bowles (Gintis and Bowles, 2011), Herbert Gintis (Gintis and Bowles, 2011), Ernst Fehr (Fehr and Fischbacher, 2003), John Roemer (2019), and Kenneth Scheve and David Stasavage (2017) have examined fairness and collective action problems in contexts as diverse as fishery management, market governance, wealth taxes, and human evolution. I seek to shift the emphasis away from collective action problems altogether to a different type of problem that groups face, showing how, at least in the context of shared infrastructure governance, the fairness problem can become a more significant challenge than collective action problems for sustaining group cooperation.

When the literature on cooperation and public goods provision has taken fairness into account, it has almost always done so by reducing it to norms of fairness shared by a group.[2] The accepted convention from an influential and

---

[2] To retain internal validity, I use the same definitions of key terms such as norms, rules, and institutions as earlier studies unless otherwise stated. Ostrom (2005) provides a thorough explanation of these terms. Institutions are a collection of working rules known to all users. A rule is a language statement that is expressed as either ignoring, forbidding, permitting, or requiring an action. Rules are typically written down and backed by punishment. Norms are unwritten but commonly

extensive body of research is that fairness matters to sustained cooperation only insofar as shared norms of fairness help groups to solve collective action problems. In contrast, my analysis of irrigation systems in Nepal shows that the significance of fairness need not derive from its connection to collective action problems, and that the problem of remaining fair is far more than that of developing shared norms. Cases in which groups possess all the necessary institutions and experience to solve collective action problems but still fail to maintain their shared irrigation systems show that solving collective action problems is not enough: groups must also address the fairness problem.

In the following pages, I aim to show how the survival of these cooperative systems eventually depends on the ability of the community to solve myriad problems in terms of remaining fair. These fairness problems are distinct from well-known collective action problems, which have received overwhelming attention in the study of cooperation. The focus on initiating cooperation among selfish individuals has contributed to this emphasis. I argue here for recognizing the greater significance of fairness problems to sustained cooperation.

Cooperation and Its Challenges

The fruits of cooperation are all around us. Many positive outcomes can only be achieved by individuals working together over extended periods of time. Our ability to survive and prosper depends on cooperation at some level, from the irrigation systems that enabled ancient humans to abandon their nomadic lifestyle to the free and open source software that undergirds the Internet. My intention in this book is to improve our understanding of sustained cooperation by showing how it depends on user perceptions that the cooperative arrangement is fair. For things like using and maintaining shared resources, simply agreeing to cooperate and successfully evoking this cooperation where previously there was none is not sufficient. A simple thought experiment suffices to underscore this point. Suppose that all who depend on the resource (the community) desire a joint outcome such as preventing resource depletion. Suppose further that they recognize that working together is necessary to achieve the goal, and then they begin to work together. Sustaining this mutual cooperation toward the shared end can still lead to new obstacles. The contours of these challenges in sustaining cooperation hew closely to the particulars of each situation, especially the features specific to each resource.

---

known rules without formal punishment (although there might be other punishments such as shunning). These terms are elaborated in later chapters.

The social factors that influence the likelihood that a community solves collective action problems through initial cooperation also affect whether and how these new challenges are met. A familiar example of this common social factor is mutual trust (Locke, 2001; Ostrom and Walker, 2003) between individual cooperators in the community. Unlike the old problems, however, this new set of problems takes on greater significance once individuals have already been cooperating for some time. It consists of the challenges associated with remaining fair (Gintis et al., 2005). These challenges deserve to be better understood. The dynamics of these dual problems and associated social factors such as trust and perceived fairness underlie successful sustained cooperation around the shared resources upon which societies depend.

These two families of challenges—those of evoking and sustaining cooperation—originate in the demands of cooperating over time. Cooperating over time typically requires that a significant proportion of the group commit to behaving in ways that will privilege longer-term, more uncertain results for the group over immediate, more certain gains for oneself. Having made this commitment, these individuals must consistently act on it, which sounds easier than it is at times. For example, there are situations in which even reason dictates that the most beneficial thing to do is to "free-ride, shirk or otherwise act opportunistically" (Ostrom, 1990, p. 29). Even more common are moments when emotion tempts one to act selfishly against one's best reason.

Thus, figuring out how each member of a group should behave in order to achieve a future outcome is one of the group's initial challenges. Consistently getting each other to behave in the desired way is another. These are examples from the first set of challenges, which pertain to initiating cooperation. Once these initial challenges are surmounted, users can begin to cooperate. As they do so, the rules for guiding their behavior also need to be updated in consonance with changing circumstances. These updates can be challenging because every rule change affects each member differently. Left as they are, however, even well-intended arrangements can lead to undesirable outcomes. In addition, the rules also need to be fair. These are examples of challenges from the second set of challenges, which pertains to sustaining cooperation.

Trust is often suggested as a way to move past both families of challenges (Ostrom and Walker, 2003), but trust has its limits. Take the example of discrimination. Even users who trust each other fully would not knowingly commit to rules that discriminate against them, nor would they continue to act in accordance with rules that produce discriminatory results (Fehr and Fischbacher, 2003; Gintis et al., 2003, 2005). This type of fairness can be difficult to pin down once and for all: In this example, how does one guess whether results will be discriminatory? Thus, trust does not ensure that groups will create fair rules to which individuals can commit to achieve future gains.

Both types of challenge can be overcome, as enduring examples of user-governed shared resources show. However, prior studies have shown that not all groups of individuals sharing a resource can overcome the initial challenges to working together, or commit themselves to rule-bound behavior over time (Ostrom, 2005, p. 282). Why is it that some of these groups are able to use and maintain shared resources over extended periods of time while others are not? More generally, under what conditions can a group of interdependent individuals sustain cooperation?

Distinguishing these two phases of cooperation—initial and sustained—further reveals that the challenges of sustaining cooperation are similar to but different from those regarding initial cooperation. The initial decision faced by the individual seeking to cooperate with another concerns whether to co-operate (Ostrom, 1990), whereas the decision faced by a long-time cooperator concerns whether to cease their cooperation. It is not obvious that the reasons for reducing one's commitment to a cooperative arrangement are related to the reasons for having committed to cooperating initially. And consequently, it cannot be assumed that the same conditions that favored initial cooperation are adequate to sustain that cooperation.

Fairness considerations undoubtedly figure into the initial decision to coop-erate or not (Fehr and Schmidt, 1999). It is commonly assumed that nobody would willingly commit to an arrangement they know is unfair to them. For in-stance, rules that explicitly discriminate against some users are typically regarded as unfair and therefore unacceptable to individuals seeking to cooperate to use and maintain a shared resource (Ostrom, 2005, p. 283). Regardless of how fair-ness considerations figure into the concerns of individuals when they initially committed to be subject to cooperative institutions, these considerations change as individuals continue to cooperate. For example, it is clearer after cooperating whether the outcomes of rules disproportionately favor some users over others, even if they were not explicitly intended to do so. In this way, sustained coop-eration in the use and maintenance of a shared resource eventually depends on user perceptions that the cooperative arrangement is fair (Ostrom, 1990, p. 171; Uphoff, 1992). More precisely, perceived fairness is a necessary condition for sustained cooperation between interdependent individual cooperators (Cole and McGinnis, 2017, p. 67).

As I aim to show, perceived fairness is not easily reduced to a single measure-ment or allocation formula. It is subjective, but also possesses more universal elements in the form of patent unfairness. And therefore, a fairness-centered understanding of cooperation is necessary to account for the critical role that perceptions of fairness play in sustained cooperation. It may also help to ex-plain why it is not unusual to find once successful user-managed irrigation sys-tems that have failed, free and open-source software projects plagued by bit rot, deteriorating community forests, and depleted common fish stock. In all of these examples, maintenance requires that a community somehow sustain cooperation to use and maintain (or govern) their shared resource. Sustained cooperation in turn requires that they continue to perceive the cooperative arrangements as fair. Those that come to be perceived as unfair have a lower chance of sustaining cooperation, even if the joint outcome continues to be valuable and desirable to the individual cooperators (Gintis et al., 2005; Poteete, Janssen, and Ostrom, 2010, p. 100). Consequently, maintenance suffers.

Theory and Practice of Cooperation

To further motivate this inquiry from a policy perspective, consider how understanding sustained cooperation is important not only to theory but also to practice. The quest to characterize the sustainability of community-managed resources is an instructive example of its importance. A major undertaking for development agencies in the past four decades has been the search for a minimal set of institutional features shared by a maximal variety of long-enduring community-governed resources. What these features are, how to evoke them, or how to instill them in various settings informed development policy as well as national policy (Chambers, 1988; Wade, 1988; Ostrom, 1990; Uphoff, 1991; Ostrom et al., 2011).

Two ideas about cooperation have been particularly influential. One is that communities of users have the capacity to self-organize to use and manage shared resources; the second is that they are likely to do so if certain conditions are met (Ostrom, 1990). The history of resource governance by state and commercial institutions is one of mixed success. So as international organizations recognized these community capacities, they began a push to enable self-governance of resources such as small-scale irrigation systems and forests by creating favorable conditions for it. One of the conditions set by international organizations was that states alter their laws to delegate greater responsibility to the users of these resources. Several developing country governments such as that of Nepal adopted laws "handing over" the control of resources to locals (Ribot, Agrawal, and Larson, 2006; Baldwin et al., 2016).

This radical decentralization agenda is underwritten by an understanding that users themselves can self-govern to use and manage a shared resource without depleting it, and that greater formal control over the resource is necessary for them to do this. One influential formulation of this idea from Ostrom (1990) is that the state should legally recognize the rights of resource users to organize to "devise their own institutions" without being "challenged by external governmental authorities." Ostrom's influential "Design Principles for Long-Enduring

CPR Resources" includes seven other institutional features that improve the likelihood of self-governance success. Of these, only one concerns state institutions: that basic institutional functions such as monitoring, enforcing and conflict resolution be available to these communities in "multiple layers" of "nested enterprises" should they need them (Ostrom, 1990, p. 90).

Overall, two design principles reduce the relevance of nonlocal actors in the governance of shared resources: (1) that states should be prevented from challenging decisions made by resource users, while (2) at the same time enabling them to make their own decisions (Mansbridge, 2014). They restrain the hand of external governmental agencies such as irrigation departments and forestry agencies in overseeing a nation's resources. They also reduce the responsibility of state institutions for the success or failure of local resource governance beyond the initial decision to devolve authority. Ostrom's list stayed relatively unchanged over three decades of research between 1990 and 2010,[3] and remains strongly influential (Cox, Arnold, and Tomás, 2010).

To look further into how theory and practice are intertwined in locally based resource governance, consider that Ostrom's design principles are derived from hundreds of cases of successful cooperation (Ostrom, 2010). Thousands more examples to support this list of principles come from a wide range of resources, time periods, and locations. These examples include fisheries, forests, pastures, groundwater, and small-scale irrigation systems (Frey, 2020). They were classified and analyzed using a set of related frameworks, the primary one being the Institutional Analysis and Development (IAD) framework (McGinnis, 2011). And these frameworks were constructed on the theoretical foundation of polycentric governance (Ostrom, 2010), which in turn rests on a particular philosophical conception of the social contract (see Chapter 4).

The frameworks for classifying these cases are built with the premise that individuals sharing a resource are not only doing the best for themselves but are also able to avoid collective action problems preventing successful cooperation (Ostrom, 1990). These frameworks challenge policymakers to recognize that users can self-govern shared resources while making no claim that they will find the best way to do it (Meinzen-Dick, 2007; Ostrom, 2007; Ostrom and Cox, 2010). They also put the onus on analysts to see particular situations through the eyes of a particular type of individual that is rational, self-interested, and fallible. This cost-benefit form of reasoning is exceptionally versatile (Elster, 1985). It also saves one the work of understanding other reasons that might direct human behavior. Any observed action is recast as due

---

[3] To see the changes, compare table 3.1 in Ostrom (1990, p. 90) and table 2.1 in Ostrom et al. (2009, p. 33). The surrounding text in the latter work provides reasons why these revisions were made.

to benefits outweighing costs. It is the task of the analyst to understand what factors into costs and benefits without entering into any more complex subjective assessments of mental processes.

In this view, a user can notice and thus be variously influenced by a range of variables. Each individual calibrates what the variables mean, individually or in combination, for their self-interest. They are then assumed to behave as though they are using that assessment to decide what to do. In cooperative situations, they can either cooperate with another user or not. The design principles, then, are an enumeration of what might convince that type of individual to behave cooperatively in order to avoid "tragedies" in a group (Hardin, 1968).

The design principles are ultimately based on an argument about institutions. This argument is that users have the capacity to (and should be allowed to) design and operate their own institutions for governing shared resources. The evidence supporting this argument consists of the aforementioned thousands of cases of surviving community governance arrangements. It is important to note that there are far fewer long-term longitudinal studies of the viability of these features than cross-sectional accounts based on a single snapshot in time.

Small-scale irrigation systems that bring water to smallholder farms are of particular interest to development agencies because of their connection to agriculture, food systems, and rural livelihoods. In the late 1970s, development agencies such as the World Bank sought to understand how communities were able to use their shared irrigation systems sustainably, while systems funded by international donors were in disrepair (Chambers, 1988; Uphoff, 1991). Having found examples of successful systems, a necessary first step for understanding why they endure and for improving community participation in general is documenting the features that they share. Ostrom's team subsequently recorded the features of those complex cases that were relevant to the IAD framework. The Nepal Irrigation Institutions and Systems (NIIS) database is a prominent example of a data set compiled to support this type of theory-informed meta-analysis of existing studies (Lam, 1998; Frey, 2020). Another such data set is the Common Pool Resource (CPR) database, which covers a wider range of resources (Poteete, Janssen, and Ostrom, 2010, p. 102). In this way, theory and policy have been intertwined.

Improving Existing Approaches

However, there are limits to what successful cases alone can reveal about the reasons for success. Here, this limitation means that it is not possible to know if those that failed shared or lacked the same features of surviving systems. In this way, using surviving examples alone to identify critical features risks generating logical fallacies: in this case, that those that survived did so because of the features they all share. Despite these dangers, generalizing based on existing cases is the best that can be done as long as long-term studies are unavailable. Among the extant data sets, the NIIS database remains the best available because of the large number of cases (233) and its strong internal validity within its framework. The cases it contains have been carefully parsed and classified according to the IAD framework. Thus, conclusions based on its analysis are likely to be more reliable than other datasets (Poteete, Janssen, and Ostrom, 2010, p. 105). Nevertheless, the only way to avoid this particular limitation is by examining the same systems over time, as I do here.

The irrigation systems in Nepal that I examine in this book include all those contained in the NIIS. Ostrom identified these systems as helping to lay the foundations of the IAD framework—the key framework to generate and encapsulate the design principles (Ostrom, 2010). For this reason, these cases are well suited to bear out the predictions of the theory. The analysis presented in this book derives from the first attempt to follow a relatively large number of long-enduring examples over decades using both survey analysis and qualitative data.[4] Over a period ranging from 16 to 37 years, some (31, or 13%) declined and disappeared, while the others continued to survive. Of the survivors, some improved their functioning, some stayed the same, and others deteriorated. This variation permits a comparison of the features of those that still endure with those that do not. One is no longer restricted to focusing on only those that still survive, which is a significant improvement over existing approaches.

This focus on farmer-managed irrigation systems as the primary examples for the empirical investigation appears to restrict the overall argument in other ways. The lessons might seem to apply most directly to only one type of shared resource in a single, small country: irrigation systems in Nepal. But the restriction to these cases is not as consequential for understanding sustained cooperation in other instances as it might seem. It has been long accepted by scholars studying cooperation that the situations faced by farmers in these specific irrigation systems are characteristic of a more general class of circumstances that cooperators face.[5] Thus the lessons from these irrigation systems in Nepal apply to situations that are created when a group of users cooperate to maintain other types of resources as well, applying at least as broadly as the framework they exemplify. They can be applied to self-governed resources more generally.

---

[4] There is another over-time data set of forest commons managed by the International Forest Research Institute (IFRI). However, it does not have interview data (Frey, 2020).

[5] For one of many statements of this claim, see chapter 1 in Gardner et al. (1994).

Institutions, Communities, and Individuals

A resource that is self-governed is the primary responsibility of the users themselves. Governance includes not only maintenance, but also other tasks such as allocating the resource to users in a regulated fashion, restricting access so that it is not depleted, monitoring each other to discourage shirking, and punishing rule-breakers. This community of users may request financial, technical, or dispute resolution assistance from state agencies or nongovernmental organizations. However, the group does not cede final control over any aspect of the resource to these authorities. In this way, the performance of user-governed infrastructure depends more strongly on the capacity of the user community to do these things than when it is managed by a public agency or a private entity (Ostrom, 2010).

Community self-governance appears to be a promising option for maintaining shared infrastructure in urban and rural settings (as well as in cyberspace, which I turn to in Chapter 6) for two common reasons. First, self-governed resources persist in diverse settings across the world. Although there is no count of how many such examples there are, it is generally accepted that even old ones are not rare. Their abundance is evidence of how adaptable communities are (Ostrom, 1990). Second, some of these resources have been in continuous use for many years. In many cases, the intervening years have brought with them myriad changes to the circumstances these communities face. This resilience highlights how community governance can persist longer than empires, states, and their governing apparatuses. For instance, some of the irrigation systems contained in the NIIS are hundreds of years old, and even those that are only two decades old have adapted to an armed Maoist revolt, two changes to the national constitution, the effects of climate change, and rapid rural-to-urban migration. I examine one such system in detail in Chapter 5 and several others throughout the book. Seen in this context, a key benefit of community self-governance or greater community participation appears to be sustainability (Agrawal, 2001).

Local self-governance is not without challenges, and capacities to address these challenges vary across groups. Therefore, community self-governance is not always the best option for avoiding deterioration of a shared resource (Meinzen-Dick, 2007). Individuals who cooperate to maintain a shared resource face predictable obstacles in working together. For example, a prerequisite for any cooperation between users is the shared understanding that there is a benefit to each of them from maintaining the resource rather than depleting it (Poteete, Janssen, and Ostrom, 2010, p. 243). After realizing this, the users encounter the problem of coordinating their actions in order to maintain the resource. Mutually accepted rules, customs, norms, and traditions commonly help, but for these guidelines to be effective, users must remain committed enough to them even in trying times that the resource isn't entirely depleted. Communities have varying capacities to overcome these challenges, and over time, not every group of users sharing a resource will be able to continue cooperating to maintain it or be willing to do so. Deterioration and depletion are also possibilities (Ostrom, 2005); and not all challenges can be predicted.

Across the variety of contexts in which they have persisted, long-enduring cooperative arrangements for community resource governance have some similar features. Communities often have rules for resolving conflicts between individuals and groups, mechanisms for monitoring each other's compliance with the rules, and ways to determine who is permitted to use the resource and who is not. There are other similarities, too, with the most general included in Ostrom's design principles—for example, that most users can participate in modifying the rules. In keeping with the literature, I refer to the set of working rules that a community uses as their institution for self-governance (Ostrom, 2005, p. 19). Working rules include those codified in language, implicit customs, shared norms, inherited traditions, and common knowledge about the resource that actually guide individual behavior in these situations. Working rules need not be written down. They need only be actually in use and be known to all users (i.e., common knowledge in the community). In cases where communities do have written rules, the working rules often differ from them.[6] These institutions can help regulate individual behavior to be more cooperative. They are also broadly similar across communities.

Community governance institutions also depend entirely on individuals for survival, but also tend to outlast individuals over time through the perpetuation of working rules. Individuals may leave the community of users, and others may join. Over a long enough period of time, all users will pass away and the membership will be entirely different. Working rules are typically passed on to new users with experience. For new users, learning the rules also means thinking in accordance with them, while acting on the rules means giving up a degree of autonomy to act independently of other users. Ultimately, it is the community of individual users that embodies, adapts, and propagates a particular community governance institution. In this way, the continuity of the institution is a result of what individuals choose to do. But at the same time, how users behave in relation to their shared resource is also shaped from the start by the working rules that they have learned. After all, by the time users are allowed to use the resource,

---

[6] The working rules and the written rules can sometimes be at odds. In one instance, the irrigation group had filed a written constitution with their local Irrigation office, as required by the Water Resources Act (1992), and later the Irrigation Rules (2000) of the Government of Nepal. The irrigators, however, did not know what was written in it.

they cannot be indifferent to the existing norms, customs, rules, and traditions governing it (Blomquist et al., 1994).

The relationship between individual behavior and institutions is thus circular. Because of this circularity, it can be difficult to study and is particularly challenging to see how individuals cooperate with one another and their institutions to use and maintain a shared resource. This becomes easier when looking at a specific example over a specific time period. The dynamics of the 233 irrigation systems in Nepal contained in the NIIS between 1976 and 2013, combined with an added set of 39 systems and 827 interviews with users help illustrate these features.

The Example of Irrigation Systems

Farmers managing a shared irrigation system are in a common type of cooperative situation in which a user's action or inaction in relation to the resource, in this case the irrigation system, indirectly affects others. The individual users are interdependent because none of them can maintain the resource alone, and without constant maintenance, the resource degrades (Ostrom, 1990, p. 38). Contrast this with another type of cooperative situation in which the key challenge is to reduce use so that the resource can replenish itself. This latter type of situation arises in the case of a shared forest or fishery. In the case of an irrigation system, users remain interdependent in this way as long as they want to keep the resource available for the future. If they do not, then continuous maintenance after they have received what water they want is not a concern to them.

The condition of farmers sharing an irrigation system that nobody owns but on which all of them depend captures the characteristic challenges of this type of cooperative situation. Figure 1 shows the branching structure of a typical irrigation system. The system is designed to collect water from a water source such as a river through an intake. Its channels then transport the water to distant fields to be irrigated. How much water is available for irrigation depends primarily on three factors: how much water the source contains, the depth and width of the intake and channels, and how well each has been maintained. The first, water availability, depends on myriad factors beyond the farmer's control. The second is decided when the system is designed, but there are few opportunities to change it after it is constructed. The third, maintenance, is entirely dependent on the farmers' willingness to inspect and repair the system regularly. I will henceforth call the entire system "the canal" for short. It is important to note that the set of users changes over time as newer generations take over, individuals migrate in or out, or the canal shrinks and grows due to, for instance, natural

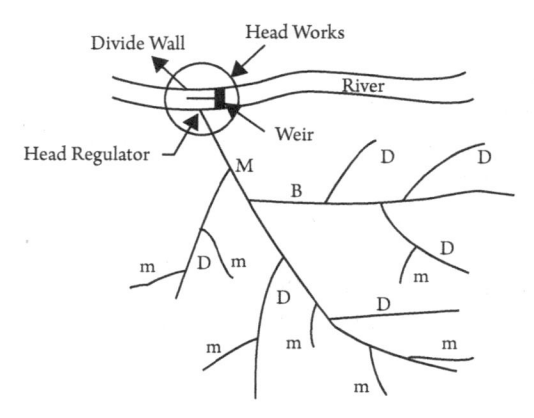

Figure 1 Spatial structure of a run of the river type of irrigation system. The headworks is the point where water enters the canal system through the head regulator and from a source (in this case the river). The weir is typically a concrete structure that spans the width of the river to control flow. The divide wall diverts some water into the main branch of the canal (M) while letting the remainder pass. The main branch divides into sub-branches (B and D) and field channels (m). The tail end of the irrigation system is towards the bottom right corner of the figure. Water flows from the head to the tail.

disasters or extensions. These dynamics are illustrated in more detail through the example of a system in mid-Western Nepal in Chapter 5. In that example, a group of downstream users intentionally broke away from the main canal. They renounced their role as users, reduced the size of the canal, and thereby changed the set of system users. I refer to the set of canal users at a given point in time as "the users."

The canal is particularly vulnerable to the selfish actions of individual users. In order to achieve greater mutual benefit in the future that comes from maintaining the resource, they must all do their parts in the present. A failure of even one of them to do so, whether for selfish reasons or not, affects the resource and possibly other users as well. For example, if one user fails to clean their section of canal, the downstream irrigators will have less water available to them. Similarly, whatever canal water a farmer upstream uses out of turn becomes unavailable to irrigators downstream. Without assurance that other users will do their part in the cooperative system and also refrain from acting opportunistically in relation to the resource, it can be difficult—even unreasonable—to depend on them. Yet without depending on them, future gains may become unattainable for the current group. If there aren't enough dependable people to inspect, clean, and repair the canal, adequate water is unlikely to be available during the planting season. This has broader effects on the agrarian livelihoods of these farmers by reducing their crop yields. They typically grow rice, which demands regular and adequate water for sustained yields.

Evoking cooperation to use and maintain a shared irrigation system is less challenging when users can believe each other's promises. Consistent with prior conventions, this ability to believe verbal promises is called trust (Ostrom, 2005, p. 98). Being able to make credible long-term commitments to cooperate without fear that others will shirk or act opportunistically can go a long way toward enabling users to work together, at least initially. It is easier to cooperate if individual users can believe each other's verbal commitment to the demands of their local governing institutions. It is difficult to expect that one who does not believe that others will do their part even after they have promised to do so will commit to binding cooperative arrangements with them. This is particularly so when the stakes are high, as they often are in the case of these irrigation systems. Even slightly less water can reduce the crop yields upon which their livelihoods overwhelmingly depend. Trust in a sufficient number of others is essential if the group is to devise and commit to institutions to meet the demands of this type of cooperative situation. This is reflected in the current systems as well.

In what follows, I present the statistical results in highly condensed form. To not break the flow of the argument, I summarize here just what is necessary to read the following tables with a fuller discussion in Appendix 1, and discuss an example. I use the Fisher's Exact Test, the discrete analog of the Chi-squared test, as follows. To look for evidence that a factor such as trust affects the performance of the systems in the sample, I first construct a contingency table and then I calculate how likely it is that table was to occur by chance alone. This is the p-value. How big a difference this makes, expressed in terms of the number of systems, is the delta value.

Consider the relationship of trust and the physical condition of the canal shown in Table 1. The rows of this table represent the three values of the trust variable (difficult, somewhat easy and easy) and the columns the canal condition

Table 1 **Baseline Relationship Between Trust and Canal Condition (Round 1): Full contingency table analysis of these two variables. N = 233 with 208 usable observations**

Trust: How easy is it to believe verbal promises?	Canal Condition			Row Total
	Poor	Fair	Good	
Difficult	0 (0.0)	12 (100.0)	0 (0.0)	12 (100)
Somewhat Easy	4 (4.88)	68 (82.93)	10 (12.2)	82 (100)
Easy	2 (1.75)	86 (75.44)	26 (22.81)	114 (100)
Column Total	6 (2.88)	166 (79.81)	36 (17.31)	208 (100)

N = 233; 25 no responses; Fisher's Exact Value: 0.089; Row percentages are in parentheses.

(poor, fair and good). The p-value for this 3 × 3 table is interpreted as the likeli-hood that this table was due to chance alone. The smaller it is, the more likely it is that the table is evidence of a relationship between trust and canal condition, and the less likely that we are seeing random chance. Comparing the number of systems in which believing verbal promises is Somewhat Easy and canal con-dition is Good to the number of Difficult-Good systems indicates the size of this relationship. In this case, there are +12.2% more systems that exhibit good canal condition and have higher levels of trust than those that exhibit good canal condition and have the lowest levels of trust. Although this seems like a large difference, this would occur about 89 out of every 1,000 times by chance alone.

This table is too likely to have been due to chance (using a generous signif-icance level of 0.05) to be evidence of a relationship between trust and canal condition. To examine whether changes in trust are related to changes in the physical condition, I calculate the standard Pearson's correlation coefficient (r) for changes to these variables (coded −1, 0, and 1 for down, same, up), and the p-value for this correlation. The remaining relationships between trust and the other three elements of performance—condition of the headworks, perceived adequacy, and perceived reliability—are summarized at the top of Table 2. It also summarizes the relationship between performance and two factors that are predicted to improve trust—prior cooperation by the farmers in both cultural and noncultural settings.

Table 2 suggests that while trust may be needed to achieve the joint outcomes, it is not enough to sustain cooperation in these situations. Consider a simplified case to illustrate this: a group of individuals sharing an irrigation system whose members all trust each other and depend critically on the system's water to sup-port their agrarian livelihoods. These are the 114 irrigation systems in Table 1 in which it was easy for respondents to trust verbal promises made by other users. However, the table also shows over two thirds of these systems do not perform well, which is an indication of non-cooperative behavior despite high levels of trust.

To see how this might be, consider how another factor—substantive outcomes of the water allocation rules—might come to matter in our simplified example. Suppose that they have devised institutions that all commit to, act upon, and up-date as needed in their dynamic circumstances. This rule-bound behavior results in more water overall for the farmers than they would get without cooperating. Over successive planting seasons, the water is allocated to farmers in accordance with their rules, as are contributions toward maintenance in terms of both labor and resources.

The jointly gained water is rarely distributed equally to all users. Farmers typically regard equal distribution of water as unfair, especially if they have contributed unevenly to upkeep, or if they have unequal plots of land and

Table 2 **Correlations of Trust, prior cooperation, and performance. Association between group variables and Performance. The values of the performance variables are poor, fair, and good. Δ% can be interpreted analogous to magnitude and direction of this association. It represents the change in the column variable when the value of the row variable changes. It is the difference in percentage of the column variable when the value of the row variable changes. P-values are from Fisher's Exact Test. For changes, Pearson's r shows the direction, and the magnitude does not have a clear interpretation; 31 in round 2 did not survive and are not included here.**

	Round 1 (N = 233)			Round 2 (N = 202)			Changes (N = 202)		
	Δ%	p1	N	Δ%	p2	N	r	p3	N
Ease of believing verbal promises (gtrust) in relation to:									
Condition of the canal	12.20	0.089	208	14.44	0.454	194	0.08	0.573	181
Condition of the headworks	−2.88	0.164	208	13.78	0.361	194	−0.07	0.146	182
Perceived Adequacy	4.18	0***	215	0.73	0.018*	188	0.17	0.216	178
Perceived Reliability	4.01	0.003**	215	−7.84	0.06	187	0.06	0.873	163
Prior cooperative activities, noncultural (ccoact) in relation to:									
Condition of the canal	12.50	0.084	189	−1.48	1	194	0.04	0.778	163
Condition of the headworks	12.18	0.071	190	30.69	0.014*	194	0.01	0.928	165
Perceived Adequacy	−18.68	0.015*	198	−12.50	0.688	188	−0.04	0.892	162
Perceived Reliability	−20.27	0.002**	198	0.66	0.751	187	−0.13	0.173	149
Prior cooperative activities, cultural (ccocult) in relation to:									
Condition of the canal	−6.56	0.271	189	10.08	0.061	194	0.10	0.087	163
Condition of the headworks	−14.30	0.06	190	−6.40	0.706	194	−0.19	0.016*	165
Perceived Adequacy	−13.69	0.104	198	8.75	0.388	188	−0.20	0.048*	162
Perceived Reliability	−7.04	0.33	198	3.77	0.934	187	−0.12	0.147	149

Note: *p <0.05, **p<.01, ***p<.001

therefore different needs. But because the water is distributed unevenly, whether based on land ownership or something else, some gain the benefits of having more water in greater measure than others. What this uneven accumulation of the joint outcomes means for the well-being of users—a substantive outcome— relative to each other is difficult to assess. This is because it depends on many other factors such as commodity prices, weather, and the demand for the crop they produce.

Additionally, the substantive outcomes of other distributional rules, not just those for allocating the resource to individual users, can be difficult to antici-pate beforehand. Myriad interconnections among a multitude of factors obscure these substantive outcomes. Concerns about them are difficult to address en-tirely with rules formulated beforehand. Not that they must be addressed be-forehand: individuals may typically find it difficult to anticipate how they will experience them. Whether or not this unevenness will matter and how unfair it will be perceived to be are both also safely beyond prediction at the time of choosing the rules, and may even be outside the set of initial concerns when first agreeing to cooperate.

The uneven substantive outcomes that result from distributional rules are more likely to matter the longer users cooperate because these results are cu-mulative, compounding year after year and generation after generation. Other developments beyond the users' control may also highlight the significance of this uneven distribution of substantive outcomes, and users can change their minds. In the present cases, for example, some users who thought the inequities in their irrigation systems did not matter changed their mind after Maoist rebels explained that they were manifestations of systemic caste-based oppression.

As these outcomes start to manifest, it is possible for individuals to assess more firmly how fair they perceive them to be. At least some individuals be-have as though they are unfairness-averse. This is evident when some farmers reduce the strength of their commitment to their institutions based on how un-fair they perceive the outcomes of their arrangements to be. They do this even when the institutions are still producing the promised greater joint gains for all. Perceived fairness is tightly linked to sustained cooperation because of this un-fairness aversion.

Individuals alter the strength of their commitment to existing cooperative arrangements based on perceived fairness. Perceptions of fairness are likely to also have been relevant to the initial agreement to cooperate, not just after the agreement has been enacted. The difference is that as cooperative behavior pro-ceeds, actual outcomes become certain, and experience can take the place of expectations in assessments of fairness. These irrigation systems show strong evidence of this dynamic between perceived fairness and levels of commitment. Even with high levels of trust, perceived fairness is most strongly and frequently associated with successful irrigation system governance by these communities of system users.

The Generality of Irrigation Examples

Ultimately, this book tells a story about why groups of farmers cooperate over decades to use and maintain shared irrigation systems, and why they stop doing so. When I looked at these irrigation canals in Nepal over thirty years, I found that after decades of working together, users stopped cooperating when they perceived the outcomes to be unfair. In fact, perceived fairness was a more important consideration than any other. Fairness is a necessary condition for sustainable resource governance, but it has become clear that community governance can be stubbornly unfair. These unfair arrangements can persist for decades, and as a result the canals become more vulnerable. On the way to presenting a fairness-based theory of sustained cooperation, I also reinterpret these influential examples from the perspective of fairness.

Farmer-managed irrigation canals are still very common in agriculture, and are in turn important for global food production. Knowing how to govern them well is therefore worthy in itself. They are also typical examples of sustained cooperation in the maintenance of shared infrastructure. My predecessors analyzed them in order to tease out how individuals could devise and commit to cooperative institutions. Decades later, they remain useful for studying the conditions under which groups of individuals can sustain cooperation. The role that these cases play in the broader effort to understand human cooperation is similar to the role that mice play in some biological investigations: as well-understood instances that provide insights for further investigation. For these reasons, these particular irrigation systems in Nepal are the examples that I will focus on for the remainder of this book.

To motivate the reader who may not be particularly interested in the details of this subset of irrigation canals in Nepal, I suggest they consider that similar cooperative situations are likely to become even more common. The human population is becoming increasingly interconnected physically in cities and digitally online. As these trends continue, sustained cooperation has taken on greater significance beyond the familiar examples of fisheries, forests, and irrigation to urban systems and digital infrastructure as well. This same digital infrastructure is reshaping every aspect of life and human society, just as a majority of the world moves to cities. Our growing interdependence and proximity to each other demands a better understanding of how individuals can continue to work together over extended periods of time.

Perceived Fairness and Sustained Cooperation

Having introduced the main elements of the argument, it is now possible to sketch the three key distinctions upon which it is built. They make it easier to see how significant fairness is to sustained cooperation. Later sections will fill in this sketch. The first distinction is between cooperation and sustained cooperation, the next between fair and unfair cooperation. These distinctions are typically not recognized in the context of user-governed resources. In the Ostromian conception, the situations of initial cooperation and continued cooperation are fundamentally the same as cooperation in general. It is also commonly assumed that mutually agreed cooperative arrangements are fair arrangements.

Applying these distinctions in the context of user self-governance reveals a class of problems that I call fairness problems, which leads to the third distinction: between fairness problems and collective action problems (Table 3). Fairness problems are difficulties to remaining fair over time, which are essentially different from collective action problems that are widely understood to be associated with cooperation. Collective action problems are the dominant obstacles to initial cooperation, but fairness problems are more significant for sustaining cooperation. So, it is possible to have unfair cooperation—that is, mutually agreed upon cooperative arrangements perceived as unfair by the cooperators are not uncommon.

Table 3 **Collective action problems and fairness problems in relation to the type of cooperation and level of perceived fairness.**

		Levels of perceived fairness	
		Low levels	High levels
Type of cooperation	Initial	Collective action problems are dominant. Fairness problems are relatively simple and concern rules.	
	Sustained	Collective action problems addressed. More complex fairness problems involving rules and outcomes are dominant and unaddressed.	Collective action problems and more complex fairness problems adequately addressed.

Distinction 1: Cooperation and Sustained Cooperation

Sustained cooperation pertains to a group of individuals who are already cooperating, not a group seeking to do so for the first time. Consider the first time that a group of people decides to share a particular irrigation system.[7] They need to induce cooperation among themselves because they have not successfully cooperated before in using and maintaining the system. After adopting cooperative institutions and using their shared irrigation system, the challenges transform. This same group would thereafter need to devise ways to sustain existing cooperation as long as they continued to want a functional irrigation system. But they would face this task having already cooperated in using and maintaining the shared resource for some time. They need not be concerned with how to convince each other to cooperate for the first time, as they would already have cooperative institutions. They would also have some knowledge of how to cooperate, some experience of doing so, and a better idea of the results of the cooperative arrangements.

Having cooperated for some time, their position would also be different with respect to the cooperative arrangements themselves. They would be considering whether or not to meet the demands of their institutions, but from a position of already being committed to these institutions. If they changed nothing, they would continue to cooperate. This inserts at the least an additional, positional variable (Sen, 1993) into the prisoner's dilemma formulation of the choice individuals face in these situations. This positional variable would need to take on at least two values, each indicating the state of the users: "in an agreement" and "outside of an agreement." Stated in this way, existing prisoner's dilemma models of collective action problems can be seen to deal with the case that the positional variable is "outside of an agreement"—that is, they are not currently in an agreement. This positional generalization is another way to make the explicit assumption that the individual by default is either cooperative or non-cooperative. From their default state, they must decide whether to change their behavior in relation to their institutions. When the positional variable is "in an agreement," the default behavior is to cooperate. So, their decision is whether to behave uncooperatively and break the commitment. After this generalization, two choices made by these individuals must be explained. One is the familiar choice between cooperative and non-cooperative behavior, and the other is the choice to reconsider one's default behavior.

There is the obvious question of whether this distinction between default states is spurious. Can it be captured by viewing sustained cooperation as

---

[7] See Coman (1911) for a description of how cooperation came about in a prominent example, the Minidoka irrigation system in the American West at the turn of the twentieth century.

subsequent stages in a repeated game in extensive form, as Ostrom has argued?[8] Attempting to do so presents difficulties. In this view, one formulates subsequent behavior as the move $n + 1$, given a sequence of n moves which are cooperative or not. The difficulty with this view is that this sequence of actions does not capture the observation that if the user does nothing to alter their default behavior, they will behave cooperatively when they are in a commitment and non-cooperatively when they are not. An improved formulation of the Ostromian view could define being in a commitment as an unbroken sequence of "cooperate" actions, but this revised approach also misses an important reality: even those in a commitment can behave non-cooperatively without abandoning their commitment. Well-known examples are non-cooperative actions taken as a form of dissent or protest of arrangements they are deeply committed to improving. A sequence of binary action variables corresponding to the actions themselves cannot capture the state in an agreement (or not) from which the actions were taken in general.

Other common conceptions of human behavior also leave space for the idea that the decision to continue to cooperate is different from the decision to cooperate initially. If we assume that individuals are cost-conscious, there is a mental transaction cost to recalculating all the costs and benefits before taking an action. This is particularly so if the situations are as complex as shared irrigation systems. There are many interactions and variables to consider. Therefore, rational, self-interested, benefit-to-cost-maximizing people in a commitment should tend to adopt default behaviors without good reason to do otherwise. One could value a reconsideration of default behavior as a cost, call it epsilon, of reweighting the options. This would include the cost of reconsidering and reprocessing a multitude of relevant variables and their interactions. This makes clear that the two options for an individual (default behavior or not) are not equally costly—at least because of the epsilon. Default behavior is immediately less costly because it does not require any additional mental work.

There are also other justifications possible for the distinction between cooperation and sustained cooperation. A person motivated by doing the right thing will also face an epsilon before breaking their commitment and discontinuing cooperation, but they will bear the cost for a different reason: a preference for doing their duty, as described by Sen (1977). Another explanation of this cost is to assume that individuals are loss-averse: that is, they weigh losing what they have more than gaining an equivalent that has the same probabilistic expected value (Kahneman, Knetsch, and Thaler, 1986). A third explanation could simply

---

[8] "In the most general sense, all institutional arrangements can be thought of as games in extensive form." (Ostrom, 1990, p. 23).

rely on the fear of uncertainty. After a long enough time period, it is likely that the individual user will not have kept a close account of all of the ways that their lives have been altered by their commitment and their reliance on the resulting joint benefits. Thus, they cannot know how their lives will change if they alter their commitment. The detrimental effects of not cooperating may only appear after the resource is no longer available to them. This adds to the uncertainty that discourages changing one's behavior and encourages the default behavior of continued cooperation.

For my argument, which is predominantly empirical, the choice of behavioral explanation is not urgent. It is necessary only that the choice that individuals face when they decide to continue to cooperate is different from the choice they face when deciding to cooperate for the first time. For those who are in a cooperative agreement, it is not whether or not to commit to these arrangements, but whether to alter their existing commitment.

In many cases of this type of cooperation, there is another prominent difference between continued cooperation and initial cooperation. It is typical in such cases, although not universal, to find that groups of users devise or adopt norms, customs, rules of thumb, traditions, and even formal rules to help them cooperate. In these cases, one of the main goals of initial cooperation is to devise a set of these working rules that are agreeable to all cooperators. Those who are already cooperating have accomplished this. However, once users have begun to cooperate, the burden of creating these institutions shifts to updating them.

To the extent that they rely on a set of working rules to structure their behavior, sustaining cooperation to use and maintain the resource also entails changing these rules to keep up with changing circumstances. Those who are already in a commitment have to sustain cooperation to update and maintain the institutions that help them to cooperate. The interested reader could jump to Chapters 2 and 5 for a detailed illustration of when this updating might become necessary and what forms these updates take. The key question here is why some appropriately adapt and change the institutions to which they have already committed and therefore continue their commitment, while others decide to lessen or end their commitment to their institution. This is related to the question of why some groups, even after updating their institutions, fail to find the "right" ones that can sustain cooperation while others do.

In this way, distinguishing initial and sustained cooperation admits of two possibilities. One possibility is that an individual's current position, whether committed or not, may influence their decisions about their future commitment. In particular, without good reason, they are likely to favor continuing their commitment. A second is the possibility that people may have different reasons for taking each of these three actions: committing to an agreement for the first time, renewing their commitment, and discontinuing their commitment. What these reasons are, whether they are related to each other, and whether they remain constant over time cannot be theoretically resolved. It is an empirical question.

The distinction between phases of cooperation sheds new light on the steps to understanding cooperation. Cataloging the factors that affect the likelihood of cooperation between individuals remains an important part of the puzzle of understanding sustained cooperation, but a missing piece becomes apparent: understanding whether the same factors that affect initial cooperation also affect its continuation. In a situation where users are already cooperating, it becomes important to ask why people continue to cooperate or stop doing so. This is because the reasons for taking each of these actions may have changed since the individual made their initial commitment to their cooperative institution. It is my contention that individuals reduce this commitment when they perceive systems of cooperation to be unfair. This is because over time, a significant proportion of people in a group appear to behave as though they are unfairness-averse.

Distinction 2: Fair and Unfair Cooperation

The second key distinction is that between fair and unfair cooperation. Although defining fairness empirically is the task of Chapter 3 and theoretically is that of Chapter 4, even with a general understanding of the word certain points can be made. Fairness and cooperation are clearly not the same, although they tend to be folded together in studies of cooperation. There is an element of truth to the expectation that if individuals are voluntarily cooperating to achieve joint outcomes, then the system of cooperation to which they are committed must be fair to some extent. After all, who would knowingly commit to an unfair agreement?[9] However, evidence from current cases shows that cooperative systems can be unfair.

The co-occurrence of fairness and cooperation is actually a special case of cooperation. It is possible for cooperative systems to be perceived as unfair at any point in time. In the present cases, perceived fairness lends a resilience to cooperation in the face of changing circumstances, while its absence makes cooperation vulnerable to unexpected situations. For example, in several instances, users were willing to contribute more than the rules required of them in order to rebuild an irrigation system whose governing institutions they perceived to be fair. In several others not perceived as fair, the users hesitated to go beyond

---

[9] This question is partly rhetorical in order to mirror the structure of a common question implied in the collective action literature: Who would knowingly be a sucker? I examine this further in Chapter 5 and 6. Until then, I will note that it is often the case that people do commit to an unfair agreement when they don't have better alternatives. Nevertheless, this question captures a common working assumption in the collective action literature.

what was demanded of them in normal times. Thus, the fact that a group of users might cooperate around a shared resource at any point in time is not a reliable indication that they perceive it to be fair. How robust the system is when subjected to changes or shocks over which the users have no control provides a better indication.

Conversely, it can seem reasonable to assume that long-enduring cooperative systems are perceived as fair. But this, too, relies on an equilibrium-type argument of the following form: over a long enough time period, the unfair systems will either decline and disappear or become fair. As appealing as this assumption is, it fails by itself to put some nagging questions to rest. For example, what is a long enough time period for the unfair systems to shake out or reform? There is no broadly accepted answer to this question, so the assumption remains untestable. It is justified instead only by its theoretical convenience. Short of this elusive equilibrium, it is possible to find shared resources that have not yet depleted, even though users perceive it as unfair. One reason for this is that the group has not yet experienced particularly challenging circumstances that could test their commitment. So while fairness is a necessary condition for sustained cooperation, perceived unfairness alone is not sufficient for decline. Persistent unfairness simply makes the irrigation systems more likely to be neglected. How quickly this neglect leads to decline depends on other factors.

Distinction 3: Collective Action Problems and Fairness Problems

The third distinction arises because of the first two. It is intended to differentiate the nature of the challenges faced by users in the two states of cooperation. Groups face challenges both before they have started cooperating and as they seek to sustain their cooperation. The former set of challenges consists primarily of problems with coordination and compliance. The latter set, which becomes more important over time, consists of problems with remaining fair.

When initiating cooperation, the group must discover what needs to be done and when in order to maintain the resource, and this includes the question of institutional supply. Then they must decipher what will convince individuals to make a commitment, which includes the problem of credible commitment (Ostrom, 1990, p. 185). Before they can actually begin to cooperate, they must additionally decide who is going to do those things and get them to do them credibly. It is well established that to initiate cooperation between self-interested individuals around a shared resource requires addressing myriad such problems, which are referred to altogether as collective action problems. As they continue to work together, the users do become more adept at avoiding or solving collective action problems that initially stood in the way of cooperation. This lessens the threat posed by collective action problems. Instead, another family of problems (fairness problems) grows more salient as users continue cooperating. These problems morph into more challenging forms because individual cooperators experience substantive outcomes that have resulted from their cooperative system. They can see how these outcomes are distributed and thus may have more developed ideas of what is fair.

Because they live with the results of their voluntarily agreed-upon institutions firsthand, they come to a better position from which to assess the fairness of their cooperative system. Two other elements of this situation change with time. One is what users regard as fair or not, and the second is how significant they regard perceived unfairness to be to their continued commitment. These two dynamic aspects of this type of cooperative situation make fairness problems particularly challenging for the individual cooperators to anticipate or address beforehand.

Based on these cases, my contention is that in the stage of sustaining their cooperation, various fairness problems come to be central to continued cooperation, while the difficulty of the challenges posed by collective action problems decreases. As a result, fairness grows into a major factor affecting the maintenance of the shared resources precisely because these groups successfully addressed collective action problems to achieve joint outcomes.[10] The new forms that fairness problems take are likely to be more significant to continued cooperation and also more persistent than collective action problems.

The predominant explanation of cooperation relates to collective action problems. This focus on collective action problems is a consequence of a particular set of commonly adopted assumptions. These assumptions are required in order to apply the apparatus of game theory to these types of situations. In game theory literature, the circumstances around a shared resource are regarded as creating a social dilemma situation in which "individuals face short-term incentives that, if followed, would lead them all to be worse off than feasibly attainable outcomes" (Ostrom, 2005, p. 70). The analysis of cooperation in these game theoretical approaches begins with a particular conception of the human individual. This individual fundamentally fears being a "sucker" by nature (Ostrom, 2005, p. 167). They are therefore wary of cooperating first without some certainty that the cooperation will be reciprocated by others. This fear is a problem for acting collectively, and only by overcoming this hesitation is

---

[10] These are related to the idea of social dilemmas that is mentioned in *Governing the Commons* (Ostrom, 1990) and later works. As Ostrom noted, "Social dilemmas are pervasive in social life, and proposed solutions to these dilemmas have occupied all great political philosophers including Aristotle, Hobbes, and Hume. There are many differently structured social dilemmas, but they all are characterized by a situation where everyone is tempted to take one action but all will be better off if all (or most of them) take another action. Studying how subjects behave in this type of social dilemma helps us understand more general questions of relevance across the social sciences than simply the study of natural resources" (2005, p. 79).

collective action possible. In this view, one way to do this offers a solution to the problem of collective action.

The Centrality of Collective Action Problems to Cooperation

There is ample evidence that collective action problems stand in the way of successful cooperation, but it is not obvious that solving collective action problems is sufficient to achieve or sustain cooperation. For instance, there may be other classes of problems that take on greater prominence once collective action problems have been solved or avoided. An example of this type of problem arises because of other human tendencies besides the deep-seated suspicion that others will not do their part. The set of problems related to remaining fair is of this type. These problems arise because some people tend to avoid remaining committed to unfair situations. Acting collectively does not automatically result in these situations becoming fair unless the collective action explicitly aims to achieve fair outcomes. So it is possible to solve collective action problems and begin cooperating without addressing fairness problems.

Following Nash (1951), I define cooperation as a pattern of behavior that arises between individuals when they can communicate freely to achieve joint benefits. One way to find these patterns is to look for phenomena that could not arise otherwise. Irrigation systems in the NIIS data set are handy examples, as those that are entirely managed by users could not have survived without cooperation between them. Initiating cooperative behavior entailed favoring longer-term over short-term ones. So these irrigators favored, for instance, taking less water than they could at any particular time so that those downstream would also have some, and because they did this, those downstream were more willing to help maintain the canal. As a result of sustaining this type of cooperation, the users were able to maintain the canal over decades. If they had behaved with short-term self-interest only, if they had not believed that coordinating their actions would lead to longer-term availability of water, or if they did not believe that enough others would do their part, the irrigation system would have stopped being functional. That these systems are still functional implies that individuals are still cooperating.

Ostrom's IAD framework is a major attempt to explain cooperation in these shared-resource situations by applying game theory. Characteristically, it is exclusively focused on collective action problems. Collective action is an action that is produced by a group in contrast to individual action, which is initiated and carried out by a single individual. A collective action is complete when all members of the collective have completed their individual actions in a particular manner. A collective action, then, is composed of actions by more than one individual. Henceforth, I use collective action problems in the sense of Olson (1965) to refer to particular difficulties that a group faces in working together to achieve a mutually beneficial outcome. In order to remain compatible with the IAD framework, I refer specifically to the difficulties created when a person fears that after doing their part, others will not do theirs despite having committed to do so.[11]

Collective action problems are distinct from but related to social dilemmas. Both are used frequently in the analysis of cooperation, but have slightly different connotations. A social dilemma game (social dilemma for short) in a game theoretical setting refers to interactions between individuals that can lead to Pareto efficient outcomes if and only if they can coordinate their actions. Ostrom explained, "They [social dilemmas] occur whenever the private returns to each participant are greater than their share of a joint return no matter what other participants do," before concluding that, "understanding how individuals interact within social dilemma situations constitutes one of the major puzzles facing all contemporary social science disciplines" (Ostrom, 2005, p. 37).

The common pool resource game is one of several types of games that involve a social dilemma situation: a game in which individuals must stop themselves from overexploiting a shared resource (Gintis and Bowles, 2011, p. 12). Ostrom referred to this game as the commons dilemma, and noted that in cases of successful commons governance, people have "broken out of the trap inherent in commons dilemmas" (Ostrom, 1990, p. 21). That is, they have devised institutions not only to help achieve joint gains, but also to distribute those gains in a particular way. When a commons dilemma has been solved, these joint gains are distributed so that over time, each person's private return is less than their share of a joint return. In game theoretical analyses of these types of shared resource situations, it is conventional to label as "cooperate" a particular strategy among a set of possible strategies in a specified, structured interaction. What distinguishes the "cooperate" strategy from the other non-cooperative ones, which are also called "defect" strategies, is that if it is pursued by all individuals, it will result in the highest payoff to all. A defect strategy does not have this feature.

This game theory-based account begins with a model of human beings and proceeds to construct situations that they face (Gardner, Walker and Ostrom, 1994). The result is referred to as the structure of the situation because it cannot be altered by the individual. Aspects of this structure of the situation can be altered by the group, primarily through institutions. The generating assumption is that of symmetry: each player is similar in all significant aspects. It follows that

---

[11] In this literature, actually being taken advantage of in this way is the definition of a sucker.

individual players perceive their situation along similar dimensions, although they may not perceive the situations in the same way. The most common model of human being used in these types of explanations of shared resource governance is "rational and self-interested" to varying degrees and strictness. Some variations are permitted for specific behaviors such as norm following tendencies or other regarding preferences (Poteete, Janssen and Ostrom, 2010, p. 222). The main task for an analyst applying game theory to these examples, then, is to see the "structure" of a situation as perceived by that type of person (Ostrom, 1990). Ultimately, in this account, the only reason people cooperate is because it is more beneficial to them over the long term than not doing so.

In this applied game theoretical tradition on which Ostrom relies, the model of individuals as doing what is best for themselves is the starting point for analyzing cooperation. Aside from parsimony, versatility, and widespread use, this model also permits a type of empathy. Rather than assume that farmers are different from the observer, we assume that the farmers are doing the best for themselves, just as those observing them are (Ostrom, 1990, p. 42). When they suspect others of not doing their part, they are merely admitting human frailties such as selfishness, opportunism, laziness, or greed. If one begins from this model of human behavior and furthermore assumes that the model is universal, then what needs to be explained is cooperation itself. The default implication of these assumptions is that people who are using a shared resource selfishly will not cooperate, so non-cooperation need not be explained. It is simply not rational to cooperate unless some other conditions are also met. In particular, they will not cooperate unless incentives are such that cooperation is more beneficial than defection. In this view, cooperation is never more beneficial by default.

Others have argued that cooperation arises from basic human nature—in short, that it is in our best interests to cooperate with others (Gintis and Bowles, 2011). This argument explains that the cooperative aspect of human nature has been honed through evolutionary processes to confer a survival advantage on our species. This explanation begins to focus on explaining why we do not cooperate rather than explaining why we do. Indeed, this evolutionary argument is perhaps enough to explain why humans are cooperative by nature, and why selfish people may want to cooperate: it makes evolutionary sense to do so. For my purposes, however, this argument still leaves open how they might cooperate. Wanting to cooperate is not enough for cooperation to arise or to be sustained, particularly if individuals are mainly concerned with their own survival and do not trust each other to keep their commitments.

I am concerned not with instances where cooperation arises but rather with where it continues or breaks down. It cannot be assumed that game theory will fit these situations. Users are already cooperating in cases where irrigation systems are still functional. If these cases of irrigation systems in Nepal have one major feature limiting their generality, it is that cooperation is already the evident default mode of behavior. They say little, therefore, about situations in which cooperation is to be evoked among self-interested people. However, by focusing on extant situations of cooperation, I avoid the debates about why they cooperated in the first place. These reasons for cooperating initially are relevant and even possibly important to the breakdown of cooperation. As I have noted, however, these reasons may change the longer people cooperate.

It is common to assert that people are naturally averse to shirking and free riding. As Ostrom noted, "No one wants to be a 'sucker', keeping a promise that everyone else is breaking" (Ostrom, 1990, p. 44). This is the universal, animating fear that this assertion attributes to human beings. In this way, collective action problems are defined as originating in an aspect of human nature that is assumed to influence human interactions in general, not just in shared-resource situations. It follows that collective action problems are central to cooperation as long as this particular aspect of human nature dominates individual behavior. For an example from an entirely different context, see Levi's description of taxpayers as strategic actors, and about whom they noted: "No one prefers to be a sucker" (Levi, 1989, p. 53).

The dangers of hewing to a game theoretical analysis of phenomena like these irrigation canals in Nepal are twofold. The first is the usual question of fit. Can we be relatively certain that the behavioral assumptions of the model and the chosen structure of the game represent enough of the significant features of the situation to be relevant for a particular purpose? The second is a question of focus. Using the type of game theoretical analysis that Ostrom applied draws attention to collective action problems by definition. It takes attention away from other conceptions of fairness not associated with social dilemmas. This type of analysis is limited to a conception of fairness in which what is agreed to is fair by definition, which is the main topic of Chapter 4. This may not seem like a major blind spot if one accepts the reasonable claim that fairness is folded into voluntary cooperation—i.e., people's voluntary cooperation is evidence that they think cooperative arrangements are fair. Fairness is a complicated and vast topic in its own right, so avoiding it only adds to the appeal of this simplified approach. Instead, it can be convenient to assume that nobody would voluntarily agree to an unfair agreement[12]. My empirical findings show how cooperation can be both

---

[12] It is important to underscore how difficult it can be to assess whether an agreement is voluntarily agreed to, and how misleading this assumption can be in certain common situations found in Nepal. Bonded laborers of Tharu communities in Nepal under the *Kamaiya* system are prominent examples. Here, the initial loan agreement to pay back the principal with labor appears to be made voluntarily and often with great relief when it enables the borrower to construct elements of a dignified and meaningful life, such as a wedding ceremony. But in light of "the severe power imbalances between the parties," the terms are likely to seem exploitative to observers (Kara, 2014).

fair and unfair, so fairness issues become difficult to avoid in cases of sustained cooperation.

The Fairness Problem

The interviews and case studies reveal that a different type of problem affects sustained cooperation. These are fairness problems, or the problems of cooperators continuing to perceive their institution as fair. The rest of this book is dedicated to elaborating fairness and fairness problems in detail, so I will simply summarize the main findings in the next three sections as an introduction. Fairness problems do not have the same structure of a social dilemma situation, as collective action problems do.[13] Instead they appear only after collective action problems have been solved or avoided. Thus, they are distinct from collective action problems that may obstruct initial cooperation. These problems of remaining fair become more significant the longer users sustain cooperation to use and maintain a shared resource. They are a less significant problem before the resource becomes functional through the cooperation between the individual users. As individuals in groups continue to cooperate, avoiding the perception that their institutions are unfair takes on greater significance.

Perceived fairness is an assessment of fairness of the institutions to which users have committed to for managing these irrigation systems. There are two aspects of this assessment: the rules, and the outcomes that arise from following the rules.[14] Fairness problems are potent because defining individual perceptions of fairness before users have committed to a set of rules and experienced resulting outcomes poses substantial obstacles. Perceptions of fairness are difficult to anticipate because the outcomes that result from cooperating according to a set of rules become apparent only over time. In addition, individuals may not be able to completely define what they consider fair, but they may be able to more readily recognize when they are in unfair situations. I address these issues in Chapter 3, in addition to the important question of how perceived fairness over time is different from iterative cost-benefit calculations.

There are also other factors that can affect the nature and potency of the fairness problem. These include how significant users consider the fairness of their systems to be, the perception of fairness that users have, norms and traditions that the groups share, broader political movements or government interactions, and how they attribute unfair outcomes. These factors are enumerated and

---

[13] The theoretical structure of fairness problems is described in Chapter 5.

[14] This differs from the perceptions of fairness elaborated by authors such as Tyler and Blader (2013) that emphasize procedural, or process, concerns over outcomes.

described in detail in the following chapters and a schematic diagram is developed in Chapter 5. In these irrigation systems, user perceptions of fairness concern five aspects of their situation:

1. **Water Gap:** This refers to the relative distribution of water between users. It includes the question of whether the difference in amounts of water received by the biggest user and the smallest user is increasing; whether some users get more water than others; whether some parts get predictably less water than others; and whether the relatively worse off have been deprived of water.
2. **Work Gap:** This refers to the relative assignment of work by the rules among users. It includes questions of whether the rules assign disproportionate duties to some subgroups of users, as well as whether users are required to contribute their own labor and assets to the maintenance of the canal.
3. **Qualification:** This refers to the rules about who is qualified to use the water and who isn't. It includes questions of whether the rules about who can be a user are well-defined, and whether the rules for becoming a user assign consistent advantage to some subgroups.
4. **Exclusion:** This refers to the exclusion or marginalization of some qualified users for long periods. This includes questions of whether the relatively worse off have been deprived of water, whether some users have been consistently disadvantaged, and whether the rules give some groups consistent advantages. Where qualification refers to the rules, exclusion refers to the implementation of rules and their effects.
5. **Outcome Gap:** This refers to a perceived unevenness in substantive outcomes that accrue to different users of the system over time. Substantive outcomes are outcomes that are significantly affected by water and labor allocation. For example, consider an irrigator who is now able to send his children to private school because, for decades, he has been getting his share of water according to the working rules. That his child goes to private school now is a substantive outcome. These rules for allocating water may have been agreed to before he had children, or they may have been decided without knowing the difference that it would make to the educational opportunities his children would have.

As I show, as a set of arrangements comes to be perceived as unfair by the individuals committed to it, these individuals tend to reduce their commitment, even if they have been cooperating for decades. If enough people in a group reduce their commitment to the institutions in this way, the irrigation system shows persistent deterioration. If that perception of unfairness persists, cooperation will eventually break down completely. An irrigation system whose users are not willing to cooperate is more likely to fail and less likely to be resilient.

In the context of these rule-bound irrigation systems, the fairness problem can be stated more specifically. It is the problem of keeping institutions for governing the system fair, as detailed in the five aspects noted previously. The fairness problem is complex because of its multiple aspects, some of which are subjective,[15] and it is dynamic because perceptions of fairness change over time. Some groups are able to continuously address such a dynamic fairness problem, while others are not.[16] When they are not, they increasingly come to perceive their institutions as unfair.

In response to this persistent perception of unfairness, individuals may not immediately leave or stop cooperating, but it will take much less to get them to do so than if they had solved or avoided the fairness problem. A reduced level of cooperation from some users makes these systems less resilient to outside shocks. The fairness problem is more or less solved for a time when this type of attrition is no longer a danger to the continued functioning of the resource. In those systems that are functioning well, users have been able to maintain a set of rules that keep the institutions fair.

Fairness Problems Eclipse Collective Action Problems

Collective action problems remain important to sustained cooperation, but working together to avoid collective action problems becomes less challenging the more the farmers do it. It is easier to trust each other the longer they work together, and having successfully cooperated in the past makes it easier to do so again. This positive relationship between the performance of the canal and both trust and prior cooperation were reflected when assessing the factors affecting sustained cooperation. Over decades, their finely crafted institutions and mutual familiarity have made cooperation rather than non-cooperation the default action. As Ostrom notes, through trust and prior cooperation, they learn to avoid collective action problems altogether (Ostrom, 1990, p. 216).

In the construction and early maintenance phases, the challenge is to devise new rules in order to begin to cooperate. In this initial situation, the problem of keeping institutions fair has a rudimentary form. It requires only that they agree to a set of rules that they regard as fair without any knowledge of how these rules will be implemented or what will result from them. When choosing the working rules that make up their institution, individuals are forced to rely on a

---

[15] For a longer discussion of subjective and objective aspects of the fairness problem, see the discussion of patent unfairness in Chapter 3.

[16] This is an urgent question, but not one that this book addresses. The intention of the book is to provide a systematic way to ask this question in specific instances of sustained cooperation.

guess about what will be fair in the future. Recall from Table 3 that the fairness problem is not as salient until people have continued to cooperate long enough to live with the outcomes of the rules, which they judge adequate or not. Before cooperating, how fair the rules promise to be is certainly one part of convincing individuals to commit to them. But this is a small factor compared to the myriad other factors that can affect whether or not people agree to cooperate such as whether they believe the verbal promises of others in the group to do their part. Collective action problems are a better representation of the dilemmas faced by would-be cooperators in the initial situation of deciding whether to start cooperating. Fairness problems are dormant in comparison. Initially, the perceived fairness of the institution involves an assessment only of the rules, not the outcomes.

Although sustained cooperation involves collective action problems as well as fairness problems, their relative significance flips as the users continue to co-operate. For example, farmers will decide whether to adopt a rule for allocating water based on how much land a user owns or the type of crop they cultivate, or they may assess whether the prescribed punishments for not doing one's part in maintenance are proportionate. This initial assessment is rudimen-tary in comparison to the complexity of the assessment after users have been cooperating for decades. As time passes in a cooperative situation, outcomes be-come more apparent. Faced with the outcomes, users can assess how fair they are. Users who have learned to successfully avoid collective action problems to achieve these outcomes then encounter fairness problems with greater urgency. Characterizing fairness problems as a social dilemma-type game captures only a part of the problem. Overall, it leads one to miss the main factors affecting sus-tained cooperation.

For instance, consider a farmer in the initial situation who is not yet com-mitted to any rules. He is faced with choosing between two possible rules for allocating water between users—for instance, in proportion to the land he owns or an equal amount to all the farmers. If he owns more land than most, he might recognize that the first will give him more water. If he owns less than most, he might recognize that the first allocation gives him less and the second more. Suppose that he can calculate in monetary terms how much value each unit of extra water is to him; for most of the farmers in this sample, the value is very high. A more complete assessment of what the two different allocation rules imply for the farmer's substantive outcomes, however, would still remain elusive. This is not only because there are still two other inputs into the agricul-tural process (land and labor) that must be factored in. The main reason is that, regardless of what he does with the water, he is limited in his ability to predict to what outcomes it will contribute in the future. In this way, the second aspect of fairness, the outcomes of a proposed set of rules, becomes clearer only over time.

Cooperation in Terms of Fairness

Fairness problems can come to dominate sustained cooperation, even though collective action problems are central to initial cooperation. Once fairness problems are recognized as central to sustained cooperation, it is possible to reinterpret sustained cooperation in terms of fairness. The longitudinal data shows that there are fewer significant associations between most of the variables from the IAD framework in the second round than the first. Furthermore, there are fewer significant associations between the changes to these variables over time than in a single time period. Instead, the variables associated with fairness problems dominate sustained cooperation over time. As will be seen, these variables show greater associations with the changing performance of these systems.

The variables in the IAD framework do not explain why some cooperative arrangements succeed or fail over time for two reasons. First, in all of the NIIS cases, the farmers had been cooperating on their systems before they were first studied. These are not cases of initial cooperation, so claims about initial cooperation cannot be tested with these cases. Indeed, the evidence to support these claims came from lab experiments designed to study initial cooperation and plausible game theory models. Second, the framework prioritizes collective action problems, which are typically less significant the longer people continue to work together compared to when they started. Thus, variables predicted to relate to cooperation using a collective action approach are likely to need to be supplemented over time.

The recognition that sustained cooperation is better understood in terms of fairness has some practical implications. Consider that perceptions of fairness can be used to characterize how robust a particular instance of sustained cooperation is over time. To do so, it is necessary only to examine changes to variables associated with perceived fairness, not the stack of variables associated with collective action problems. Overall, however, the demands that the fairness approach to sustained cooperation makes of researchers are greater because it will take longitudinal studies to verify the theory. Without at least two observations per case, changes cannot be detected. Since these studies will have to be conducted over decades, or as long as it takes for the outcomes to manifest and the institutions to change, it will require collaboration over time between researchers to study long-term trends. The frequency of these types of studies will increase if researchers can revisit work done by others decades ago in such a way that fairness can be isolated.

Recognizing fairness will involve at least one further demand on researchers. They will have to maintain the openness with which they do their work. Without having access to earlier data, documentation, and the study parameters, follow-up studies are difficult to design. This one was possible only because the original researchers had documented their work thoroughly. Without a long enough gap between observations, it will be impossible to properly assess temporal theories like the one presented here.

Finally, after recognizing the central role of fairness in sustained cooperation, concerned government agencies can understand and explore strategies to support fair local arrangements. The persistence of unfair cooperation should be of interest to state agencies concerned with justice for its citizens, but it is not clear what state agencies or other actors can do to help these groups make their cooperation fairer. So, how can locally-based institutions and substantive outcomes of the institutions be rendered more fairly? That question and many like it take on more force in the fairness-centered understanding of sustained cooperation presented here.

Reconsidering Community Governance

The collective action approach to cooperation, beginning with the assertion that communities of users can self-organize to solve collective action problems, provides a strong argument for decentralization. When applied to infrastructure governance, the policy recommendations dovetail with a type of decentralized governance called polycentrism (Ostrom, Tiebout, and Warren, 1961; McGinnis, 1999b, 1999a; Aligica and Tarko, 2012; McGinnis and Ostrom, 2012; Cole and McGinnis, 2014). In polycentric governance, administrative jurisdictions are formed around specific services or resources, not necessarily geographically or according to historical boundaries (Ostrom, 2010). These many centers of governance are then combined in a bottom-up fashion into larger governance structures. The ability of groups of users to solve collective action problems is what gives rise to the benefits of polycentric resource governance (Thiel, Blomquist, and Garrick, 2019). If the fairness problem is central to sustained cooperation instead of collective action problems, then the benefits of polycentrism to successful resource governance are less clear.

Some communities may possess a distinct advantage for avoiding collective action problems in the use and maintenance of shared resources, but this advantage does not automatically mean that they can avoid fairness problems. It is possible that a group of individuals successfully sharing a resource may not always be able to resolve or avoid these fairness problems on their own. Thus, the solution to the infrastructure governance puzzle—i.e., how best to govern shared resources—cannot be to leave it to the locals. At the same time, because some communities can remain fair, it is imperative to understand both the fairness problem and the role of communities in continuously addressing it.

User governance also has different justice implications when examined through the lens of fairness problems. The first concern is that it takes time for unfair cooperative systems to become fair or to deplete. If left to themselves, users can be subject to unfair systems of cooperation for arbitrary periods of time simply because the system has not yet experienced challenging circumstances. This possibility raises a normative concern, particularly when those who perceive the system as unfair have been historically subject to other forms of injustice as well such as class, race, or caste exploitation. This also highlights the central normative concern with leaving fairness to the locals: How long is it reasonable for users to wait before a system self-corrects to become fairer? Until it corrects or dies out, these users would continue to be subject to a system of cooperation they perceive as unfair. Furthermore, this system would be backed by the state itself—unless, that is, there are other means for communities to solve the fairness problem.

Introducing or strengthening participatory processes is the usual recommendation from policymakers and development agencies who want resources to be governed sustainably and in an adaptable way, but this is not certain to be effective. As these irrigation systems reveal, ensuring processes such as elected local bodies for resource governance coupled with voting mechanisms to change the governance rules do not ensure fairness in these types of cooperative situations. It is well-established that groups of individuals can self-organize to devise and commit to a system of self-governance around shared resources, and furthermore, they often will do so if the conditions are right. However, considering the fairness problem, it quickly becomes clear that they might not be able to remain fair as often as they might be able to cooperate. We know far less about the conditions under which these cooperative systems can remain fair than we do about the conditions that will encourage self-governance. So, what is to be done with locally governed systems that are unfair but persist, or those that are in decline because they are not perceived by their users to be fair?

Map of the Book

In this chapter, I introduced the book and provided a broad overview of its argument by highlighting the key elements. I began by emphasizing the necessity of collective action to human survival and underscoring a distinction between initial cooperation and sustaining cooperation once it has been achieved. I introduced the irrigation cases in the context of decentralization policy pursued by development organizations over the last four decades, and I highlighted Elinor Ostrom's "Design Principles for Long Enduring CPR Resources" as a very influential set of ideas for achieving successful collective action. I then explained how the rest of the book engages in conversation with that school of thought and summarized the main argument centered on the fairness problem.

In the second chapter, I move further into the details of irrigation systems. I first present a grounded account of one system and illustrate how collective action becomes necessary at each stage of using and maintaining it over time. I then connect these features into patterns that appear across the systems in this sample. I use this to explain how these systems in Nepal had all the requirements of successful collective action before presenting some unexpected results that show variation in their success over thirty years. I then show how the level of cooperation relates to the variables included in Ostrom's collective-action focused framework (Poteete, Janssen and Ostrom, 2010, pp. 235–237). I report that none of them prove adequate for explaining cooperation over time before examining the implications of this unexpected result. This sets up the puzzle that motivates the rest of the book.

Against this backdrop, in two chapters that follow (Chapters 3 and 4), I develop an explanation based on perceived fairness both empirically and theoretically. I do this by illustrating two general approaches to deducing what fairness is in these Nepalese irrigation systems and comparing them. One is the empirical approach, which analyzes responses to the question of why individuals reduced cooperation with their institutions (Chapter 3). It results in a conception of fairness based on the reasons people have for rejecting the existing rules. The other is the theoretical approach taken by Ostrom (Chapter 4) in which one looks for agreement, assumes users are broadly rational, and identifies fair rules as those that were agreed upon to use and maintain the irrigation canal. In this approach, one faces the task of modeling agreement among rational individuals, while the conception of fairness that arises from it attempts to capture the reasons that people might agree to rules. These two approaches support different conceptions of perceived fairness.

In the third chapter, I argue that people reduce their commitment to cooperation when they perceive the system of cooperation to be unfair. I begin by explaining how, in these cases, the level of cooperation among members of a group is directly visible in two ways: through the functioning of the shared canal, and through changes to the institutions that accompany successful cooperation. Using this insight, I add more texture to the empirical findings introduced in the first and second chapters. I argue that interviews with canal users provide a better understanding of why individual irrigators reduce their level of cooperation. I show that they do so when they perceive the outcomes of the cooperative institutions to be unfair, a tendency that I call unfairness aversion. I next assess the multi-dimensional nature of this revealed perception of fairness while highlighting that some of the elements of this perception are mutually incompatible. I then end with a question: what type of framework can accurately incorporate the complexity of actual perceptions of fairness?

In the fourth chapter, I argue that a contractarian conception of fairness and cooperation such as Ostrom's cannot accommodate this perception of fairness. I begin by showing how this dominant framework borrows a conception of fairness from Buchanan's contractarian tradition of Social Contract Theory (Congleton, 2014), which can in turn be traced to Hobbes (Nagel, 1959; Hobbes, 1996). Next, I illustrate that this tradition draws too sharp a distinction between the procedural and outcome aspects of fairness, while emphasizing the former. I show how this framework of variables and their relationships is built on the idea that a fair allocation of burdens and benefits per the rules consists of what the cooperators actually agree to, not in their adherence to an external standard. I explain how this conception of fairness is at odds with the dynamic perceptions of fairness encountered in the third chapter. I then argue that in relation to sustained cooperation, which includes the idea of time, this contractarian idea of fairness must be extended in significant ways, such as from measured inequality alone to perceived outcomes more generally, and based on a different conception of human motivations. I end by identifying the properties that a usable concept of fairness must have for thinking about fairness over time.

In the fifth chapter, I combine the theoretical discussion with the empirical findings to define the fairness problem. I argue that the problem of remaining fair becomes more important than collective action problems to sustained cooperation. I also note how sustained cooperation hinges on the ability of communities to solve the fairness problem. I begin by explaining how cooperators are grappling with the perpetual problem of figuring out what fairness means and then what rules will avoid unfairness. To illustrate this, I show how rule changes or changes in institutions are also attempts to grapple with the fairness problem. There are also factors outside of the group that can alter these dynamics, however. To explore some of the key factors, I trace how these systems adapted to the decade-long Maoist conflict in Nepal. I then explain that local communities may not be able to solve complex fairness problems on their own, even when they have solved collective action problems. Consequently, this variability opens up a wider range of roles for state institutions in shared resource governance than dominant understandings permit. I end with a discussion of how governments and local communities might address fairness problems.

The aim of the sixth and final chapter is to examine the implications, limits, and possibilities of this fairness-centered understanding of sustained cooperation. I begin by emphasizing the core insight of this book: that cooperation and fairness are not the same thing. I then give a restatement of the key claim that perceived fairness affects the quality of cooperation, which then renders the institutions of cooperation more or less robust to changes. I then illustrate how perceived fairness is a key to a better understanding of why some of the irrigation systems continue while others have declined, even though all of them exhibited the institutional prerequisites for solving collective action problems. I then show how this approach leads to a classification of the robustness of cooperation in examples beyond the cases in this study, exploring what a fairness-centered understanding of cooperation means for our understanding of user-governed infrastructure as well as for future studies. I end by summarizing the argument with examples for how and why the search for fairness must be central to our understanding of sustained cooperation in physical and digital spaces.

2

What Affects Sustained Cooperation?

It is helpful at this point to consider an example that illustrates what it means for users to sustain cooperation and for their irrigation system to perform well over time in the face of changing circumstances. There are two key aspects where sustained cooperation is critical and most visible. The first is in the actual day-to-day operation of the system. The second is in relation to the rules. In particular, in the updating of the rules to changed circumstances, enforcement of the rules, and compliance with the rules. The following example illustrates these aspects and also conveys myriad factors affecting cooperation in a typical system. With the dynamics of a relatively simple system in mind, data analysis across cases, and the more theoretical developments to follow are better motivated. I present the general features of sustained cooperation, and then present a specific example.

General Features of Sustained Cooperation

Cooperation in Everyday Canal Operation

Successful canal management by farmers resembles a well-synchronized dance. Each canal has its own version of the performance, and this is most visible during canal cleaning days. Usually well before the rainy season, farmers gather to perform a ritual to begin the planting season. Then they break up into groups and move to different parts of the canal, carrying shovels. One of them uses his stick to measure out, end on end, how much each person needs to clean, although this can vary. The same stick is used every year, and is the unit of measure for assigning cleaning work. In most cases, a farmer who irrigates twice the land that another does is assigned twice as many stick-length units of canal to clean. They might also work in groups sharing the work between them and alternating roles. The groups might be small teams of four or five people at various locations along the canal, or a majority of users working in a particular location at once. If so, at

Beyond Collective Action Problems. Atul Pokharel, Oxford University Press. © Oxford University Press 2024.
DOI: 10.1093/oso/9780197755792.003.0002

each location, one man stands in the canal and shovels mounds of sand out of the channel, and onto the ground alongside it. They break for a midafternoon meal (*khaja*), work through the remaining daylight, and go home as the sun sets. These labor days go on until the canal is clean and ready to carry water to their fields. Throughout these work days, the individual farmers behave as though they know exactly what needs to be done, and what other farmers will be doing.

This synchronicity continues into the planting season. The morning of the first day of watering, the owner of the plot closest to the canal's water source starts the day by diverting the channel to his fields. He leaves, and comes back to meet the next person in line at their appointed time with a greeting and conversation, usually about the canal or the water. He stops the diversion of water into his land, leaving the next in line to divert the water to their fields. This diversion may consist of a hole in the mud lining of the channel, or it may be a more advanced control structure such as a metallic gate that is lowered and raised by twisting a handle. A third man walks along the canal regularly to make sure that the canal is operating as it should, checking for cracks and blockages. As each person in line alternates into the irrigator position, all the fields become watered down to the very end of the canal. It usually takes a week to water all the fields depending on the crops, the amount of water, and the rules for distribution. Months later, depending on what the users have planted, crops all over the irrigated area mature in sequence of their watering, ripening and changing color reflecting the order in which the farmers got their water—a closing scene that can be awe inspiring.

The pattern of performance rarely plays out in similar fashion every year. Rivers change course, are flooded, farmers leave for work; new people who don't know the rules buy land in the command area; arguments become heated; someone may complain that they are not receiving enough water, and so on among many other possibilities. Sometimes, the farmers may need to temporarily adjust their performance. At other times, they may need to alter the rules governing their practices. Every change has uneven effects on farmers. For instance, some may end up getting less water, others may end up with a more preferred position in line, yet others might end up with a higher burden of cleaning.

Nevertheless, the farmers remain uncertain about what new conditions may arise and how that might affect the water they receive, and ultimately, the crops that they will be able to grow. The working rules that farmers use to synchronize with each other are subject to changing circumstances, mostly beyond the farmers' control. Yet, to keep the canal functioning they must coordinate their actions and work together. The result of dancing to different tunes is often a season of reduced crops, tightened belts, borrowing money, and possibly wage labor as porters in town.

Cooperation in Canal Governance

Of course, the set of rules the farmers follow to coordinate their activities has no agency of its own, even though it might outlast individual farmers and be passed on across generations. It is the farmers themselves who must ultimately change the rules that they use in response to changing circumstances. This too requires cooperation between the farmers. Before farmers can cooperate with the system's rules in order for it to function as intended, they must cooperate with each other to choose or alter their rules.

There are many complex circumstances to which rules may need to be adapted by their users, including changing relationships between users, external conditions of their environment, political changes,[1] and technology among others. Some of them are specific to particular institutions or locations. For example, about 20% of canals in the sample are frequently damaged by natural disasters such as floods and landslides while the remaining 80% are not. The rules must accommodate these conditions. In the GD Canal, which I describe next, it was only after a new headworks had to be built because the old one was damaged by a flood that the group adopted a rule specifying what was required of users in emergency situations such as building a new headworks. In a similar way, a location's particular history is one of the reasons that the specific rules of these systems differ even though, on the whole, they are all intended to help manage the canal.

Along with these differences, there are also circumstances that most of these systems are likely to have encountered. For example, an existential decision that a group of users must take is who qualifies to use the water from their canal and who does not. In nearly all of the cases, this criterion is expressed as a rule. The specific criteria used to grant access to the canals in this sample are shown in the first column of Table 4. It is common to find combinations of these requirements, such as both the ownership of land to be irrigated and the payment of a seasonal water fee. Most systems in this sample have rules concerning the allocation of water, of work that has to be done on the canal, and for punishing rule breakers, monitoring activities, and resolving disputes. Similar to the variety of rules that define eligibility, there is a range of specific rules that address each of these situations.

---

[1] Prior work using this data set scarcely mentions party politics although more recent work on shared resource commons is catching up to the political process. This is admitted in the idea of "winning coalitions" and negotiation of rules, although the word "political" remains mostly absent. See for instance Poteete et al. (2010) for an Ostromian take and Bardhan and Mookherjee (2020) for a broader summary of the frontiers of a more politically aware approach.

Table 4 **The number of systems that have a particular requirement for becoming a user. The leftmost column contains the various requirements. The remaining two show the number in the first and second visits with percentages in parentheses. The second round of visits shown includes the added sample of 39 systems together with the 202 that are still surviving from the original sample.**

Requirements for becoming a user*	First survey (N = 233)	Second survey (N = 241)
Be a resident of the locality	3 (1.3)	46 (19.1)
Be of a certain ethnic group or caste	0 (0)	1 (0.4)
Be a member of a certain organization	54 (2.3)	39 (16.2)
Own shares in the canal	4 (1.8)	12 (5.0)
Own or lease rights to water	12 (5.2)	17 (7.1)
Pay a seasonal water fee	20 (8.6)	52 (21.6)
Own or lease land in the location	193 (83.8)	146 (60.6)
Have continuously used water in the past	4 (1.7)	19 (7.9)
Use water only for agriculture	21 (9.0)	23 (9.5)
Get rights through a lottery	0 (0)	1 (0.4)
Own shares in an organization	1 (0.4)	2 (0.8)

*78 (33%) in the first round and 100 (36%) in the second had multiple criteria.

This table shows that even the most basic rule about who qualifies as a user likely changed during the decades between the first and second observations. Indeed, this intertwined complexity of change, copying, learning, trial and error, and adaptation is common to all durable canal management institutions (Simon et al., 1962). But it can also be highly specific to particular systems. To understand the cooperation needed to make these sorts of rule changes, I describe the dynamics of the GD canal next. It is important to keep in mind that these dynamics take place against the cyclic backdrop of the cooperation involved in everyday canal operation.

GD Canal: A Typical Example of Sustained Cooperation

The GD Canal in Western Nepal has been in continuous use for nearly 60 years. A year after it was upgraded to have a large concrete weir at the headworks and handed over to the users to manage in 1995, it was severely damaged by a flood.

Funding for this project had been provided by the Agricultural Development Bank, a major government bank. The handover was implemented as part of a "Community Irrigation Project" funded by multiple international donor agencies through the setting up of "federated" user's associations that were formally registered with the Department of Irrigation of the Government of Nepal. As part of the handover, and with help from the Department of Irrigation, the users adopted a constitution that stated the rules for how the canal was to be used.

Nested Water User's Associations

Each village had its own Water User's Association. Four villages jointly managed the canal through an umbrella association that had representatives from each village, in proportion to the division of water between them. Each of the four associations had its own constitution, written at the time of the handover. The constitution followed a common template. These constitutions allowed for the election of a local chairman although users reported that these leaders were chosen by consensus before the election, which was seen as a formality. This position was usually assumed by the largest landholder, or the person who already held the position of leader in the local government of the area, such as the former *pradhan pancha*.[2]

A concrete aqueduct that carried water over the river to fields on the other side was among the parts damaged by flood. This relatively advanced—and expensive—structure served two villages. More importantly, the headworks itself was also damaged. The umbrella association eventually received money for the repairs from the Department of Irrigation. The users repaired the headworks and created a diversion to bypass the aqueduct and get water to the two villages. The new diversion was damaged the following year, this time stopping water from flowing to one of the two villages on the other side of the river. Because the required repairs served only a single village, the umbrella association decided that the village association should bear the costs. The repair that resulted was temporary and unreliable, primarily because the users in this village did not know how to repair it properly, and had less money available to do so than the parent association would have had.

[2] Five years after moving to a democratic constitution from an absolute monarchy, villages in Nepal were still dominated by families that had governed during the Royal Administration, or the Panchayat System. For donors who were looking for efficiency, and because of the practical difficulties of holding elections for these Water User's Associations, letting villagers choose a leader by "consensus" was the most reasonable and practical thing to do. Few locals wanted to upset locally powerful families by opposing the candidacy of the former leaders, or *pradhan panchas*.

A Village Breaks Away

After being neglected by their parent association, the users in this fourth village that was left to itself decided around 2007 at their General Assembly meeting that they would formally separate from it. By this time, "The People's War" waged by the Maoist Party had forced large landholders to stay away from the village for months at a time. Consequently, the landowners' influence over the Water User's Association in this village had weakened and the chairman, who had been the chairman from the very beginning and was a prominent representative of the largest landholders, stepped aside "to give others a chance," as he put it.

The new chairman—also chosen by consensus[3]—was the head of two other local organizations. He was the elected chairman of the Village Development Committee for his village, which is the lowest level administrative body of the Government of Nepal.[4] But more importantly, he was the chairman of the local branch of the Nepal Communist Party (UML), one of the two largest political parties in the country.[5] This new chairman had proposed the separation from the parent association after being confident that he would get alternative forms of support because of his formal and informal connections with the District Development Committee and the UML.

The Centrality of Politics

Prior to the split from the parent Water Users Association, it had been difficult for him to justify using resources from the Village Development Committee (VDC) for the canal because it was the formal responsibility of the parent Water User's Association. His party superiors had also indicated that the funds that they had secured for him through administrative channels should be used for other things such as seed distribution.[6] This was a logical way to counter the power that the other political parties[7] had gained through their dominance of

---

[3] Although nearly all of the canals had formal mechanisms of elections for leaders—a required feature of donor-supported Water User's Associations—they seemed to use elections only to resolve difficult disputes. At other times, the elections merely formalized agreements that users had already reached amongst themselves and outside of these formal, and foreign, mechanisms.

[4] There were many wards per village, many villages per district, and 75 districts in the country.

[5] This party is also called the UML, or Untied Marxist Leninist which is different from the Maoist Party. As the major opposition party at the time, the UML had been in and out of power multiple times since the country had moved to a multiparty system in 1990. During the People's War, the UML was also targeted by the Maoist rebels.

[6] This emerged through interviews of the chairman, as well as party functionaries at the district level.

[7] In this case, the major party was the National Democratic Party (RPP), and the Nepali Congress.

the umbrella Water User's Association. But in the face of changed circumstances, discussions with his fellow comrades turned up a new idea: repairing the canal in the name of the party in order to fill the political vacuum that was being created with the departure of the old chairman.

By showing the promise of support from his party, and with Rs. 5,000 of discretionary funds[8] from the VDC, he could now ask other users to contribute toward the construction of a new headworks downstream from the aqueduct. According to this plan, a simpler headworks was to be built with stones and twine. It would be in such a position on the river bank that it could funnel water into a part of the old channel that was sufficiently upstream from the village to irrigate most of the fields that used to be irrigated. Once approved by a meeting of users, the committee hired brick and cement workers (*mistris*) from a nearby town. Other villagers carried stones and other materials as needed to save on wages that would have been paid to day laborers. The same group of users also donated materials such as stones and brick, loosely based on how much land each user irrigated.

According to the rules of their institution, none of these additional contributions were required from users. In fact, the old rules did not address emergency situations in which a new intake had to be built. Instead, there was an informal understanding between the representatives from the four user's associations that they would all help each other as needed. Thus, this was the first change in rules because of the shock. The institution now requires mandatory contributions to cover emergencies and unexpected circumstances in proportion to the water that a farmer uses.[9]

The most difficult contribution to secure, and also the most contentious, was the land to build the new intake. None of the farmers whose land could have been used for this purpose wanted to lose a piece of fertile land bordering a canal without being compensated adequately. However, paying them market rate would have made the whole project unaffordable. Here again the UML came into play—other officials in the local party organization convinced a farmer who was also in the party to donate some land for a token amount.[10]

Eventually, all the different dynamics came together and the headworks became functional. Despite money coming from the Village Development

---

[8] This was about 70 USD in 2007. The monthly salary of an entry level government employee at the time was around Rs. 5,000.

[9] According to users, the General Assembly adopted this rule because a user had seen that other similar groups also had it.

[10] Respondents would not disclose what the deal entailed, but it was clear in interviews with the farmer in private as well as the other party members that he had been promised something in return by the district level party organization.

Committee, and all of the other contributions of labor, materials and land coming from users, the common refrain amongst farmers was that "our own party made it." The role of a non-local political party in the resilience of local canal governance institutions like this one is very common but also relatively invisible to a passing observer in part because users tend to hide it.[11]

New Rules for New Conditions

The new intake created a new set of operational challenges. As described earlier, the new structure was not as advanced as the original one and less water was available to users. It was also less reliable because it could be more easily blocked by rocks and debris; and it was more prone to damage from yearly swelling of the river. In turn, this meant that for water to reach the tail end users, others had to limit their usage more than before. There were many who were reluctant to reduce their share, especially those who lived closer to the head, because they were used to taking as much water as they wanted.

The rules stated that each farmer would receive water in proportion to the land they irrigated, and in return each user was required to contribute labor in proportion to their irrigated land. When the old canal was functioning, anyone could take as much water as they needed during their time slot. At the beginning of the time slot, the next person would make sure that the opening before theirs was closed before directing the water to their fields. Because of the abundance of water, it was common for the next in line to wait until morning even if the handover time was in the middle of the night. During a time of relative abundance, the turn-based sequence was primarily intended to make sure that everyone got water in time. It hadn't been intended to limit water use.

With the new headworks, and the much smaller amount of water available, the turn-based system turned into a way to limit the amount of water that each user took. Before the new headworks, the general feeling amongst users was that they were all making do with a temporary arrangement. However, having invested heavily in a new construction, all expected more than was available.

---

[11] In the GD Canal one of the chairman's strengths was that he could communicate with donors and consultants who came to study the canal, and evaluate their aid investments. As the chairman admitted, and some users concurred, one of his qualifications was that he "knew the answers." His job was also that of an ambassador who, with help from people he knew in his party, understood what the donors were looking for. Across canals, the chairmen noted that he knew that "working together," "voluntary villager contributions," "cooperation," "local resolution of disputes," "regular meetings," and "inclusion of ethnic minorities" were keywords to be mentioned. He knew never to talk about the contentious involvement of political parties, but to always stress harmonious local cooperation among users.

Monitoring of handovers became stricter. The guard who was responsible for checking for damage to the canal now started enforcing penalties for overuse. Arguments between users over water became common, and there were incidents of vandalism: the most common form was taking a shovel to another's field channels, preventing them from taking water in turn. The next user in line would sometimes camp out all night to make sure that he got his water. If the prior user did not stop drawing water, there could be a physical confrontation. And the issue would be brought up at the meeting of the User's Association, making these meetings more contentious and longer than before. Paying the fine for taking more water became seen as a necessary cost by some farmers who could afford it: after all, once water had been absorbed into the soil, there was no way to take it back. Increasingly, some wealthier farmers upstream began taking more water than they were allowed. Reduced water use also reduced the amount of labor that people contributed to maintenance. The length of canal that had to be maintained was the same, but fewer resources were available to maintain it.

Another set of institutional challenges came from the location of the new intake. Water now entered the canal further downstream from the original intake. Before, the water would flow over a long length of canal before reaching the village, and would deposit silt along the way. But now water reached the village directly from the river, thereby carrying more silt into the village's channels. This demanded cleaning more often lest the volume of the canal decrease. The headworks also required more maintenance and oversight as it was no longer a permanent structure. Any damage to the headworks would eventually result in less water in the canal, so users had a good reason to detect problems early. But increased inspection meant more work for users.

Conflicts had also increased with nonusers. For instance, a group of people from Rolpa, a mountainous district to the North, had fled the People's War and settled upstream of the new headworks. They made a living by operating a water powered grain mill, which diverted a substantial amount of water from the river when it was in use. This hadn't mattered before because the previous intake was upstream of the mill. But now, their water use had caused direct confrontations with the users of this canal. A group of five to ten farmers would occasionally visit these nonusers at night and demand that they stop. Not many farmers wanted to go on these intimidation missions, and their rules did not require it or compensate them for their extra effort.

The old rules were not working with the new conditions. The result of mixing old rules and new conditions was that the canal began to deteriorate. Much less water was available, especially to downstream users; fewer workers were available to maintain the canal; and the group of users became highly suspicious of each other. The user's group meetings were dominated by disputes between farmers. Yet, the institution changed eventually and still exists. There were three elements of this adaptation: experimentation, withdrawing of cooperation, and another political party.

The new canal intake required more labor input to maintain, increased the expectations of users, and demanded voluntary contributions from farmers whose time was already scarce in the planting season. In response, the farmers at various points along the canal—the head, middle and tail- adopted different strategies to cope with these changes.

The users who were closer to the head were also wealthier, and had larger plots of land. The chairman's plot was in the middle of the canal, but closer to the head than the tail. His was also the area where the UML was strongest, and even those with smaller plots in the middle had more influence now because of their party's control of the Water User's Association. But the rising prominence of the UML in the canal's association had made it more difficult for party members to punish each other for breaking the rules and taking more water.[12]

Those farmers who were further downstream began to lose hope that the canal would serve them. They were normally the poorest, and belonged to an indigenous ethnicity, not the now dominant Tharus. Although the largest land-holder had his land close to the tail, his family had not returned to the village with the same power as before the People's War. One of the main reasons water continued to flow downstream toward the tail was because this man owned land there. So, his relative powerlessness resulted in less water at the tail. Instead of working in agriculture, the tail enders began to seek work for a daily wage in the nearest town. The journey was too long to make frequently, and so they began spending more time away from the village.[13]

In the past, most of the workers for upper parts of the canal had come from these villages at the tail. Farmers at the head end had sent their children to schools in town, or were themselves teachers and grain merchants. Their families, although large, were not in the village regularly. In fact, although the institution's rules didn't allow it, these users often hired wage laborers from other villages and towns to work on the canal instead of family members as required. However, that these users were breaking the rules had never been a point of contention with the other users—"they were doing their own things, we were doing our own things," was how one tail-ender described it. But now the tail enders used this as an example of how the powerful people "always broke the rules" and they also claimed that "the rules are just to keep us poor."

---

[12] Interestingly, this suggests that in this case, political homogeneity made enforcing rules more difficult, which is in contrast to the prediction that heterogeneity is more of a challenge to local self-governance than homogeneity (Varughese and Ostrom, 2001; Bardhan and Dayton-Johnson, 2002).

[13] Prolonged absences were not explicitly allowed in this system, although they were in many others.

Another change had resulted in alternative economic and social options for the tail enders. A few years before, Christian missionaries had begun to convert people living at the tail with the promise of a better living and also instant freedom from an oppressive caste system. Those affiliated with this new religion appeared economically better off, and received regular support from Christian organizations in Kathmandu and abroad. Priests in particular were paid a regular salary, and others received training in sewing, crafts, and other work. This was drawing more and more tail enders away from agriculture, especially the younger ones who enjoyed the singing during church, as well as the camaraderie of bible reading gatherings.[14] Indeed, the poorest tail enders—those who were most likely to work on the canal for wages—gradually began severing all interdependence with those further upstream, effectively distancing themselves not only from the canal institution but the society of canal users as it was.

As the tail enders began to move toward other occupations, they effectively withdrew their cooperation with the system. Consequently, a major source of labor dried up too. This made it even more difficult for other users to keep the canal in functioning order. Another direct result of this was that the user's association changed its rules to allow hiring labor from outside to do work on the canal. This turned an activity from the realm of rule breaking to the norm, because it seemed to work in this new situation. Other users even relied on the networks of people that the former rule breakers had used to secure workers. But this was not a solution: not everyone could afford paying for workers, and without willing workers from amongst the canal users, the shortage continued to he felt.

As those furthest from the head stopped engaging in agriculture, those who were previously in the middle of the canal became the new tail end canal users. There were many in the former middle who still engaged in agriculture, and unable to receive regular water or speak up at the user's association meetings they tried another approach. In town, a few of them met with members of a second political party, The Nepali Congress, to try to broker a deal with the leaders of the UML controlled user's association.

However, the users who had turned to this other party later felt the effort did not work primarily because the Nepali Congress was not powerful enough to force a compromise. In fact, they said that turning to another party had made it more difficult to be "heard" by the leaders of the user's association. However, the

---

[14] There was also a visible difference in villages in which Christian missionaries had organized the locals. They were defined by a prominent church made of concrete, and bright colors. And homes could often be seen displaying portraits of Christ that were placed directly adjacent to the main entrance so as to be visible to passerby, as if to announce independence from generations of religious and economic oppression.

chairman who had overseen the building of the new canal eventually stepped aside. Like his predecessor, he said it was "to give other people a chance." It is also possible that his party had come to sense that a political opportunity was opening up for an opposing party.[15]

Under the new chairman, the rules changed again. The boundaries of the canal were now drawn closer to the head. This excluded those at the furthest end of the canal, the former tail-enders, from the user's association.[16] They changed their rule for allocating water between the remaining users. Instead of the users at the head end receiving water first every season, they alternated with the tail. If this season, those at the head end took water first and the sequence moved down, then next season those at the tail would take water first and the sequence would move up. The leaders of the user's group also came to an agreement with the mill owners upstream to divert a certain percentage of water to them and the remaining to the canal users.

This modified rules appear to be meeting the needs of users so far, and those who are using it report that the canal is functioning in a relatively timely, adequate and reliable manner. The physical condition of the canal is also good, although the headworks is damaged almost yearly. However, the users have repaired it quickly every time so far, with financial assistance from the Village Development Committee.

A Chain of Rule Changes

Over decades, most conditions that affect a resource and its users change. In the case of canals in Nepal, the changes have been rapid and multidimensional. On average, the survey shows that each canal has experienced 4 such changes since it was first visited. These changing conditions have led to variations in the specific rules over time. Consequently, none of the systems have remained unchanged in this period. Amidst this complexity, some groups of users simply may not have the capacity to come up with appropriate rules that can continue to elicit cooperation. Yet, even after rules have been devised and users have committed to cooperating with the rules of the institution, there is always the question of whether the change will work. After all, the behavior that results from following the institution must keep the canal adequately functioning. Even if the rule change was imported from another canal, it may not have the desired effects in the new case. Table 5 summarizes the key changes that occurred in the GD canal between 1995 and 2013.

---

[15] This was suggested by other users. Because the change had taken place in the two years prior to the interviews, no one appeared to want to directly confirm what had happened.

[16] This was decided at the general assembly meeting which those downstream had not attended, having stopped taking part in the system.

Table 5 **Old rules, new conditions, and problems, as well as rule changes that arose from them, in the GD Canal.**

Old rules	Changed condition	Resulting problems	New rules	Resulting solutions
Association was governed by an umbrella association, which received funds from government agencies for repairs to member canals.	Repeated damage to the intake of this village's Canal reduced water availability and reliability.	This village was forced to repair the damage on its own without assistance because the damage did not affect the other villages.	Formal separation from the umbrella association.	This allowed the group to make decisions independently of the umbrella association, and receive direct funds from government agencies.
No specific rules requiring the contributions for emergency repair.	A new headworks had to be built because of repeated damages to the old one.	Farmers were not willing to contribute. They were unclear about how much or what to contribute, and whether others would also contribute.	Rules requiring voluntary contributions for emergency repairs. Contributions in proportion to land irrigated by each farmer.	This made it more clear what an emergency situation was, and what each farmer would be required to contribute.
Mandatory labor contributions from farmers in proportion to the land irrigated. No outside labor used.	A smaller intake, made of temporary materials. Less water in the canal.	Less water available meant less land was irrigated. This reduced the amount of man-days of labor available for maintenance.	Allow the use of hired labor from outside of the village.	This increased the available labor pool beyond what users were willing to do.
Water applied to the fields based on time slots that were enforced by users themselves.	Less water available, downstream users camping out at night to make sure transfer was on time. Increased user vigilance.	Increase in arguments and suspicion between users. Relationships between users becoming contentious.	Rotate yearly whether the tail end gets water first or the head.	Users were more confident that they would get water. But the rule changes alone did not solve the contentious relationships.

In the face of this complexity and unpredictability, how do users know what rules to change, and how do they know what to change the rules to? A version of this problem is regarded in the literature on institutional emergence as the problem of institutional supply, as opposed to the problem of compliance (Ostrom, 1990). In this literature, the prevalent hypothesis is that local users learn which rules work by trial and error. This leads to a process in which the rules are changed, the results assessed, and the change either kept or rejected, or changed further. Over time, this process of "search" is predicted to result in rules that "fit" given conditions most appropriately.[17]

Like the cooperation required for everyday functioning of the system, continuous adaptation of mutually agreed upon rules to meet the demands of changed conditions while still providing users adequate reason to continue to cooperate also requires sustained cooperation. This example serves to illustrate the nature of cooperation and the myriad, seemingly highly unique, dynamics within which cooperation must be sustained. As noted earlier, Ostrom's approach provides one way to parse the complexity and systematically classify irrigation systems in order to focus on the factors that most affect cooperation in these settings. Given the seemingly unique circumstances of each system, such a framework becomes indispensable for comparing many cases.

Elements of the Empirical Approach

Using the IAD framework, Ostrom predicts that three classes of variables affect cooperation in sequence: first, external shock variables, then group variables, and then behavioral variables. Consider the properties of a study that can statistically test these predictions about what factors affect sustained cooperation. Such a study requires observations for at least two points in time per case, as well as a comparable set of variables recorded for that set of cases. This set needs to be representative of the universe of shared-resource situations. Furthermore, the survey should have strong internal and external validity. The observations also should be separated by a reasonable time period, in this case of the order of decades. The reason for this range of time is to allow these types of institutions to change, according to the new institutional literature upon which Ostrom has drawn (Williamson, 2000).

---

[17] This argument about the opaque complexity of local conditions is similar to the argument laid out in Hayek (1945) against centralized planning. They both rely on the presumption that at least some information relevant to the task—devising appropriate institutions in the former and allocating resources efficiently in the latter—is unavailable to nonlocals. There are many accounts of how rules change in the literature on institutions (Mahoney and Thelen, 2010), and the notion of search that is implied here is described in Simon (1962).

The set of cases that I use come from the Nepal Irrigation Institutions and Systems (NIIS) data set. This is a set of 233 irrigation systems in Nepal originally compiled, coded and analyzed by Elinor Ostrom and her team at Indiana University. The NIIS includes systems in 30 of Nepal's 75 districts. The mean canal length is 618 m with a standard deviation of 324 m and the number of users fluctuates over time. This data set does not meet all the conditions of an ideal study that could test these predictions statistically, but it comes closer than anything that is available as of this writing.[18] An authoritative account of the history and aims of the NIIS research program can be found elsewhere (Poteete, Janssen and Ostrom, 2010, pp. 102–107; Frey, 2020). Summary statistics are included in the Methods Appendix.

This data set has several shortcomings compared to the ideal features noted above. Namely, the sampling favors accessible systems and is not representative of the universe of shared-resource situations. The data set also contains only one type of system in one country. However, the data quality is high because it was supplemented with fieldwork. In particular, the authors note that the NIIS data set provides a high degree of internal validity to the concepts measured in it (Poteete, Janssen and Ostrom, 2010, p. 105). The NIIS has a higher quality of data compared to other data sets such as the precursor Common Pool Resource (CPR) database. For this reason, even though the CPR database contains different types of shared resources beyond irrigation systems, the NIIS makes a better starting point for adding a second set of observations. It is important to note that the CPR database was entirely based on the IAD framework, and so was the NIIS. The latter benefitted from lessons learned while compiling the CPR data set and can be considered an improvement over it. The NIIS was intended for a "model-centered metaanalysis" (Poteete, Janssen, and Ostrom, 2010, p. 91). That is, it was designed to capture all of the variables deemed relevant to collective action problems by the IAD framework. This enabled the authors to say of the NIIS that "all major variables" (according to the IAD) are included there (Poteete, Janssen, and Ostrom, 2010, p. 103).

The NIIS has 509 variables per case (which is greater than the total number of cases).[19] With such a large number of variables to investigate statistically, there are the usual challenges of variable selection and of multiple comparison, so some care is needed to avoid these two pitfalls by using the appropriate statistical tests.

---

[18] Complete details on the methodology and data characteristics can be found in the Methods Appendix.

[19] In the second round, there are 1,116 variables, accounting for before and after questions about Maoist conflict.

To meet the multiple observation condition, I resurveyed all these paradigmatic cases of irrigation canals in Nepal between 16 and 37 years after they were first studied. Details of the sampling process can be found in the Methods Appendix. This resulted in two observations per system, separated by at least a decade. I also reasoned that without formal training in the IAD framework and with the opportunity to interview respondents myself, I might regard different observations as salient or ask different questions.[20] This would allow me to examine the claim as to whether all relevant variables were included in the IAD framework.

It is standard practice to assess prior results using a smaller random sampling of the original cases. A small sample assessment is often the most efficient balance between effort and rigor. However, a small sample approach is less useful here since the original case selection was, as explained above, neither random nor representative of a larger population, so a smaller sample wouldn't offer the same confidence for checking results derived from the bigger sample. Moreover, the main intention is not to audit the IAD framework but to understand the phenomenon (cooperation) that it intends to capture. In particular, the aim is to assess whether a collective action-centered account of cooperation can correctly capture the factors affecting sustained cooperation. I do this by examining the significance of the variables identified by the IAD framework. To maintain high internal validity of the survey, I conducted interviews with the respondents to augment the survey data collection. I also refrained from using any frameworks other than the IAD framework, based on which the survey was designed. This is a different approach from Lejano (2023), who begins with a relational model of human beings in order to build a fundamentally different framework to explain the same types of cooperation that the IAD framework does.

In order to make up partially for the unknown nature of the biases in the original sample, I added a new sample of 39 additional canals chosen randomly. One canal was selected from each of the 39 districts left out of the original NIIS sample, as shown in Figure 2. The upper map in this figure shows the number of systems sampled by district in Nepal in the original NIIS, with district numbers bracketed. The lower map shows the predominant terrain-type in each district with district numbers in each district boundary. The terrain also corresponds with the climactic zone: Terai with Subtropical, Hill with Temperate and Mountain with Alpine. The first round had systems from 30 districts out of 75, and the second round 69. Six districts were inaccessible because of extreme weather. There was no pattern to this selection, although there were a few likely influences. First, the enumerators were bound, just as in the original study, to

---

[20] A danger is that it is misunderstood, or that important parts are underemphasized if not missed altogether.

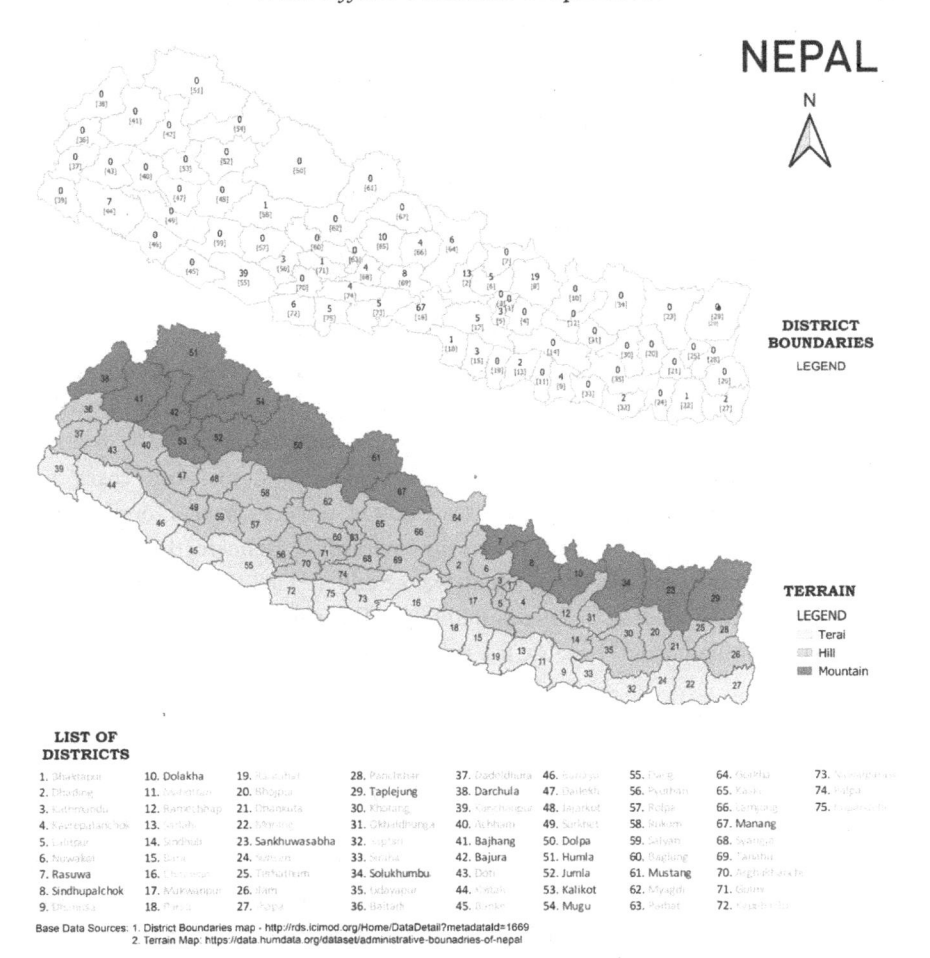

Figure 2 Locations sampled. The upper map in this figure shows the number of systems sampled by district in Nepal in the original NIIS, with district numbers bracketed. The lower map shows the predominant terrain-type in each district with district numbers in each district boundary. The terrain also corresponds with the climactic zone: Terai with Subtropical, Hill with Temperate, and Mountain with Alpine. The first round had systems from 30 districts out of 75, and the second round 69. Six districts were inaccessible because of extreme weather.

survey systems that they could reach and study within a reasonable amount of time. For the added systems, a reasonable amount of time was approximately two days from the nearest town by foot. This pulled the sample toward those systems that were closer to towns while systematically excluding those that were further away. Despite adding another sample of 39 cases, the external validity remains as limited as the original NIIS. Much can be learned about cooperation from this combined set of 272 irrigation systems, but the characteristics of this data set—namely, the convenience sample and the restriction to one country and one type of resource—limit the types of inference that can be drawn from it. In particular, only non-stochastic interpretations can be considered reliable. That is, the strongest type of statistical statement possible is that the patterns presented are important to consider. Other claims such as the reasons that people stop cooperating are beyond the capacity of the numerical data to support. Instead, they are supported by interviews with irrigators as well as the ethnographic study of two systems.

This study had several iterative stages of data collection and analysis. They resulted in two observations each for 233 irrigation systems separated by between 16 and 37 years and one observation each for 39 systems. Additionally, there were recorded interviews with 827 respondents (approx. 1,200 hours), and detailed case studies of two canals. I use "canals," "systems," and "cases" interchangeably. The survey portion of this study is in the form of a longitudinal data set of 509 variables per case at two time periods.[21] Henceforth, the second round refers to the second survey, which was conducted in 2013. The first round refers to the data collected in the original NIIS. The sampling in the two rounds resembles a "spilled panel" because the second-round sample covers and extends beyond the first.

Analysis Methods

Of the three general approaches that have been applied in the past—agent based modeling, regression analysis and non-stochastic analysis—I use the third. The weight given to the results from each approach hinges on the extent to which one believes that the unknown sampling could be a significant source of selection bias. I discuss the last two approaches here—first assuming that the sampling cannot be reliably modeled and second assuming that the sampling can be largely accounted for. I regard the results of the former—using contingency tables—to be the most reliable, although they are also the most limited. This is because, as indicated above, this is a convenience sample of irrigation systems even though the data for each system is longitudinal and each variable has strong internal validity.

To justify the nonstochastic (or nonparametric) approach that uses contingency tables, one can argue that I had no control over the sample selection in the survey done by Ostrom's team. Since this study stands on that one, there is good

---

[21] I refer the reader to the Methods Appendix and Expanded Results Appendix for more details and summary statistics of the variables.

reason to use exact tests to look for significant patterns in the non-stochastic approach (Freedman and Lane, 1983). In the analysis that I present, multiple comparisons are not corrected for in order to minimize the risk of ruling out possibly significant regularities. Variable choice is thus critical, and so I rely on prior studies and the broader literature to identify comparators. In this scenario, the exact tests render the data usable by allowing for the identification of significant regularities that are unlikely to be due to chance alone. This approach imposes a smaller set of assumptions on the data than regression analysis for instance, and can be used with unknown sampling, although it severely limits the inferences to tests of independence (Agresti, 2012, pp. 75–80). This is a necessary trade-off because the results of probabilistic modeling would likely be meaningless or irresponsible to interpret. In all hypothesis testing scenarios, the null hypothesis to be tested could itself be misleading without knowing how the initial sample was chosen by, and before, Ostrom. For example, it is not possible to confidently rule out survivorship bias or the ecological fallacy based on the original sampling alone. With multivariate analysis of this type ruled out, I control for two or more variables by using nested contingency tables.

For the sake of completeness, I must note that if one can make it past the problematic sampling—a move that I argue is unjustified given the properties of the sample and the aims of this book—then a larger range of regression analysis opens up. Although I do not rely on the results of these models in this text, they do allow one to both control for particular variables and examine their relative significance. No special techniques are needed aside from linear transformations of variables, but at the cost of yet more assumptions about the structure of a data set whose sampling is already unknown, as well as the disqualifying of a significant number of observations (Powers, 1999, pp. 179–182). In particular, by including variables that could have influenced sampling in the regression, one can attempt to control for sampling errors. I leave that level of conjecture for the future in order to avoid unnecessary distraction from the findings presented here. Given the fundamental unknowns regarding the sample and data collection, the regression models serve to highlight the myriad assumptions made of the data that would need to be met but are not. I hope their clear shortcomings invite the interested reader to design a longitudinal study that can support these more sophisticated methods.[22] A fuller discussion of these assumptions can be found in the Methodological Appendix.

---

[22] One could argue similarly for and against a logistic regression with mixed effects and its variants. It would not need to drop so many observations, but they are not only the least reliable within the present study constraints, they also give inconsistent results and still layer on additional unrealistic data assumptions (Hosmer Jr., Lemeshow, and Sturdivant, 2013, pp. 315–318). I do not include the results of that analysis here.

Some Surprising Results

Irrigation system user groups in these cases were able to sustain their cooperation over decades, even in the most challenging circumstances. A majority of systems were resurveyed between 20 and 25 years after the first survey, with the most recent one surveyed 16 years ago and the oldest 37. The period of time between 1988 and 2013 was particularly convulsive for Nepal institutionally, politically, and economically. During this time, Nepal's irrigation systems were exposed to rapid, exogenous changes, failure to transmit working rules between generations of users, easy access to external funds, corruption, and lack of supportive large-scale institutional arrangements. These are precisely the types of shocks predicted using Ostrom's framework to pose the most serious danger to this type of cooperative system (Ostrom, 2005, p. 272). Instead of being localized in particular parts of the country, these changes swept across it. There were two new constitutions with a third being drafted, multiple changes of government, and a change from a monarchy to a constitutional monarchy to a federal republic. The country went through a period of economic liberalization, mass out-migration of labor, a torrent of development assistance, rapid road-building, and urbanization. These political shifts and labor dynamics are also detailed by way of an example in Chapter 5. After all this, 202 (87%) groups of individuals were able to keep their systems functional by sustaining their cooperation, while 13% (31) of the canals stopped functioning altogether. This proportion lends support to the claim that local users have the ability to adapt in order to sustain cooperation.

While they did not become defunct, some of these 202 systems declined in performance while others did not, as shown in Figure 3. These systems' changes in performance[23] were not significantly related to the number, frequency, or type of external shocks, as would be expected in Ostrom's view (Table 6, Table 7, Table 8, Table 34, Table 35). As I explain shortly, those that declined did so because the users couldn't or didn't cooperate in maintaining them, and others fended off decline by continuing to cooperate.

There are a few other remarkable features of the ability of these groups to sustain cooperation to use and maintain their shared irrigation systems. First, their ability to sustain cooperation depends on how long they have been cooperating. In particular, the more shocks they are able to adapt to, the more likely they will adapt in the future. Table 8 shows the significant (Fisher's $\alpha = 0.05$) relationship between the time between observations and whether or not the systems survived. The longer the gap between the first and second observations, the more shocks they may have experienced given the myriad changes occurring in the country at the time. Where the predictions lead us to expect that the more the shocks

---

[23] Performance is measured along two broad dimensions of perceived functioning and physical condition of the canal.

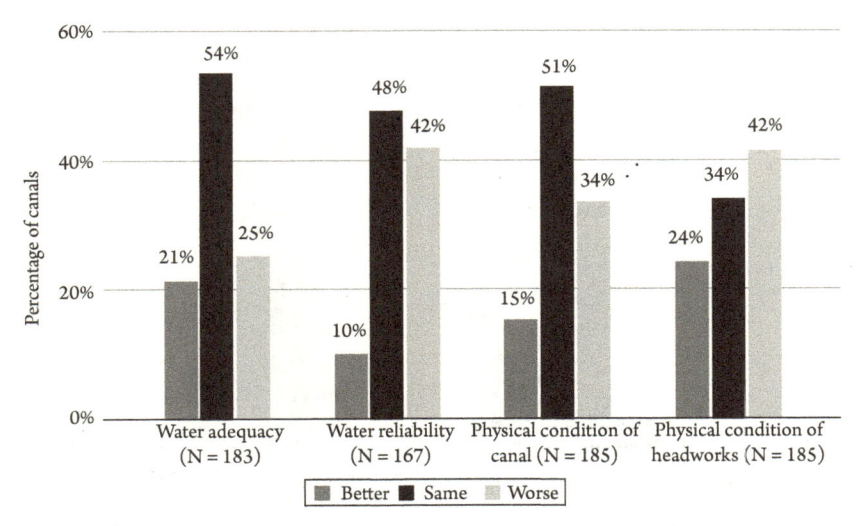

Figure 3 How canal performance has changed in farmer-managed irrigation systems in Nepal (1976–2013): This figure shows changes in the four aspects of canal performance (Water adequacy, Water reliability, Physical condition of canal and Physical condition of headworks) within cases between the first and second surveys. Changes to each of the aspects are computed by subtracting their values in the two surveys.

that are experienced, the less likely they are to survive, the opposite is the case. This is not the full story, however. What is not shown is that the shorter the time between observations, the more likely it was that the systems were younger. The older the systems were the more likely they were to survive, possibly because

Table 6 **Survival proportions by type of shock experienced: Each row in this table represents one of the reasons that users of defunct canals cited as a cause of decline. The final column shows the total number of canals that faced similar types of changes, based on user responses. This total is broken down by the number that survived and did not survive in the remaining two columns. Row percentages are shown in parentheses. (N = 233)**

Type of shock	Survived	Stopped	Total
Decreased agricultural activity	36 (85.7)	6 (14.3)	42
Land used for other purposes	144 (96.0)	6 (4.0)	150
Physical damage	177 (95.7)	8 (4.3)	185
Use of private pumps	–	10	–
Out-migration	146 (98.6)	2 (1.4)	148
New roads	132 (97.8)	3 (2.2)	135
Water to urban areas	24 (96.0)	1 (4.0)	25

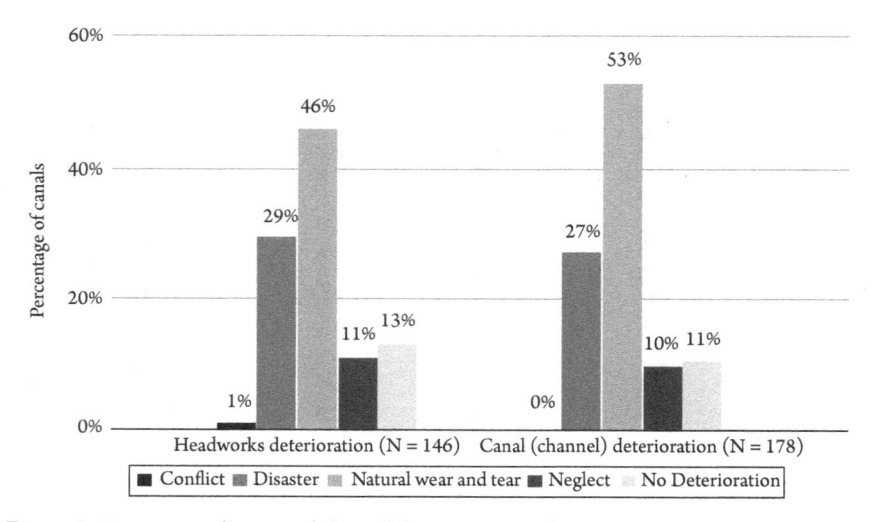

Figure 4 User-reported causes of physical deterioration in farmer-managed irrigation systems in Nepal (1976–2013). This figure shows user-reported causes of physical deterioration in these cases. Natural causes refers to normal wear-and-tear that users expect to repair.

they had robust rules.[24] Second, as to the exogenous shocks hypothesis—that these present the most challenging conditions for sustaining cooperation—the supporting evidence is weak. Users cited these shocks as reasons for failure in particular instances (Figure 4), but looking across all the cases, many more survived than declined after having experienced them (Table 6).

Table 7 **Survival rates with time between observations: The longer the gap between the first and second observations, the more likely the systems were to survive. There is a significant (Fisher's exact = 0.009) inverse relationship between the years separating observations and whether the system is still in use. A longer duration indicates that the systems have likely been subject to more shocks since the baseline. They also typically correspond to older systems. (N = 223)**

Years between observations	Not in use	Still in use	Total	Survival rate
16 to 20	23	76	99	76.7%
21 to 25	7	87	94	92.6%
26 to 30	1	25	26	96.1%
31 to 35	0	3	3	100%
36 to 40	0	1	1	100%

[24] These regularities are among the more prominent reminders that the sample of systems in the NIIS is likely skewed toward systems that are more likely to be robust.

Table 8 **Factors relating to changes in canal performance (1976–2013):**
Table shows the correlations between changes in performance and
other characteristics. Changes in performance are coded worse,
same, or better. (N = 202)

	Changes to			
	Condition of canal pcanalchange	Condition of head pheadchange	Adequacy padeqchange	Reliability .prelchange
Number of changes (*numshocks*)	0.040	0.068	-0.102	-0.060
Years between obs. (*duration*)	0.120	0.051	0.341***	0.168*
Time on other activities (*msubnot2*)	-0.04	0.09	0.12	0.14
Length of canal (*mlength*)	0.04	0.20*	0.14	0.16
External Assistance (*massist2*)	0.028	0.065	0.01	0.09

Note: $^{*}p<0.05$, $^{**}p<0.01$, $^{***}p<0.001$

To set the stage for the more detailed results. Some of the most immediate factors that could affect sustained cooperation—the length of the canal, whether they received external assistance, how long ago they were surveyed, and how important agriculture is to their livelihoods—are shown in Table 8.[25] These are only loosely related to performance changes.

Based on the collective action-centered understandings of cooperation in these situations, there are also two other sets of variables that could possibly be responsible for variation in ability to sustain cooperation. These are the group- and individual-level variables that affect the ability of groups to sustain cooperation, none of which exhibit particularly significant relationships to sustained cooperation. I approach these findings systematically below.

It is important to note that there is a much longer journey from observing these mismatches between prediction and observation to understanding their

[25] Even though the ability of these groups to sustain cooperation does not correspond to the nature of the external shocks, there are other aspects to consider. In particular, none of this rules out that these external shocks or their combinations, could be qualitatively related to the cooperation underlying these systems. But the statistical relationships presented so far are not as stark as one might expect based on the emphasis they are given in collective-action based framing.

cause. But first it is necessary to address systematically some of the most immediate concerns about the initial observations presented so far. This will help to sharpen the question of why, even when the conditions for solving collective action problems have been met, some groups sustain cooperation while others do not. That question of what lies beyond collective action problems motivates the rest of this book.

What Theory Expects

User-governed irrigation systems are fundamental to the current understanding of commons governance institutions (Ostrom, 2010). The literature predicts that the primary reason for decline in long enduring user-managed irrigation canals is rapid and complex "exogenous" changes (Ostrom, 2005, p. 272). That is, long-lasting commons governance institutions begin to deteriorate primarily due to external conditions: factors beyond the control of the users themselves. The reason that these are considered primary is that the institutions, because of the fact of survival, are understood to have rules that very precisely align individual incentives to cooperate—resulting in an equilibrium state in relation to the existing conditions.

Although more recent work (Bastakoti, Shivakoti, and Lebel, 2010) has examined the mechanisms by which these institutions mediate some market and regulatory shocks, a rapid, unexpected shock can still misalign incentives and not afford the users enough time to adapt to changed circumstances. Since surviving institutions are argued to have aligned the incentives of individual users to make long-term commitments rational through mutual monitoring and proportionate punishment, this misalignment can lead to decline if it exceeds their capacity to adapt. There are no panaceas for shared resource governance (Meinzen-Dick, 2007; Ostrom, 2007; Ostrom, A and M, 2007).

The capacity to adapt is affected by group characteristics, the secondary set of reasons that the literature predicts can lead to decline in these systems. In theory, between equilibrium states, individual incentives are momentarily more unaligned because the rules have yet to be adapted to altered conditions. During this time, characteristics of the group are predicted to have a greater influence on whether or not a group is capable of making the required changes to their institutions to restore equilibrium (Ostrom, 1990, pp. 43–45).

The literature identifies four general features of groups that can improve the adaptability of shared irrigation systems. The first is whether the users know each other, facilitated by repeated interaction and having worked together before (Poteete, Janssen, and Ostrom, 2010, pp. 225–226). The second is whether they can communicate, for instance by speaking the same language or by meeting regularly (Ostrom, Walker, and Gardner, 1992). The third is whether they can trust each other to reciprocate, for instance when someone cooperates and another promises to in the future (Ostrom and Walker, 2003, pp. 19–79). And the fourth is whether they can get accurate information about their situation including each other, again by communicating or keeping written records (Ostrom, 2005, pp. 104–109). These aspects are related to the umbrella term "social capital" because they contribute to it or indicate the presence of it, but they also have distinct characteristics (Ostrom, 1990, p. 184).

Overall, without the possibility of communication between users, the entire framework loses its relevance (Ostrom, 1990, p. 48). Many have noted that heterogeneity within groups of users can make communication difficult, and thus raise the costs of organizing collective action (Varughese and Ostrom, 2001). However, the effects of heterogeneity on collective action appear ambiguous (Baland and Platteau, 1999; Baland, Bardhan, and Bowles, 2007). The most important heterogeneities for irrigation governance are: income, caste, ethnicity, gender, language, politics and religion (Bardhan and Dayton-Johnson, 2002).

One of the ways to overcome possible challenges from heterogeneity is for users to learn more about each other, usually through prior cooperation or interactions in other contexts. Whether or not users have cooperated in the past on activities unrelated to the maintenance of the canal gives an indication of how well the users know each other. This relates to trust and to whether they have developed working rules, tacit understanding and heuristics (Locke, 2001, p. 20). Both trust (Ostrom, 2011) and prior-cooperation (Gardner, Walker, and Ostrom, 1994, p. 69) have also been identified as relevant to the type of cooperation observed here. Trust in the behavior of others facilitates long term planning and coordination. It gives users reason to comply with rules regulating their behavior rather than acting selfishly with only immediate gains and losses in mind (Arrow, 1974; Ostrom, 2011).

Following external shocks and group characteristics, the ultimate reason for decline in long enduring user-managed irrigation canals are predicted by the literature to be factors affecting an individual's perception of their costs and benefits. These norms, beliefs, incentives and expectations of the users are included in the broad idea of "local conditions" to which institutions must adapt (Ostrom, 2007). Thus, appropriate rules which are credibly enforced are understood to match both these internal conditions with the external conditions of the canal and the environment in order to render cooperation rational for users (Ostrom, 2005, p. 125).

Finally, the literature predicts that users' willingness to cooperate with a given set of rules is influenced by a comparison of what they would expect to gain from cooperating with what they would need to contribute. Indeed, this "cost–benefit calculation" has been assumed to reliably, although not entirely, guide user actions (Ostrom, 1990, p. 193). Here norms and commitments (Ostrom, 2005, p. 112) are understood as imposing an intrinsic cost on individuals. It is important to reiterate that the literature relegates the characteristics of the group and the reasoning process of users to a secondary and tertiary role respectively in explaining variations in common pool resource governance outcomes, after external shocks.

Perceived fairness is also recognized to affect commons governance outcomes (Ostrom, 2005, p. 263). In the IAD framework, fairness and justice are considered shared norms (Poteete, Janssen and Ostrom, 2010, pp. 222–225) represented as "internal" variables that alter the individual's perception of cost and benefit. It is gradually receiving greater attention (Frey and Rusch, 2014). Recent work has examined different "types" of actors, such as selfish, altruistic or conditionally cooperative in lab settings and controlled field experiments, but direct observations in the field are scarce (Poteete, Janssen and Ostrom, 2010, p. 163). Researchers typically assume that norms are shared by members of the group (Ostrom, 2005, p. 272). In the literature, there is comparatively little discussion of cases where there isn't a clearly dominant norm of fairness within the group, or when there aren't shared community norms of both behavior and fairness (Ostrom, 1990, p. 55). Where it is addressed, this type of norm heterogeneity within a group is regarded as posing challenging difficulties to collective action (Poteete, Janssen and Ostrom, 2010, p. 224).

It is well documented that unequal distribution of resources is a type of within-group heterogeneity relevant to perceived fairness that is related to co-operation and collective action around the operation and maintenance of irrigation canals (Varughese and Ostrom, 2001; Bardhan and Dayton-Johnson, 2002; Baland, Bardhan, and Bowles, 2007). Lam (1998) treated "equity" as an indicator of system performance and found that it was an outcome associated with successful collective action in a subset of the cases in the NIIS. Overall, norms—both of fairness and action—are considered to change the internal value that individuals place on actions and outcomes (Ostrom, 2005, p. 122). Several variables related to norms of fairness are included in the IAD framework—such as whether some receive much more water than others, or the rules punish some users more than others. I examine nine of these in detail in the findings below.

Individuals perceive the impact of institutional rules, also called working rules, differently (Ostrom, 2005, pp. 243–245). The literature has typically assumed that long enduring irrigation systems have mechanisms for resolving these possibly different perceptions of fairness of new rules proposed in the process of adaptation. For instance, the IAD framework has assumed that rules are chosen by these sub-groups based on "winning coalitions" (Ostrom, 2005, pp. 246–247) and through a process of voting or other rule-bound process (Ostrom, 1990, p. 141). In this way, dispute resolution is essential to cooperation. This approach prioritizes fairness in process over substantive fairness, or fairness in outcomes (Rawls, 1972, pp. 84–85). Yet, it is precisely the differential outcomes of the institutional rules that become apparent over time. Further, there is very little empirical evidence of the efficacy or dynamics of these voting mechanisms for resolving fairness differences over time (Poteete, Janssen and Ostrom, 2010, p. 225). Understanding the types of heterogeneous norms as well as how users resolve these differences in order to cooperate over long periods of time presents theoretical challenges for the IAD framework (Ostrom, 2005, pp. 123–127; Poteete, Janssen and Ostrom, 2010, p. 225).

A more basic question is what the various forms and relative effects of perceived fairness on commons governance outcomes in the field are. There continues to be comparatively fewer studies examining this latter question because the main empirical efforts in this literature have concentrated on identifying structural features—external and group variables—of successful local self-governance arrangements. Overall, the literature suggests that understanding perceptions of fairness in more detail requires broadening attention to precisely those "in the mind" variables that are under-represented in the IAD framework (Ostrom, 1990, p. 193).

Apparent Reasons for Decline

Turning now to the empirical observations, in those 31 cases where the canals were no longer in use, former users[26] gave various accounts of why. Users were more likely to cite multiple reasons (80%) as being responsible for the decline of their canal than a single one. The most common reason was that agriculture had become less important, and so the gains of cooperating in using and maintaining a canal were no longer worth it. In many cases, the land had been used for other purposes such as housing, or the soil for brick production. In these cases, the canal provided convenient[27] public land on which to build a

---

[26] These former users identified themselves. There was no way for enumerators to verify if indeed they were past users, although older respondents who had lived continuously in the area were more likely to have been users in the past.

[27] According to an engineer at the Department of Roads of the Government of Nepal, it was convenient for two reasons. As he put it, "We need the same slope to build it [the road]. So we usually

road. In other instances, the water was used for urban drinking water, while in others, the canal had been damaged by a natural disaster or the source had dried up, but the users had lacked the resources or the willingness to repair it. A few were also reported to have declined because there were not enough people to maintain and repair them. At the same time, those who continued to need water for agriculture had dug private bore wells. Consequently, the canal had fallen into further disuse and disrepair. It is also interesting to note that none of the reasons concerned the Maoist conflict, and those reasons are enumerated in the first column of Table 6.[28]

On their own, the reasons given by users sound convincing in terms of canal decline. After all, it is reasonable to expect institutional adaptability to have its limits. With enough external changes or shocks of sufficient effect or sequence, any institution would become dysfunctional. For example, it is conceivable that a flood could damage the canal to such an extent that users lose the ability to make it operational again with their resources. These responses from former users appear to support the claim that the canals that are already user-managed are likely to decline because of changes beyond their control. However, these reasons alone look less convincing when the conditions experienced by surviving canals are examined.

Uncertain Surprises

Table 6 shows how many canals in the entire sample experienced each of these shocks. The shocks in the first column were cited as reasons for decline in the now-defunct cases. It also shows how many of them survived or did not survive. The table shows that these shocks were faced even by canals that survived.[29] Furthermore, of those that experienced each shock, many more systems survived the shock than declined. Take, for instance, those that were reported to have experienced decreased agricultural production. Only 12.7% of them stopped functioning. Similarly, only a small proportion of canals that experienced

---

just build over it [the canal]. It isn't owned by anyone. Sometimes, it helps to drain runoff so it's even better." (2/13/2013 interview) First, the land was already public, and second, the canal's path followed a gradual gradient in hilly terrain that roads also require.

[28] There may be a question here of how to classify a system that falls into disrepair and declines but is then revived and once again becomes functional. If the users are largely the same and the system has not been unused for too long, I take this to be an instance of continued cooperation and not initial cooperation.

[29] This is based on user responses to questions about whether they had recently experienced each of these changes.

physical damage, out-migration, the opening of roads, or a combination of these stopped functioning.

Thus, based on user responses, it appears unlikely that facing these changed conditions alone would cause breakdown in cooperation. The reasons that former users associated with the demise of their canals still leaves open the question of why it was that in the face of similar types of changes, some institutions declined while others did not. But it does begin to turn attention away from external conditions, which appear similar across the cases in this sample, toward the effects of the internal characteristics of the group over time.

Every institution in the sample experienced at least one of these changing conditions. Indeed, the surviving systems experienced an average of 4 of the changes cited as reasons for some to have failed (Table 34). Thus, the changes in external conditions given as reasons for failure were pervasive across all canals, surviving and not.[30] Additionally, there was no significant statistical relationship between the number of external shocks and the present performance of the system (Table 8). Thus, in these cases, external changes alone do not appear to identify those that are likely to fail. The factors affecting how the irrigators responded to these shocks can improve this identification, as I discuss shortly.

All of the canals that stopped functioning did so before I surveyed them a second time. Therefore, without reconstructing their history through sources other than the data set, it is not possible to examine systematically the changes to most of the variables documented in the first study. For example, it is not possible to know what the physical conditions were right before the users stopped using the canal. However, looking at canal performance allows viewing survival and failure as two ends of a continuum. While complete time-series data for those that are no longer in use is not included in this data set, detailed data for those that are declining but have not yet stopped is included. This allows for a finer examination of the factors affecting sustained cooperation.

From Survival to Performance

Varying levels of performance among surviving canals give a better indication of varying levels of cooperation. As expected, some of these groups were able to sustain cooperation better than others. How well they were able to sustain their cooperation is directly reflected in the performance of their irrigation systems. Unless the canal comes to an abrupt stop such as through a catastrophic disaster such as

[30] There could be several other reasons for decline that cannot be examined here because there is limited data about those that have declined. For instance, there is no information on the intensity of the changes or the sequence in which the changes occurred.

widespread flooding or a large rockslide, there are two dimensions of the canal that would likely exhibit decline before the canal itself stops being used. The first dimension is the physical condition of the canal (including the intake or headworks), and the second is its ability to distribute water.

Overall, the surviving canals show variation in both physical condition and performance. Indeed, 90% of the canals show some sort of physical deterioration (Figure 4). There are four causes that users cited for this deterioration: difficult conditions created by the "People's War"[31], natural disasters, neglect, and normal wear and tear that has yet to be repaired. Of particular interest is that the large proportion of the surviving canals have deterioration due to neglect or that have remained unrepaired after a disaster (about 41%). These are directly indicative of a lack of maintenance by users. It is not clear whether users will repair the deterioration that is attributed to normal wear and tear, so this is not unambiguously indicative of a lack of maintenance.[32]

In order to assess how likely the users are to repair the deterioration, I use two different variables. The first is the physical condition of the canal as assessed by the enumerator by walking along it and after discussions with users to evaluate how likely they are to repair it. The second is a similar variable for the physical condition of the headworks (Figure 5). Looking at the canal in this way is appropriate because the canal and headworks affect different users. The physical condition of the headworks affects every user because it determines how much water is available to all. A point along the canal, however, only affects those downstream from it. Thus, while the stretch of canal between the headworks and the first user affects everyone, the parts downstream do not affect the water received by those upstream. The canal usually takes more physical work to maintain than the headworks does, as well as much more cooperation between users. On the other hand, depending on the technology used in the headworks, it might be more expensive to maintain than other parts of the canal. Because of this difference in who is affected by damage to the headworks versus a point along the canal, the physical condition of the headworks is likely to be much better than that of the canal.

Looking at performance, it becomes possible to examine whether canals experiencing more challenging conditions faced more difficulties sustaining cooperation, something that was not possible with a simple binary distinction between survival and non-survival. The physical condition of the canal is not

---

[31] The armed insurgency between 1996 and 2006 was referred to by the Maoists as the "People's War."

[32] It is more likely that users will not repair it because the canals were visited between the end of February through June. Repairs are usually done in the dry months preceding February. Thus, this table likely overstates how many will be repaired.

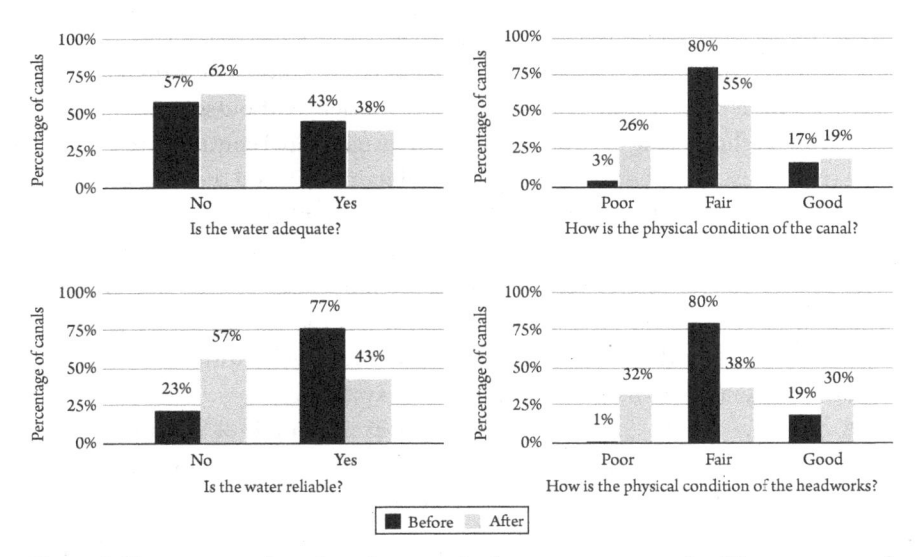

Figure 5 Four aspects of canal performance in the two survey rounds of farmer-managed irrigation systems in Nepal: four aspects of the performance of the irrigation system (the primary commons governance outcome) in the first (before) and second (after) rounds.

significantly associated with the number of shocks that the canals experienced (Table 8).

A second dimension of canal functioning is its ability to distribute water according to the needs of users, irrespective of its physical condition. For example, although the physical condition of a canal might appear poor to an observer, users might assess that its ability to deliver water is adequate. Thus, in order to examine user assessments, I use variables that encode how users perceived canal adequacy and reliability. Adequacy refers to whether the amount of water users receive from the canal is adequate for their needs. Reliability refers to user confidence that the water will be available on time and in the amount that they need. Overall, there is significant variation in these characteristics of water availability across the different surviving canals, as shown in Figure 5. Just as with physical condition, this is indicative of varying levels of cooperation.

Using these indicators of water delivery, it is now possible to understand the significance of the finding that user-perceived functioning of the canal bears no significant relationship to the complexity of external shocks that the canal faced.

These aspects of canal functioning—perceived functioning and actual physical condition—are closely tied to the institution for governing the canal. The institution is responsible for enabling individual users to work together on maintenance and upkeep by altering the costs and benefits of alternative actions to favor cooperative behavior. I assume based on earlier studies that without these institutions, cooperation between users would be irrational and therefore unlikely in these cases. I also assume that in the absence of outside assistance or catastrophic shocks, the only reason a user-managed canal continues to function well is if the users cooperate in using and maintaining it, and the only reason for decline is if they fail to do so. Based on these assumptions, I take institutional performance to mean the extent to which it can elicit required cooperation. I further take institutional performance to be indicated by canal performance. Using these conventions, it is possible to interpret the varying levels of performance as reflecting the extent to which community-level institutions are able to sustain cooperation to use and maintain these systems.

A consistent story comes into view after examining how sustained cooperation is affected by external shocks—that is, whether a group that can sustain cooperation is not significantly determined by challenging circumstances beyond the cooperators' control. These groups have differing capacities to sustain cooperation that are independent of these external shocks. They are certainly not impervious to their circumstances, but they are evidently more resilient to the primary challenge to solving collective action problems in the way of continued cooperation that Ostrom predicts: complex and rapid external shocks.

The results are more mixed for internal variables, although the story remains familiar. They provide little support to the expectation that group variables are the primary reason that individuals reduce their cooperation with existing arrangements. There are few associations between key features of the group such as trust, prior cooperation (Figure 6) and group heterogeneity (Figure 7) with sustained cooperation. Of these, trust is the most significantly associated with sustained cooperation, as expected based on Ostrom's framework. Taken together these group-level variables relate infrequently to variations in the performance of the canals overall, with 13 of 120 comparisons resulting in significant associations (Table 9).[33] Most of these significant (Fisher's $\alpha = 0.05$) associations with performance arise from trust and prior cooperation (8 of

---

[33] Given the unknown sampling procedure, I rely on correlations, primarily the Fisher's exact test due to the preponderance of categorical variables, to examine the relative salience of variables at a moment in time as well as across time. This approach imposes the minimum set of assumptions on the data and can be used with unknown sampling. However, the inferences are limited to tests of independence. I do not apply adjustments for multiple comparisons for three reasons. First, the common correction methods are better suited for experimental designs in which the comparisons to be made are decided beforehand. Second, the purpose of the numerical analysis is to identify factors to direct future research. Third, due to the unique set of circumstances that made this study possible, I did not want to reject plausible new hypotheses even at the risk of false positives (Freedman and Lane, 1983; Agresti, 2012, pp. 75–80).

Table 9 **Relative significance of factors affecting commons governance outcomes (Perceived Fairness, Group Heterogeneity, Trust and Prior Cooperation) to the Performance of the Irrigation System. This table summarizes the results of performing a total of 216 statistical correlation tests. Each test compared one of 18 subfactors (8 for perceived fairness, 7 for heterogeneity, 3 for trust) against one outcome measure of irrigation performance (adequacy of water delivery, reliability of water delivery, canal condition and headworks condition). For example, 8 variables of perceived fairness were each tested against all 4 performance variables in each of the two rounds ($8 \times 4 \times 2 = 64$ tests). In addition, changes in these variables between round 1 and round 2 were separately tested against changes in all four performance variables between rounds ($8 \times 4 = 32$ tests). This results in 96 tests for perceived fairness. All three groups of factors show more significant results than would be expected by chance (alpha = 0.05). I use the Fisher's exact test for Round 1 and Round 2, and standard correlations to compare changes between them. The full tables are in the Appendices.**

Factors affecting commons governance outcomes	Total number of statistical tests for each group of variables	Number of significant test results in Round 1	Number of significant test results in Round 2	Number of significant test results comparing differences in values between Round 1 and 2	Total number of significant test results (α=0.05)	Expected number of significant test results due to chance alone (α=0.05)
Perceived fairness (8 variables)	96	11	5	8	24	5
Group heterogeneity (7 variables)	84	2	2	1	5	4
Trust and prior cooperation (3 variables)	36	4	2	2	8	2

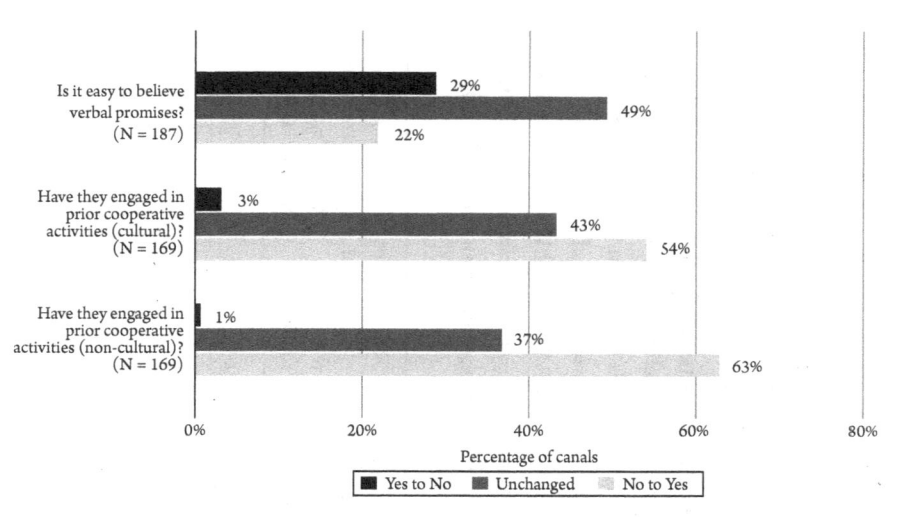

Figure 6 How trust and prior cooperation have changed in farmer-managed irrigation systems in Nepal (1976–2013): changes in three indicators of trust (belief in verbal promises, prior cultural, and noncultural cooperation) within cases between the first and second surveys. Changes to each of the aspects are computed by subtracting their values in the two surveys.

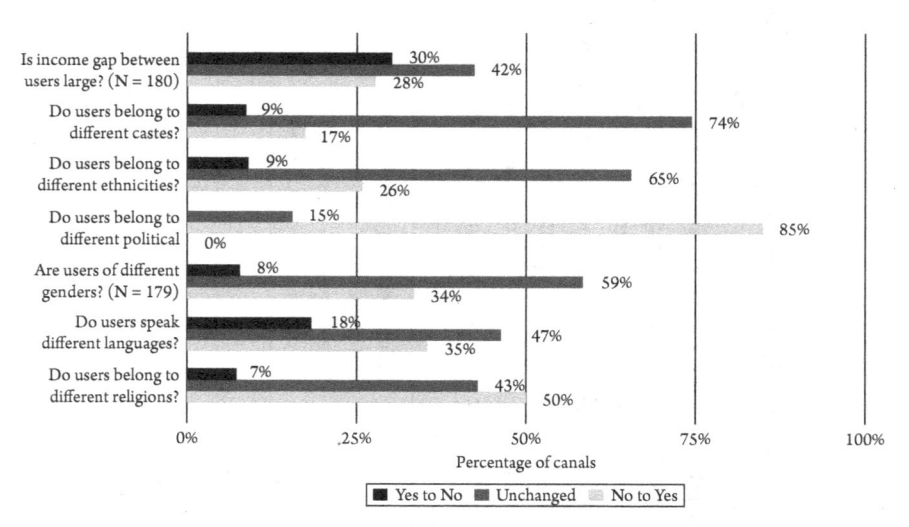

Figure 7 How within-group heterogeneities have changed in farmer-managed irrigation systems in Nepal (1976–2013): changes in seven aspects of group heterogeneity within cases between the first and second surveys. Changes to each of the aspects are computed by subtracting their values in the two surveys.

36 comparisons are significant), not heterogeneity (5 of 84 are significant). Beyond the significance of the associations to the direction of the relationship, there is also a more mixed picture with some variables exhibiting a negative or positive relationship at different times and with different indicators. None, not

even trust, retain their significance to sustained cooperation between the two rounds of data collection (Table 9).

Overall, prior cooperation as a group in cultural or non-cultural activities showed a mixed relationship with current cooperation (Table 2). Prior cooperation in cultural activities such as religious rituals like those commonly held at the beginning of the planting season does not show any relationship in either of the two rounds, and shows a significant ($\alpha = 0.05$) but inverse relationship to the condition of the headworks and perceived adequacy. Prior cooperation in non-cultural activities such as community forest management relates to perceived performance significantly, although negatively. In the second round, it shows a significant (Fisher's $\alpha = 0.05$) and positive relationship to the condition of the headworks.

Here, recall that trust is directly indicated by whether users feel that other users in their group tend to honor verbal agreements (variable *gtrust*).[34] It shows significant (Fisher's $\alpha = 0.05$) relationships with perceived functioning in the first round and adequacy (Fisher's $\alpha = 0.05$) in the second round, both in an expected positive direction. The significant relationships are relatively frequent (3 of 12), but trust is unrelated to the physical condition of the canal. Overall, trust and prior cooperation show relatively frequent significant associations with performance (8 of 36 comparisons). The directions are more mixed than expected. Overall, the relationship of trust to performance is less ambiguous at points in time, although it is not significantly associated to changes between them.

I use user perceptions regarding the diversity of gender (*hgender*), ethnicity (*hethnic*), caste (*hcaste*), religion (*hreligion*), language (*hlanguage*), income (*fecogap*), and political parties (*hparty*) within their group to indicate heterogeneity. Heterogeneities show infrequent (5 of 84) significant relationships, and significant ones are relatively weak (Fisher's $\alpha = 0.05$). Most prominently, heterogeneity of income (*fecogap*) is not significantly associated with performance, despite findings that it can be a primary cause of breakdown.[35] Caste heterogeneity (*hcaste*) does show a significant (Fisher's $\alpha = 0.05$) negative relationship in round two to canal condition. The most frequent significant associations (4 of 12) are shown by ethnic heterogeneity (*hethnic*), although it is intriguing that in the first round and over time, it shows a positive association with indicators of perceived performance. That is, the more ethnically diverse the group is, the greater their ability to sustain cooperation. It shows a significant

---

[34] In places, I have referred to the variable name used in the data set in order to facilitate cross-referencing.

[35] In this analysis, I consider it an indicator of fairness rather than an element of group heterogeneity. This is because income distributions can change over decades, and in these cases are likely to do so as a result of a change in water availability.

negative relationship (Fisher's $\alpha = 0.05$) in the second round with the physical condition of the canal, however. Thus, although it retains its significance over time, the direction of the relationship is not maintained. For ethnic heterogeneity, the relationship is not uniform, although it is frequently significant. Taken together, however, there is scant evidence of an association of heterogeneities of these types with performance (Table 41).

The puzzle of what corresponds to sustained cooperation is now much clearer. But is the puzzle created by choosing the wrong subset of variables from the IAD framework to test? Given how fundamental the identified mismatches are, this question needs to be addressed. Indeed, there is a distinct possibility of getting the variables wrong with a framework that contains 84 different factors that could affect cooperation, with each factor having many different operationalizations, thereby resulting in hundreds of possible variables to inspect. To avoid this danger, the variables examined above were selected based on the literature on the general IAD framework, the literature on local governance of irrigation systems, and prior studies on irrigation canals in Nepal (Meinzen-Dick, 2007). Many of the studies of these same irrigation systems were conducted directly by Ostrom and her students, so it is unlikely that all of these studies have also chosen the wrong variables. It is much more likely that these studies have been restricted to variables identified by the IAD framework, which is designed to focus on variables that are most likely to be significant to the ability of a group to solve or avoid collective action problems.

A Confirmatory Investigation

The findings so far show that there aren't the expected associations between the variables that, using the IAD framework, are regarded as the most likely to affect cooperation. In almost all cases, except for trust and ethnic heterogeneity, there are far fewer significant associations with system performance than expected. Moreover, the predicted variables show even fewer associations with changes in performance over time. It is changes in performance over time that indicate the ability of these groups to sustain cooperation. By any measure, these mixed results are surprising, leaving the reader with the question of what factors are associated with sustained cooperation.

Before moving ahead, it is important to note that the study described above was designed to have a high chance of confirming the predictions of Ostrom's collective action-focused approach. The cases were the same as those used to develop the framework, and the protocol was also the same. The data set used was regarded by Ostrom herself as having a high data quality and internal validity for measuring the concepts in the IAD framework. Gaps in the data and protocols were filled so as to increase the chance of supporting earlier findings. For example, villages closer to the headworks, which normally have much more water available than the tail ends and therefore better performance, were chosen for this survey. This direct replication would have a good chance of confirming Ostrom's results, but the actual results provide only mixed support at best. This fact underlines the lack of association between canal performance and the variables most likely to affect the ability of these groups to solve or avoid collective action problems over time.

It is unlikely that these variables are not related to collective action problems. They were identified through the analysis of hundreds of documented cases of successful shared-resource governance. The framework as a whole was developed through an extraordinarily thorough examination and analysis of the collective action literature over decades. More broadly, it was carefully updated to reflect insights from the social dilemma literature that incorporates recent developments in game theory. The framework was developed with great care for the nuances and complexities of collective action problems in these types of cooperative situations. It is therefore more reasonable to argue that collective action problems themselves may not remain the central concern in sustaining cooperation over time, and therefore the variables associated with them do not appear as significant over time. But if it is not collective action problems that most strongly influence sustained cooperation, then what does?

The implications of this reach to the very roots of the Ostromian approach to gathering and coding data, down to the framework itself. If there are variables that relate to sustained cooperation but not to collective action problems, then the IAD framework may not contain them. The NIIS data set contains only those variables included in that framework. Out of necessity, the cases were coded using this framework, and other details were intentionally left unrecorded. The central aim of the entire enterprise was to record those variables that the IAD framework identified as possibly affecting the ability of groups to solve or avoid collective action problems in social dilemma situations. If sustained cooperation depends on other variables that might not relate to collective action problems, then it is likely that the NIIS data set is missing the necessary information to study them. Because of this, it is possible that despite containing 500 variables, at least some of the variables relating to sustained cooperation—not only the initiation of cooperation—might not have been included. This is where the other data sources come in. My interviews with irrigators and ethnographic studies of specific examples provide information about these irrigation systems that is not restricted in the same way that the NIIS is.

Perceptions of Fairness

The first step to assessing the theoretical conception of fairness in the Ostromian framework is to analyze the ideas of fairness that appear in these cases. The path to do this starts form the concrete tasks of canal maintenance, leads to an examination of user motivations and then to a concrete idea of perceived fairness. Looking at these motivations through perceived fairness reveals a type of motivation I call unfairness aversion. Building on unfairness aversion, it is possible to systematically assess the extent to which seeing these cases though Ostrom's framework captures the dynamics of perceived fairness as empirically derived from interviews, case studies and longitudinal analysis. Its shortcomings become clear at the end of this empirical chapter, and they motivate a deeper examination of Ostrom's theoretical conception of fairness in the next chapter.

The Significance of Maintenance

In built systems such as irrigation canals, survival, decline, and variation in performance are all consequences of maintenance. The fact that 87% of these systems survive (202 of 233) but that some perform[1] better than others is primarily because some groups are more willing to maintain their systems regularly than others. Over a period of 16 to 30 years, some surviving systems have declined in performance while others remained the same, and yet others have improved therefore reflects changes in how willing users are to maintain. Users who are less willing to regularly inspect and repair normal deterioration allow these relatively minor problems to build up, which results in reduced performance. Physical problems with the canal such as cracks and silt accumulate and eventually impact

---

[1] I use performance here to refer to the four aspects of performance regarding a decline in any of the aspects to indicate a decline, no change to be the same, and an improvement in all of them to be improvement.

Beyond Collective Action Problems. Atul Pokharel, Oxford University Press. © Oxford University Press 2024.
DOI: 10.1093/oso/9780197755792.003.0003

the adequacy and reliability of the water that it conveys. As this wear and tear is allowed to persist for longer periods of time, it hastens the spiral of decline: as less water is available, total user contributions to maintenance decline, more day-to-day inspection and cleaning is neglected, and even less water is available next time. Most groups are able to perform the basic maintenance tasks demanded by their irrigation canals at a level that keeps it functional, despite facing the very conditions that make dealing with collective action problems most challenging. However, only some are able to sustain the cooperation required for adequate or reliable water delivery.

The performance of an irrigation system depends on its physical condition. The condition of the channels and of the intake or headworks affects water availability and reliability at various points along the canal. Cracks and obstructions in the channels reduce water available downstream, while a damaged or heavily silted intake reduces the amount of water that enters the canal in the first place. In this way, the physical condition directly impacts the productivity of the canal because it determines the adequacy and reliability of the water available to users. The physical condition typically gives a reliable indication of how well a canal is working.

In turn, the physical condition of artificial structures such as canals depends on regular maintenance. It is a common experience that in the absence of regular upkeep, such resources fall into disrepair, their performance declines, and they become useless. In order to be useful, an irrigation canal first requires that it be cleaned in order to remove silt that has been deposited along its floor, the weeds that may have grown there, or branches and leaves that may have fallen in. It must also be checked for cracks and leakages, and these must be repaired before the canal can transport water. The headworks (or intake) also requires regular inspection. When the headworks is made of temporary materials such as a Gabion box with rocks and twine or wire, it is common for it to be washed away by the previous year's monsoon rains and needs to be rebuilt every year. These activities require an investment of work and other materials in proportion to the canal's length. In the current sample, this ranges from approximately 500 m to 50 km, with the average around 4 km. Based on user estimates, the canals in this sample require the equivalent of at least 10 days of work per user to maintain per year, excluding emergency repairs. The average was 200 "person-days," which is 10 days of work for 20 people. These aspects of maintenance are illustrated in Figure 8.

The amount, type, and timing of maintenance activities required by a canal typically depends on the materials used to construct the system, technology, and design, including its length. Whatever the qualities of the canal, it is also subject to factors beyond the users' control such as geography and climate. All of

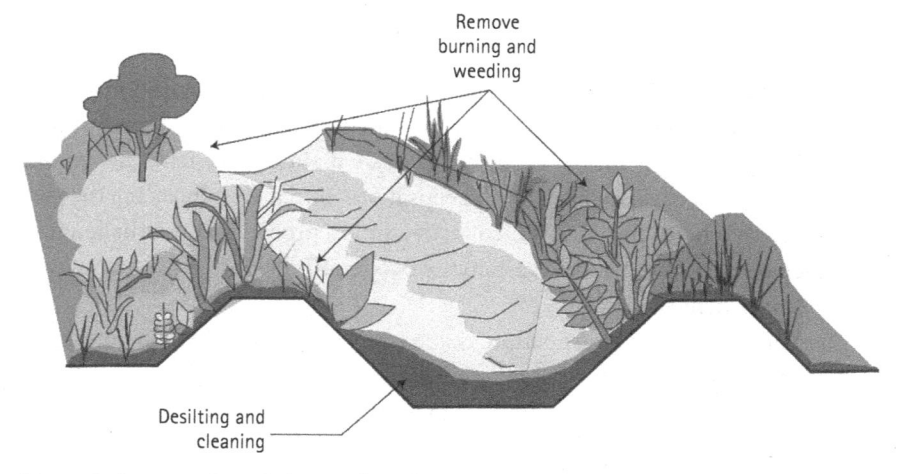

Figure 8 Aspects of canal cleaning based on a handbook on canal maintenance published by the United Nations' Food and Agriculture Organization (FAO, 1985) It was intended for users of canals and government extension officers. It illustrates the different cleaning related tasks a canal requires. These tasks must be performed along the entire length of the canal, which in this sample averages about 4 km. Failing to clean a part of the canal has effects on those downstream from it.

these factors affect how demanding the system is. I discuss the relationship between out-migration, labor availability and canal condition in Chapter 5. Here, it is important to note that the implications of system design and environmental factors for regular maintenance are not straightforward. For instance, advanced systems with professionally designed headworks are typically the most difficult for users to repair and maintain. Similarly, a headworks made of twine and stone can sometimes be the most appropriate when the water source exhibits seasonal fluctuations that change the appropriate intake location. Yet, the former is clearly more durable than the latter so it requires far less maintenance after seasonal flooding. In this sample, 51% of the systems have a temporary intake not made of concrete, 23% of the channels are made entirely of earth without cement lining, and for 88% of the systems the water source is primarily a river with the rest relying on rainfall, springs, and groundwater.

A Willingness to Cooperate

Maintenance in turn depends on the willingness and ability of users. In the case of built, user-managed resources such as irrigation canals, physical deterioration is a direct consequence of how willing users are to contribute to maintenance. In those instances where the demands of canal maintenance have not changed, any deterioration must be because less of what is needed—such as labor, resources or expertise—is available to users, or users are less willing to contribute. A well-maintained canal indicates that contributions continue to be made in required measure, although who is contributing what might not remain the same.

Willingness alone may not be enough to ensure that a system continues to function if users don't have the ability to do so. There are limits to what any group can do cooperatively. Their capacity for maintenance depends in part on what resources users can access and in part on their ability to cooperate to marshal these resources. Certain types of damage are beyond the abilities of the users to fix because they require too much investment, work, or inaccessible expertise. For example, when a flood damages elaborate concrete intake structures such as weirs built by engineers, users often do not know how to repair it. When a group's capacity does not measure up to the demands of maintenance, the irrigation system will continue to show deterioration, even if users are actively repairing it.

Disentangling inability and unwillingness presents a dilemma for any explanation of why some systems function better than others: to what extent is any observed deterioration due to inability or unwillingness? Exacerbating this difficulty is that in the most common instances of persistent deterioration, it is not possible to know what a group is capable of before they attempt it.[2] The case of a natural disaster decimating miles of irrigation canals is easy to explain as inability because such severe damage would be challenging even for government corps of engineers to rebuild, but the typical instances of deterioration in these systems are far less severe. Recall from Chapter 2 that about one-third of surviving systems were in disrepair in 2013 (34% headworks, 30% canal) because of damage that users attributed to natural disasters, while the remaining two-thirds were attributed to the Maoist conflict, normal wear and tear that was yet to be repaired and general neglect. The category of neglect is the only one clearly arising due to unwillingness. Furthermore, willingness is related to an assessment of ability. That is, users who assess that they do not have the ability to maintain a system may be less willing to try to do so. As Mr. Aryal, a user of a system whose headworks was damaged by a flood explained it, "Why should we try to fix it? Even if our cows and goats came [to help] we couldn't do it."

There are several reasons why willingness to maintain is likely to be the key systematic reason for persistent decline across these cases. First, the water from these systems remains important to the livelihoods of users of the systems,[3] so they have good economic reasons to maintain it. Next, as Chapter 2 showed, the

---

[2] For a memorable exposition of this theme of revealed capacity, albeit in a different context, see Hirschman's Development Projects Observed (1967).

[3] See the questions: How valuable is a little bit more water? (s32) What percentage of the group spends time in non-agricultural activities? (s18, s19, s20).

groups of users managing these systems display a remarkable ability to cooperate despite the most difficult challenges—in particular, frequent, unpredictable changes to "contextual factors" related to market pressures, government intervention, technological changes, demographic changes, and ecological changes (Poteete, Janssen and Ostrom, 2010). Furthermore, natural disasters are not a systematic reason for canals to stop being functional. Finally, the groups have also cooperated in the past, so they possess the proven ability to do so. Across these cases, therefore, the main reason for canals becoming defunct is not damage that is beyond the group's ability to repair. Most likely, persistent deterioration is due to changes in the collective willingness[4] of users to maintain their systems.

If the significance of the collective willingness of subgroups of users to maintenance is critical, the willingness of every user is not equally important to the continued functioning of their canal. Although less common in the past, it is now typical that there is a division of labor among the users of these systems, as explained below. Some perform labor intensive tasks that directly impact the canal such as repair and cleaning, while others perform tasks more indirectly related to the canal's productivity such as the job of the Water User's Association (WUA) secretary. The willingness of users engaged in maintenance more immediately impacts the functioning of the canal than that of those who are not. At the same time, the unwillingness of some users to work on the canal matters less if there are others who are willing to work in their stead. There is often a difference in the quality of work done by users and non-users: those who don't interact with the canal regularly are not as familiar with it and lack the intimate knowledge of the canal that makes user contributions more effective, so irrigators tend to prefer that other users maintain the canal rather than those from outside the group. Despite this well-founded preference, groups across systems have changed their rules to allow the hiring of others, typically non-users, for tasks such as cleaning and repair. This has the effect of further weakening the significance of any individual user, while it strengthens the significance of those who have the means to hire workers.

Nevertheless, although there are many ways that a canal might be damaged, such as by floods or landslides and even normal wear and tear, there is only one reason that this damage will persist in these cases: the unwillingness of users to repair it once the problem has been detected. In the 16 to 37 years since these canals were first studied, their main source of labor and money for regular upkeep has remained relatively unchanged. Occasionally, government agencies or donor

---

[4] I use collective willingness to denote the willingness of the group taken together rather than the individual willingness of any particular user.

agencies provide assistance, but these are far from reliable sources of support for self-governed systems like these canals. In cases like these where the power to govern resides with the groups themselves, most of the resources for regular upkeep and maintenance also come from the users themselves. In this way, built resources self-governed by users are particularly sensitive to factors that affect the willingness of users to continue cooperation.

Thus, in the case of built, user-managed resources such as irrigation canals in this study, deterioration is a direct consequence of how willing users are to contribute to maintenance. This relationship between maintenance and performance persists throughout the life of the resource. Within the limits noted above, some perform better than others because people stop repairing and cleaning some of them. Users vary in their willingness to maintain their shared systems, and so the key question here is why some users continue to cooperate to maintain their resource while others don't.

The Collective Action View

The collective action approach to cooperation, elaborated in Ostrom (1990, 2005), gives one explanation of why some users stop cooperating: they no longer expect the result of cooperation to be of net benefit to them. There are many scenarios that could lead to this pessimistic assessment. It may be because users no longer believe in their ability to solve collective action problems, so the likelihood that they will cooperatively achieve joint gains is reduced to the point that the expected benefit is less than expected cost. Without a belief that cooperation is likely to bring about joint gains, users can be discouraged from continuing to cooperate. For instance, because of disagreements over political ideology sharpened by electoral politics, some users may stop believing the promises—regardless of what they are about—of users with different allegiances. Without this type of trust, they will find it difficult to make credible commitments to each other about regulating use and contributing resources for maintenance. Without the ability to make credible commitments, they are less certain that one's cooperative behavior will be reciprocated, which in turn makes it unlikely that joint gains in terms of long-term water availability for all will be achieved. Users may also stop cooperating because the expected benefits to them of their share of the joint gains that are likely to be achieved is outpaced by the expected costs of cooperation. For instance, the expected future benefit of rice cultivation may no longer seem compelling compared to the expected benefits foregone by not taking as much water as they can and selling it to a water tanker supplying a nearby city.

This conventional view of non-cooperation begins with the assertion that the individual user faces the exact same choice every single time he considers how to act: cooperate or not (Ostrom, 1990; Gardner, Walker, and Ostrom, 1994). Next, every individual is assumed to behave as though they are guided by the costs and benefits to themselves of particular actions in all circumstances, so the reasoning process of individuals faced with this choice consists of assessing and comparing the expected costs and expected benefits of the two options: cooperating or not.[5] The main task in understanding why a user decides to not cooperate, then, is to glean why they expect cooperation to be more costly than beneficial. The cost–benefit assumption is remarkably versatile and is also impossible to disprove empirically because of its basis in an individual's subjective perception of cost and benefit. Any choice made can be said to have been perceived by the individual as beneficial overall. This is true even for actions that users admit were not guided by net benefit to themselves. For example, if an individual admitted that they took an action explicitly in violation of this principle, this admission would still fail to contradict the assumption. It could still be said in defense of the universality of the cost–benefit view that the satisfaction of behaving against the cost–benefit principle in that instance is of net benefit to the individual. It could also be said that the verbal account of the individual is incorrect, and they were acting in a way that benefited them. On its own, the principle does not provide a logical end to the recursion that it generates.

This view further recommends that to understand why cooperation is not expected to be of net benefit, the analyst primarily relies on objectively measurable variables that are likely to affect the expected costs and benefits of cooperation such as the frequency and complexity of external shocks. The reliance on observable variables to explain behavior comes from the assertion that the "internal, in the mind, subjective variables" are too difficult to measure (Ostrom, 1990, pp. 37–38). Observable variables, in contrast, are objectively visible and therefore considered to be at least slightly more reliable for explaining human behavior than unobservable ones. For instance, it is too difficult in this view to measure the extent to which individual reasoning processes have an arithmetic structure, or whether the same person can use different basic reasoning processes at different times, such as before they have made a commitment and after decades of being committed. It is easier, in comparison, to measure how large of a fine would induce a user to not take water out of turn.

There is no reason from the conventional collective action viewpoint to interview individual users about why they reduced their cooperation, with one

---

[5] This overall schematic of the internal reasoning process of individuals in the conventional view is given in Figures 6.2 to 6.5 in Ostrom (1990, pp. 197–206).

important exception. In this view, it is beneficial to interview people in order to discover what variables are included in their expected cost–benefit assessments such as monetary value of the crops they produce and what factors envelop their cost–benefit calculations overall, including group norms, discount rates, whether they can trust verbal promises made by others, or the psychological value of an equal distribution of water. For example, if people can no longer believe each other's promises to cooperate in the future, then they are unlikely to cooperate now (assuming that they are conditional cooperators) (Ostrom, 2000). This disbelief can result from interactions outside of those around the irrigation systems of interest. A large body of literature on common governance, irrigation governance, and these specific irrigation canals has identified a large list of variables affecting expected cost and benefit and classified them into two groups: external shocks and group-level variables. The full list of these variables and mechanisms is included in the Institutional Analysis and Development (IAD) framework.

Recall that there is an unremarkable proportion of significant numerical associations between the most widely accepted measurable, objective variables—external shocks and group variables—and levels of cooperation in these current irrigation systems. Faced with these contradictory findings, the conventional approach directs one to look for other measurable variables that might be more closely associated with performance and therefore sustained cooperation. There are close to another five hundred variables in the NIIS data set to choose from, but supporting an existing theory by mining for significant associations when the predicted ones fail can scarcely be considered an adequate measure of correctness. With so many variables to test, spurious associations are more likely without a firm basis—theoretical or empirical- for looking at other variables. Cost–benefit reasoning is a convenient and versatile characterization of human reasoning. It is also one of many types of reasoning about a choice of actions that can be attributed to cooperators and is treated as such in what follows.

Reasons for Not Cooperating

Where the collective action-based explanation offered one set of reasons that users stopped cooperating, the users of these systems gave other reasons. Before examining user reasons, it is important to note that the interviews presented next are not assumed to reveal the elements of an internal cost–benefit assessment that guides user decisions. To do so would implicitly project the collective action-based explanation onto their reasons for action. A comparison of overall cost and benefit no doubt approximates the logic structuring some of the reasons that the users give both for making a commitment or stopping.

However, understanding why individuals stop or reduce their commitment to existing institutions doesn't require assuming that a respondent always reasons in the same or even comparable ways when thinking about starting and then stopping cooperation. The analysis of these interviews is informed by the discipline of foregoing convenient assumptions about human reasoning such as that they act when it is of net benefit to them. More specifically, I do not assume that a significant number of respondents hide their purely selfish reasons behind a set of apparently "noble" responses. I examine this concern at length in Chapter 4. The intent of these simplifications of human motivations is usually to ease the modeling process, as the Ostromian project illustrates. However, if one is interested in first understanding user reasoning, then simplifications of the reasoning process are not as critical to the task ahead as they might be if one wanted to model behavior.[6] This approach proves its value by leading to the very fairness related variables that are systematically correlated with sustained cooperation over time that have been underemphasized so far.

The most common reason users stopped committing to the canal came from a comparison of their economic conditions with those of others who used the canal. Notably, they had come to recognize the many ways that other users had become better off over the years than themselves. This difference in substantive outcomes would not have been as perceptible to prospective users at the time of committing to the institution as it had become after decades of following its rules. The following is a typical conversation with former users of the canal.[7] It offers a starting point for examining why people stopped in other instances.

> I used to work on the canal. Everyone who used water had to work. For many years, I worked. I have a small amount of land. That was enough for us. My brothers and I worked all day sometimes. They paid us.
> Interviewer: Did everyone have to work as much as you?
> (His tone turned serious and hinted at resignation). I can't speak about others. Our houses (pointing to the cluster of ten houses nearest his), you see how they are. (pause) You also talked to others, so you saw how they are. How much

---

[6] The account of interviews with irrigators that follows is aimed at understanding the reasons that existing institutions exhibit adaptation, resilience, and decline. How the institution came about is an important part of the answer, but explaining why certain conditions led to its emergence is not the focus of enquiry. In the traditional setting, there is a group of individuals who are self-motivated and share a resource. When revisiting these cases, however, the group of users has already collectively managed a resource for decades through institutions and is facing changing circumstances.

[7] The questionnaire was not designed to survey reasons that individuals or groups stopped working on the canal, but there were incidental interviews with former users in cases where the canals were no longer in use. Most of these conversations occurred during the detailed case study conducted after the survey.

they worked on the canal, you probably know better than me. They are able to send their kids to boarding schools. . . (he tapered off into silence and peered down at his hands).

It is notable on first reading how the respondent appears to not answer the question. However, this is a typical way of "saying something without saying it,"[8] a mode of speaking in certain parts of the country, especially by less powerful people. Despite not making the comparisons himself, he suggests doing so, and in his tone he also suggests the results of his own comparisons, which also remain unsaid. However, Mr. Darai's response is typical in how it draws on implicit comparisons the respondent associates with the canal's rules.

The first comparison is between the respondent's economic condition and that of others. Mr. Darai compares his family with those who are far better off. During the interview, he revealed that he has three sons with two living in a foreign country doing low-skilled work, and the third one is unemployed. One is a construction worker in Qatar, and the other is in Malaysia. Their mother had passed away after giving birth to the youngest, who stayed with his father. The families to which he was comparing his own also did not have their youngest members living in the village. A typical family had a son working as a journalist and another as a middle-man for "manpower" agencies that recruited potential migrant laborers. Their fields, which were larger than Mr. Darai's, were fallow. People that Mr. Darai knew used to work the fields for them, but refused to do so now.

Mr. Darai also remembered how in the past everyone—including "they"[9]— worked physically on the canal. It was common at the time for all users to contribute labor themselves. This included cleaning, inspection, and repair work on the canal. It was also more common than it is now to require that every user perform an equal amount of work, measured by the length of canal that they cleaned or the number of days that they served as a guard. This universal participation lent a sense that the conditions of most users were similar with respect to work. There were also large landlords then who would oversee the work, but they were regarded, according to Mr. Darai, as always being "different from everyone else."

The shift that Mr. Darai describes is typical. Across cases, these rules for allocating labor have changed toward requiring work in proportion to the amount of water used from requiring everyone to work equal amounts. In many

---

[8] This is a colloquial phrase in Nepali that refers to how not saying something can be as remarkable as saying it.

[9] I explain shortly who this "they" is. Mr. Darai refused to identify the people in these groups explicitly out of fear of retaliation.

Table 10 **Changes in rules for allocating work, showing how the percentage of cases in which rules were allocated according to one of four rule-types changed between the two time periods. The rules used before are in the first column. Each cell shows what percentage of those that had a particular rule before moved to a particular rule after.**

Rules used before (%)	Rules used After (%)				Total
	Equal	Land	Water	Mix	
In equal amounts (Equal)	31.82	51.52	4.55	12.12	100
In proportion to land irrigated (Land)	19.39	68.37	7.14	5.10	100
In proportion to the water used (Water)	33.33	66.67	0.00	0.00	100
A mix of the above two (Mix)	28.57	50.00	7.14	14.29	100
Percentage of Total	24.86	60.77	6.08	8.29	100

canals, this change happened because those with less land did not want to do a disproportionate amount of work. Overall, 64% of the institutions now have rules that require work in proportion to the amount of land the users irrigate or the amount of water they use. In the past, only half of the canals had this kind of rule. The broader pattern across cases is apparent in Table 10, which shows that about two-thirds of those groups that used to divide the work equally between all users no longer do. There are large shifts away from using equal allocation toward proportional allocation. There is also a large shift away from allocating work based on the amount of water used toward the amount of user's land that is irrigated by the canal. This is likely because it is difficult to measure how much water is being used, but easier to check how much land is being irrigated: this is reflected in how much land has crops.

The second comparison suggested by Mr. Darai refers to the emergence of two user subgroups. One subgroup consists of those whom he remembered having worked on the canal in the past but stopped, and the second subgroup consists of those who still work on it. Mr. Darai compared this past where everyone worked on the canal to a present where only some work while others do not. This pattern of some users doing most of the work was also consistent across cases. Indeed, users preferred hiring other users to do extra work on the canal when needed instead of hiring outsiders because they believed that the former's familiarity with the system would result in more effective work contributions and would require little or no supervision.

During the first round, it was common for institutions to have rules requiring each household to send someone to work. Most often, users sent their own family members. When they could not, they would hire others to work for them.

Table 11 **Changes in labor substitutes. The percentage of cases in which one's labor contribution would be substituted by hiring others, paying a fee, or something else.**

Substitutions before (%)	Substitutions after (%)			
	Labor	Money	Other	Total
Hired Labor	15.56	84.44	0.00	100
Money	14.29	78.57	7.14	100
Other	16.98	77.36	5.66	100
Total	15.58	79.87	4.55	100

However, paying money to their user group instead of finding someone to work was rare: it was expected that a family member, relative, or friend would cover. Users normally associated hiring a stranger with paying a penalty, or understood it to indicate an unusual circumstance. As shown in Table 11, there is now a much greater proportion of canals where users are required to pay money instead of sending someone to work in their place. This signals the greater acceptability or necessity of looking beyond relatives for help. It also indicates that it is more difficult for individual families to find contract workers. Of those institutions that required users to find someone to work in their place, 84% now require the payment of money instead.

Finally, Mr. Darai identifies an "us" that he feels are like him as distinct from 'them': those who did well and don't have to work on the canal if they don't want to. This hints at a greater sense of closeness to his people who do most of the work, and a greater sense of distance from others who do not work but pay money instead. This specialization is also apparent across cases. Users of 26.8% of systems reported that some people do much more physical work than others. The emergence of a subset of users who do most of the physical work has resulted in less interaction between those who increasingly work because they can't pay someone else to do so and those who can. Often those who do physical work on the canal are paid to work extra, as in Mr. Darai's case. This is, again, because users consider it better than hiring outside workers who lack experience with the canal.

These apparent inequalities in the amount of physical work that users perform also overlap somewhat with ethnic divisions. This is because in every case in which an increasing number of users pay money instead of physically working, the work is given to particular ethnic groups and not to others. Those chosen are usually considered of "backward" ethnicity or "lower" caste. Mr.

Darai's "us" appears to refer to a mix of three groups: the group of people of his ethnicity (the Darai), the group of people who appear to do most of the work on the canal (mostly Darai, but also poorer non-Darai users), and the group of people who have not done as well as others by using the canal (a mix of castes and ethnicities).[10]

Interviews such as this one were first conducted with users who were most willing to talk. These initial interviews were then supplemented by walking along the canal to the headworks where reachable and interviewing other users, particularly those living in relatively less "pukka" or permanent dwellings (usually also with smaller plots). On average, there were three respondents per system. Multiple interviews were intended to address the fact that those who were the first to talk at any location were often better off, or had an official role in the governing Water User's Association. These ranking members would most often be called to join in and given the responsibility of speaking on behalf of users.[11] Only a handful of users in each group are ranking members of their associations, however. So, speaking to other users along the canal helped reveal broader opinions than just those of the officers.[12] Table 12 shows topics that appeared in interviews with users and non-users, grouped by type of comparison.[13]

Table 12 also enumerates the reasons individual users gave for stopping their cooperation or significantly reducing it. Statements in Group A concern the difference between what poor users are promised—explicitly or implicitly—by the rules and what they actually receive. As expressed, users also tended to attribute this gap to more powerful users not giving the poor what they were entitled to and not, for instance, a reduction in available water because of a landslide. Group B consists of comparisons among how much work different groups of users do. As expressed by those who did more than others, the responses in this group indicated not only that the speakers felt that they were contributing more than others were, but also through phrases like "If we don't do it, who will?" that the respondents felt they were solely responsible for carrying an essential burden—that of contributing physical labor to maintenance—whereas others

[10] This is apparent in variables o62 (Do takers hire workers from outside to do labor on the canal?) and o63 (Who do they usually hire?).

[11] The discussions that occurred around the actual interviews often involved disagreements between those present about what the answers to questions should be. Any officeholders present would be given the final word by other users.

[12] See the Methods Appendix for a tabulation of respondent characteristics.

[13] This method gets at a roughly "collective understanding" more than an individual understanding because of the study design. I did not distinguish whether characteristics of the respondents led them to make certain connections and not others between the concepts. So, I take the respondents interviewed as representative of the "local" understanding of fairness. This is akin to assuming that the working rules are "common knowledge."

Table 12 **Reported reasons for stopping or reducing cooperation. Recurrent user reported reasons for stopping or reducing their individual involvement in canal maintenance. They are grouped by comparisons that the respondents appear to be making. The example phrases are illustrative excerpts from interviews. Responses from the added sample are included. The table is compiled from a total of 827 interviews from 266 systems. The phrases are translated from the Nepalese by the author.**

Group	Comparison	Example phrases from interviews
A	Whether the poorer members receive their share of water.	"They don't give the poor their water"
B	Whether some people do much more physical work than others.	"Everyone doesn't do the same amount of work" "We are the ones who work" "If we don't do it who will?"
C	Whether the rules are appropriate for the current situation. The word translated into "appropriate" is "uchit," which also includes an idea of legitimacy.	"Rules are not appropriate to the situation." "Rules are not acceptable, they are not ok." "The don't rules match the conditions." "The rules are not satisfying to one's mind" (the phrase used was "chitta bujhdo")
D	Whether or not there is discrimination by the rules against some users, particularly the poorest.	"The poor are treated badly." "They give some a lot and others less."
E	Whether the rules favor the wealthy and those with more land.	"They give benefits to the wealthy." "The wealthy get water first."
F	Whether the rules are easy to understand.	"The rules are not easy to understand." (in the sense of how they led to the present situation)
G	Whether the rules treat people uniformly.	"The system doesn't treat everyone in the same way." "The customs don't give some water to everyone." (the word for custom was "niyam," which translates to a particular rule or set of rules)

were unwilling or unable to do so. A more complex assessment, the appropriateness or acceptability or "fit" of the rules, is included in Group C. Here users compared the rules to what they expected in the particular situation. This is a broad, seemingly impressionistic comparison that included views of whether the punishments were appropriate for changing times, and whether the rules allowed users to hire others to work in their place (so that they could work more profitable jobs, for instance). For example, user complaints that confiscating the cows of a poor user who had taken water out of turn wasn't something they expected to see in modern times would fall into this category.

Group D consists of statements assessing whether the rules disadvantage some users consistently. This is not limited to consistently less water received, but to whether, for instance, some were consistently more severely punished than others for the same rule violations. Group E resembles Group D, but concerns whether wealthier users appeared to receive advantages that others did not. For example, it includes whether wealthier users always received water first instead of last when there was a shortage, as some systems required. Group F concerns whether users could understand how the rules resulted in the present distribution of outcomes. This was typically expressed to indicate that the respondent found it difficult to understand how the rules led to the present situation and had stopped trying to understand, instead accepting his fate in the current system. Finally, Group G consists of statements about whether the rules treat users uniformly. These statements resemble those in Groups A, B, D, and E, but were expressed neutrally without pointing to some individuals or groups who were advantaged or disadvantaged as a result. These comparisons only suggest that there was a difference in how uniformly the rules in their implementation appeared to treat individual users.

These seven reasons appear significantly different from those for stopping one's cooperation that are suggested by Ostrom's collective action-based framework. The reasons here are both comparative and normative. For instance, these observed reasons do not refer to the benefits a user expects to receive from their share of water and the costs they incur from their share of the necessary burdens of maintenance. Instead, the reasons refer to what others receive. It is unclear how these comparisons can be included in a cost–benefit framework without introducing a subjective value that individuals assign to the results of these comparisons. For example, one way to include the reasons in Group B in the Ostromian framework is to assume that users have a preference for particular distributions of labor across users, and not just a preference for a particular allocation of labor to themselves in proportion to the benefits they receive.[14]

---

[14] See the discussion on norms and their adequacy in Poteete, Janssen, and Ostrom (2010, p. 224).

Yet, a preference for distributional outcomes alone does not capture several other aspects of reasons for not cooperating. Consider that users of different systems that are not otherwise related gave other overlapping reasons for stopping their cooperation such as whether the rules treat everyone uniformly. To fit this regularity into the IAD framework, one could assert that the set of seven reasons is evidence of group norms of fairness. Group norms are a common extension of the traditional collective action view and are represented variously as intrinsic preferences for particular variables not clearly of individual benefit.[15] The difficulty of this group norm-based explanation is in defining the group. The interviews have identified a set of commonly connected elements of norms of fairness across all groups in this sample, so to what group would the norm of uniform treatment of all users by the rules belong?

Taken together across all 272 cases, most of the 827 respondents have not had contact with each other and live in geographically distant places. They are also from a wide variety of ethnic groups, castes, and cultures with wide regional variations. Thus, if these seven reasons constitute a norm then it must be of a type that is not limited to neighbors, communities of practice, or ethnic groups. This type of norm cannot arise from the usual sources: repeated interactions among members of a group, cultural inheritance, or social capital between individuals. It would have to arise from other commonalities between individuals or groups in this sample: for instance, psychological such as inequality aversion, or situational such as a cooperative situation around the sharing of resources, or the state. This suggests that these seven elements may appear more universally in reasons for individuals to stop or reduce their cooperation beyond just these cases. Overall, it cannot be a group norm, normally understood as specific to the users of a particular shared resource, unless the group is defined more broadly to include people who share the norm but are otherwise unrelated. Yet, after this modification, the idea of a group becomes much broader to include strangers.

The Structure of Reasons for and against Cooperation

In this way, users deployed comparative reasons in explaining the negative (why they stopped cooperating) but not the positive (why they started or continue to cooperate). Similar to the example of Mr. Darai, across cases the responses to the negative question of why individuals stopped working on the canal reveal comparisons of how one's condition has changed to how others' have changed.

---

[15] "By norms, we mean that the individual attaches an internal valuation—positive or negative—to taking particular types of action in specific situations." (Poteete, Janssen, and Ostrom, 2010, p. 224)

When the positive questions were asked, respondents referred to their continued need for water for agriculture, its significance for agrarian livelihoods, a desire to grow crops, or a lack of alternatives to their agrarian way of life. They stressed how working together worked well for all villagers, and in some cases how if they were to survive, they should continue working together. Overall, they tended to refer to what we may recognize as economic reasons. The reasons for starting to work on the canal or continuing to work on it appear to be reliably characterized as the reasons for individual or collective economic benefit.

Comparisons do not appear in interviews where current users are asked the positive question of why they continue to work on the canal or started doing so many years ago. In response to questions such as "Why do you continue to work on the canal?" no respondent suggested reasons involving comparative concerns over time. For example, no respondent noted that they remained committed to the canal because the poorer people receive the share of water promised by the rules or that the rules treated all users uniformly. Additionally, no respondent reported that working on the canal helped them to send their children to private schools, just like wealthier users. Furthermore, no respondent mentioned what comparative results they expected after working on the canal for many years. They did not report, generally, that they expected that by continuing their commitment they would keep up with other users socially or economically.

This pattern of mentioning distributional concerns when explaining why they stopped or reduced their commitment, but not mentioning them when talking about why they continue (or started) was common across interviews with users of otherwise unrelated systems. It emphasizes that the reasons for not using the canal may be related not just to one's own economic benefits, but also to a comparison of one's benefit with those of others over time. Thus, even if an irrigator perceives that their economic benefits from using the canal outweigh the costs, they may still reduce their commitment if the comparison of the benefits they receive with those that others receive may lead them to perceive the system as unfair. A misalignment of economic incentives that renders not cooperating more personally beneficial than cooperating can also lead to non-cooperation, but it is misleading to assume that a reduction in cooperation is a result of this misalignment by default.

The Effects of Being Committed

Overall, the interviews reveal that the reasons for starting or continuing to work on the canal appear to be substantially different from the reasons that former users gave for not continuing to work on it. While it was not possible to interview users right before they made a commitment, three other types of respondents highlighted different reasons for starting and continuing to maintain their canal, or stopping their involvement in maintenance.[16] The first type were current users who had continued their involvement by either keeping it the same or increasing it. The second type were former users who no longer worked on their canal; the third type were current users who had for one reason or another reduced their involvement with the canal. These second and third types of user reported reasons for stopping or reducing their commitment to maintenance, while the first type reported reasons for continuing. All three gave reasons they initially started.

The difference in the decisions faced by farmers in a commitment and those not in one explains the fundamental difference between the reasons farmers gave for starting (or continuing) versus stopping their cooperation. Farmers who share these irrigation canals in the NIIS are in the situation of having committed to a set of working rules to govern their relationship to it. The farmers using the irrigation systems have behaved cooperatively for decades. They are familiar with the rules governing their systems as well as what behaviors the rules require of them. For these farmers, the decision that is most consequential to the continued functioning of the canal is whether or not to cooperate less with their existing institution. The irrigation system will begin to deteriorate as fewer people cooperate in using and maintaining it. However, unless these committed farmers reconsider their commitment for some reason, they do not have occasion to consider changing their behavior to not cooperate with the prevalent rules. Their default behavior is to remain the first type, and possibly become the second or third.

In a different situation is the farmer who is not already committed to a cooperative system. This farmer is either deciding whether to commit to an existing cooperative system or whether it is worthwhile to cooperate with others to devise an institution to which they all commit. For this uncommitted farmer, the successful functioning of the canal depends on whether he decides to make or continue a commitment. This farmer's reasons are likely to be similar to those given by the first type. The canal will only remain functional or become so after a significant number of farmers decide to cooperate. In this way, whether to enter a commitment is different from the question of how one acts on an existing commitment.

---

[16] It is important to note that the reasons for starting were collected from irrigators who had already committed at some point. None of them were asked at the point of starting. There are two questions here: whether this is an accurate way to assess why individuals not in a commitment join one, and also whether to consider the answer they give to be indicative of someone who has never committed.

The dominant convention in the collective action approach to understanding cooperation is to assume that there is no qualitative difference between the situations of being committed to an institution or not. Therefore, the only difference is that the expected costs and benefits of each of the alternative actions may have changed in the interim. This means that whether the farmer has already committed to an institution or not, he faces the exact same decision every single time: cooperate or not. For instance, within this conventional view, there is no need to reconsider the extent to which individuals will continue to behave as benefit-seekers or cost-avoiders. Instead, on this assumption, there is a greater need to measure changes to the factors that could affect expected costs and benefits.

If there is a difference in the type of reason that users give for starting or continuing versus reducing their cooperation, then it will be problematic for the collective action-based view to include it. The symmetry of reason that the cost–benefit view requires makes unreasonable demands of the individual cooperator. To assume that the reason not to do something is the inverse of the reason to do it—that is, that reasons are symmetrical—asks too much of an individual cooperator. That would assume that an individual not only has available all possible reasons for not cooperating prior to the point of initial commitment, but has also assigned weights to them. In this view, the observation that someone has stopped or reduced their cooperation would be offered as the reason for not continuing gaining greater weight. There is contrary evidence that the reason that accounting for these distributional concerns beforehand is challenging is that they are very difficult to guess. Mr. Darai's example illustrates one reason why these substantive outcomes cannot be fully taken into account when initially deciding to commit to an institution: there may be too much uncertainty as to what they will be.

The Structure of Reasons to Not Cooperate

If the comparative structure of negative reasons distinguished them from the positive ones, the negative reasons had additional structure. Not only were the reasons to reduce cooperation comparative; they were also related to each other. The assessments listed in Table 12 enumerate a group of topics that appeared connected to each other in the expressions of respondents. When one of the topics in this group came up in the course of an interview[17], at least one of the others was also often brought up by the respondent themselves. For instance,

---

[17] These connections were found not just in relation to having stopped or reduced their commitment, but in responses to other questions as well.

Mr. Darai was asked to compare how much work different groups of users did, and then, without prompting, he compared whether the rules favored some groups over others over time.

The groups of statements listed in Table 12 were interconnected with the frequencies shown in Table 13. This table of interconnections was compiled by listening to each interview and marking when a comparison was made, followed by a reference to another comparison without prompting by the interviewer. For example, if the interviewer asked whether some did more work than others, as in Mr. Darai's case, the answer would be a comparative statement. However, to be included in this table, the respondent would have had to mention another of the comparative statements also in the table without prompting when answering the question.

Table 13 shows how many times one comparison led to another without prompting in the interviews. For instance, if the user subsequently mentioned on his own that the rules benefited the wealthy, as Mr. Darai did, then this would be noted by increasing the number in Row 5, Column 1 by 1 to record the connection. Each comparative statement may have been connected to many others in the same interview. The table does not include those statements that were not connected to any others. In 103 interviews, there were no connected statements primarily because the respondents were not eager to engage in an open-ended interview but were willing to answer only the narrow questions they were asked.

Thus, Table 12 shows the elements of an inductively constructed concept of fairness. The concept finds the intersection of what I recognize as fairness on the one hand and on the other, those distributional or comparative notions that respondents referenced in their speech. In other words, this concept is the users' perception of a group of elements that I recognize as and thus call fairness. The elements of this concept appeared together in a connected fashion. More specifically, users responded to a question about one of them by also mentioning another one without prompting. Recall that not every user made these connections, nor did any single user connect all of them.

The topics in Table 12 enumerate what was perceived as unfair such as discrimination, bias, and partiality of rules. The pattern of interconnection between these concerns shown in Table 13 suggests that the users, taken together across all systems in the sample, also indicate a connection between these topics. Nevertheless, it is important to emphasize that because there isn't a direct translation of fairness into the Nepali language—and in fact, the mother tongue for many respondents was not Nepali but other regional languages—effectively, those conducting the study supply the notion. This process of importing ideas of fairness into studies of shared resource situations in this way is not unique to this study. The approach was also used by those who compiled the NIIS data set

Table 13 Frequency of connections between comparative statements. The left of the Total column shows the number of times the comparative statement listed in each row (labeled accordingly) corresponded to another one indicated in the first row of each column. The numbers in each column refers to the numbered statements in the rows. Each number indicates how many times the statement in its row corresponded to the statement in its column. The right half of the figure shows the row percentages for the corresponding cell in the left half of the figure. There were 827 individual interviews of which 724 contained connected statements about reducing cooperation.

Reason for Reducing Cooperation	Group	A	B	C	D	E	F	G	Total	A	B	C	D	E	F	G	Total	
Poorer users receive water	A		91	60	113	97	48	117	526		17.3	11.4	21.5	18.4	9.1	22.2	100	A
Some do more work than others	B	91		129	52	22	76	106	476	19.1		27.1	10.9	4.6	16.0	22.3	100	B
Rules are appropriate	C	60	129		49	114	45	111	508	11.8	25.4		9.6	22.4	8.9	21.9	100	C
Rules discriminate against the poor	D	113	52	49		45	58	54	371	30.5	14.0	13.2		12.1	15.6	14.6	100	D
Rules favor the wealthy	E	97	22	114	45		72	81	431	22.5	5.1	26.5	10.4		16.7	18.8	100	E
Rules are easy to understand	F	48	76	45	58	72		60	359	13.4	21.2	12.5	16.2	20.1		16.7	100	F
Rules treat people uniformly	G	117	106	111	54	81	60		529	22.1	20.0	21.0	10.2	15.3	11.3		100	G

when they decided what questions to include in the questionnaire. Designed to facilitate a theory-informed meta-analysis, variables in the NIIS were explicitly coded using concepts of fairness from the IAD framework. This severely restricts how useful the data contained in the NIIS can be for examining other ideas of fairness that users may express, but that the collective action-based theory embodied by the IAD framework does not recognize and therefore the NIIS does not record.[18] The only difference with the approach used here is that the concept of fairness is constructed inductively from interviews by combining conceptions of fairness that users express rather than looking for evidence of a single conception based on theory.

There were individual differences in which comparisons a particular user conveyed as connected in this way. However, across all 827 individuals interviewed, at least two of these notions were likely to appear in a connected fashion. If these same respondents were to learn English and then be asked to talk about 'fairness' in this new language, they might not touch upon the same elements, and their understanding of the term may thus be different. However, these findings would lead one to expect an overlap between how they would respond and the elements listed above.[19] Thus, it can be said now that users reduced their cooperation when they perceived the system as unfair.

The Perception of Fairness

Relying on interviews with users, one is not left with a clean, universal, or objective metric of fairness. Instead, perceived fairness emerges as a cluster of seven subjective assessments of particular aspects of the rules. These assessments recur in interviews with users across cases, but understanding what fairness means in each situation requires reasoned judgment of the results of each of these comparisons in each instance. Which ones are more relevant than others can be surmised more accurately with time and familiarity with the particular situation in question. Each of these comparisons can be made in each case. However, there isn't an equally rigorous basis for combining them into a single measure

---

[18] Poteete et al. (2010, p. 91) note "In model-centered meta-analysis, theory—in this case, the IAD framework—guides the identification and definition of variables to be coded based on information contained in the case studies. The IAD framework directs attention to the actors, rules or institutions, relationships among actors and among institutions, actions, and outcomes associated with a collective-action situation." I explore this further in Chapter 4.

[19] While tracing the connections between these comparisons gives the sense that they are related to each other, a more complete indication would come from comparing these connections to their connections to other concepts as well. Something like a Multitrait-Multimethod-Matrix (MTMM) would be useful, but the limited data does not allow for its construction.

of fairness, or for reducing them to a smaller number of components.[20] It is precisely because of the difficulty of reducing these comparisons to a smaller number—both for the observer and for the individual cooperators—that a multidimensional idea of perceived fairness can evoke greater understanding of the situations faced by cooperators. Stopping short of a single unit of fairness forces consideration of what relative weighting of each aspect might be most appropriate in each case.

Approaching cooperation through fairness entails a different understanding of human actions than is possible by assuming that all humans are doing the best they can for themselves. The collective action approach demands of the analyst that they try to see through the eyes of one behaving as though they are doing the best for themselves. By assuming that everyone is doing the best for themselves to the best extent they can carries the implication that all people, including observer and user, are fundamentally the same in that regard. Through the question "What would a selfish, rational person do in this situation?" the observer is asked in the collective action approach to recognize that others are just like themselves in their motivation (Ostrom, 1990). The fairness approach begins from the even more basic question of what is important to others. Critically, it allows for two new possibilities. First, not everyone's conceptions of unfairness can be entirely accommodated at once. Second, even a single user's conception of fairness can consist of demands that are incompatible in particular situations. As a consequence of this generality, using this approach becomes a more complex process.

By way of illustration, consider the rule for allocating water in the SP canal in Tanahun, Nepal.[21] The rule states that each user receives water in proportion to the land they own. An implication of this rule is that during times of scarcity, those who own smaller plots do not receive enough water to grow any crops, while those that own more land get enough water to grow at least some (although far less than they might normally). In the past, this scarcity has been rare. In the last decade, changing rainfall patterns have made scarcity more frequent. Now, it is more common that some of the poorer users cannot grow any crops. Some users see the current water allocation rule as favoring the wealthy and therefore perceive it as unfair (Table 12, Row E). Others do not see it as unfair because the rules are being applied uniformly to everyone in all circumstances, as originally agreed (Table 12, Row G). Here it is not clear how both conceptions can be accommodated at once in this new situation of scarcity.

---

[20] These components for this reason are incommensurable.

[21] I spent a month living in a village at the tail end of this canal, and had a chance to interview users and observe them in more detail than the interviews and surveys permitted in other cases.

An individual user can have conflicting ideas of fairness as well. A relatively wealthy older user who favored uniform rule application, Mr. Aale, at the same time also believed that the poorer members should receive a greater share of water during scarcity. Therefore, for him, the system was not as fair as it could be because poorer users were not currently receiving the share of water they deserved (Table 12, Row A). Over multiple interviews, he explained that even though fairness requires uniform rule application, it also requires giving everyone at least enough water to grow some crops, no matter what is demanded by the principle that "we are all brothers and sisters. So, everyone should get at least something." Here, "something" referred not to water, but to cultivated rice. During meetings, he explained it differently to other users. He used the phrase, "purkha ko chalan" or the traditions of the ancestors, when justifying the idea in public. Respect for the traditions of the elders is not an explicit principle stated in the working rules of the group, nor is the idea that all users should receive enough water to grow at least some crops.

Furthermore, during the last four meetings of the Water User's Association, Mr. Aale threatened to withdraw from the association because of this.[22] An important member of the group not just because of his wealth and age, but also because of his knowledge of how the outside world worked, there was a general recognition that he was a critical member of the association. The other users didn't oppose him publicly although their hesitation to agree was also clear in their relative silence during meetings, but these two views gathered supporters beyond Mr. Aale. At the same time, some users also felt uncomfortable with this idea that they should receive less water during times of scarcity. This sentiment was shared particularly by some of the less wealthy (but not poor) users, for whom even a slight reduction in water could impact their livelihoods to a large extent. Mr. Aale's argument that giving everyone at least some meaningful amount for growing crops is more important than the current working rules left them uneasy that they would bear the burden of this idealism.

The fairness approach asks that an observer recognize the universal aversion to being treated unfairly, consider what fairness means to different individuals in the group, and how as a group they can struggle successfully with the conflicting demands of fairness. Where the collective action approach of Ostrom recognizes the struggle that results from having to resolve individual desires to do the best they can for themselves given that there isn't enough for everyone to get as much as they want, the fairness approach addresses a different struggle. The fairness approach recognizes the challenges involved in convincing users who possess

---

[22] A retired soldier from the Gorkha regiment in the British army, he did not need the low-lying land that this system was irrigating. He had land in other command areas as well. On top of that, he also received a pension.

different perceptions of what is fair to continue cooperating to use and maintain shared resources, given that some of these perceptions will likely be at odds with each other and that even individuals can believe in fairness demands that are not always compatible.

Assessments of Fairness

Factors outside the control of the group such as political movements, interactions with government agents, and activities by NGOs can all provoke a user to reassess how fair their institutions are. Take the example of a canal in the district of Dang. The headworks of this canal was located in a stream nestled in the nearby forested, uninhabited hills on the Southern border between Nepal and India. Crossing over the hills, one can make an easy, undetected, entry into India. Partially for this reason, a contingent of Maoist army members used the headworks area as a campsite for several months. During this time, they implemented a strategy of periodically "re-educating" villages in the surrounding area by abducting male members and requiring them to attend evening educational camp meetings in the nearby forests. These nighttime programs included talks, discussions, and plays that emphasized one of the Maoist party's central objections to all existing governance institutions: that they were systematically dominated by upper-caste Hindus and in turn oppressed others.

A 34-year-old respondent, Mr. Chaudhary, who had also attended this camp described the effects this had on him: "I had not noticed why [poor] people like us always got less water and did work. The comrades [Maoist rebels] showed me that we are being oppressed." This response highlights how fairness assessments can be provoked by factors outside the group of users. Like Mr. Darai before, this user had noticed that people like him "got less water and did all the work." However, he hadn't assessed whether this was fair or not. Second, the situation did not offend his sense of fairness to the extent that he automatically perceived it as unfair upon noticing this unevenness. The Maoist influence here did at least two things. First, it altered his sense of fairness so that he recognized the uneven distribution of work as unfair; second, it forced him to assess the existing situation using this updated sense of fairness.

Consider another response from a 16-year-old user, Mr. Basnet, for the same canal. He had only started representing his family as the head of the household a year ago after his father fell ill. When asked what he thought about the Maoist intervention, he noted, "I liked it a great deal. . . . This water is everyone's. It is not theirs alone. Using weapons, we should recapture our Water User's Group because it has been captured by feudal forces." While it is not possible from this response to attribute his sense that "they" are monopolizing the water to the

Maoist influence, the second sentence is clearer. Using the language of the Maoist party, he asserts his willingness to act violently on his sense of unfairness. The Maoist programs appear to have heightened his sense that his perceived unfairness of the Water User's Group is significant. It appears to be significant enough not only for him to reduce his commitment to the governing institutions, but also to violently act against it.

The perception of fairness is different for other users of the same canal, however. Some upstream households of the DBA canal were targeted by the Maoist militia for reeducation, while a large number of downstream users did not attend these sessions because they lived too far away from the rebel camp. Consequently, none of the downstream respondents spoke of feudal systems or oppression, even though they were subject to the same institution and Water User's Association for canal governance as upstream users. Instead, a typical response was more forgiving of the same unevenness that those upstream had perceived as unfair.

For example, when asked whether everyone performed the same amount of work on the canal, one of these downstream respondents, Mr. Aryal, replied, "Sometimes. Sometimes. But it is not like before, . . . We did work but we didn't get any water when there was a shortage. Now, when they get water we get some water. Our group is improving. Slowly, slowly." He optimistically refers here to a change in the rules for allocating water in that particular system. The previous rule—that those upstream took water first in proportion to the work they contributed—made no allowance for disasters or scarcity. Thus, when scarcity did happen, those downstream (usually poorer users) did not get water, although they were still required to help clean and repair the headworks. A new rule was adopted as a compromise after the headworks was damaged by a landslide and those downstream refused to help repair it. This modified rule for allocating water specifies a different process during scarcity: everyone is allowed a minimal amount of water, and those downstream would take water first. Although he may still perceive the current situation as unfair, this respondent indicates that it is less unfair than in the past, and seemed to be getting better.

Although I have given two examples here of how the Maoist influence provoked fairness assessments, the fact that people gave fairness reasons to stop is not limited to these cases. Many more cases were not affected by the Maoist movement than were. The example of Mr. Darai represents this vast majority of other cases where there was no reported Maoist influence, although it is not clear from his interview why he had come to perceive his institution as unfair.[23]

---

[23] I provide some possible explanations in Chapter 5.

The Power of Perceived Fairness

The perceived fairness of an institution for user self-governance contains seem-ingly conflicting features. It is universal in the sense that at least one of its con-stituent comparative assessments appear in every case where a user reduced their commitment, and most likely in at least two cases. However, it is also subjective in that these assessments are made by individual users. It is also un-clear whether the seven dimensions can be reduced to a smaller number. Most likely it cannot be. It is also likely that some subset of these seven dimensions of perceived fairness will occur in other examples of sustained cooperation be-yond irrigation systems.[24] Thus, the perception of fairness is not entirely unique to the individual, nor is it general enough to be applied across cases without tweaking. The dimensions appear to be universal, but the specific assessments are more local.

The tension between the universal nature of the contours of this concept and the specific nature of its content gives rise to its particular power for assessing institutions aimed to sustain cooperation. Before it can be applied to instances of sustained cooperation, one must decide which aspects of the compound con-cept are relevant and whether a reduction in dimensionality of the concept is warranted. If in the collective action approach, the analyst is asked to perceive the situation of an individual cooperator through the eyes of one guided by costs and benefits, the perceived fairness assessment demands a related type of empathy. The fairness-based approach asks an analyst to consider what users consider fair in the seven dimensions, as well as what factors might affect their assessments of fairness. Since fairness assessments can vary within groups, this variation opens up the possibility of different, even conflicting, assessments of the perceived fairness of an institution for self-governance among users in a single group, or even for the same user at different times. This diversity, circumscribed because it is pinned to the seven dimensions instead of being arbitrary and basically in-comparable, forces one to examine in specific instances how such differences are prevented from derailing cooperation in successful cases.

The conception of fairness as consisting of seven dimensions but ultimately subjective in its specific content provides a discursive basis for a framework to understand why some instances of cooperation persist while others don't. As will be seen, it is more accurate in describing the complex reality of sustained cooperation precisely because it does not provide a fully objective basis for a deterministic framework, but requires that the analyst understand the reasons of individual users or groups. This is the opposite of the dominant collective action

---

[24] What these are is an empirical question for future researchers.

approach, which privileges objective, measurable variables rather than "in the mind, subjective" ones (Ostrom, 1990, p. 38). By using the fairness approach to cooperation, one trades convenience and elegance for greater understanding.

Tracing the connections between notions of fairness in the responses of a single user and then gathering elements that appear connected when all interviewee responses are considered together has led to a multidimensional idea of fairness. This method has not narrowed down on a universal notion of perceived fairness across all cases of cooperative local self-governance, or even farmer-managed irrigation systems in Nepal. But it has delimited a set of seven comparisons from which at least two are likely to appear in any individual notion of fairness that users of these irrigation systems might convey. This narrowing facilitates examining these ideas of fairness numerically by first identifying questions in a survey that indicate separate comparative statements, and then examining how user responses to these questions relate to continued cooperation.

Unfairness Aversion

This suggests that a significant number of cooperators behave as though they are unfairness-averse, not just cost-averse. That is, they display a basic aversion to remaining committed to situations that they perceive as unfair, even if the commitment remains of net benefit to them. It is true that at least initially, individual farmers resemble conditional cooperators whose assessments of other farmers are likely to influence their decisions about what they themselves will do (Ostrom, 2000). For instance, farmers who are constitutionally averse to shirking, free-riding, and opportunism will likely seek credible assurance that others will not behave in these ways before they commit to cooperating. Conditional cooperation is behavior that is conditional on the likely behavior of others. Eventually, farmers also respond to their experience of how the existing cooperative arrangements are turning out for themselves in comparison to other users, not just whether it is of net benefit to themselves, or whether the rules meet the condition of adequately deterring opportunism by others. That is, they appear to condition their behavior on that of the institution toward themselves and others. This falls outside of conditional cooperation. This assessment of how the system behaves with respect to fairness joins considerations of how others will behave with respect to cooperation in affecting individuals' motivations to continue cooperating.[25]

---

[25] Here, it is worth noting that perceived fairness may affect trust in governing institutions.

Thus, those systems survive in which institutions avoid unfairness. Sustained cooperation depends on a perception of fairness primarily because at least some people in shared-resource situations behave as though they are unfairness-averse. In these cases, the extent of dependence is a result of how many people are unfairness-averse and how much they affect the functioning of the canal. For example, in Mr. Darai's irrigation system, those who did most of the physical work on the canal wielded this power. Perceiving the system as unfair, they reduced their cooperation, which in turn resulted in canal deterioration for all users. In this way, as unfairness-averse cooperators begin to perceive their institutions as unfair, they lessen their commitment to it in some way and thereby reduce their level of cooperation. This tendency toward unfairness aversion is akin to the widely acknowledged aversion to being a "sucker" upon which the collective action understanding of cooperation is built. The difference is that if this sucker-avoidance is apparent in the initial stages of cooperation, unfairness aversion only manifests itself over time and with respect to outcomes, rather than just rules. Nobody prefers to be treated unfairly for an extended period of time.[26]

Some Further Aspects of Unfairness Aversion

As the examples so far have illustrated, unfairness aversion does not mean that an individual will automatically act on their perception that the institution is unfair. In the example above, it took a Maoist reeducation campaign to convince users to act on long-perceived unfairness of their system. Not only did these external actors encourage disadvantaged users to act on their perception of unfairness by challenging the authority of the WUA; they also offered to provide armed support for it. This example, while atypical, clearly illustrates the significance of factors outside the group. While it is possible that the system of cooperation will be perceived as so unfair that an individual's directly offended sense of fairness alone might provoke them to act, this is unlikely for reasons I explain in Chapter 5. The same power relationships that prevent poorer users from speaking out at meetings would likely induce enough fear of retaliation from wealthier users to discourage them from acting on perceived unfairness. More likely than outright revolt is that users will reduce the quality of their involvement. They might do lower quality work, be less punctual attending group work sessions, or show less enthusiasm for punishing others who break the rules. All of these indicate reduced commitment. Cumulatively, these personal

---

[26] This is a modified version of Levi's (1989, p. 177) observation.

micro-protests can also affect the functioning of the canal, even in the absence of a sudden revolt similar to Scott (2008).

It is also important to clarify what the users perceive to be unfair. For them to act against the system of cooperation or reduce their commitment to its institution in some way, they must attribute at least a part of the unfair distributional aspects of their cooperative arrangements to the system itself. In this way, they regard the system as unfair. For example, it is also possible for them to attribute unfair distribution that results to a disaster or a natural cause, not something caused either by the people currently implementing the system of cooperation or the system itself. Unless they blame the system for the perceived unfairness, it is unlikely that they will reduce their cooperation. In the absence of this attribution, even if users should decide to act on perceived unfairness of aspects of their current situation, some may do other things targeted at individual users. It is common, for instance, for some users who notice that other users are stealing water from them to vandalize the gates that regulate water, or intentionally damage parts of the canal or headworks to spite other individual users whom they blame for perceived unfairness. Thus, the mechanism connecting a perception of unfairness and reduced commitment to a cooperative system requires that the user at least partially attributes unfair individual or comparative outcomes to the rules, and in this way perceive the system as unfair.

This attribution of causes of perceived unfairness is also particularly open to influence from factors outside the group. As the 34-year-old respondent indicated above, the Maoist training program convinced him that their unfair situation was a consequence of the system itself, not because the system was being implemented unfairly by the current WUA, whereas for the 16-year-old, the blame lay squarely on the WUA and those currently in control. In the same example, the destruction of the headworks resulted in reduced water for all users. According to the existing rules, this often meant no water for those downstream. This suddenly increased water gap between upstream and downstream users was attributed by users to natural causes—a landslide. While this landslide gave the opportunity for some users to threaten to reduce their commitment to a system that required that all users contribute after a disaster, the reduced water available to those downstream was not blamed on upstream users not following the rules.

Institutional Fit Reconsidered

Incorporating the unfairness-averse tendencies of users into an understanding of cooperation forces a reconsideration of the role of institutions in cooperation. Those systems appear to survive whose institutions not only give reason to benefit-seeking individuals to cooperate but also remove the reasons that would cause unfairness-averse users to stop cooperating. An institution is a set of working rules intended to guide user behavior whose outcomes can be difficult to predict. In the early stages of cooperation, before users have experienced the cumulative outcomes of their working rules, the institutions can only make a credible promise to users that they will not be treated unfairly under them, but as the users gain experience with their institution, experience the consequences of regulating their behavior in their own lives, and compare these to other users, this changes. Over time, users condition their cooperation on actual comparative results. Thus, institutions that fit local circumstances not only continue to alter the costs and benefits assessed by individual users to render cooperation rational. They also credibly and continuously remove the fairness reasons that users may have for reducing their cooperation over time. This implies that effective institutions for cooperation also address the elements of perceived fairness.

Now for a slight detour. So far, I have discussed perceived fairness and argued that institutions have to address the reasons of unfairness in order to effectively sustain cooperation. However, it is well known through the work of E. Ostrom and many others that institutions also have to perform a range of other functions to help users maintain their shared resources. Overall, they have to fit the circumstances in such a way that the incentives of selfish users are aligned toward making cooperation beneficial (Gardner, Walker, and Ostrom, 1994). Before returning to fairness, it is useful to examine these other demands. I will then combine these demands with those of fairness to show how it becomes necessary to reconsider what it means for institutions to "fit."

Credible institutions stand between a group of individuals and the depletion of their shared resource. A well-functioning canal is typically accompanied by a well-functioning institution. Institutional credibility comes from at least three features. First, users must be relatively certain that opportunists will be discouraged from acting to the detriment of the longer-term viability of the resource. Second, users must be convinced that behaving in accordance with the institution's working rules will actually result in the long-term availability of the resource. Third, users must continue to believe that the institution will not treat them unfairly. It functions well when it is able to alter user behavior to produce a desired pattern, usually maintenance of the shared resource. So, a canal governance institution can be said to fit well when it alters the incentives faced by individual irrigators in such a way that they continue to maintain the canal, and actively removes the reasons of unfairness that might compel them to stop.

The specific types of rules that an institution should have in order to "fit" derive from the ways in which the users depend on each other. Consider the nature of their interdependence in the case of the irrigation canals in Nepal. All of the users need water from the canal to grow their crops. Without regular inspection, cleaning, and repair, the physical structure of the canal will deteriorate, and the amount of water it can transport will decrease. The average canal in this sample is about 4 km long and would take one person 200 days a year to maintain, so a farmer who receives water from the canal must depend on the cooperation of other farmers to maintain it. At the same time, the amount of water that the downstream farmers receive depends on how much the upstream farmers use. Because of how important the allocation of work and water is to the farmers, farmer-managed irrigation systems all typically have rules that specify how the necessary maintenance work is assigned and how the water is distributed to users. The specific allocation rules are not the same across cases, however. This variation is due not only to the fact that different canals require different amounts of work, but also due to the fact that each user benefits differently from the water, and they will be willing to bear different expected costs in order to receive their share. For instance, in some locations work volume is assigned based on the amount of land one owns, while in others the work done is split equally between them.

Allocation of the resource is one aspect of governance that well-fitting institutions have rules to govern. Other aspects of shared resource governance are listed in Table 14. This collection of working rules that address these aspects altogether constitute the institution that governs the shared resource.

The types of rules that these institutions consist of derive from these aspects of governing shared resources in Table 14. Qualification refers to the rules as to who qualifies to use the resource. These rules determine who can be included in the community of users and who cannot. When less of the resource is available

Table 14 **Aspects of governance of shared resources. Examples of rules for key aspects of governing irrigation canals. There is wide variation in the specific rules across all 266 groups. Those listed below are illustrative and not representative. (Adapted from Uphoff, 1991.)**

	Aspect	*Example rule from irrigation canals*
1	Qualification	Must own land adjacent to the canal in order to use it
2	Inspection	Each should inspect as much as they can and report damage to the WUA
3	Maintenance	Must work in proportion to the water that they withdraw from the canal
4	Allocation	Can withdraw water in proportion to the area of their land
5	Enforcement	Each farmer is required to monitor other farmers
6	Punishment	The first time a day of work is missed results in a public rebuke
7	Adaptation	Rules can be changed with a majority vote at a general meeting

than potential users might want, it is typical for there to be rules delineating who is allowed to use it. Related to this is Allocation, which is concerned with how the resource is distributed among qualified users. Inspection, Maintenance, and Enforcement concern specific types of tasks that must be done for the resource to remain functional, and to not deteriorate. When it is not possible for one or a handful of people to do all these tasks, it is typical for there to be rules allocating these necessary burdens to users. These rules also specify how these tasks are to be done. In some situations, it is easier to regard these three aspects— Inspection, Maintenance, and Enforcement—together as the contributions that users are required to make in return for being allocated a proportion of the resource. As users learn and their situations change, they may need to update the rules to more appropriately address the prior six aspects of governance in new circumstances. Adaptation concerns the process by which prior decisions as encoded in the rules are to be updated.

Institutional Origins of Unfairness

Just as institutions present a solution to collective action problems, they also present new problems. Without the rules regulating user interdependence, farmers would likely not be able to achieve reliably and consistently the desired joint outcomes or avoid unfairness. Collective action problems would probably prove insurmountable. In these cases, users wouldn't be able to maintain a fully functional irrigation system that can provide water to fields at a distance from a water source in a way that is not perceived as unfair by the users. However, more than one rule will typically achieve the desired user behavior in relation to each of the above aspects of governance. Any rule that is chosen to govern each of these aspects has different effects on different users. Thus, any choice of rule can be perceived as unfair by some users.

Consider how in order to address these aspects of governance, rules have to be tailored to address the particular mix of reasons that users have to cooperate or not. Focusing on the aspect of punishment, which is particularly important in the literature on social norms (Elster, 1989; Bicchieri, 2005), consider how different user tendencies put different constraints on the working rules governing it. When irrigators are uncompromisingly calculating and selfish, any arbitrary punishment won't do for altering particular behaviors such as stealing water: the punishment must be calibrated so as to cancel out the benefits of not cooperating by engaging in that particular action. In general, any punishment greater than the benefit that a cost–benefit driven user expects to get from their share of water would be enough to shape their behavior. The punishment could entail a small monetary fine to months of social shunning or confiscation of cattle. In contrast, irrigators who are concerned about the "good name" of themselves or their family, or "ijjat" in Nepali, will be deterred by a wider range of punishments, not necessarily those carefully tailored to them or to a particular action. This is because for such users any punishment whatsoever is understood to ruin the good name of the family. When users are unfairness-averse, they will also consider the pattern of enforcement of the punishment. For instance, they will assess whether some groups are punished differently than others for similar violations (Group G in Table 12). They may even reconsider whether to enforce the rules.[27] After all of these considerations, the rules must direct enough user behavior to result in the canal being maintained.

Any particular institution may not initially address all seven aspects of governance robustly, although it will eventually mature to have rules that address more of them. Table 14 also shows the most common rules governing each aspect of the irrigation canals in this sample. Regardless of the type of resource, these are the key decisions that are made at some point or another by users who seek to govern it over time. Because a group may not face these decisions all at once, rules encoding what they decided are not all present at once either.[28] Users typically begin cooperating using a subset of these, such as rules for allocation and maintenance, but as users encounter unexpected circumstances, they will develop new rules. In this way, the institution matures as rules are added to address these other aspects as well. For instance, the users of the CM canal in the Terai region did not have any rules governing allocation in 1990. Users could take whatever they physically could whenever they wanted, but twenty-three years later, they faced a thirsty urban center nearby and the increasing cultivation of a variety of rice colloquially called Tai-Chin, or Japanese sushi rice, which is considered more suitable for making the delicacy *kheer* (rice pudding) than other long-grained varieties, but is also more water-intensive. To address the increased conflict over water between users, the Water User's Association modified the rule so that users could only take a fixed percentage of the total water available.

Each rule affects each user differently. For instance, some users may have less cash than others, and so the same monetary fine may be more difficult for

---

[27] The sociolegal literature on compliance and punishment is too large to adequately summarize here. However, recent literature on punishment and compliance in forest commons settings has found local rulemaking to be a key factor driving compliance (Epstein et al., 2021). It is suggestive that in both the first and second surveys that I present, there is a large proportion of irrigation systems in which users responded that rule breakers were not likely to be punished (33% in the first and 46% in the second).

[28] An exception is the case of systems that are "handed over" by Government Agencies to farmers' groups, or that come to be formally organized by following a template for their constitution. In this case, rules are present.

some to pay than others (Ostrom, 2005). Yet others may be more capable of physical labor than others, and so a rule to punish infractions through increased labor contributions would be more difficult for the latter. Due to these disparate effects across users, it is distinctly possible that unfair outcomes can result from any initial choice of rules. Yet, without rules the users would be unlikely to avoid situations that are patently unfair and thus likely to maintain their canal.[29] For instance, it is well-established that selfish users who don't have rules to regulate their behavior are more likely to deplete their shared resources than those that do. The main challenge, then, is discovering what rules will achieve maintenance while also not exacerbating the reasons for unfairness as given in Table 12.

What Institutions Do

Thus, mature institutions address these seven aspects of shared resource governance, independent of the type of resource that is being governed. They do more than shift around a subjective unit of cost or benefit to compel people to achieve goals. For an illustration of what else institutions do, consider the comparison of artificial and natural resources, which have many similarities. In both cases, the institutions might provide for key roles such as that of monitor or guard, as well as leaders (elected or otherwise). There are likely to be rules determining how one qualifies to use the resource, rules specifying punishment for violating the rules, rules for allocating necessary burdens such as maintenance tasks, and rules for allocating the resource. Looking at the structure of the institutions alone reveals more similarities than differences because the aspect of shared resource governance is similar for the two types of resources.

Although the aspects of governance are similar, an institution's rules are different for the two types of resources. The main challenge for users of a shared renewable resource is to devise rules that stop users from using too much so the resource may replenish itself, whereas when the resource is built, the main objective of the rules is to encourage regular contributions from users in the form of work or money. Institutions for governing built resources also seek to stop users from using water out of turn or from using too much water, but the purpose is different. It is not so the resource will be available for use, as in the case of natural resources. Instead, it is to ensure that water reaches more people and, as a consequence, the chance is increased that minimal labor and resource

---

[29] Rules play other roles as well, such as passing on knowledge between generations about how to govern.

contributions needed for the canal to remain productive will be forthcoming. That is, in the case of built resources, the rules intended to stop individual people from overusing it are actually intended to increase the chance that adequate labor will be forthcoming, not to ensure that it has a chance to replenish itself. This difference is due to the need to first "produce" a built resource before it can be distributed.

For the sake of simplicity, one might argue that evoking willingness is the real task of institutions, and that the distinction between the tasks required by natural versus man made systems is frivolous. Based on this, one might regard the general task of institutions in both cases (natural and artificial resources) as being the same. They appear to be regulating natural human tendencies in order to produce patterns of behavior that will eventually be more beneficial to all (Ostrom, 1990). In one case, the "regulation" prevents overuse, while in the other it prevents laziness—both common human tendencies. One could further argue that in both cases, the users are exercising their wills.

However, even this shorthand use of the word "regulation" misses a critical difference in what the institutions are required to do. In one case, the institution is asked to give reasons to users to stop using a resource in which they have invested nothing.[30] In the other case, the institution is tasked with the opposite: it is asked to first give users reasons to invest in a resource to be made usable. Without a critical number of users invested in maintaining the canal, it cannot function for even a single season due to siltation and blockages. This is why the canals are cleaned before the rains every season. Furthermore, the sources of water are also typically at some distance from the nearest fields. This means that often even the first user depends on the canal condition, although less so than those further downstream. Thus, it is most often the case that a group of people is required to make it even minimally productive every season: one or a few can rarely do it themselves.[31]

The loss of meaning that a one-sided use of the word 'regulation' entails is now more clear: one ends up conflating incentivizing and preventative functions. It is important to understand why users stop or reduce their commitment to co-operative systems to maintain the broader meaning of regulation as patterning behavior generally, without implying only the prevention of undesirable behavior. The type of mistake that one would otherwise make is illustrated by the following example.

---

[30] Examples of this type of natural resource and institution for governing it are prevalent in the literature on the commons.

[31] If it is hit by natural disasters such as landslides or floods, its productive interval shortens further.

Suppose one was to use the preventive meaning of what an institution is expected to do to explain a deteriorating canal. Suppose further that after studying the costs and benefits of a well-functioning canal to these users, it appeared that all of them would benefit from maintaining it collectively. In other words, everyone would be better off without making anyone worse off. A reasonable conclusion would be that either their institutions would need to be adjusted to align the incentives of individual users in such a way as to produce the behavior that would result in the desired maintenance by preventing laziness, or the canal is beyond the ability of the users to maintain, given the resources available to them. This line of reasoning leads to a focus on the undesirable behavior of users such as "shirking, free riding, or otherwise acting opportunistically." Indeed, this is the classic formulation of collective action problems defined in terms of the postulates of rational choice theory. This was how these canal governance institutions were first studied. The logical diagnosis would recommend finding ways to counter the temptation to engage in these activities through punishment and monitoring.[32]

The logical diagnosis would recommend finding ways to counter temptations to engage in these activities through punishment and monitoring.[33] Thus, relevant questions raised by the broader meaning of regulation are ruled out by using the narrow meaning of regulation as prevention of certain behaviors. In the first instance, it does not appear important to ask why fewer potential users were now invested in the canal (and therefore the institution) compared to the past. In the second instance, it does not appear important to ask why or how the commitment of users to institutions that had been successful in the past had now changed. In effect, one would be turning to their assumptions about why people behave as they do for an explanation, instead of trying to find out why it was in this case, and this narrow meaning leads one to commit a systematic error. Consequently, questions that may have tested our theory about human

[32] This is the standard analysis of the framework in Ostrom (1990, 2005). Opportunism is defined in Williamson (1975).

[33] A classic analysis of why individuals do or don't do things is Becker (1968). In this model, the act of breaking the law is modeled as a cost–benefit calculation by a rational individual seeking to maximize his utility function. For any person, the variables determining whether they comply or not is their expected utility from not complying, the probability of conviction per offense, the monetary punishment per offense, and income (monetary and "psychic") from the offense. Every rational individual might therefore break the law for the same reason that they comply with it: the benefits of doing so. By leaving the "psychic" component in our assumptions, we are able to simplify human motivation. However, we also close off the possibility that the reason for not doing something having once started might not have much to do with cost or benefit, even though the initial decision to start might have.

motivations do not appear significant, and we risk assuming our theory of why people cooperate is true even in cases where it may not be.[34]

Past studies of these cases have struggled with this distinction because they sought the conditions that might lead uncommitted people whose reasons for action were well-understood to make a commitment to a collective agreement. A change in rules is typically simplified as analogous to committing to a new set of rules from a position of not having committed. It should be noted here that the question of institutional change is folded into the question of institutional emergence in traditional approaches. Distinguishing institutional emergence and change leads to two new possibilities. First is the possibility that an individual's current position, committed or not, may influence their decisions about their future commitment. Second, people may have different reasons for taking each of these three actions: committing to an agreement for the first time, renewing their commitment, and discontinuing their commitment.

In view of this distinction, any empirical explanation of sustained cooperation (not just initial cooperation) will need to seek potentially different reasons that users may give for committing to a canal institution for the first time, and stopping or continuing to do it after having once started. It should also recognize that the significance to the users' decision-making process of these different reasons might not be related.

The Requirements of Fairness

Institutions not only alter incentives, but also inform users how to cooperate so that their behavior results in the maintenance of the resource and at the same time prevents the institutions from being perceived as unfair. Table 14 enumerates the governance-related aspects of a cooperative system that institutions have to address in order to keep the irrigation system functional. These categories group the specific tasks that have to be done to maintain any shared built resource and are based on significant literature documenting the maintenance and continued performance of irrigation systems in particular and shared built resources in general. Whatever else an institution does, it should give reasons to users to perform these tasks so that joint gains are achieved. In addition, the common elements of fairness in Table 12 provide a basis for identifying the fairness-related aspects of a cooperative system that institutions need also to address in order to avoid the perception of unfairness, and avoid a reduction of cooperation by users. The specific types of comparison that users made to justify reducing their level of cooperation refer to the five fairness-related aspects of a shared resource situation enumerated in Table 15.

---

[34] This situation would be analogous to a Type I error, where a false positive is generated.

Table 15 **The five fairness-related aspects of canal governance, giving examples of the five aspects of a cooperative system that users compare to assess the fairness of their system. The comparisons that users make refer to one or more of these aspects and can be grouped accordingly.**

	Aspect of the system	Description
1	Resource Gap	This refers to the relative distribution of water between users. It includes the question of whether the difference in amounts of water received by the biggest user and the smallest user is increasing; whether some userpartss get more water than others; whether some parts get predictably less water than others; and whether the relatively worse off have been deprived of water.
2	Work Gap	This refers to the relative assignment of work by the rules amongst users. It includes questions of whether the rules assign disproportionate duties to some subgroups of users; and whether users are required to contribute their own labor and assets to the maintenance of the canal.
3	Qualification	This refers to the rules about who qualifies to use the water and who doesn't. It includes questions of whether the rules about who can be a user are well defined; and whether the rules for becoming a user assign consistent advantage to some subgroups.
4	Exclusion	This refers to the exclusion, or marginalization, of some qualified users for long periods. This includes questions of whether the relatively worse off have been deprived of water; whether there are some users who have been consistently disadvantaged; and whether the rules give some groups consistent advantages.
5	Outcome Gap	This refers to a perceived unevenness in substantive outcomes that accrue to different users of the system over time. Substantive outcomes are outcomes that are significantly affected by water and labor allocation. For example, consider an irrigator who is now able to send his children to private school because, for decades, he has been getting his share of water according to the working rules. That his child goes to private school now is a substantive outcome. These rules for allocating water may have been agreed to before he had children, or they may have been decided without knowing the difference that it would make to the educational opportunities that his children would have.

Grouping the seven elements of fairness in terms of the five fairness-related aspects of a cooperative situation is not an attempt to reduce the elements of fairness in Table 12. This reduction is not possible without losing important information because even though two comparisons may refer to the same aspect of a cooperative system such as the outcome gap, specific comparisons matter. For example, whether poorer members receive their share of water (Table 12, Row A) and whether the rules favor the wealthy and those with more land (Table 12, Row E) could refer to the Resource Gap (Table 15). However, they are distinct reasons for stopping or reducing cooperation because addressing one does not imply that the other has been addressed. It would be mistaken to assume that because a rule addresses the outcome gap, it automatically addresses the elements of fairness that refer to it. Thus, the set of fairness-related aspects of a shared resource situation in Table 15 is a way to group those specific reasons by the fairness-related aspects of the cooperative system, but the seven elements of fairness are still necessary to address.

Giving a reason to cooperate and removing reasons not to cooperate by avoiding patent unfairness are distinctly different objectives for institutions. This difference stems from the difficulty of defining fairness: users may not know what they perceive as fair, but they learn to better recognize unfairness when they experience it. In contrast, they typically find it easier to define benefits in terms of what they want (either water or the results of having water) from the canal. So, institutions can be designed to give reason to cooperate by aligning the incentives to make cooperation appealing, but on the fairness side, the best a well-functioning institution can do is to reduce the possibility of the most patent types of unfairness and thereby not give users a reason to stop cooperating due to perceived unfairness.

What makes governing these fairness-related aspects of a cooperative system challenging is that users have difficulty defining what is fair, but they can still recognize unfair situations.[35] For example, rather than possessing a value for what the water gap should be, they behave as though they have a sense of when the gap is too wide when the gap seems to favor the wealthy, or seems to indicate that the poor don't get their share of water (as in Mr. Aale's case). In this way, they assess whether the particular fairness-related aspect of an existing situation offends a sense of fairness that has become sharpened through experiences of unfairness. The resulting assessments, possibly more than one for each aspect, comprise a perception of fairness that then affects the level of commitment of an

---

[35] It is more likely that they behave as though they assess these five aspects of what results from the system for them and others against their sense of what these should not be. Therefore, rather than having predetermined ideas of what each of these aspects of a cooperative situation should be, they appear to develop a sense of what they should not be.

individual user to their system of cooperation. The quality of their contributions to use and maintenance reflects this commitment.

It is important to emphasize that fairness does not imply equality along these five aspects of a cooperative situation—that each person gets the same amount of water, contributes the same amount of labor, and so forth. If it did imply this equality, then the rules pertaining to each fairness-related aspect could simply say so, which would go a long way to ensuring that the system would not be perceived as unfair. None of the systems have rules that suggest that there be equality for all users in all these aspects, although there are systems that specify equality in water allocation or labor contributions. It is almost impossible for there to be no water gap or work gap in a rule-bound cooperative system such as these, in which the users are already unequal in terms of land ownership, volume of agricultural activities, and position along the canal. In fact, it is typical that there is persistent inequality—that is there is always a resource gap and work gap. This inequality in itself does not seem to be perceived as unfair. Instead, when the inequality increases (or decreases) to something they are not used to or comes to appear patently unfair, it contributes to a perception of unfairness.

Addressing the fairness-related aspects of a cooperative system in Table 15 through rules or other measures demands information that is not possible to know beforehand. To illustrate this, consider the position of individual irrigators attempting to devise rules that would induce them to cooperate and convince them to continue cooperating—that is, rules that would solve collective action problems also meet these conditions of fairness. Consider the simplified case that they believe the seven elements of fairness in Table 12 would justify reducing their commitment to these institutions. This is a simplified case because the irrigators who currently use the rules in these cases were never in a position to devise them, although they may later have made changes to working rules. Second, they do not typically know why particular rules were put into place, although they might know the rules themselves.

Even in this simplified situation, it would be nearly impossible to remove the reasons that the system might be perceived as unfair by using rules alone. This is because the reasons in Table 12 refer to realized outcomes and also the nature of implementation of the rules, two of the fairness-related aspects of these systems enumerated in Table 15. How could an irrigator or a group of irrigators know how the rule they selected for allocation of water would affect the outcome gap? Or know that the gap would be so uneven as to be perceived as unfair because they came to be seen as favoring the wealthy (Table 12, Row E)? Similarly, it is impossible to know that two decades later, poorer members would fail to receive their share of water, or that the rules would seem to favor the wealthy. Yet, in light of the evidence so far presented, it is not reasonable to deny that these realized outcomes and the implementation of the rules come to matter to the level of a user's commitment, irrespective of how initially obscure they are.

The Design Principles and Perceived Fairness

The question turns to what institutions can meet these dual demands of sustaining cooperation: one, that the resource be maintained, and two, that it not be patently unfair. The features of institutions that will help users avoid or address unfairness have not received as much treatment in the literature compared to what institutional features pertain to the functional aspects of governance. Even though Ostrom's Design Principles (Table 16) for successful commons governance also focus on the functional aspects, they provide a starting point for approaching the fairness question. To what extent do systems

Table 16 **Design Principles for Governing Sustainable Resources Derived from Long-Enduring Studies of Institutions. (Adapted from Ostrom et al., 2009.)**

	Principle	*Description*
1	Clearly Defined Boundaries	The boundaries of the resource system (e.g., irrigation system or fishery) and the individuals or households with rights to harvest resource units are clearly defined.
2	Proportional Equivalence Between Benefits and Costs	Rules specifying the amount of resource products that a user is allocated are related to local conditions and to rules requiring labor, materials, and/or money inputs.
3	Collective Choice Arrangements	Most individuals affected by harvesting and protection rules are included in the group that can modify these rules.
4	Monitoring	Monitors, who actively audit biophysical conditions and use behavior, are at least partially accountable to the users and/or are the users themselves.
5	Graduated Sanctions	Users who violate rules in use are likely to receive graduated sanctions (depending on the seriousness and context of the offense) from other users, from officials accountable to these users, or from both.
6	Conflict Resolution Mechanisms	Users and their officials have rapid access to low-cost local arenas to resolve conflict among users or between users and officials.
7	Minimal Recognition of Rights to Organize	The rights of users to devise their own institutions are not challenged by external governmental authorities, and users have long-term tenure rights to the resource.
8	Nested Enterprises (For resources that are parts of larger systems)	Appropriation, provision, monitoring, enforcement, conflict resolution, and governance activities are organized in multiple layers of nest enterprises.

that embody the design principles succeed at avoiding patent unfairness? The results are mixed.

First, a note on the design principles. They describe features of processes that the cooperative system should have if it is to help users avoid collective action problems. To the extent that collective action problems are the dominant obstacle to cooperation, successful systems should share these features. Ostrom provided a summary of how these principles fit together:

> When the users of a resource design their own rules (Design Principle 3) that are enforced by local users or accountable to them (Design Principle 4) using graduated sanctions (Design Principle 5) that define who has rights to withdraw from the resource (Design Principle 1) and that effectively assign costs proportionate to benefits (Design Principle 2), collective action and monitoring problems are solved in a reinforcing manner. (Ostrom, 2000, p. 151)

"Conflict resolution mechanisms" should be local because they are less costly to irrigators, and they perform the function of allowing users to resolve differences in rule interpretation. Nested structure refers to a way of keeping local decisions local but coordinating at higher levels across systems.

These eight design principles do not directly address the five fairness-related aspects of cooperative systems. They do not allude to elements of perceived fairness given as reasons for users to stop or reduce their commitment either. The principles concern the rules alone, not the outcomes. For example, *Design Principle 2: Proportional equivalence between benefits and costs* comes closest to referring to the outcomes of the collective agreement, but only goes as far as the allocation of the resource. It does not refer to the cumulative outcomes of this allocation. In this way, the design principles describe procedural features that these institutions share and do not refer to the purpose of these rules. The purpose is filled in by the analyst: to increase the likelihood of avoiding or solving collective action problems.

However, without an explicit mention of these outcome-based aspects of fairness, the question turns to whether the mechanisms of institutional change proposed by these principles are adequate to meet the fairness conditions in Table 12. The fairness conditions stipulate that when institutions can ensure that the disadvantaged obtain the water promised to them (Table 12 Row A), work is allocated proportionally across users (B), no users are consistently disadvantaged (D), the wealthy are not consistently advantaged (E), all users are treated uniformly by the rules (F) and it is not confusing to the users how the current outcomes could arise from having followed the rules (G), users are more likely to continue to cooperate with their institutions. Ideas of proportional, disadvantage, advantage, and uniformity are normative.

The only normative conditions included in the Design Principles are: Clear Boundary Rules (Rule 1), Proportional Punishment (Rule 2), and Minimal Rights to organize (Rule 7). What is clear, proportional and minimal are all defined by the users. Of these, Rule 7 pertains to securing the rights of locals to fill in what counts as proportional punishment and clear boundary rules. Overall, the design principles place the levers for addressing the fairness-related aspects of shared resource systems largely in the hands of local users and ensure that they cannot be taken away. This still leaves the question of how one knows that the locals have discovered what is proportional and clear. In the Ostromian[36] view, if they agree to the rules, then normative conditions have been adequately met.

In Ostrom's view, the Design Principles should be adequate to incorporate fairness concerns to the extent that fairness matters to users—or, more precisely, to the dominant coalition of users that has the voting power to change the rules. Every choice of rules will result in unfairness at some point. The mechanism by which these systems are suggested to change and adapt to unfair situations is through voting. Users propose changes to the rules, which are then voted on by eligible members. Since every change in rules affects different groups differently, winning coalitions emerge victorious and get to adopt their rule. These coalition-driven mechanisms are characteristic of the collective action approach (Ostrom, 2005, pp. 204–206). In collective action approaches like Ostrom's that recognize the importance of fairness, there is an implicit assumption that fairness will result from these voting mechanisms. The implication is that instances of voluntary cooperation are fair by definition because if fairness is important to users, they won't cooperate without it. That is, fairness is an element of collective action problems such that addressing collective action problems also addresses fairness concerns.

There is nothing in the design principles that will ensure that users will devise rules to address the five fairness-related aspects of governance, let alone specific elements of fairness. In the Ostromian view, if such rules are adopted, it will be because those who have the ability to alter the institutional rules (usually, the majority or other group decision rule) want these normative properties in place. Yet, in such heterogeneous groups, a diversity of normative beliefs is the norm. So for these design principles to result in institutions that will meet the requirements of fairness, these requirements should be part of the dominant norm among users. Thus, in the Ostromian view, if fairness matters to sustained

---

[36] I use "Ostromian" to refer to the set of views developed by Elinor Ostrom in the context of shared resource governance, as well as the work of Vincent Ostrom on polycentrism that influenced that work. In this sense, I follow convention in that community, as illustrated by Aligcia and Tarko (2013). It is also called the "Bloomington School" of political economy (Cole and McGinnis, 2014).

Table 17 **Significance of Individual Design Principles to Performance. Shown are the associations between the systems meeting each design principle in Round 1 and their survival, as well as their performances in Round 2. None are significant at the 0.05 level.**

Principle	Survival	Canal Condition	Headworks Condition	Reliability	Adequacy
1. Clear Boundaries	0.65	0.9	1	0.34	0.22
2. Proportional Cost–benefit	0.86	1	0.3	0.58	0.63
3. Collective Choice Arrangements	0.35	0.1	0.34	0.29	0.51
4. Monitoring	0.32	0.52	0.26	0.2	0.11
5. Graduated Sanctions	0.47	0.81	0.29	0.31	0.23
6. Conflict Resolution*	–	–	–	–	–
7. Right to organize	0.43	0.53	0.07	0.3	0.06

*There were no questions asked to assess whether there were low cost, local conflict resolution mechanisms available to users

cooperation, it is that form of fairness that is the dominant norm or is shared by those that can impose rules on the entire group.

Focusing now on irrigation systems that embody all these design principles and have the necessary deliberative structure, there is variation in survival and performance. None of the design principles by themselves corresponded to whether the system survived or performed well (Table 17). Systems that have survived and are performing well vary with respect to the number of design principles that they satisfy (Table 18). Those that are performing well need not satisfy all of the design principles, and of those systems that do satisfy all of the design principles, a significant number are not performing well (Table 19). As Chapter 2 showed, this variation in performance is also not a result, across cases, of the most significant external variables affecting collective action problems. This suggests that these groups are able to solve collective action problems, but that the ability to do so is not enough to perform well over time.

The design principles are thus not sufficient for avoiding patent unfairness, although they may be adequate for dealing with collective action problems. Next, collective action problems themselves become less important over time. The empirical mismatch documented so far between the predictions of the collective action approach and these cases leads to the question of whether the mechanisms outlined in the Design Principles are sufficient to address perceived

Table 18 **Frequency of Design principle adherence in Round 1 among well-performing systems in Round 2.**

Number of Design Principles met	Survived (N=194)	Good Canal Condition (N=143)	Good Headworks Condition (N=131)	Reliable (N=74)	Adequate (N=71)
0	1	1 (0.7)	1	0	0
1	3	3 (2.1)	3	3	3 (4.2)
2	11	9 (6.3)	8	6	6 (8.5)
3	15	13 (8.4)	11	6	6 (8.5)
4	56	40 (28.0)	31	19	20 (28.2)
5	69	51 (35.7)	48	23	20 (28.2)
6	39	27 (18.9)	29	17	16 (22.5)

Table 19 **Varied Performance of systems in Round 2 that embodied all the design principles in Round 1 (N = 39).**

	Poor (%)	Fair (%)	Good (%)
Canal Condition	30.8	48.7	20.5
Headworks Condition	30.9	35.6	33.5
	No (%)	Yes (%)	
Adequate	59.0	41.0	
Reliable	52.8	47.2	

unfairness. That cooperation and fairness may not always go together also marks a fundamental departure from the assumption that the fact of agreement itself indicates fairness of the resulting outcomes, an assumption that underlies the collective action problem-centered approach to sustained cooperation.

If these principles are not enough to rectify or avoid unfairness, one danger of sticking to them as currently formulated is that they rationalize existing agreements, irrespective of how fair they are. There is a certain logic to this argument: instrumental human beings do the best they can, and existing institutions that are in accordance with the Design Principles are the best they can do. However, this chapter has suggested that we may need to reconsider the basic behavioral feature of human beings that gave rise to the design principles in the first instance. Not everyone behaves in all situations as though they are boundedly rational, instrumental, selfish actors who also have other preferences and norms. As they cooperate, at least some in the group resemble instead moral beings making collective decisions acceptable to the group about nontrivial fairness-related decisions involved in governing a shared resource over extended periods of time. The design principles do not appear to capture the features that enable these groups with diverse moral orientations to come to agreements that continue to be perceived as fair.

Conclusion

Ostrom's framework is derived from an understanding of cooperation constructed around collective action problems. Despite its strengths, this collective action approach to cooperation does not yet include the ideas of fairness that users of these shared irrigation systems express. This is because a collective action-based framework conflates the reasons that an individual may have for taking three distinct actions: starting, continuing, or stopping a commitment to an institution. The simplification offers a convenient way to draw attention away from the myriad reasoning processes of individuals to the situational variables that could predict behavior—i.e., features of the group and the environment. In this way, it not only permits but also requires the use of a typical human being to represent different individuals, a move that reduces the complexity of human reasoning considerably while allowing for greater complexity in social situations.

This elegant approach to cooperation leaves one at a loss in cases like irrigation systems, when user behavior isn't primarily affected by the variables thus derived. It therefore becomes necessary to alter this approach to understanding cooperation. After walking back the simplifying assumption that human reasoning is fundamentally unitary, these cases reveal seven comparative reasons that people stop or reduce their commitment. These reasons consist of comparisons of five outcomes of an individual's cooperative situation. Together, these comparisons comprise the perceived fairness of the system of cooperation.

Analysis of data showed that perceived unfairness is a significant reason that people reduce their commitment to an existing institution for shared resource governance. These institutions aid in the maintenance of shared resources and also impact aspects of fairness. For this reason, avoiding the perception of unfairness makes additional demands of cooperative systems and the individuals that design and maintain them. In particular, the rules need to reduce or avoid the perception of unfairness at the same time that they contribute to avoiding collective action problems. These additional conditions of fairness are only partially addressed by collective action-based characterizations of the sustained cooperation seen in successful systems. One of the most prominent of these characterizations is Ostrom's design principles, which inadequately emphasize perceived fairness. This suggests that a more complete list of features conducive to sustained cooperation should include descriptions of the distributional outcomes of local self-governance. As I show next, however, this will require building a framework for assessing the fairness of local self-governance arrangements based on a different philosophical foundation than dominant approaches.

Conceptions of Fairness

The findings so far lead to the question of what type of framework can accurately incorporate the complexity of actual perceptions of fairness. To answer this question, it is necessary to descend the ladder of concepts on which the Institutional Analysis and Development (IAD) framework is built from variables to concepts to philosophical foundations in order to find an appropriate level for the foundations of such a framework. Here, I begin by dissecting the Ostromian conception of fairness and identify it as having, at heart, the features of a social contract within a particular philosophical tradition of Social Contract Theory—the Contractarian one (Gauthier, 1987, 2007; Locke, 1988; Hobbes, 1996). I show that a framework to adequately incorporate the aspects of perceived fairness revealed by the empirical analysis should rebuild from at least at the level of the social contract, and possibly deeper at the level of human motivations. I then illustrate how this might be done by suggesting one possible approach that involves a different tradition within Social Contract Theory called Contractualism (Rousseau, 1968; Scanlon, 1982, 2000; Southwood, 2014).

There are many ways to conceptualize fairness outside of the Social Contract tradition (Rawls, 1958, 2008), and even within it the division between the Contractualist and Contractarian traditions can appear strained (Rawls, 2005; Sen, 2009). Rather than broaden the discussion in this chapter to incorporate many more conceptions of fairness, I take the approach of comparing the empirical conception of fairness developed in the previous chapter to the Ostromian conception of fairness as developed in the literature. Focusing on these two helps to identify aspects of perceived fairness that the Ostromian framework is too narrow to fit, but that might be incorporated by a different one. I choose a Contractarian conception as an illustration of how this could be done, although there may be better candidates outside of the Social Contract tradition altogether. Not straying too far from the Ostromian conception that underlies the IAD framework also largely preserves the internal validity of the current longitudinal data set.

Beyond Collective Action Problems. Atul Pokharel, Oxford University Press. © Oxford University Press 2024.
DOI: 10.1093/oso/9780197755792.003.0004

Ostrom's Conception of Fairness

Ostrom's framework for the analysis of cooperation[1] contains a notion of fairness conceived of as the uniform application of a set of mutually agreed-upon rules across all users of a shared resource, describing various aspects of a cooperative agreement. In this context of a group of cooperators, fairness is: (1) a property of the various rules (Ostrom, 1990, p. 214; Poteete, Janssen, and Ostrom, 2010, p. 100) and procedures (Ostrom, 2005, p. 14) of a collective agreement between them; and (2) a property of how the rules are applied to members of the group in cooperative situations characterized as thoroughly bound by rules. Consequently, the idea of perceived fairness pertains to several different aspects of these situations (Ostrom, 2005, p. 263), and it is useful to identify these different uses in order to illustrate how they are applications of the same idea of fairness.

In Ostromian accounts, "fair" or "unfair" commonly describe the method of allocating the benefits from cooperation (Ostrom, 2005, p. 87) such as the resource itself (Ostrom, 1990, pp. 32, 74, 126). For example, the rules that describe how much water everyone receives from these irrigation systems can be fair or not. The fairness of the water allocation rules is assessed by each person regarding what they get, not what others get. Fairness is also used to describe the resulting distribution of resources (Ostrom, 1990, p. 88), together with the resulting distribution of duties and rights to users (Ostrom, 1990, pp. 48, 65). Consider a system where each user gets water in proportion to the area of land that they irrigate. The resulting distribution of water across users might be fair or not, depending on the size of the gap between users who end up getting the most or the least water. Here, the fairness of the distribution and ultimately the fairness of the rule behind it are assessed by each person by comparing how much every individual in the group gets to how much others do. In this second usage, fairness describes not only the rules themselves but also some of the results of enforcing them. In its most general sense, then, fairness in this framework is used to describe the distribution of costs and benefits across users from enforcing the rules (Ostrom, 2005, p. 263; Poteete, Janssen, and Ostrom, 2010, p. 156). This generalization entails two conceptual moves. First, it translates the resource, as well as the labor involved in these situations, into either a benefit or cost respective to a particular individual. These costs and benefits can also arise from more general sources than just the resource, such as those that accrue from a

---

[1] Henceforth, I use "Ostrom's framework" to refer to the commonalities across all three versions of the Ostromian framework—the Common Pool Resource (CPR), Institutional Analysis and Development (IAD), and Socio-Ecological Systems (SES) frameworks (Poteete, Janssen, and Ostrom, 2010).

good reputation of trustworthiness and the psychological costs of feeling guilty for defying a social norm when nobody is watching.[2] Second, it recognizes that nearly every rule can be understood as altering, possibly in a uniquely personal way, the costs and benefits to each individual.

This generalization extends to the domain of fairness. A general interpretation of rules as rearranging, when enforced, the perceived costs and benefits to an individual following them (or not) also makes the idea of fairness apply yet more broadly to anything that alters the distribution of costs and benefits. This broadening in turn permits the idea of fairness to be applied to several other aspects of a cooperative situation, in addition to the current rules. This is how fairness can be used in the Ostromian approach to describe not just the rules that have already been adopted but also those that are proposed for adoption. Different from the fairness of rules already in use, the fairness of proposed rules is assessed in terms of how the rule is expected by each person to rearrange the costs and benefits they associate with actions. This assessment incorporates expectations about how likely the rules are to be enforced, or how uniformly they will be applied. When fairness is used to describe proposed rule changes in this way, it is understood to describe different proposals for sharing these costs and benefits within the group (Poteete, Janssen, and Ostrom, 2010, pp. 224, 243).

This general conception of fairness also describes the interactions of individuals with their environment (Ostrom, 2005, p. 14) and the constraints that the rules place on them (Ostrom, 2005, p. 244). The action of taking water from the irrigation system out of turn might be considered fair or not. At the same time, the restriction that water can only be taken from the canal during one's turn might be considered fair or not. Fairness can be used similarly in the context of various processes of governing the shared resource such as monitoring, enforcement, and conflict resolution. It can describe judgments about what rule-breaking is (Ostrom, 2005, p. 21), about the enforcement of rules through the application of penalties (Ostrom, 2005, p. 77), and about the mechanisms for resolving conflicts between users (Ostrom, 2005, p. 272) and communities (Ostrom, 2005, p. 279). Applied to the way in which these conflicts are resolved, fairness describes the formula for addressing competing claims on the resource (Ostrom, 1990, p. 114; Poteete, Janssen, and Ostrom, 2010, p. 230).

Perceived fairness plays an important role in Ostrom's world and is thus ubiquitous within this framework. The main reason that it is so important is that perceived fairness is understood to influence the extent of user cooperation; it motivates individuals to cooperate (Ostrom, 1990, p. 32; Poteete, Janssen, and

---

[2] It is important to note here that if something is not perceived by an individual as entailing a cost or benefit to them, it is irrelevant to their decision to cooperate.

Ostrom, 2010, p. 224), while perceived unfairness causes them to reduce their levels of cooperation (Ostrom, 1990, p. 48). Rules perceived as unfair are difficult for users to commit to (Ostrom, 2005, p. 214), and conformance to such rules may decline (Ostrom, 1990, p. 101). Even unfair rules that are difficult to commit to can alter individual behavior (Ostrom, 1990, p. 101), but when the rules are perceived to be fair, more individuals are willing to comply with them, thereby building trust in each other's promises (Ostrom, 2005, p. 263). Users are more likely to perceive rules as fair when they have participated in their formulation (Ostrom, 2005, p. 263; Poteete, Janssen, and Ostrom, 2010, p. 100). Overall, examples of successful cooperation are understood to have avoided perceived unfairness (Ostrom, 1990, p. 56). To stress the significance of this, the absence of fairness is regarded as a threat to small-scale resource governance systems (Ostrom, 2005, p. 272). Conversely, fairness is regarded as a critical attribute of robust systems (Ostrom, 2005, p. 263).

This framework stops short of describing the content of fairness. Perceived fairness is fundamental to the framework even though it provides no guidance to recognizing what fair rules, distributions, interactions, constraints, monitoring, enforcement, or conflict resolution processes might look like. Fairness is typically used interchangeably with equitability (Ostrom, 1990, p. 214; Poteete, Janssen, and Ostrom, 2010, p. 100, 123), which also lacks a single definition.[3] The framework's seeming compatibility with any substantive definition of fairness is an implication of assuming that each individual is potentially unique in their preferences, desires, and aversions—and so, it is only possible for them to know in meaningful detail what they perceive as fair. Despite this uniqueness at the individual level, groups are understood to share a morality that is to various extents internalized by its members. It is therefore possible for members of the group to evaluate whether rules are fair by assessing how they accord with the group's shared morality.[4] With this general morality in view, fair rules are regarded as evolving from social norms that derive from the specific shared morality of the group of users (Ostrom, 2005, p. 67). The cause of disagreement between users over rules is not, therefore, a moral one. Instead, these disagreements are about what specific rules most appropriately instantiate a shared morality.

---

[3] For instance, an equitable distribution of water amongst groundwater basin users might meet Selten's general equity principle or something else. Ostrom emphasizes that equitable formulas are not universal because they "take into account a variety of specific problems" that would arise if a single formula was applied uniformly across cases (E. Ostrom, 1990, 230, notes 7 and 8). It is not clear, however, what these problems are.

[4] Morality is used here, as in the Ostromian tradition, to denote belief in right and wrong. It is implied that cooperation is difficult without this shared, dominant morality (Ostrom, 2005, p. 153).

In that approach, the content of fairness is specified by users when they choose their rules. The framework defers to what rules the members of the group choose, as well as to the distributions, processes, and interactions that result from their uniform application to every individual in the group. It does not define fair rules in general or attempt to characterize them. A group of cooperators shares a collective idea of fairness that becomes known to those outside the group (and perhaps even to some of those inside it) only after the rules have been negotiated and consented to. The group's idea of fairness is understood to be expressed in the rules that the group has agreed to, using whatever standard of consensus they have previously agreed to or inherited. If the agreement defines fair rules, then fairness is what results when most users adhere to them (Ostrom, 1990, p. 126). To encourage adherence, fair rules are to be enforced strictly and uniformly for all users (Ostrom, 1990, p. 126), with some tolerance for exceptional individual circumstances or honest human failings (Ostrom, 1990, p. 101).

Fair is measured against shared group conceptions of fairness. Overall, rules, processes, or interactions are themselves fair when they meet these shared conceptions of fairness within the group (Ostrom, 2005, p. 263). This shared conception derives from the "general morality" of the users (Ostrom, 2005, p. 67) and refers primarily to whether the individuals view their own costs and benefits as proportional in some way (Poteete, Janssen, and Ostrom, 2010, p. 100). The actual content of fairness is thus specific to each group. This is because the general morality and shared conceptions of fairness that derive from them are specific to a group's history and present circumstances. On Ostrom's view, the shared conception is so localized that it is unlikely that nonmembers will know what it is in sufficient detail (Ostrom, 1990, p. 214) to infer fair rules for the group. It is, however, known to all of those in the group to some extent (Ostrom, 1990, p. 74). This assertion that shared conceptions of fairness are local knowledge (Aumann, 1976) underlies the Ostromian push toward self-governance by resource users as a means of achieving fairness.

In this sense, fairness is regarded as a group-specific social norm (Ostrom, 2005, p. 287; Poteete, Janssen, and Ostrom, 2010, p. 224) internalized—like any other social norms—to various extents by each individual (Poteete, Janssen, and Ostrom, 2010, pp. 174, 224, 250). This means these individuals learn, in part, because of the institutions themselves (Ostrom, 2005, p. 287), to attach emotions to complying with them. They may, for instance, feel guilty for neglecting to participate in group meetings or for not reciprocating altruistic behavior. Because of this internalization, fairness is regarded as being reflected in the decisions individuals make, and the social norm of fairness in particular is reflected in the rules these individuals agree to adopt (Ostrom, 1990, p. 214). Further, there are various psychological costs related to adopting unfair rules, although these psychological costs are not enough to reliably change behavior, especially where the benefits of defying a norm are high. What is more, a norm's lack of specified punishment is said to risk allowing disproportionate punishment for breaking it, an asymmetry that can carry great risks for continued cooperation. It follows that to be effective, these norms must evolve into rules with a priori punishments. Such concerted rules are assumed to be fair, and the outcomes they lead to are also described as fair if they were primarily the result of these fair rules being enforced uniformly across all users.

Ostrom's conception of local fairness derives from the idea that each or most of the individuals in a group share an understanding of what fairness looks like. The challenge of formulating fair rules is thus reduced to agreeing how these shared norms of fairness are to be expressed as linguistic statements. Different users might disagree about what formulation of a rule best embodies the norm of fairness that they share. They are indeed likely to disagree, given the imperfect nature of language. In the case of disagreement, the users are taken to rely on majoritarian voting or other such rules for aggregating rule preferences. These are examples of higher-level "collective choice rules" (Ostrom, 2005, p. 253), which define the process of rule selection (Poteete, Janssen, and Ostrom, 2010, p. 224). In this view, as long as these rules for choosing rules are considered to be fair, then the resulting rules are considered fair as well.

A more challenging scenario for this framework is one in which significant differences exist among members regarding what fairness is. In this case, even if users rely on concerted collective choice rules, they may not reach an agreement as to what other rules to adopt (Poteete, Janssen, and Ostrom, 2010, p. 156) because of substantive disagreement on what fairness is, and not just because they disagree on how a shared conception should be stated in rule form. A case of disagreement about the collective choice rules themselves poses an even more difficult scenario. This type of indeterminate result is regarded as less likely if groups of individuals share a general morality or a clearly dominant social norm of fairness (Ostrom, 2005, p. 112) that can be imposed on the minority through force of majority or quickly learned by the former. Nevertheless, the Ostromian framework classifies groups of individuals with different norms as less likely to reach an agreement about what is fair (Ostrom, 2005, p. 87) and therefore, as less likely to sustain shared resources.

Whatever the specific content of the fair rules, Ostromian fairness is maintained if those rules are uniformly applied to all individuals who are party to the agreement. Importantly, the fairness of the lower-level rules pertaining to interactions between users and resource derive from the fairness of the higher-level ones pertaining to rule changes. Thus, in this framework for understanding cooperation, fair rules are adopted and changed to remain fair through local rule-bound processes which are themselves considered to be fair, by these same individuals, and in which most of them participate. User agreement with the rules is also understood to be hierarchical: users first agree to the highest-level constitutional rules,[5] then collective choice rules, and then the actual rules governing their interactions with the shared resource. In this arrangement, where one set of rules is nested within another in a hierarchy of institutions, the perceived fairness of lower-level rules is inferred from the faithful application of higher-level rules already perceived as fair. This is illustrated, for instance, by the role of collective choice rules in resolving disagreements about other rules. Thus, fairness of process begets fairness of outcomes.

This is a primarily *procedural* as opposed to a substantive conception of fairness. For this reason, the framework is concerned more with the process used to choose rules and with the processes set up by the rules than with the outcomes of these processes. Fair rules are those that are agreed to by using higher-level fair rules. Fair distribution of resources results from the uniform application of fair rules. Fair interactions among individuals, whether with each other or with the environment, are either in conformance with fair rules or regulated by a dominant shared social norm of fairness (which is, itself, a more rudimentary form of rules). These rule-imposed constraints on behavior are fair when the rules are fair. Monitoring, enforcement, and conflict resolution processes are thus fair when regulated by fair rules.

Fairness and the Social Contract

The theoretical IAD framework appeals to the idea of fairness by agreement—the characteristic feature of a social contract—to explain the relationship between fairness and sustained cooperation.[6] To focus on fairness in this framework it is helpful to analyze it as a contract-based approach to collective action around shared resources. Social contract theories typically start from observations about a model of human being and a state of nature in which they exist. Ostrom's conception of fairness can be similarly described.

In the IAD framework people are assumed to be broadly rational and norm-following, yet mostly self-interested (Ostrom, 1990, p. 37); that is, although they may have some altruistic motivations, they primarily seek their own benefit by examining the costs and benefits of actions and outcomes over some time horizon, long or short (Ostrom, 1990, p. 89). In shared resource situations that are

---

[5] Indeed, the content of fair rules is understood to be specified by cooperators in a way that does not violate the constitution of the country in which these resources are located.

[6] From the *Internet Encyclopedia of Philosophy*: "Social contract theory, nearly as old as philosophy itself, is the view that persons' moral and/or political obligations are dependent upon a contract or agreement among them to form the society in which they live" (Friend, no date).

unconstrained by rules, it is rational for those seeking short-term gains to behave so as to deplete the resource (Ostrom, 2005, p. 132). This is the rule-less state of nature that Hobbes describes and that Ostrom rejects as atypical (Ostrom, 1990, p. 140). To solve the practical conundrum of achieving greater joint gains and escaping the prisoner's dilemma situation, users must regulate their behavior in relation to the resource: they must share benefits and burdens in such a way that enough of them remain committed to the arrangement (Ostrom, 1990, pp. 48–49) so the resource does not deplete (Ostrom, 2005, p. 221). In Ostrom's account, they do this by agreeing to mutual monitoring (Ostrom, 1990, p. 45) and enforced rules (Ostrom, 1990, p. 51) that will bring out these greater benefits in that particular situation. In short, they consent to be governed.

In these circumstances, it is rational to commit to a contract. Thus, rational norm-following individuals come to a mutually binding contract (Ostrom, 1990, pp. 15–18) that acceptably allocates the necessary benefits and burdens of cooperation (Poteete, Janssen, and Ostrom, 2010, p. 100). They seek to cooperate because it makes them all better off (Ostrom, 1990, p. 29), and the rules are deemed worthy of being followed because they are necessary if rational people are to cooperate (Ostrom, 2005, pp. 210, 219–221). This set of mutually agreed-upon rules that rational people will accept in each particular situation—on the condition that others accept them as well (Elinor Ostrom, 2000)—is both indicative of fairness and constitutive of it. After all, as implied in this approach, nobody would voluntarily agree to a set of rules that they perceived as unfair, and it follows that nobody would voluntarily agree to the uneven application of fair rules. Individuals agree to be bound by this set of rules because it is beneficial to them that everyone else is committed to them and because it mitigates the fear of opportunistic behavior. However, they actually follow the rules because the rules are credibly enforced, and it is therefore rational for them to avoid punishment. In this type of rule-bound situation, reciprocity and altruism become rational,[7] whereas in the rule-less state of nature where rational action leads to depletion, they are not. In Ostrom's view, mutual cooperation is much more likely in groups whose members share norms of reciprocity.

In Ostrom's state of nature, that is, the normal state of affairs, individuals use and maintain these shared resources collectively to varying degrees of

---

[7] They become rational because they can thus gain longer-term benefits. Not behaving in this way would make others less likely to do so, thereby reducing the chance the longer-term gain will be achieved. Also, credibly enforced rules (by other users) with appropriately calibrated punishments (set not by outsiders but by the users) increase the chance that others will also comply, and the chance that the expected loss from punishment exceeds the expected benefit of not behaving this way (Becker, 1968).

success.[8] They do this by using their capacities to solve problems rationally and to make binding commitments.[9] This state of nature can devolve into one where individuals are depleting rather than managing the resource. In this degraded state, they compete ceaselessly with one another over it, motivated only by short-term self-interest.[10] This devolution into a Hobbesian rule-less situation is triggered when a user acts opportunistically to claim what is rightfully someone else's—whether by shirking one's responsibilities, free-riding and thereby stealing residuals of other people's contributions, or being otherwise grasping—and others reciprocate this behavior. Unable to trust that their rights will be respected, other users begin to act similarly as demanded by rationality and lock themselves into a prisoner's dilemma. When the Ostromian state of nature degrades in this way, the resource is sequentially overused, as each takes as much as they can, whenever they can. Having no external authority to prevent or manage this situation results in the depletion of the resource. Since there are no impersonal rules to guide punishment, and it is no longer rational to follow social norms, individual norms may lead to disproportionate punishment. This in turn will only exacerbate mistrust, thereby reinforcing mutual conflict.

This gets to the main reasons for individuals in Ostrom's world to agree to form a contract, and through it a sort of civil authority established by users to regulate user behavior and to enforce property rights regarding the resource. First, users can see that through a contract they avoid this depletion scenario and can enjoy the available resource for a longer time. In brief, they recognize that they can achieve their instrumental aims through an implicit or explicit contract. They are also able to encode and transmit their knowledge of continuous trial-and-error to calibrate delicate matters of coordination and compliance, such as appropriate punishment.[11] Thus, in Ostrom's state of nature, shared resources are normally maintained not depleted. They deplete in the fashion described by Hardin (1968) when the normal situation devolves into a conflictual state. Avoiding this unusual but mutually destructive state of conflict is among the key reasons, in Ostrom's conception, why individuals agree to a social contract for the use and maintenance of their shared resource.[12]

---

[8] Since this is precontract, the users rely on heuristics, customs, repetition, and learning—all the reasons it is possible for people to cooperate without institutions.

[9] This is what makes them different from Hobbes' (1996) humans.

[10] Because the users are naturally in a better state than they could be, Ostrom's degraded state of nature is akin to Locke's state of war.

[11] See Design Principle 5, "Graduated Sanctions" (Ostrom, 1990; Ostrom, Ingram, and Hong, 2009; Cox, Arnold, and Tomás, 2010). This has remained completely unchanged over the years.

[12] Note the distinction with Locke, for whom we end up in a state of conflict or war in the state of nature because we cannot impartially adjudicate our property conflicts (Locke, 1988).

For Ostrom, then, boundedly rational, self-interested individuals have their own reasons to commit to mutually agreed-upon rules to use and maintain shared resources.[13] This framework for variables and the relationships between them is built on the idea that a fair allocation of burdens and benefits by the rules consists in what the contracting parties actually agree to, not in their adherence to an external standard of fairness.[14] This is the characteristic assertion of social contract theory. Furthermore, people act in a way that others perceive as fair not because, for instance, they are seeking to justify their behavior to others or because they respect others as free and equal parties, or even because it is what they are due. People are considered to be primarily self-interested and to follow norms of fairness because the rational strategy for attaining greater long-term gains is to act in a way that others perceive as fair. In Ostrom's view, although both depletion and maintenance of user-governed resources are possible, depletion is less common among existing systems because over the years they have learned how to sustain cooperation.

A Contractarian Conception

The conception of fairness that appears in the Ostromian framework is contractarian. The contractarian approach to social contracts offers explanations of why even instrumental, selfish individuals would have reasons to cooperate to achieve long-term gains.[15] This subjectivity of reasons for consenting to be governed is a crucial part of the contractarian school (Sen, 2009, pp. 69–71). Users are understood to have their own good reasons for doing so, which have no relationship to some idea of what objectively good reasons might be, should such an idea exist. In an analogous argument, Ostrom's framework is primarily aimed at illustrating how local self-governance of shared resources is similarly viable. Echoing the contractarian view, a key argument is that these governance arrangements can emerge and be sustained among even the most eminently self-interested people.[16]

---

[13] It is worth noting that Ostrom traces a line of thinkers whose ideas need to be developed further to Hobbes (Ostrom, 1990, p. 216).

[14] Note that this does not rule out that what unrelated contracting parties actually agree to could have some features in common as was found in Chapter 3. I develop this distinction theoretically shortly when discussing nonlocal fairness.

[15] This contrasts with the Contractualist social contract approach, which begins from the premise that people are irreducibly moral. These are rough classifications, but they serve an important illustrative purpose in the current argument.

[16] See Ostrom (1990, p. 34): individuals are broadly rational, and are also motivated purely by cost and benefit to themselves.

In this view, fairness is mutual agreement. For Ostrom, the existence of a contract shows that rational individuals acting to advance their own interests will, as a matter of course, consent to be governed because of self-interest alone.[17] Ostrom goes further by showing they can do so on their own and thereby prevent deterioration of a shared resource without assistance. This contradicts the premise of policy that anticipates the prisoner's dilemma, a situation designed to lead inevitably to noncooperation and tragedy.[18] Ostrom claims that individuals can escape the Hobbesian state of nature that arises among humans sharing a resource, or avoid it altogether through a social contract among themselves.[19] Over time, those groups able to devise and commit to appropriate contracts survive, while others disappear. Unlike Hobbes, then, Ostrom's state of nature is characterized by the existence of myriad collective agreements, those who are unable to make such agreements having perished. In this state, groups have various levels of success at maintaining shared resources and are not doomed to deplete them.[20] Overall, consistent with the contractarian tradition, what is fair in Ostrom's conception is defined by mutual agreement among users, not by anything external to them.[21]

Thus, seen from within the contractarian tradition in Social Contract Theory, the central question for Ostrom—"How can a group of principals who are in an interdependent situation organize to govern themselves so as to obtain continuing joint benefits, when all face temptations to free-ride, shirk or otherwise act opportunistically?"—can be understood as asking two questions.[22] First, what conditions favor the emergence and sustenance of these mutually enforced second-level contracts, irrespective of the presence of a protective state? Second, what do these contracts look like? Ostrom's design principles can then be seen to partially answer this second question.

---

[17] This is similar to the argument put forward by James Buchanan, prominent member of the contractarian tradition: "Individuals will be led, by their own evaluation of alternative prospects, to establish" (1965, p. 26).

[18] Ostrom's disagreement with Hardin's formalization is abundantly clear, as well as with its implications. Ostrom seeks to replace the idea of tragedy with something else. This distaste appears in several places (Ostrom, 1990, p. 9; 2010b). The Ostromian project in some ways aims to rectify the damage that Hardin's formulation and its use has caused.

[19] For a direct comparison to Hobbes, see Ostrom (1990, p. 140). Ostrom notes that a CPR situation in which there are no rules to forbid or require any actions is equivalent to the Hobbesian state of nature in which every action is permitted.

[20] However, unlike Buchanan, Ostrom is concerned with the specific contracts that govern a particular resource and its users. These are, at most, a subset of Buchanan's general collective agreements that govern social relations between individuals in a society.

[21] See Ostrom (1990, p. 33, para 1): "Without a fair, orderly, and efficient method of allocating resource units."

[22] See Ostrom (1990, p. 36) where Ostrom uses Williamson's (1975) definition of opportunism.

Again, to Ostrom, individuals are rational, norm-following, and primarily self-interested (Ostrom, 1990, p. 37). They do the best they can with what they have—that is, they maximize their interests in a bargain with others. This bargaining takes place over the choice of governing rules in what Ostrom terms "institutional choice situations."[23] Fair rules are those that are consistent with a dominant group morality, or the "generally accepted moral fabric of a community" (Ostrom, 2005, pp. 17, 242). Moral behavior is whatever is mutually advantageous for the group, whatever is required to maximize its joint interest, and also whatever is required for it to be instrumentally rational. That is, fairness consists not only of those rules that lead to joint returns, but also those that incorporate norms of fairness. Similarly, norms are followed because they are necessary to achieve joint returns, whether because others expect it or because the pattern of behavior it engenders is favorable to the use and maintenance of the shared resource. Fair rules are justified by the fact that they lead to maximal joint gains. Individuals follow these rules because it is the rational thing to do, considering the punishments they would have to face if they did not. In this way, moral behavior is strategic. Whether an agreement is considered fair is indicated by acceptance from all parties. Ultimately, in this view, reasons for behaving fairly can be reduced to instrumental reasons for achieving greater long-term gains.

Mismatches with Perceived Fairness

I have presented two general approaches to deducing what fairness is in these Nepalese irrigation systems. One is the empirical approach, which analyzes responses to the question of why individuals reduced cooperation with their institutions (Chapter 3). It results in a conception of fairness based on the reasons people have for rejecting the existing rules. The other is the approach taken by Ostrom in which one looks for agreement, assumes users are broadly rational, and identifies fair rules as those that were agreed upon to use and maintain the irrigation canal. In this approach, one faces the task of modeling agreement among rational individuals, while the conception of fairness that arises from it attempts to capture the reasons that people might agree to rules. These two approaches support two different conceptions of perceived fairness: the empirical and the Ostromian.

The empirical conception of perceived fairness suggests that at least some individuals are unfairness-averse, in addition to behaving as though they are performing a rough cost–benefit calculation. They will reduce their commitment

---

[23] See Ostrom (1990, p. 242), ch. 6, note 5. See also Ostrom (2005, pp. 44, 245–247).

when they perceive local institutions as unfair, even when continuing to use the irrigation system would be valuable to them. Despite a perceived benefit to cooperating, they do not do it, or do so less because they perceive the agreement as unfair. A second feature of empirical perceived fairness suggests that individuals have motivations that are not oriented toward maximizing benefit to oneself: the reasons for stopping their cooperation are asymmetric to their reasons for having started. Although impossible to verify using the present study's design, the reasons for devising and consenting to rules could be plausibly characterized as driven by the pursuit of joint benefits, particularly if individuals are considered to be rational and self-interested. The subsequent discovery that they are committed to an unfair agreement, albeit one that provides the promised joint benefits, appears to have compelled some to stop. Thus, even if the relative costs and benefits to cooperating may not have changed, users might develop reasons to cease cooperation that do not depend on its net benefit to themselves. This realization is very difficult to anticipate before making the commitment and enjoying the joint gains, in part because individuals can detect unfairness but have difficulty defining fairness. Because it is possible that individuals failed to anticipate that they would perceive the agreement as unfair in a particular way, it could not have been included as a necessary condition for cooperation (Malthouse et al. 2023). Users may have had a general desire to not be treated unfairly, but they likely could not have anticipated in what form unfairness would present itself. At least some users appear to be oriented away from perceived unfairness and not just toward their personal benefit.

Another difference between the Ostromian conception of perceived fairness and its empirical counterpart is that in the latter, commonalities in the elements of fairness exist across individuals and groups. This is not a commonality that dissolves into a specific ordering or combination of elements of fairness that remains the same across groups. Instead, as I have shown, there is a common set of seven elements that appears repeatedly (Chapter 3, Table 12). How these elements are related and which are more significant are probably questions with which every group and user grapples. For unfairness-averse individuals, however, a blatant violation of any of these is a sort of patent unfairness, serving as an indicator of unfairness recognized by most unfairness-averse individuals, regardless of their locality, and this perceived unfairness is likely to cause them to reduce their cooperation. What constitutes patent unfairness seems to be shared among all irrigators in this way, although this shared set may change over time. If any of the seven conditions are violated, therefore, it is likely that at least some users in any group would recognize it as patently unfair and reduce their cooperation. This type of shared conception across unrelated groups of what is fairness is possible within the Ostromian framework, but it is certainly not a defining feature. Recall that instead of relying on some objective standard of fairness, which the idea of patent unfairness approaches, the Ostromian conception depends on a concept of fairness defined by agreement among a particular group of users.

The elements of perceived fairness between conceptions also differ. The Ostromian conception emphasizes fairness in process. Rules are chosen through a fair process, and these fair rules then result in fair outcomes when applied to all users. If these rules come to be perceived as unfair because they result in the unfair distribution of duties and resources, the rules are changed through a rule-bound bargaining process. In this way, fair rules beget more fair rules. Several of the elements of empirical perceived fairness refer to fairness of process that Ostrom emphasizes. Whether poorer people get their agreed-upon share of water (Group A), or whether the agreed-upon rules are applied indiscriminately (Group D), both refer to rule-bound processes. Other references to process among the elements of perceived fairness refer to a failure of the rules to keep up with changing ideas of what is appropriate (Group C), for instance, whether the rules continue to discriminate on the basis of wealth (Group E), or whether punishments such as public humiliation or ostracism (Group C) are indicators of unfairness of process too, regardless of how they are enforced. All of these aspects of perceived fairness can be seen as referring at least in part to the properties of rule-bound processes to which users have committed.

Unlike the Ostromian model, however, empirical perceived fairness mixes process and outcome-related reasons. These outcomes may be long-term: for example, whether the repeated application of the rules over decades results in some groups doing a majority of the work (Group B), or an even weaker condition of whether or not people do roughly the same amount of work (Group G). These conditions can only be assessed after the rules have been agreed to, followed, and outcomes made manifest. The outcome-based reasons of unfairness may also be intergenerational, as in the case of Mr. Darai, who was concerned that his children did not receive the same opportunities as those of wealthier families (Group D). In that instance, his perception of unfairness includes an assessment of the actual lives that not only he but his sons are able to live. His concerns thus extend beyond outcomes narrowly defined as "the distribution of water across users." Nor is this empirical perceived fairness restricted to the unequal distribution of water or work across users. Mr. Darai's example illustrates that it can also include substantive outcomes to which the rules for allocating water or labor were but one contributing factor. Other reasons of perceived unfairness are consistent with the view that users are owed something as a matter of being a user and not because it is of instrumental benefit to themselves or others that they be given their due. Whether everyone gets at least some water (because they deserve it, Group D), or the wealthy are treated more favorably under the rules (Group E), both suggest that users have a notion of what others are due merely as equal members of the group of users, and not necessarily because it would be personally beneficial to them.

The empirical and Ostromian accounts are also different in explaining why people appear to follow the rules. These accounts are closely related to how each conception of fairness is derived. According to Ostrom, perceived fairness is something users seek in rules. It is necessary that a set of rules appears fair in order for people to agree to them. The entire intellectual apparatus is geared toward indirectly elaborating on what fairness is by examining what people agree to. The Ostromian conception of fairness primarily captures the reasons individuals agree to a set of rules. The empirical approach leads to a conception of fairness that is indicated by the absence of reason to reject a set of rules. It takes a direct approach to identifying the reasons people stop or reduce their cooperation—that is, it identifies reasons for the rejection of existing rules. Therefore, the Ostromian conception attempts to model agreement and the empirical one, a lack of rejection.

Because of this difference in what the approaches to fairness attempt to capture, it is not surprising that they lead to different explanations of why individuals accept fair rules and then act in a way that is perceived as fair by others (and themselves). In Ostrom's account, people agree to rules that require them to act fairly because it is rational to accept them. In short, agreeing to and abiding by rules will lead to joint gains. In contrast, it is not possible to identify why people agree to a set of rules using the empirical approach. In the case of the systems here, it is most likely that these rules were simply inherited. These systems are old enough that the founders have long passed, and the original reasons for adopting particular rules largely have been lost with them. In most cases, the current users inherited the rules but not the knowledge of why the rules were chosen in the first place. Current users might know why newer rules or rule changes were adopted, but these systems always consist of a mix of old and new rules. Most often, when asked the positive question about why they agreed to rules, users indicated that they could achieve a greater benefit by doing so: that water was necessary in order to continue with agricultural livelihoods, that it was the "way it is"—referring to norms deriving from customs—that they had a deference to tradition and the instructions of elders, and that following the rules was a matter of habit.

Although the two models of fairness are not incompatible, taken together they introduce an uncomfortable asymmetry. Furthermore, there was no evidence to contradict the view that at least some people actually complied through fear of punishment or because others also followed the rules. The reason that people are likely to comply with rules is fear of punishment—whether psychological (such as feelings of guilt and shame) or financial (such as a fine or ostracism)—and not a desire for fairness. The reasons they are likely to not comply include perceived unfairness independent of punishment.

Taken together, then, the idea of perceived fairness that at least some users actually convey suggests that they regard others, particularly poorer users, as having something due to them. For instance, users perceive rules that do not give poor people their share or do not give a minimal amount of water to everyone as unfair. This is expressed without regard to what those poorer users actually contribute to the maintenance of the canal. Similarly, other seemingly fair rules for allocating water, like its proportional allocation based on labor contributions or with preference to those who most contribute to the irrigation system, could be perceived as unfair if they result in some obtaining no water. It is important to note that these reasons of unfairness are not expressed in terms of cost and benefit, and that they do not appear to depend on whether the system is functioning well or not. Indeed, even people who were receiving joint benefits according to the rules expressed some feelings of unfairness for reducing their cooperation.

Ostrom's conception is built on the view that human nature is more instrumental than moral in these types of cooperative situations. Whatever else they are, in this view individuals are uncompromisingly strategic. It is therefore unlikely that these farmers in Ostrom's conception would have reasons of unfairness that are not reducible to cost or benefit to themselves. They are moral in that they follow social norms, which in turn mirror locally shared morals, because they have been conditioned to do so and it would be psychologically or physically costly for them not to. However, because of this reliance on the supremacy of local norms, it is not clear what this local shared morality is based on aside from mutual agreement. This leads to the conclusion that these social norms, like the rules, are whatever has been historically and locally agreed to. For Ostrom, any shared morality can ultimately be reduced to instrumental reasons: norms deriving from shared morals typically reduce costs of agreement, monitoring, enforcement, and proposing new rules. There are no objectively good norms, although norms of reciprocity come close, and there are bad norms if they increase the likelihood of violence, although norms are overwhelmingly considered to be beneficial to cooperation.[24]

In contrast, the empirical conception of perceived fairness is more consistent with the view that users believe that there are certain things that others are due, independently of how these norms affect the achievement of joint gains. This could be, for example, because these systems are but one part of rural life. Based on these cases, these are: poorer people get their share, nobody has to do so

---

[24] See Ostrom's (1990, p. 73) discussion of how norms of honor among Valencian irrigators are more likely to lead to violent conflict than without the norm.

much work that it is disproportionate when compared to others, there shouldn't be discrimination on the basis of wealth or class as far as water allocation is concerned, wealth shouldn't entitle one to favorable treatment by the rules, and everyone deserves at least some water. Finally, a broad sense of legitimacy or appropriateness of the rules, whether or not they are "uchit" (meaning appropriate to the current circumstances) is a significant element in the perceived fairness of rules. This suggests their justifiability to other members in general is at least part of the assessment of how unfair the rules are.

An Illustration of the Mismatches

As revealed in the interviews, several aspects of perceived fairness seem to differ from its conception in the Ostromian framework. How far can it be accommodated in the present one? The NIIS data set is a good example of an application of the framework to an actual set of cases because it was designed by Ostrom's team and continues to be regarded as having high internal validity (Poteete, Janssen, and Ostrom, 2010, p. 105). It is designed to include only those variables deemed significant by the IAD framework to cooperation, which makes it useful in examining this question. Mapping the elements of perceived fairness onto this data set shows that only parts of perceived fairness can be captured by it, while other aspects are left out. Standing in the way of a better fit are deeper conceptual differences between the contractarian conception of fairness and the empirical idea of perceived fairness. The reasons of unfairness uncovered empirically are not emphasized in the IAD framework, primarily because they are not obviously relevant to collective action problems. The mapping of their reasons onto the variables included in the framework is therefore uneasy.

There are several variables already in the framework that correspond to aspects of perceived fairness. Equity, for instance, is equated with fairness and considered likely to impact the level of individual cooperation. It is regarded as typically requiring proportionality in the benefits and costs of resource allocation and contribution of required inputs.[25] Other variables from the Ostromian framework roughly map onto the reasons of empirically derived unfairness, as shown in Table 20. In this table, the elements of perceived fairness are grouped according to the comparisons they imply, and the groups are mapped further into questions from the NIIS survey as much as possible. It shows the existing variables are plausible indicators of some aspects of perceived fairness, while

---

[25] "Rules that respect proportionality are more widely accepted as equitable. Perceived inequity may lead some participants to refuse to abide by rules they consider to be unfair" (Poteete, Janssen and Ostrom, 2010, p. 100).

Table 20 **Mapping the elements of fairness: the elements of fairness deduced from interviews can be grouped by closely associated variables from the IAD framework. The variable is encoded Yes/No unless otherwise noted. The elements of fairness were deduced from Nepali language interviews; the survey questions were in English.**

Group	Comparison	Nearest survey question	Variable name
A	Whether the poorer members receive their share of water.	Are there any users who have been consistently disadvantaged in this period?	*fdisadv*
B	Whether some people do much more physical work than others.	Have members of this group invested their own labor or other resources in maintaining or improving the structure of the appropriation resource? Do the rules assign substantially unequal duties to some subgroups than others?	*fevenwork* *fselflabor*
C	Whether the rules are appropriate for the current situation. The word translated into "appropriate" is "uchit," which also includes an idea of legitimacy	Are the rules perceived by members as legitimate?	*flegit*
D	Whether or not there is discrimination by the rules against some users, particularly the poorest.	Have the relatively worse off been deprived of their benefits from this resource or substantially harmed?	*fworsedeprived*
E	Whether the rules favor the wealthy and those with more land.	Do the rules assign substantially unequal privileges to some subgroups than others?	*fadvantage*
F	Whether the rules are easy to understand.	How complex are the rules?	*fcomplex* (Simple, Relatively Complex, Very Complex)
G	Whether the rules treat people uniformly.	Do the rules assign substantially unequal duties to some subgroups than others?	*fevenwork, fspace*

others are not captured directly. In total, there are nine variables (in italics) from the IAD framework (included in the NIIS data set) that capture aspects of perceived fairness as expressed by the users of these systems, even if in some cases, more than one variable is needed to capture the comparison being made. The table also shows that one of the reasons for this difficulty is that the perception of fairness as it emerges from the interviews mixes both procedural and substantive conceptions, while the IAD framework's use of fairness refers to one or the other, but primarily to process.

Overall, this is an uneasy mapping. Some comparisons map almost directly onto Questions A, C, D, E, and F. Others are approximated by more than one question in combination: B and G. The mapping is less accurate than it seems, considering that the grouping of reasons for stopping into groups of comparisons in Table 12 also entailed some loss of meaning. Translation causes further loss of meaning. For nearly all of the survey questions, the mappings reflect how the English language question was understood by respondents after it was translated into Nepali and the response translated back into English. This can diverge from the English meaning of the question. For instance, for Group A, it is not obvious without some explanation why the nearest survey question was understood as asking about poorer members and not just any user. Similarly, it is not clear that the word "uchit" means much more than the English translation to "appropriate" captures. Comparing the reasons for stopping cooperation and Table 20 also shows that some meaning is lost between the actual fairness-related reasons users gave and the questions derived from the collective action framework that were actually asked of them. Group D, for example, asks whether there is any discrimination by the rules, focusing on income-based discrimination. However, many users expressed that they had reduced their commitment due to other forms of discrimination such as caste, gender, and ethnicity, even though they were not asked directly about them.

It is clear that a survey designed to examine explicitly fairness-related reasons for rejecting an existing commitment could have better captured these factors, although this would have required a framework using a different conception of fairness. The current framework emphasizes certain types of variables over others, and this selective emphasis is a result of its peculiar conceptual constraints. Examining these constraints sheds light on why certain variables were included in the IAD framework and others were not.

The first of these conceptual limitations derives from one of the axioms of the collective action approach: namely, that people guide behavior in terms of cost and benefit to themselves. Broadly conceived, this is a supremely versatile general behavioral assumption. For the analyst, it also plausibly simplifies analysis through a reasonable assumption that is also empathetic (Ostrom, 1990, p. 42) about why people do what they do by imparting a universality to the question of predicting behavior: what would you do in that situation? It particularly succeeds in directing the observer's attention to variables outside the mind of the individual that affect individual behavior. This permits any subsequent analysis to focus on the factors structuring behavior, instead of, as Ostrom maintains, "the subjective in-the-mind variables" (Ostrom, 1990, p. 38).[26] It requires of the analyst only that they model behavioral tendencies in terms of how individuals regard expected costs and benefits, how well they can estimate them, and what their biases are.

A consequence of this cost–benefit assumption for understanding sustained cooperation is that it obscures an obvious behavioral observation: the reasons for doing something may be and often are different from the reasons for stopping having started. This assumption imparts an ultimate symmetry to the reasons for starting and stopping one's commitment, which can be misleading, since this symmetry is derived from the conversion of all reasons into costs and benefits. Interpreted in such terms, stopping one's commitment is simply the result of that course of action having become more beneficial to oneself. In other words, commitment becomes too costly, or the results of commitment are not beneficial enough. Given this underlying logic, it is difficult to justify turning to interviews—as was done in Chapter 3—to identify the actual reasons people stopped their commitment. This in turn would have obscured perceived fairness in the interviews. Because the basic reason people reject a set of rules and stop cooperating is assumed to be known (benefits outweighing costs), one would listen instead for how certain variables affecting perceived costs and benefits of the available actions have changed. One may also listen for how user responses reveal different behavioral tendencies, albeit in a limited way that does not include unfairness aversion, as I will discuss shortly. In other words, under this assumption of costs and benefits, no qualitative difference exists between the reasoning process of someone who is in a commitment and that of someone who is not, and people are not recognized as behaving fundamentally differently in either situation. Indeed, this lack of recognition leads to the symmetry in reasons for starting and stopping, a shortcut that ends up conflating the reasons for the acceptance of a set of rules with those for not rejecting them.

The second feature of this approach more directly prevents one from examining what perceptions of fairness might mean. The collective action approach taken by Ostrom requires the analyst to implicitly assume that the meaning of fairness may not be knowable to outsiders or for it to become knowable to them

---

[26] Ostrom notes that the rest of the analysis is intended to follow Karl Popper's advice to "empty" the "rationality principle" (Ostrom, 1990, p. 38). As the Ostromian literature illustrates, the advice proves supremely useful for understanding the collective action problems that arise around initial cooperation.

once the agreement is reached, not before. This is because it is assumed that individuals will not commit to rules that they perceive as unfair and so the terms eventually agreed to are fair. Another way to state this assumption is that fairness is what all (or most) individual users agree to. Among the examples here, fairness in each case is what people have agreed to. The content of fairness is thus relative to every instance of collective action because users can conceivably come to different agreements that reflect the significant particularities of each group and their circumstances. Indeed, the same uniqueness of local situations that places state institutions at a disadvantage in devising and enforcing rules for resource governance would seem to demand different agreements. Empirically, however, there is far less variation in the elements of fairness than this relative view suggests. Based on the interview findings, there is enough commonality for it to make sense to speak of patent unfairness.

The Ostromian view only accommodates a nontemporal idea of fairness in that it is compatible with ideas of fairness as characteristic of the rules that can be known before they are implemented. This is inherent to the contractarian approach: whether the rules prescribe proportional punishment, graduated sanctions, or demand uniform enforcement are all relevant to fairness of this type. In Ostrom's view of fairness by agreement, it is assumed that users can accurately assess these aspects before reaching an agreement. After the agreement, fairness is a question only of implementing the rules agreed to. This is, once again, a procedural concept of fairness that, if one is generous, could be plausibly extended to include how the rules are implemented, and not just the statement of the rules. It is, however, unclear how to include the outcomes of the rules, particularly substantive ones, into this nontemporal framing, since outcomes might be difficult to imagine, not just predict.

An explanation of why only certain fairness-related variables are included in the NIIS and not others is now within view. Recall that the current approach to the question of sustained cooperation began empirically with extending the data set compiled by the NIIS team. As part of a theoretically informed meta-analysis (Poteete, Janssen and Ostrom, 2010), this dataset was in turn constructed using variables identified by the IAD framework. In turn, the data that the framework is used to generate such as the NIIS is selected primarily to capture this idea of fairness. It is a desirable feature of the IAD framework and the NIIS database that only the variables that the IAD framework identifies as relevant to solving collective action problems are coded and therefore included in the NIIS.[27] Poteete et al. (2010) noted in describing the approach of the NIIS that "the IAD

---

[27] Chapter 4 of Poteete et al. (2010) describes this process in detail. On Page 92, they note, "The IAD framework ... helped the team develop coding protocols that reflected theoretical concepts and made sense in a wide variety of field settings." The description of the NIIS begins on page 102.

framework guides the identification and definition of variables to be coded," and in this way "directs attention" of the analyst to these variables and not others (Poteete, Janssen and Ostrom, 2010, p. 91). A further consequence of this, however, is one is forced to assume that only this conception of fairness is related to collective action problems. In this way, the IAD framework defines the rows and columns of the NIIS, filtering details of the case studies into the cells of the NIIS data set while leaving other details out. Thus, by design, the IAD framework only contains variables thought to be associated with the Ostromian idea of fairness and not others. Any other conception of fairness will fit uneasily into the framework's variables, if at all.

Consider, for example, Question G4d of the "Operational Rules Coding Form" that Ostrom's team used to input the irrigation systems into the NIIS. It asks, "In your estimation, are the rules-in-use perceived by members of this subgroup as fair? (Yes/No)." This question immediately runs into problems if one considers that there is no direct translation of the word "fair" into Nepali. Thus, the enumerators who encoded this aspect of these 233 irrigation system case studies into the NIIS made a judgment about how fair the users perceived their system to be, and they did so without interviewing individual users in most cases. So what did the enumerators consider fair? Those who coded the cases into the NIIS were trained to apply the IAD framework and its underlying concepts, including Ostrom's contractarian conception of fairness.[28] They were consequently directed by the framework to focus on rules and processes rather than outcomes, and to code variables that were thought to impact the likelihood of agreement with proposed rules and not with a lack of rejection of rules already agreed to.

As a result of being restricted to a particular idea of fairness, the IAD framework can accommodate only a subset of the elements of perceived fairness, as expressed by users in Chapter 3. The IAD framework's conception of fairness is circumscribed by the assumptions of the Ostromian approach to human nature and deliberation. These assumptions ultimately miss significant aspects of the perception of fairness that users actually express as reasons for reducing their cooperation. They do not even attempt to capture Mr. Darai's perception of the unfairness of the differences in opportunity available to his children, compared to the children of those who have historically received more water under the allocation rules that were mutually agreed to explicitly or implicitly before his time. Major differences concern

---

[28] More precisely, the coders were helping to develop the IAD framework, and the specific meanings of particular concepts were being actively discussed. There is an implicit assumption that fairness could be assessed without speaking to the individual users—something the enumerators could not do. This already suggests that their assessment overwhelmingly is based on the rules and their structure.

individual behavioral orientations, the extent of shared conceptions of fairness, the elements of perceived fairness, what reasons each conception aims to capture, and whether people are moral or instrumentally rational.

Three Conceptual Fixes

There are three conceptual avenues for expanding the Ostromian approach to account for some of these differences without descending into the philosophical foundations: other-regarding preferences, norms, and evolutionary convergence. Neither of them goes as far as explicitly incorporating the type of multidimensional perceived unfairness that arose from interviews, or swapping out the underlying cost–benefit calculus that is attributed to human nature. The first two modify the behavioral assumptions underlying the model to significant effect. One modification is to regard people as capable of altruism through other-regarding preferences. Another is to give a greater explanatory role to norms of behavior such as trust, reciprocity, and fairness. The third approach, evolutionary convergence, characterizes the state of nature to explain how different groups might develop similar norms or conceptions of fairness.

First, other-regarding preferences. More recent versions of the Ostromian framework allow for individuals to have preferences for other people's benefits and costs, or other-regarding preferences for short.[29] In particular, Ostrom augments the understanding of "rational individual" to encompass individuals whose preferences include those related to the benefits others receive (Ostrom, 2005, pp. 111–112). These preferences are represented as internal valuations on outcomes that others may receive.[30] Other-regarding preferences are one way to model altruism without departing from the assumption that individuals are selfishly rational (Fehr and Fischbacher, 2003; Cooper and Kagel, 2016). Thus, care about the well-being of others along with themselves can be explained in terms of their preferences, which include a consideration of the outcomes that

---

[29] "While it is not possible yet to point to a single theory of human behavior that has been successfully formulated and tested in a variety of settings, scholars are currently positing and testing assumptions that are likely to be at the core of future developments. These relate to (1) the capability of boundedly rational individuals to learn fuller and more reliable information in repeated situations when reliable feedback is present, (2) the use of heuristics in making daily decisions, and (3) the preferences that individuals have related to benefits to the self as well as norms and preferences related to benefits for others"(Ostrom, 2010b, p. 430). See also Poteete et al. (2010, chap. 9) and Ostrom (1998).

[30] See Ostrom(2005, p. 292), Note 4 for references to the behavioral economics literature that Ostrom relies on to make this inclusion. See also E. Ostrom (2005, p. 121) and Poteete et al. (2010, 223).

others experience (Dimick, Rueda and Stegmueller, 2018). This technique can capture some of the elements of perceived fairness such as whether some people do much more physical work than others (Group D). It can also explain why those who are not disadvantaged might support changing the rules to not disadvantage the poor (Groups A and E): they would be understood to have a preference for a particular distribution of opportunities across members in the group (Poteete, Janssen, and Ostrom, 2010, p. 153). This modification to the basic cost–benefit model explains moral behavior without going so far as to introduce noninstrumental motivations (Fehr and Fischbacher, 2002; Tricomi et al., 2010; Fehr and Leibbrandt, 2011).

A second approach is to extend the idea that people are norm-following to include norms of behavior such as trust, reciprocity, and fairness. Norms pertain to beliefs that affect discount rates, the relative importance of the future compared to the present, and the acceptability of actions and strategies such as opportunism (Ostrom, 2010b, p. 35). Norms are represented as internal valuations of actions and strategies, not outcomes, as with other-regarding preferences in and of themselves, without regard to immediate consequences (Ostrom, 1990, p. 35). They enable people to not expect that others would always behave opportunistically, or enable them to consider longer-term consequences and contingent strategies (Ostrom, 2010b, p. 36). Later refinements incorporated a more general conception of norms as a simpler form of rules: norms differ from rules because they don't provide a guidance for punishment should one violate them. They are what distinguish groups that have lived together for a long time from those that are relatively new (Ostrom, 2005, p. 224). For example, everyone getting their share of water in practice can be a norm that is not written in the form of rules but that people are nonetheless expected to follow in a particular group. The content of norms varies widely: they can specify anything, from whether opportunism is appropriate to how much participation is needed and what sort of rules are legitimate (for instance, those formulated with user input) to the importance of trust and reciprocity. These norms of trustworthiness and fairness can explain some behavior that is counter to the rational egoist assumption (Ostrom, 2005, p. 112).

It is important to note how similar rules and norms are in this conception, and how alike the reasons are that people follow them. Norms are rules without a specified punishment (Ostrom, 2005, p. 140), and people follow these norms because they attach internal value to their following or an internal cost to not doing so (Ostrom, 2005, p. 121). These can take the form of public shaming, ostracism and shunning, or other forms of psychological punishment, as well as actual punishments such as fines, all based on a shared sense of morality within a group. Rules are followed for a similar reason in Ostrom's view: punishment is costly. Social norms are shared by the group, and internal norms are specific to the individual. The extent to which an internal norm reflects a social norm will depend on how socialized the individuals are; that is, on how much psychological weight in the form of pride or guilt the individual assigns to the social norm. They are considered to be rudimentary rules because they are insufficient to foster cooperation (Ostrom, 2005, p. 138). Finally, norms evolve over time in the face of long-term survival pressures, while rules are designed by users in response to local conditions to be consistent with local norms. This distinction between the evolution of norms and the design of rules is actually less stark than it appears because rules are attempts to formalize local norms. Nonegoist behavior and norm-following behavior can be indistinguishable in practice. However, norms are ultimately followed for the same strategic reasons—and for the same instrumental reasons of benefit to oneself—that rules are. Other-regarding behavior is a consequence of this self-directed behavior when the social norm demands it and when the internal norm for each person attaches a strong weight to it.

Norm-following behavior is one example of the Ostromian framework's compatibility with any behavioral model of the individual that possesses a minimal set of characteristics (Fehr and Schmidt, 1999; Poteete, Janssen and Ostrom, 2010; Gintis and Bowles, 2011). The first is that humans behave as rational choosers consistent with calculations of cost and benefit to themselves. The second is that they discount future returns while overvaluing immediate returns. Last but not least, their valuation of alternative actions and strategies are susceptible to norms. This means that existing valuations of actions and strategies can affect (1) the perceived alternatives and (2) the contextual valuations of cost and benefit for each of these alternatives. These rational choice assumptions serve as the interface between the framework and the behavioral literature in psychology and economics. While the early versions of the framework operated under the assumption that individuals had minor behavioral differences, later versions allowed for greater behavioral variance within the group. Because of this interface, it is likely that the framework will continue to be updated as behavioral models improve. It is also likely to include individuals with a greater variety of behavioral tendencies, whereas now it has broadened to include two types: norm-following and nonnorm-following individuals.

So far, I have described attempts to explain why people may behave in ways that appear to be different from those of the simple rational egoist, while retaining the perspective that individuals are primarily self-interested, cost–benefit driven, and strategic. It is also necessary to address how common elements of fairness across groups can be explained by extending the Ostromian approach. This is the third avenue for explaining the empirical findings: evolutionary convergence (Axelrod, 1986; E. Ostrom, 2000; Platteau, 2000; Gintis et al., 2003; Skyrms, 2004; Gintis and Bowles, 2011). A possible explanation based on this assumption is as follows: because rules are designed in response to local conditions, the similarities between irrigation systems specifically deriving from the use and maintenance requirements of this type of technology led disparate users to develop at least some similar rules. In short, the response of these diverse groups to similar conditions was to develop similar rules. Furthermore, these rules were responsible for their survival. In this way, the social norms themselves evolved to confer a survival advantage on those groups that had adopted them (Axelrod, 1986).[31] This argument would continue that those who had different responses and failed to develop these common types of rules didn't survive. Over time, those that survived would all have similar norms of fairness.

This evolutionary convergence argument permits one to regard the common elements of fairness as due not to an irreducible, common morality that motivates human action, but to the similar physical demands of maintaining a shared irrigation system (Bicchieri, 2005; Skyrms, 2014). Although there is no way to test whether the common demands of the same technology selected for the same idea of fairness without cases where users have maintained multiple types of resources, it seems like a plausible argument. The same argument can be extended to norms in general: these situations of sharing an irrigation system are similar enough that particular norms conferred a survival advantage to those groups that developed them. Those that failed to adopt these norms did not survive, and the evolutionary process selected for groups with these norms (Elinor Ostrom, 2000).

The existence of shared elements of fairness doesn't contradict contractarianism so much as qualify it. A shared sense of patent unfairness is possible in the contractarian conception if the groups and their resources are similar in all significant ways. Taken together, these fixes—norms, other-regarding preferences, and evolutionary convergence—address some of the mismatches between Ostrom's conception of fairness and that expressed by the irrigators themselves without abandoning the central tenet that individuals are guided by at least a "rough cost-benefit calculation" (Poteete, Janssen and Ostrom, 2010, p. 226). They have the advantage that each can be applied without significantly altering the framework. They also have major shortcomings.

Limits of Other-Regarding Preferences

Tinkering with the preferences that underlie the cost–benefit assessment, a type of fairness can be introduced that allows individuals to have a preference

---

[31] This advantage could be, for instance, because the norms better evoke compliance (Sigmund, 2012; Hilbe et al., 2018).

for particular distributions of resources, labor, and outcomes across members of the group (Fehr and Schmidt, 1999). So, if a particular distribution of outcomes results or not, their cooperative or non-cooperative actions respectively can be explained. This comes close to the more substantive idea of fairness that is indicated by the interviews to be among the several reasons for perceived unfairness represented in terms of work and resource distribution. For example, it can be asserted that individual irrigators have a strong preference for a distribution of water where poorer users receive their share, or a distribution of work in which everyone does a similar amount. This incorporates the element of fairness into Groups A and B, although it moves only one step away from the assumption that people regard only their own cost and benefit by attaching a cost or benefit to that of others. In other words, individuals are understood to have coupled preferences.

Incorporating a preference for distribution falls short because fairness is still understood as a particular distribution of resources and not as the substantive outcomes experienced by others that might result from this distribution over decades. Although it could be asserted that people prefer substantive outcomes of the sort (Binmore and Shaked, 2010), this alone is an inadequate response, since these substantive outcomes entail significant uncertainty and subjective assessments of what is substantive. The allocation of labor and water, for instance, factors into nearly every substantive outcome imaginable for these farmers because the irrigation system plays such an important role in their current lives and prospects. Of these possible futures, adequate opportunity for further education for one's descendants is but one aspect. Another might be adequate savings for retirement. To be able to specify what someone else considers to be a more significant substantive outcome requires an intimate knowledge of another's preferences over future substantive outcomes or that all significant future outcomes are known. This is an unreasonable demand without an attendant assumption to make it possible, such as that everyone has similar preferences for certain substantive outcomes, so that knowledge of one's preferences for future substantive outcomes provides information about those of others. Knowledge of another's preferences for future substantive outcomes is further complicated if one does not know what these outcomes might be, so it makes little sense to speak of preferences or, therefore, of knowledge of another's preferences over them.

It is a strength of this preference-based approach that it can be used to justify any behavior after the fact: one simply has to assert that those individuals had a preference for the particular outcome that they were observed to favor. To meet the objection above, the argument could again be modified to affirm that these subjective assessments by others, with all their attendant uncertainty, are also included in an individual's preferences. There is thus no end to what might be incorporated into them.

However, pushing this too far presents the concept of preferences as all-too malleable and all-inclusive. There are problems with this approach of allowing the idea of self-interest to include anything by simply assuming that the individual has a preference for it. If anything can be included in self-interest, such as the interests of others, the boundaries between the concepts of the "self" and "other" become blurred. This causes the very notion of "self-interest" to lose meaning because the set of things not in one's "self-interest" would be an empty set. If no difference exists between what is in my self-interest and what is in the interest of others, then there is no notion of "self" as opposed to "nonself." A result of fully incorporating the preferences of others into one's own is that there is little left of the egotist who is primarily other-regarding. If, however, there is a difference and the notion of "self" is to have meaning, then there will be things that are in the interests of others that are not in my own. There thus appears to be a conceptual limit to how other-regarding an individual can be if the self is to survive.

The distinction between self and nonself might be built into the structure of preferences by applying relative weights to one's own and distinguishing them as "self" and "other"-regarding. It could be asserted that within the limits noted earlier, this split between self and other-regarding preferences varies by person. Some may be primarily other-regarding while others may be primarily self-regarding, with some others assigned to gradations in between. But this nuanced approach of attributing fine weights to how other-regarding someone is takes us into the realm that Ostrom sought to avoid: inside people's minds. A foundational feature of the Ostromian project is to "use observable variables to reject our theories, rather than internal, in-the-mind, subjective variables, which are far more difficult to measure" (Ostrom, 1990, p. 38). Pushing the idea of other-regarding preferences so far that it includes perceived fairness undercuts this aim.

Limits of Norms

Allowing individuals to be norm-following also permits a greater range of behavior that apparently deviates from cost–benefit logic to be explained by the framework. Norm-following tendencies can explain why aversion to actions that would seem to be most beneficial to individuals in the immediate future are sometimes not chosen by them. In Ostrom's view, norms "reflect valuations placed on actions and strategies in and of themselves, not connected to immediate consequences" (Ostrom, 1990, p. 35). They also affect how alternative actions are perceived and weighted. Norms can be understood as inducing a preference over actions (not outcomes, as the case with other-regarding preferences). Norms are social and individual, with the latter a reflection of the former, and they are represented in language as rules without rule-bound punishment for not following them. This lack of formal punishment is what makes norms less effective than rules in helping groups solve social dilemmas. To explain the empirical finding of unfairness aversion, one might regard unfairness aversion as a norm. If this approach is taken, then one must include an aversion to each combination of the seven aspects of perceived unfairness as a different, possibly contradictory, norm. Another approach could be to recognize aversion to patent unfairness as a norm. Both of these approaches admit of the possibility that subgroups of irrigators might adhere to different unfairness-aversion norms, and further that these norms might clash.

It is with regard to norm diversity within the group that the framework's most significant shortcomings begin to emerge. Consider that even in Ostrom's example of norms against opportunistic behavior, some are predicted to disobey the norm (Ostrom, 1990). In Ostrom's view, a diversity of individual norms is unfavorable to cooperation unless there is a clearly dominant social norm within the group. This is because norms are viewed instrumentally as reducing the costs of coming to an agreement, and a diversity of competing norms might significantly increase the cost of resolving them, thereby adding to the cost of coming to an agreement. When there is a diversity of norms within the group, there must be some way to resolve competing norms. Indeed, the idea that people can have different norms—or more generally that individuals are not the same with respect to "all strategically relevant variables"—is noted as a difficulty faced by this approach (Poteete, Janssen, and Ostrom, 2010, p. 225).

There may be reasons of tradition, custom, and/or socialization for individuals to accept a norm, but the reason they disobey it is—according to this framework—a matter of cost and benefit: a high enough benefit to disobeying. This conception of the costs of disobedience is built into human models as an internal delta parameter that alters the perceived cost of various actions. The point here, however, is that this is a finite real number that is included in a cost–benefit calculation using the operators of arithmetic: addition, multiplication, division, or subtraction. Norms thus do not fundamentally change the conception of human motivation in the framework: norm-following people are instrumentally rational and behave strategically according to costs and benefits to themselves. By introducing this delta parameter, norms can explain why some actions leading to short-term benefits are foregone by some users, or why some actions that appear to have no immediate benefit are favored. It does not give them the ability to have genuine moral values that cannot be reduced to costs and benefits to oneself. Human moral reasoning is fundamentally assumed to follow the logic of decimal arithmetic. Thus, the inclusion of norms does not include noninstrumental reasoning of the type that perceived fairness suggests, nor does it allow for nonstrategic behavior of the type that unfairness aversion includes (Bicchieri, 2016).

This leads to a primary difficulty with Ostrom's lack of norm diversity. The framework assumes that there is a uniformity of norms within groups, at least among the group of users underlying the contract, however this uniformity is achieved. Within a group that shares the same norms, the difficulty is one of aligning incentives and generating commitment against normal·human temptations—a practical difficulty, not a moral one. One can see this more clearly by asking how differing norms are resolved within the framework. The framework offers no answer to this question, and even a generous application of the methods of resolving different views of rule changes described above results only in problematic possibilities. Is the resolution of norms also ultimately subject to the relative power of subgroups, just as choosing rules is? This question is left unresolved, so dropping this assumption of norm uniformity causes a range of problems. One of the most immediate is that it stresses the mechanism by which groups resolve these norms, a mechanism that is unexamined in the Ostromian framework.[32] It follows that the inclusion of a variety of individuals with different norms in the framework will require working out to a greater extent the model of agreement used in the framework. What are, for instance, the conditions on human nature that are assumed to apply in order to use the framework and guarantee a solution to the bargaining problem? Rawls (1958) uses information restrictions on parties to the deliberation,[33] while others like Ostrom use behavioral restrictions such as norms and information restrictions to ensure a solution. Currently, the difficulty in specifying how rules (and norms) are chosen is vaguely handed off to Rawls as a difficult problem to address (Ostrom, 1986, 2005, p. 303 note 8, 2007, 2010a; Poteete, Janssen and Ostrom, 2010, p. 225), but it is, in fact, the central problem of not just social contract theory but also of collective action. To allow for significant norm diversity by dropping the requirement of a dominant social norm would make this moral question central to the framework, and take attention away from the current practical question of how norm-following individuals (who follow the same norms, or can be made to do so) devise institutions to avoid collective action problems.

Some have argued that the Ostromian approach adequately addresses the problems caused by a diversity of normative beliefs within a group through polycentricity. As Aligica and Tarko (2013) note,

[32] Rules are negotiated, but norms are not. Because norms are prior to rules, and because they are a property of individuals and groups, it is unclear how dominant norms change to accommodate minor ones. At most, individuals are described as assimilating—that is, learning the dominant norm and adopting it.

[33] See Rawls' use of the 'veil of ignorance,' an important information restriction in the original position.

"We can look at polycentricity as a structural solution to this problem. People with different values and perspectives, once allowed the freedom, gather and cooperate in particular co-production processes for the provision of public goods at different levels and in different circumstances. Indeed aggregation continues to be a problem, yet, now it is dispersed at multiple levels, segmented into a multitude of possible solutions.

Thus, the Ostromian approach isn't to propose mechanisms by which legitimate self-governing groups resolve norm heterogeneity, or propose that certain norms are inviolable, but to find the "best way in which heterogeneous, incommensurable, and incomparable values can coexist and, if not enrich, at least not undermine each other." Implicit is that across different groups there will be a multitude of solutions to how this is to be done, and, provided the normative view is locally decided, is to be considered a legitimate normative perspective that should be permitted to coexist with other views. They continue, "the polycentric approach is concerned with *the possibility of creating valued states of affairs from as many normative perspectives as possible.* Rather than asking only which voting system or deliberation and aggregation procedures leave the least number of people unsatisfied with the result, we have to ask this more general question: Which structure of political units, each with its own collective choice system, leaves the least number of people unsatisfied with the production and provision of public goods, club goods, and common-pool resources?"

But polycentricity inadequately addresses the significant role of patent unfairness along seven dimensions that is significant to sustaining cooperation in these cases.

Limits of Evolutionary Selection

The idea that certain ideas of fairness are selected for by evolution can help explain why perceived fairness shows seven common elements across unrelated groups, albeit with difficulties. As noted earlier, this argument relies on two similarities across groups: the basic physical similarities of the irrigation systems and the shared nature of human beings. For evolutionary convergence to lead to similar ideas of patent unfairness across groups, one would need to assume that local groups are similar in all relevant ways so that it is precisely these norms that conferred a survival advantage and not others. But any claim of similarity strains against the other characteristic assumption Ostrom makes: namely, that the specific conditions of these localities are unique enough to confer an information advantage on locals in crafting fair rules. In short, the reason locals are better able to craft rules that are perceived as fair is that they know better than any outside agent what fairness is. This implies that the particular expression of fairness norms as rules is group-specific. But these two claims—that they are similar in all aspects relevant to perceived fairness, and they are different in all other relevant aspects—are at odds. Furthermore, if we are able to identify shared conditions of fairness through an idea of patent unfairness across groups, this weakens the initial contractarian claim that fairness is defined by what groups agree to, and not by an external standard.

The Fixes Fall Short

Although individual fixes to these fairness-related shortcomings in the Ostromian framework might go some way toward including more aspects of perceived fairness, each brings its own challenges. Viewed individually, these challenges might not seem significant enough to demand that the foundation of the framework be altered. At worst, this post hoc fixing of the framework might render it clumsy, where among its key advantages are its elegant assumptions on human behavior and decision-making in situations of uncertainty. Taken together, though, these fixes stretch the framework too far because of the modifications needed to make them work together. This generates two other problems more serious than inelegance. First, these modifications risk rendering the claims of the framework untestable. Second, if these patches are all incorporated, there's little left of Ostrom's views on cooperation. Ultimately, the available fixes fall short of enabling the Ostromian framework to incorporate perceived fairness. I take each in turn before explaining the major problems with incorporating all of them.

The mapping above (Table 20) illustrates some of the limits to how well a data set generated to focus on collective action problems can be used to study perceived fairness, and the mismatches leave a difficult choice for the analyst using the IAD framework to examine perceived fairness. They either illustrate the limits of the framework, or they stretch the assumptions of the collective action approach too far. If Table 20 is regarded as a reasonable mapping of actual responses to variables identified through the collective action approach, it is more significant that these variables were never considered central to collective action problems. This is a theoretical difficulty. If, instead, these fairness-related questions are considered to already be a part of collective action problems, then these collective action problems are of a distinctly different flavor than in Ostrom's account: they taste strongly of fairness. In particular, if unfairness-averse individuals are to be included in the Ostromian approach, then the sucker-aversion assumption about human nature would need to be modified to allow that remaining committed to an unfair situation is to be a sucker.

To extend the intended meaning of sucker-aversion to accommodate a fundamentally different human nature, unfairness aversion, would render the concept needlessly ambiguous. It would also represent a dramatic alteration of the meaning of a term that in the collective action approach refers to being taken advantage of by others who do not regulate their behavior while one does. It is possible, and most often the case, that unfair outcomes are realized only after joint outcomes. By definition, joint outcomes are only possible if everyone does their part—that is, if the group acts collectively. The group can act collectively if nobody is a sucker. In this way, unfairness aversion manifests after collective action problems have been solved or avoided and joint gains achieved. To extend being a sucker to incorporate unfairness aversion would imply that one can be a sucker even after everyone has done their part to the full extent required to obtain joint gains.

The next obstacle is an empirical limitation borne of necessity: the reliance on cross-sectional data to test predictions of the theory and to generate the framework. I began this chapter with an example illustrating how using variables from theory to classify new examples can reduce the possibility of finding variables that challenge it. An overwhelming majority of the studies used to develop and test the IAD framework were cross-sectional. For those that were not, the data between time periods is comparable in a limited way. None are as directly comparable as this one. Using cross-sectional data to identify the variables corresponding to existing cases and limiting oneself to existing cases, gives little ground for challenging the other two assumptions about cost–benefit behavior and fairness by agreement. Evidence challenging the former arises from interviews about why people stop their cooperation, and evidence questioning the latter only arises over time. The type of data required by the collective action approach imposes certain limits to this search for fairness because it was collected to understand what conditions might induce individuals to begin cooperating, not to understand what conditions might lead them to stop.

A final concern is that if the reason to base the framework on descendants of *homo economicus* was elegance,[34] then with all these necessary accoutrements— myriad norms and other-regarding preferences—the model is far from it. So, asking whether we can find a simpler explanation in the context of sustained cooperation like unfairness aversion might be reasonable, if not necessary, for the same reason. To be compelling, this new explanation would have to explain more elegantly some phenomena that the older approach could not. The desire for the simplest explanation that can adequately account for phenomena is at least partly responsible for the popularity of *homo economicus* and her descendants, and for missing significant aspects of the nature of perceived fairness in these

---

[34] Ostrom calls it the rational choice model (Ostrom, 2005, p. 103) and has high regard for it as a useful starting point for analysis.

cases. The evidence presented here suggests favoring unfairness aversion as an explanation of non-cooperation for a similar reason.

Moral Motivations

This pushes one further down the ladder toward a different philosophical foundation for understanding the cooperation that users in these cases exhibit: the contractarian one alone appears inadequate for explaining the empirical findings. This new foundation would need to rest on a different understanding of human behavior than one ultimately reducible to costs and benefits to oneself. That some users exhibit unfairness aversion suggests less that they are primarily self-interested and more that they respond to some sense of what is right or wrong. It also suggests that this sense can clash with what is instrumentally beneficial to oneself. The mutually agreed-upon rules reflect these commitments to an adequate extent, even if individual ethical values might differ between individuals or subgroups within the user group. So, even though these rules may deviate from the dominant morality of the group, this very deviation could render the rules less likely to be rejected by a moral minority. Moreover, rather than accepting the rules reached through a process of interest-group bargaining, these cooperators seem to assess the rules together with the substantive outcomes they contribute to against a sense of what is justifiable to others in the group, not just whether they were agreed to initially.

The significance of this last condition of fairness that the rules remain justifiable is most directly indicated by the fact that the rules may not be "uchit," which includes a conception of being justifiable under the current circumstances, is an aspect of patent unfairness. Recall that the notion of the appropriate or justifiable was illustrated by the example above in which a group reconsidered a punishment: temporary confiscation and subsequent public display of cattle belonging to the accused. From a purely instrumental perspective, it could be considered appropriately "graduated" to local conditions to be effective at deterring rule-breaking behavior without seeming to be heavy-handed. But, in rejecting this type of punishment, respondents indicated that it was no longer justifiable given current circumstances.

Together with "uchit"-ness, these reasons for unfairness are motivationally effective in that they motivate people to act, despite not being of net benefit to them. This can lead to a mismatch between what is personally beneficial and what is morally correct, and this gap also suggests that the sense of right and wrong is not entirely reducible, for at least some of these individual users, to costs and benefits to oneself. Rather than regarding binding agreements as fair because of the fact of agreement, at least some users see fairness as outcomes that avoid particular conditions of unfairness—that is, they avoid patent unfairness. It further suggests that people also act because they hold these actions to be the right thing to do, and not because these actions are instrumentally valuable to achieving their personal gain in the long or short term.

Based on the interviews, fairness seems to be not just what is agreed to. Several aspects of perceived fairness, notably those that concern whether everyone gets some share of the water, suggest that fairness is not just what is initially agreed to or what is reached by uniformly applying rules previously agreed to, including the rules for choosing rules. The shared elements of perceived fairness suggest there are conditions recognizable to a significant number of irrigators, regardless of where they are located or to what group they belong, that can be used to assess whether an agreement is patently unfair. For instance, at least some irrigators assess the fairness of these agreements based on whether the outcomes of the rules give everyone their due as members of the group. The avoidance of patent unfairness as well as the idea that the fairness of rules is indicated not just by agreement, but also by a lack of rejection, underline the need to move to a different conception of fairness than the contractarian one included in the Ostromian framework.

The shortcomings of the most promising fixes also point to starting from a different model of human being. Taken together, these necessary shifts imply that the assumption that at least some people are irreducibly moral could be a more favorable point of departure to explain sustained cooperation. Users possess a sense of right and wrong that is not unchanging and is not universal, but that is also not reducible to costs and benefits to oneself whether in the short or long term. This is different from recent modifications to the framework that account for norm-following and nonnorm-following individuals (Poteete, Janssen and Ostrom, 2010) because in those cases, the starting point remains the model of individuals as rational choosers of net benefit. This ultimately means that any and all moral behavior must be understood as instrumental in the service of one's own eventual benefit, the difficulties of which I have detailed above. The evidence suggests instead that analysis of these groups include a different type of person: one who has irreducibly moral beliefs that are also genuinely motivating. Avoidance of patent unfairness provides a starting point for understanding what some of these moral motivations might be.

Moving to a framework built around a diversity of moral individuals presents two practical advantages for the analyst. First, one no longer has to carry the burden of testing hypotheses about why people accept an agreement, as is needed for using the cost–benefit model of man. The current analysis provides a clear example of why this is so burdensome. For existing cases selected precisely for endurance, it is impossible to verify why the rules were agreed to, although it is easier to verify why people continue to follow them. The latter may have very little to do with the former, even in Ostrom's account. With a different framework that admits of unfairness aversion, the explanatory burden shifts to why people reject agreements and what conditions are necessary for people not to do so. Divining human intention is equally challenging in both cases, but in the latter it is more likely to find individuals who have rejected the agreement compared to individuals who first agreed to it. The evidence also suggests that there are commonalities in the conditions that individuals seek as embodied in the aspects of patent unfairness. So this is the second advantage that this fairness approach confers: it becomes possible to separate the conditions of fairness from any particular group and to speak of at least some types of fairness separately from them. To be clear, it does not negate the local nature of rules, norms, or shared moral understandings. It does, however, set some constraints on them that are more broadly recognizable than by the members of the group alone.

Assuming that at least some people have irreducibly moral beliefs does not negate the existence or analytical importance of the individual benefit maximizer that drives the Ostromian frameworks. Even from the fairness-oriented view, those who hold that costs and benefits to oneself as the universal guide for morality would be considered to be a type of moral person. Their devotion to even a rough cost–benefit calculation leads to a type of instrumental morality in which it is moral to act in a way that is beneficial to oneself in the long term and in which the uniform application of rules is paramount.

Stated this way, it is clearer how Ostrom's account of cooperation only applies to a special case of cooperation. It deals only with cooperation in groups of those who share a same instrumental morality, or in which those who hold this instrumental morality are dominant. When a diversity of morality within groups is accounted for, the framework itself will also need to be modified in the direction sketched here.

It is also important to note that assuming that individuals are motivated by an irreducible morality is also distinct from arguing that people are infallibly moral. That is, while some individuals may be motivated by a sense of right and wrong, they are unlikely to always do the right thing. Indeed, Ostrom's characterization of deeply flawed and imperfect human beings would continue to apply even after this assumption is applied. Any aspects of the framework designed to counter human tendencies that can interfere with rule-following behavior—temptation, greed, lack of self-control—would remain in place. This generalization would leave a role for carefully calibrated punishments and penalties. The biggest difference would be in our understanding of why people obey rules, what rules are fair, why people reject rules or fail to follow them, and what conditions must be met in the process of choosing rules to get to fair ones.

Once individuals are regarded as possessing an irreducible moral sense, the central question of sustained cooperation takes on greater force: how do they remain fair? Continued cooperation, then, appears as a feat of continuous moral adjustment and accommodation. This recognition, then, reveals an aspect of successful cases of sustained cooperation that is hard to unsee. Rather than seeing these cases as examples of groups of self-interested individuals bargaining to devise institutions to self-govern by avoiding collective action problems, they can be seen to have solved a different problem: that of remaining fair. From this viewpoint, these groups of moral individuals have practically and continually addressed their moral differences to the extent that they can effectively use and manage a shared resource over decades.[35] This can be a far more difficult challenge than would be faced by groups that are morally homogeneous, as Ostrom implicitly assumes.

In the more general setting of moral heterogeneity that I propose here, the use and maintenance of shared resources shows that groups of individuals with at least some irreducible moral beliefs have adopted and continue to update a set of rules that are justifiable enough to all of them that they continue to cooperate with each other by cooperating with the rules, despite the deeply motivating nature of unfairness aversion, rapidly changing circumstances, and generational shifts in beliefs. What the individual users are doing appears not primarily as pursuing an abstract idea of what is fair, but as avoiding in specific ways, concrete experiences of patent unfairness. This generalization from rational benefit maximizers to irreducibly moral individuals focuses on the conditions that will lead to fair agreements, and makes achieving fairness—or more precisely, continuously avoiding perceived unfairness—central to the framework. It also provides some basis for the external evaluation of local collective agreements on the basis of fairness by nonusers because of the common elements of perceived unfairness.

Perceived fairness can thus be better incorporated into existing frameworks by using a broader conception of fairness than contractarianism allows. This does not require moving so far away from the contractarian conception as to abandon the Social Contract tradition. For example, these findings could be viewed in a Contractualist way to include a conception of fairness that emerges from the view that individuals are irreducibly moral. A major advantage of this shift is that the aspects of the framework built around the conception that these groups self-govern by contracts that they mutually agree to do not need to change, although one can continue to understand decline differently from what the Ostromian frameworks suggest (Harsanyi, 1976; Scanlon, 2000).

Consider one of the most immediate implications of this broader conception of fairness: how minorities within a group of users are regarded. Moving to

---

[35] It also opens up a largely neglected aspect of inquiry—how do they do it?

a Contractualist conception allows one to find justification for addressing the grievances of the minority[36]. In Ostrom's contractarian account, it should not matter whether a minority of users perceive the system as unfair as long as the rules have been agreed to using collective choice rules that these minorities have previously agreed to. This is because these rules are assumed to adhere to the dominant shared moral understanding within the group and a moral minority that disagrees is expected to honor their commitment to the group's process of decision-making even if it systematically disadvantages them. In case this shared dominant understanding changes over time, the rules are appropriately updated so that the fact of agreement and the underlying instrumental justification remain intact. In this account, a declining system in which a minority of users perceive it as unfair would not be seem to be a failure of the rules to be designed correctly or applied uniformly. It would simply be the normal result of a prior collective agreement about how rules are made. And those who would intentionally subvert a collective agreement—or refuse to cooperate with prior agreements—would be considered opportunistic knaves (Brennan and Buchanan, 1986; Buchanan, 1987; Congleton, 2014) who threaten the long-term stability of the contract underlying group cooperation.[37]

A Contractualist conception allows for an argument that the numerical minority's perception of unfairness should be considered even when these systems continue to perform because a failure to do so would result in non-cooperation from users who perceive it as unfair. This point is critical for any attempt to diagnose the robustness of these systems. Furthermore, that moral reasons can exist outside of the particular agreement—that is, even an existing agreement might still be legitimately perceived as unfair—allows for the possibility that these "knaves" are actually principled dissenters, disobeying the rules for genuine moral reasons. In this way, well-performing systems are recast not only as instances where mutually agreed upon rules that derive from a shared morality are uniformly enforced and compliance mutually monitored as the collective action approach suggests, but also ones where there is a diversity of moral beliefs and the moral minority has their views considered to the extent that they do not resort to noncooperation as a form of rejection as the perceived fairness approach suggests.

Two other immediate implications are important to highlight. First, a Contractualist foundation draws greater attention to how agreement is reached

---

[36] This minority may, for instance, have agreed to a set of rules because they had no other choices due to their poverty but that they've increasingly perceived as unfair during their time subject to them. Or, for instance, it could be a numerical minority who opposed a set of rules that the majority adopted through voting (a process that the minority had agreed to).

[37] Ostrom's analogous analysis is in (Ostrom, 2005).

between those who have differing ideas of what fairness is, rather than deferring to the fact of agreement alone. For example, in the case of the Brangdi Tallo Kulo System in the next chapter, it would no longer be considered detrimental for an external government agent to question whether the rules equating a share of water to uneven labor contributions from two different villages were reached fairly. Second, the Contractualist view also permits for different conceptions of fairness to have common elements across groups because, for instance, it is what others are due as equal members of any user group. The presence of these common elements is something that even nonmembers of a particular user group can know to some extent. This new understanding allows state institutions, for instance, to unilaterally intervene in a local agreement that enshrines caste discrimination in the use of irrigation water on the grounds that it is patently unfair, even if all of the users profess voluntary agreement with it. This example, too, is discussed in greater detail in the next chapter.

Nonlocal Fairness

With this broadening of the framework to include moral diversity, it becomes possible for nonusers to meaningfully recognize rules that are unfair but that have been agreed to. Recall how this differs from the Ostromian approach to local sovereignty over shared resources. According to that view, the extreme localization of fairness renders meaningless any discussion of the actual content of the fair rules in general by nonusers. Instead, fair rules are characterized by being voluntary and unanimous (Ostrom, 1990, p. 65) or near-unanimous (Ostrom, 1990, p. 126) agreement by the users. Rules are fair when most users voluntarily agree to them. When procedures are perceived as unfair, users change the rules by using other rules (Ostrom, 2005, p. 14). Indeed, enforcing rules that result in a distribution that is perceived as unfair can be seen as unfair (Ostrom, 2005, p. 77). Counter to this, incorporating individuals with irreducibly moral motivations that are different from strategic cost–benefit to oneself takes attention away from the enforcement of fair processes. Because certain conditions appear to be necessary for any process to avoid unfairness, such as the meaningful inclusion of the views of a moral minority, it becomes possible to ask about the fairness of processes quite independently from whether users agree to them. This is in contrast to Ostrom's framework, in which it is of no significant consequence to the fairness of the rules whether a different group of users would also consider them fair, and it is most often also inconsequential—both from the perspectives of fairness and sustainability— whether a minor number of users in the group also do (Poteete, Janssen and Ostrom, 2010, p. 100).

Once perceived fairness becomes central to the framework and becomes meaningful to discuss independently of any particular group, other questions can be asked about community governance that could not be asked when using the contractarian approach. Most of these questions stem from the fact that perceived fairness is allowed to incorporate elements specific to the locality as well as elements that are not. An example of this type of question is: what affects the capacity of groups to continually avoid unfairness, particularly elements that indicate patent unfairness? In the old understanding, this has an obvious answer: anything that increases the likelihood of effective rule enforcement. In this new framing, however, the answer isn't a general one and the old enforcement-focused answer above pertains only to the special case of groups with a high degree of moral homogeneity.

Capacity to Avoid Unfairness

One of the implications of the fairness-centered view of cooperation is that the capacity to avoid unfairness is divorced from the capacity to reach agreements about who should do what. It now becomes important not only to ask whether they can come to an agreement, but also whether they have the capacity to avoid unfairness despite an agreement. The separation of fairness from the fact of agreement allows assessing an agreement on the basis of unfairness avoidance and, in particular, on whether it exhibits patent unfairness. These assessments need not be restricted to users alone to be valid.

In Ostrom's view, there is an assumption that those aspects of fairness that matter will eventually bubble up in the form of collective action problems. For the fairness concerns that arose in the interviews, this means that eventually, if they are significant, they will come up as a condition for acting collectively. For example, that the poor do not get their share of water (*fdisadv*) would be expected to arise as a concern as part of collective action problems later. That is, some would refuse to cooperate unless this was addressed. Yet, there is no reason to assume that it will be addressed despite the refusal, particularly if the process for changing the rules is the majoritarian, coalition-based bargaining process that Ostrom emphasizes (Ostrom, 1990, 2005). Furthermore, if the agreement was congruent with the shared moral sense of the majority, not addressing these minority concerns would be justified. In other words, if those who are concerned about this discrimination against the poor in practice wanted to change the rules but were not numerically powerful enough to do so, that would be the end of it. They would instead be required to accept the desires of the numerical majority, or the more powerful group, on the grounds that they agreed to the process and must accept the results, provided the rules were uniformly applied. This does not mean that they would still perceive it as fair, but most likely they would not. They would also see that the rules are incapable in practice of addressing their concerns. Because they would continue to perceive it as unfair, it would likely affect the quality of their work and their level of commitment overall and thus detrimentally impact the canal's functioning.

The faith that these fairness concerns will eventually bubble up as collective action problems and that they will thus be resolved or at least addressed is misplaced. Fairness concerns that do emerge through collective action problems remain inadequate in comparison to the broader perceptions of fairness that drive individual behavior. As we see, there are numerous instances where systems survive despite being perceived as unfair. Once fairness is measured against more objective standards, this finding suggests that groups do not have a similar capacity to remain fair. This focus on fairness in turn raises the question of the capacity of communities to avoid unfairness, which refers to the ability of groups to avoid prolonged periods where a substantial number of users continue to perceive the system as unfair. They can do this in two ways. One is to adjust when it is clear that some users perceive it as unfair. The other is to avoid through foresight a perception of fairness altogether. The former might be considered to solve the fairness problem, while the latter avoids it.

Fairness of Self-Governance

Even putting aside the difficulties of assuming that fairness concerns will ultimately bubble up as collective action problems, there are other important questions to ask. Should all relevant fairness concerns eventually bubble up in the form of collective action problems, this process of emerging as an issue is unlikely to be immediate. In the meantime, while the issue hasn't yet surfaced in the agenda of the governing body, the poorer users will be stuck in an unfair situation. This is doubly troubling. On the one hand, the locals are tasked with figuring out for themselves and addressing their fairness concerns, even though they may be in a weaker position to do so. On the other hand and in the meantime, they are subject to state-endorsed unfair situations because in Ostrom's view, the proper role of the state is to endorse local agreements. In this scenario, the burden of waiting for fairness falls disproportionately on the poorer users— and this inappropriate distribution of burdens comes to be backed by the state through its recognition of the rights of locals to self-organize. Ultimately, there is not an obvious answer to the question of whether users should be left to discover these concerns and their solutions, whether this should be preempted by experts, or whether all should wait until the matter is expressed in the form of collective action problems within their group. It also becomes less certain that local governance, to the extent that it can be regarded as "self-governance" as proposed by Ostrom, is the correct response when this type of persistent unfairness toward moral minorities is likely.

In light of this, what is the role of state institutions in the fairness of local arrangements? Recall that Ostrom's use of social contract theory focuses on the division of authority between the local government and the external one. It focuses on the contents of the two or multiple levels of contract and how they relate to each other. In Ostrom's view, the existence of locally governed resources is evidence that the locals have the ability to self-govern and that they have the innate capability to avoid social dilemmas. The external state (the first-level contract) is not strictly necessary to support cooperative arrangements to self-govern shared resources, although when it is present, it is to respect local collective agreements where they arise. Where these local collective agreements have not yet arisen, the role of the state is to enhance the capability of the locals to self-organize. The only authority given to the state after the collective agreements have come into existence is to formally recognize them.[38] Once the agreements are recognized, they will be enforced with the powers bestowed on the state, preferably by the citizens themselves. More specifically, all authority pertaining to the resource resides locally with the group, and some of it may be voluntarily given to the state, although the state will have no unilateral claims to the resource.

In this polycentric view, the only exceptions to complete devolution of authority are when the local agreements do not treat individual users in a manner consistent with the rights granted to all the citizens of the state (Ostrom, 2005, p. 283), with the right to property and the right to enter into voluntary contracts being specifically the focus of Ostrom's writings. On the scale of citizen participation in governance, this form of participatory governance lies closer to one extreme of complete devolution of authority to local decision-making bodies. It is not unreasonable to argue that Ostrom's formulation is intended to preserve individual liberties as far as possible—including the liberty to enter into voluntary agreements (such as those for governing a shared irrigation system)- because in this way, the innate capabilities of individuals and their groups are believed to be best unleashed.

Role of State Institutions

In Ostrom's view, correct state policy should (1) recognize individual abilities and (2) facilitate the development and expression of these abilities instead of

---

[38] In the absence of which they can be frail - See *Governing The Commons* (Ostrom, 1990) Chapter 1, note 21; and chapter 5 in the same book.

trying to shape human behavior.[39] When they do this, state policies can bring out what Ostrom sees as people's best traits: they would be innovative, learning, adaptable, trusting, and cooperative. As a result, this sort of policy is expected to potentially facilitate "effective, equitable and sustainable" outcomes[40] by allowing individuals to express their capacities to solve problems without interference from outside powers. With this aim of maximum individual freedom in mind, the object of investigation for the Ostromian project is an example of "polycentric governance": shared resource governance by users themselves through mutually agreed-upon institutions embedded within but conceptually separate from the broader institutions of the state, and formally delegated with exclusive authority over the resource or other limited areas but no more.[41] Polycentric institutions are a type of decentralized governance where the ultimate jurisdictional boundaries are drawn around the geographical area served by individual resources or services (Thiel and Moser, 2019). This results in many centers of decision-making below the state apparatus, each with discretion over a particular resource or service.[42] Importantly, this form of governance enshrines the belief that what is substantively equitable or fair is a result of a collective

---

[39] Ostrom contrasts this recommendation with the behavioral economics literature (e.g. Camerer(2011)), and in particular singles out the idea of "nudging" (Thaler and Sunstein, 2008) as being incompatible with the central lessons of the Ostromian project. Ostrom notes, "Designing institutions to force (or nudge) entirely self-interested individuals to achieve better outcomes has been the major goal posited by policy analysts for governments to accomplish for much of the past half century. Extensive empirical research leads me to argue that instead, a core goal of public policy should be to facilitate the development of institutions that bring out the best in humans."(Ostrom, 2010b, pp. 664–665)

[40] "The most important lesson for public policy analysis derived from the intellectual journey I have outlined here is that humans have a more complex motivational structure and more capability to solve social dilemmas than posited in earlier rational-choice theory . . . We need to ask how diverse polycentric institutions help or hinder the innovativeness, learning, adapting, trustworthiness, levels of cooperation of participants, and the achievement of more effective, equitable, and sustainable outcomes at multiple scales" (Ostrom, 2010b, p. 665).

[41] Ostrom also refers to this pattern of decentralization as "nested enterprises," noting that "These (self organized resource governance systems, i.e. polycentric units) are nested in several levels."(Ostrom, 2005, p. 83)

[42] Polycentric governance was introduced in an influential paper on municipal governance by Vincent Ostrom, Charles Tiebout and Robert Warren(1961). Ostrom's usage is explained in Ostrom (2005, p. 283): "By polycentric, I mean a system where citizens are able to organize not just one but multiple governing authorities at differing scales. Each unit exercises considerable independence to make and enforce rules within a circumscribed domain of authority for a specified geographical area." The reason for focusing on it, rather than other forms, is in section 2 of the Nobel Prize Speech (Ostrom, 2010b). In particular, Ostrom argues that the firm and state explanations of governance were flawed in that they emphasize centralized decision making on the prediction that many centers of decision making leads to chaos. In Ostrom's view, the idea of polycentricity rescues many centers of decision making (hence "poly"- centric) from chaos, while allowing for its complexity.

agreement between these users because the users have the authority to design their own institutions to govern the shared resource.

A belief in the capacity of local, nonstate actors to solve complex problems underlies the argument that locals should be given maximum autonomy to govern themselves.[43] It is important to ask what sort of problems they can solve better than others. That they have the capacity to solve complex collective action problems around institutional design, enforcement, and monitoring is clear. Less clear, however, is how the ability of such groups to address these problems relates to their ability to remain fair. Indeed, the type of problem Ostrom recognizes locals as having the capacity to solve is distinctly practical, not moral.

The primary problems the Ostromian framework focuses on are problems of institutional supply, credible commitment, and mutual monitoring (Ostrom, 1990, p. 42). These in turn arise from the following logic: individuals need rules, the ability to commit to rules, and the ability to monitor them. Provided everyone follows the rules, the desired result will come about to the extent that the rules are the right ones—that is, that they fit the circumstances. These are three broad problems that apply to any sort of rule-based governance system. The rules must be right, they must be followed, and compliance must be monitored. Now, a more specific question is what the rules are right for. Recall there are three distinct problems here. First is the problem of figuring out what is required for the resource to be sustainably used and maintained. Next is the problem of coordination, of who should do what and when. Finally, there is the question of how these rules will be enforced—that is, the problem of commitment. This last problem is addressed by creating rules that will both convince the users to commit, while dissuading them from breaking their commitment. The second problem, getting people to perform their tasks, is a practical one. It is the first problem, that of devising rules that will lead to the resource's sustainable maintenance, that is a bit more complicated.

If we admit that perceived fairness is an important part of sustained cooperation, then the rules must be such that they continue to be perceived as fair. Addressing fairness in unforeseen circumstances is a moral, not a practical dilemma. What rules will continue to be perceived as fair? What is fair? As discussed, if the users don't differ in their morality, then this is not a difficult question. However, when they do differ, this is clearly a more difficult matter than figuring out the incentives that will give instrumental individuals good reason to comply with a set of rules resulting in the maintenance of the

---

[43] For a clear version of this argument in the context of climate change, see Cole (2015). The author identifies two key strengths of the polycentric approach: that it facilitates experimentation and learning; and that it increases communications between entities involved in different levels of polycentric governance.

resource. Therefore, at the very least, a group that possesses the ability to solve the problems of collective action- practical problems—need not also have the ability to solve the fairness problem—a significantly more ethical one. It follows that unless these groups also have the capacity to solve the fairness problem, Ostrom's main piece of advice—to give the locals maximum autonomy to exercise their problem-solving capacities—may be asking too much of them in terms of remaining fair.

This is not to deny that locals have the capacity to solve problems that could exceed the capacities of a distant government, nor is this argument one that justifies constant involvement of nonlocal state institutions in resource governance. It does, however, lead to the question of whether the same autonomy to self-govern is warranted on the grounds that locals possess untapped potential to solve all the types of complex problems they might encounter in seeking to cooperate. This opens up the possibility that there may be grounds to devolve less authority to local groups than a hopeful application of the Ostromian lessons would recommend. In order to augment the abilities of locals to avoid unfair situations, there may at least be grounds to devolve authority conditional on their success at avoiding patent unfairness.

This empirical investigation has shown that while perceived fairness is necessary for sustained cooperation, systems perceived as unfair do not automatically decline. There are certain types of shocks that will reveal their fragility in comparison to ones that are perceived as fair, and until these arise the system is likely to drag along in a lower-functioning state. Even when these systems have the features that are enumerated in the design principles, they may remain persistently unfair. So, from the perspective of fairness, this raises a separate possibility: there may be strong grounds for higher-level state institutions to temporarily take back control over local arrangements that have been permitted to self-govern, if and when they are persistently perceived as unfair and do not readjust. This would require that Design Principle 7 (Minimal Recognition of the Rights to Organize) be qualified to permit governmental authorities to challenge the institutional designs agreed to by users. Furthermore, grounds to do this would remain even if doing so lessens the chances of the system's continued survival, which leads to a moral question entirely outside Ostrom's framework: are there grounds for not encouraging the continued use and maintenance of a shared resource, even when it continues to be maintained, if some users continue to perceive it as unfair? This question can only be answered with respect to the question of who the irrigation system is for.

Consider a typical example. In the ND canal most users had a shared morality that, among other things, conveyed an understanding of fairness based on ideas of caste and karma. Lower castes, outcasts, and menstruating women were considered polluted and therefore unfit to touch the main irrigation system, and any water that they touched was deemed to be polluted. Local legend had it that many years ago, the irrigation canal had dried up because a woman violated this restriction. An expensive ceremony expressing penance by the villagers followed, and the water returned to the fields. It was unclear why lower castes were subject to the same restriction, but it seemed, nevertheless, to be an accepted norm that during particular times of the year corresponding to particular religious festivals, lower castes were not allowed to touch the water directly or to work on the canal. More frequently, women were also not allowed to touch the water during their period, with lower-caste women facing the harshest penalties. Common belief was that it was because of actions in their past lives that they were in this position now, and although they could not do anything to change their position in this life, they could dutifully follow the rules to be born into a higher caste in their next one.

For most of the canal's existence as such, this form of discrimination on the basis of caste and gender was consistent with the morals enshrined in the Kingdom of Nepal, and formally expressed in Nepal's Civil Code of 1854. Caste-based discrimination was formally outlawed in the 1964 Legal Code, though de facto discrimination persisted in these systems, the ND canal included. When the system was first surveyed in 1987, it was still persistent.

During interviews in 2013, some of the users expressed that they had come to believe that the rules for allocating water and labor consistently and inappropriately discriminated against poorer users. It was not clear what had led to this change in perception, although the most plausible explanation seemed to be the pro-democracy movement in the 1980's, Maoist activity, and exposure to other countries. Some users had reduced their commitment to the system because of this. While many lower-caste individuals had migrated to urban centers in the south of the country, those who stayed behind were typically poorer than the higher caste farmers. Women also complained of discrimination preventing them from continuing to participate fully in farming while their spouses were abroad for work. Wealthier, upper-caste women had solved this problem by hiring laborers to represent them. Lower-caste women who were typically poorer were typically unable to do this. Those who actively believed that this discrimination was inappropriate appeared to be in the numerical minority. Some had gone so far as to convert their religion to Christianity, thereby rejecting the shared morals of the dominant group. Yet the system continued to function well over the years, perhaps because these dissenters were in the minority.

In the ND canal's case, ruling out any form of state intervention to make the system fairer to these minority users because state intervention can lead to deterioration and decline of the system is not an obvious position. Would it be more beneficial to these minority users of the ND canal not to be discriminated against in everyday life than to receive a share of water? In this situation, asking higher-level state institutions to recognize the rights of the ND canal's users to self-organize and to devise their own institutions by endorsing and guaranteeing enforcement of their local rules is to impose a moral choice on them. Yes, the state would be impartial in its recognition of the rights of locals to devise institutions that reflect locally dominant norms of fairness, but from the perspective of the minority users of the ND canal who have faced persistent discrimination, it would also be impartially wrong. These local norms are different from what might be agreed to if every user of the ND canal viewed all other users as free and equal persons, who were due at least some water at all times just for being users of the system. In the case of the ND canal, its continued functioning indicates the users had the capacity to solve complex collective action problems. Though some users perceived it as unfair and may have discussed this objection at meetings, the rules for choosing rules gave no grounds for their concerns to force a rule change. However, these users do not appear to have the ability to remain fair, as evidenced by persistent unfairness, and therefore, they do not have an adequate capacity to address fairness problems.

Toward the Fairness Problem

Recognizing the importance of remaining fair to sustained cooperation appears to create more puzzles than it solves. This is because the fairness problems are in an entirely different class of challenge from collective action problems. The two overlap only in particular instances, such as when unfairness gets effectively incorporated into the conditions that individuals set for continued collective action. This can happen, for instance, when a majority perceives the rules as unfair inside a majoritarian system. But this is a special case: it is possible that a numerical majority's, which is a minority from the perspective of effective power to change the rules, perceptions of unfairness remain unaddressed while they continue to profess a commitment. And at the same time, whose lower level of cooperation in practice cumulatively reduces the system's functioning. So, systems that appear to be functioning well at a point in time may not be perceived as fair by all who are committed to them, and they can persist like that until particularly challenging circumstances arise.

Despite this, even if a functioning system is not guaranteed to have avoided unfairness, some groups have succeeded in doing so; that is, they have addressed both the fairness problems and collective action problems involved in sustained cooperation. This lends a sharper focus to the main puzzle: With this distinction between fairness problems and collective action problems in view, what institutional features would make them more likely to avoid unfairness? The Ostromian approach and the empirical one suggest two different answers to this question.

The Ostromian approach arrives at a set of eight design principles. Provided these are adhered to, the chance that fairness issues will be resolved increases. There is, consequently, a well-developed analysis and framework based on this claim. As I have shown, this framework of variables and their relationships is built on the idea that a fair allocation of burdens and benefits by the rules consists of what the cooperators actually agree to, and not in their adherence to an external standard. This leads to a focus on collective action problems and the formulation of a set of design principles that favors solving them. That the design principles are enough to ensure fairness insofar as it is relevant to the individuals is at the core of Ostrom's recommendations for how local groups can remain fair, but evidence shows the design principles are not enough. Even those systems that meet all the design conditions show variation in fairness and even persistent unfairness over time. So we know that systems that adhere to the design principles cannot always address the fairness problem. In particular, when fairness problems diverge too far from collective action problems such as in cases of moral heterogeneity, solving the latter won't mean that the former is solved.

The empirical approach suggests explicit rules to avoid unfairness. It starts out similarly to its Ostromian counterpart but takes a different direction by focusing specifically on the fairness problem. As with Ostrom, it recognizes both the uniqueness of these individual instances of sustained cooperation and their common features, which are inferred by "looking through" the eyes of a particular type of person. But where the Ostromian approach chooses the boundedly rational individual, whose actions are primarily driven by a rough cost–benefit calculation, the empirical one begins with the broader set of moralities that users profess in practice. Seen through the former, these situations appear to have the structure of various games that in turn demand strategic interactions from rational individuals. Because of this chain of implications, the core problems in the way of cooperation seem to be collective action problems. Seen from the latter, these situations appear to primarily involve avoiding fairness problems by continuously avoiding or addressing patent unfairness—that is, the problems of remaining fair that groups with people holding heterogeneous moral beliefs but common recognition of patent unfairness encounter.

The answer to the question of what regularities correspond to the avoidance of collective action problems in these cases results in the design principles of the Ostromian approach. Instead of design principles, the empirical approach affords explicit rules to avoid patent unfairness, which may not relate to their ability to solve collective action problems. For instance, the empirical approach suggests explicit triggers for rule revisions should patent unfairness threaten to arise, and also more conditional devolution of authority to user groups. More work needs to be done to develop this empirical, fairness-centered approach. For instance, what new roles the state can play in facilitating fair arrangements. In contrast to the collective action approach, there is no comparable framework or example analyses to rely on.

Whether one assumes that collective action problems include fairness concerns at some point, the key question remains: do all groups have the same ability to solve fairness problems, or strongly fairness flavored collective action problems? In other words, do these groups have the capacity to remain fair? And second, what features of institutions would make them more likely to remain fair? Again, these two questions take on greater significance once it is admitted that at least some people in these groups have moral motivations that are not generally reducible to cost and benefit to oneself.

Even without elaborating further on the notion of fairness problems, which I do in the next chapter, it is now clear that Ostrom's conception of the moral composition of these local groups is a special case in which groups are assumed to be morally homogeneous and in which any moral reasoning can be expressed in decimal arithmetic. This is a moral position aligning with the Contractarian school of Social Contract Theory. There are other views, at least one of which—the Contractualist school of social contract theory—I have shown to better describe the expectations of a significant number of users in some these groups. Thus, while Ostrom's framework deals well with groups of users with either a homogeneous morality or a clearly dominant one, a more general understanding would attempt to understand the implications of morally heterogeneous groups. This explains the empirical mismatches between the reasons that users give for reducing their cooperation and theoretical predictions.

Although my proposed alteration to Ostrom's approach to cooperation is relatively minor, its implications are sprawling. This is because, as I noted earlier, Ostrom's framework is built around the perspective of a single model of man. While I have argued that several of Ostrom's recommendations must be reconsidered once this change is made, it is necessary to trace how the framework itself must change more systematically to accommodate this new model of human and the fairness problems she perceives. It is beyond the scope of this book to trace all of the changes that are necessary. However, an immediate change is for the focus of the framework to turn to the fairness problem—that is, to the problem of continuously avoiding patent unfairness among groups of users who use and share a resource.

The unfairness users grapple with as they continue to cooperate is complex. It is so complex that it amounts to an insurmountable challenge even for some groups that have demonstrated the capacity to solve multiple and complex collective action problems by cooperating around shared resources in situations of scarcity. It includes substantive and procedural considerations. It is not entirely global nor entirely local. Across cases, it has seven aspects in common, though their relative salience and significance varies with user groups and over time. Violations of these conditions indicate patent unfairness, but perceived fairness does not remain a settled matter after the initiation of cooperative behavior. Perceived fairness might not otherwise have been so important to sustained cooperation, except that it is directly reflected in the shared system's performance. Individuals behave as though they are unfairness averse. Avoiding the unfair situations that they have committed to, likely unknowingly, around their irrigation systems entails lessening their commitment to it and thereby hastening its deterioration. So, any concern with the continued functioning of these systems translates to a concern about how fair they are perceived to be quite independently of any normative concerns about justice in these systems.

The key challenge is that the collective action focused contractarian approach exemplified by Ostrom cannot be easily amended to incorporate perceived fairness. The framework only offers three amendments—norms, other-regarding preferences and evolutionary convergence—which, taken together, still fall short. They are inadequate for permitting the framework to represent the centrality of the fairness problem although they do capture some of its flavor. Though removing or adding variables, altering the behavioral models of users in the usual ways viz.: conditional cooperation, altruistic, norm-following, preferring distributions, and introducing more than one model of individuals, does capture some of the fairness problem, they overall call for another approach. The type of framework that centers on collective action problems misses some of the aspects of perceived fairness and, with it, the significance of the fairness problem. Furthermore, the features of the situation that encourage users to self-organize—the aforesaid design principles- do not meet all the demands of remaining fair.

Incorporating the problem of remaining fair requires a philosophical shift to a different foundation for the framework that admits to the possibilities of patent unfairness in these systems. I have examined the possibility of Contractualism, although there are likely to be others. This shift will allow the analyst to more naturally focus on how groups reach agreement without abandoning the insight that there are broad bounds that enclose an idea of patent unfairness across cases. However, it will require moving away from the assumption that fairness is whatever the group agrees to, and closer to the recognition that some outcomes are patently unfair even if arrived at through a commitment to a contract that is itself reached through mutual agreement. Not everything that groups agree to might continue to be perceived as fair because continuously avoiding patent unfairness is a complex undertaking. The next chapter examines these complexities.

5

The Fairness Problem

Approaching the Fairness Problem through Chherlung

In this chapter, I begin with a long running irrigation system that possesses all the prerequisites of successful collective action, including those in the Design Principles for Long Enduring CPR Resources.[1] Of 39 systems that met all these conditions (Table 16), it is one of the best documented and was among those referred to by Ostrom in her Nobel Prize speech as inspiring the development of the design principles in the first place (Martin and Yoder, 1987; Pradhan, 1989, 1990; Tang, 1991; Benjamin, Lam, and Ostrom, 1994; Lam, 1998; Shivakoti, 2002; Ostrom, 2010). Users of this system faced a wide range of changes that occurred in Nepal between 1983 and 2013, particularly the People's War (1996–2006) and its aftermath (Adhikari, 2014). It survived these challenges and still exhibited all the design principles three decades later.

However, its performance had deteriorated. To understand why a system that possesses all the prerequisites for successful collective action might underperform, I trace its trajectory in detail. This helps to identify some of the fairness-related mechanisms underlying decline. With a clearer view of the role of fairness obtained by narrowly analyzing this case, I broadly examine these patterns across all 266 cases for evidence of the significance of the fairness problem. Next, I sketch a basic framework for the fairness problem that incorporates lessons from the examination so far. I then explain the elements of this framework using the effects of the Maoist conflict as an important example, and I end by venturing into some of the implications of this fairness-oriented view of institutional survival and breakdown.

---

[1] Of the several versions of this list, I use a more recent version that is updated by the original author to incorporate two decades of research since the first list was published (Ostrom, Ingram, and Hong, 2009, p. 33).

Beyond Collective Action Problems. Atul Pokharel, Oxford University Press. © Oxford University Press 2024. DOI: 10.1093/oso/9780197755792.003.0005

The Physical Structure of the Brangdi Tallo Kulo System

The Brangdi Tallo Kulo System,[2] or Tallo Kulo for short, is in the district of Palpa in the Western Hills of Nepal (presently in Lumbini Province). This is a historically remote region that has only recently been connected to the rest of the district via roads. Given the limited quantity of water throughout this region relative to demand, and given the variability of rainfall, such intense (300%) agricultural use would not have been possible without systematic irrigation (IIMI, 1989). The physical structure and the technology used in the system are essential elements for understanding the institutions governing this system and the fairness concerns that have come to dominate its performance.

It is a continuous flow system that serves four subcommand areas, of which Taplek is closest to the intake with Pachariya, Chherlung, and Artunga following in sequence (Figure 9). The intake is from the Brangdi Stream, which drains into the Kali Gandaki River at Rani Ghat. Thulo Kulo is another canal in the area. Its intake is located upstream of Tallo Kulo's, and the land it irrigates is below the land Tallo Kulo irrigates, as shown in the figure. The first canal in the area was the Taplek canal, which was diverted from the Brangdhi stream and served only Taplek. It was extended to Pokhariya in 1932. Tallo Kulo was constructed incrementally in parallel with this older canal. Construction on Tallo Kulo from intake to Chherlung ended in 1938. It was merged with the Taplek canal in 1977. Construction of the Chherlung-Artunga extension was completed in 1981. The canal is approximately 9km long from headworks to last user. The distance from intake to first user is about 1km. The terrain is hilly, and the channels are located on steep hillsides. About half the canal is lined, and the headworks is temporary. It has easily accessed control points along the canal. Water is apportioned using a *saacho* (or key in Nepali), which is a notched length of wood inserted into the channel at six control points to divide the water. The changeable width and depth of notches can precisely apportion flow into branch canals. These notches make it look like a key (Martin and Yoder, 1983).

Water is available year-round, but there can be significant differences in water availability from one year to the next. Water availability gradually worsens along the length of the canal from the point of intake. The system currently irrigates

---

[2] The intake (head) is at 27°54′31.0″N 83°32′22.2″E and tail is at 27°55′15.1″N 83°29′27.3″E. The following account is based on P. Pradhan (1989), U. Pradhan (1990), Martin and Yoder (1983, 1987, 1988), IWMI (1989), and field interviews with irrigators.

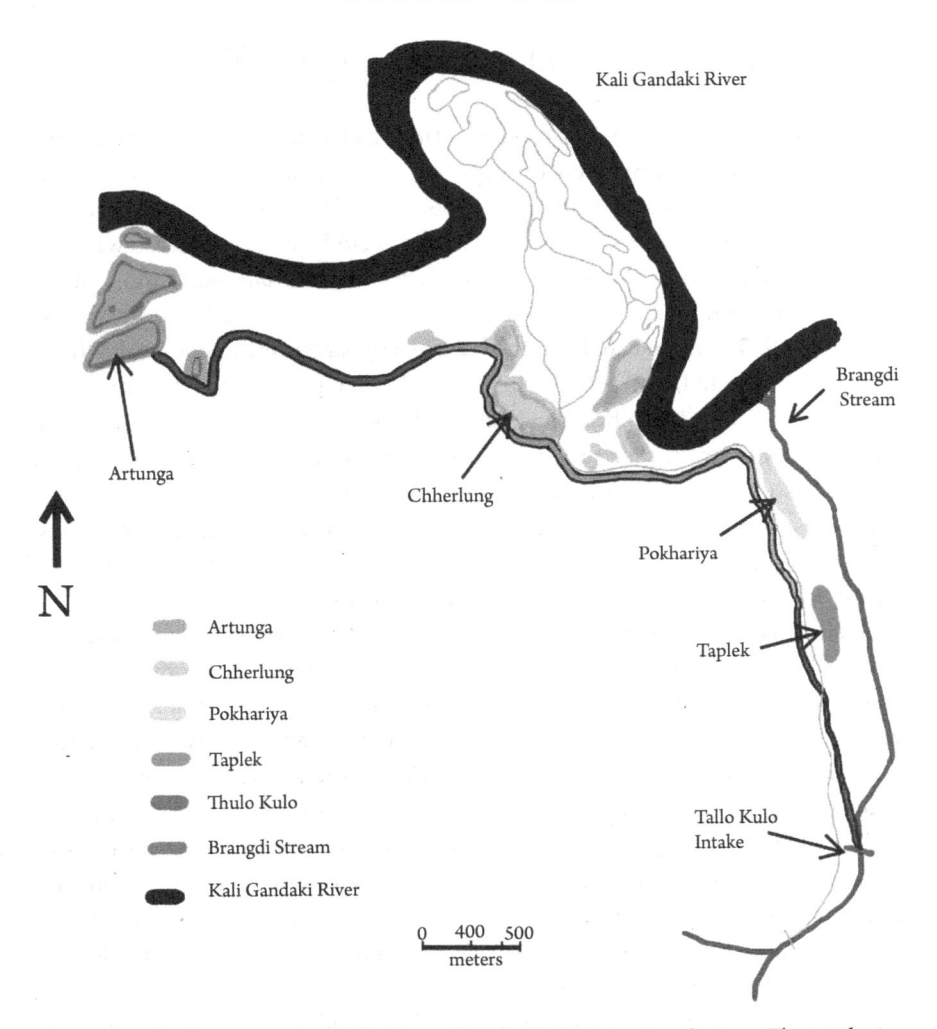

Figure 9 The four segments of the Brangdi Tallo Kulo Irrigation System. The intake is on the Brangdi Stream, which drains into the Kali Gandaki River. Tallo Kulo irrigates the subcommand areas of Taplek, Pokhariya, Chherlung, and Artunga, in that order. The main canal is enclosed in black contours, and the corresponding segments are the same color as the command areas. Branch canals are not shown. The Thulo Kulo and its command area are shown in grey. Adapted from Pradhan (1989).

about 48 hectares. Users grow rice, wheat, and maize, with amounts varying along the length and overall cropping intensity at 300%. The terrain makes the headworks prone to flooding and the entire canal prone to landslides, erosion, siltation, and obstruction, particularly during the monsoon season. The canal is typically damaged every year and requires significant effort to repair before use.

The Irrigation Institutions Governing Tallo Kulo

The original system was constructed entirely by farmers, with later extensions and improvements supported by various government agencies. The system exemplifies all the design principles (Table 21). The main canal is governed by a 130-member Water User's Association (WUA) that is registered with the Department of Irrigation and represents every household using the system. To be a member, you must own a share (or a fraction of one) and be at least 30 years old. The main canal committee is responsible for the main canal from intake until the tail, but ends at the point of diversion into the subcommand area branch canals. Each branch canal has its own governing association made up of irrigators from that subcommand area only. The main canal WUA is a focused association that does not provide other social services to its members. Members elect a single *adhyaksha* (chairman) from among the members during a general meeting held every April and May.[3] There is usually a broad consensus about who will be chosen for the position. Elections generally function as a mechanism for removing an existing chairman rather than installing a new one. Political parties are not involved in the selection, and no higher governmental body has the authority to remove the chairman. The chairman stays on until removed by vote, and the chairman can be reelected and receives water and a labor reduction in proportion to their service to the association. The current chairman is politically active with the United Marxist Leninist party (UML), is one of the larger landholders in the Chherlung subcommand area, and is also the leader of other local organizations. The association receives money primarily from membership fees, fines levied for various infractions, payments that substitute for labor input, and special fees charged for extraordinary needs such as emergency repairs.

The founding irrigation committee devised the rules for managing the canal and aligned them with local custom as well as national laws. These rules are now available in written form and were considered easy to understand by the users. Membership in the irrigation organization for the main canal consisted of shareholders, including owners of fractional shares. In Nepal, rights over water have historically been tied to land. However, in this system, they are tied to shares and detached from the land. Shares could be bought and sold again at the price set by the main canal's managing committee, and all share transactions and land to be irrigated were carefully recorded by the secretary. Thus, while the

---

[3] The current chairman explained that in the past, the head was called the *mukhiya*, but as the population grew and agricultural activities spread, the users felt the need to form a formal WUA. This association had grown from 9 to 11 members.

Table 21 **Correspondences between Tallo Kulo and the Design Principles. The Tallo Kulo exemplifies the design principles.**

Number	Principle	Tallo Kulo features
1	Clearly defined boundaries	Fixed number of shares. Shareholders have access to water. The names of shareholders and the number of shares held are meticulously recorded. It is always clear who can and cannot take from the resource and what lands are within the command area.
2	Proportional equivalence between benefits and costs	A share entitles an owner to a proportion of the water. It requires a fixed labor contribution. Other costs and benefits are tailored to the specific conditions of this system.
3	Collective choice arrangements	Rules of organization are revised at the annual general meeting of members. Decisions are reached by vote among members.
4	Monitoring	Members enforce payment of fines. Hired guards patrol canal during peak season.
5	Graduated sanctions	Cash fines range from Rs. 5 to Rs. 50 depending on seriousness. The organization can deny water. Members exert social, physical, and psychological pressures calibrated to the infraction.
6	Conflict resolution mechanisms	Conflicts resolved at the annual meetings, or by the chairman if the conflict is less serious or requires faster resolution. Reporting is easy, resolution is fast.
7	Minimal recognition of the rights to organize	National laws pertaining to irrigation governance permitted the users to devise their own rules for managing the resource and have consistently recognized these rules despite changes in regime type. Users are also guaranteed long-term tenure rights to the water in accordance with these local rules.
8	Nested enterprises	A single-tier system, so this does not apply strictly. However, branch canals and the main canal have their own WUAs.

boundary of the resource is not unchanging, at any time it is always clear who can and cannot take from the resource and what lands are within the command area (Design Principle 1). Farmers outside the command area are fined for using Tallo Kulo's water, and the committee aggressively preserves their rights and keeps others out. Transactions are recorded by the secretary of the Association, reflected in notches in saachos (Pradhan, 1989).

Each share entitles the owner to withdraw the same proportion of water from the canal, and it also carries the obligation to contribute labor during maintenance. Members of Chherlung are required to contribute one worker per day per share, members of Artunga are required to contribute four per share, and the other two areas are not required to contribute workers at all. If extra workers are needed on the main canal, the canal committee requires each member household in all four areas to send one man to work, regardless of how many shares they own. This typically occurs only in case of emergencies such as large landslides or floods. Streams fluctuate with the yearly monsoon rains; the diversion structures get damaged, and canals are frequently obstructed by landslides and silt. It is also the time of peak use. So, during the monsoon rains, two guards—usually nonusers—hired by the committee and paid in cash patrol the main canal and intake to detect damage quickly.

Water allocation rules between the four subcommand areas are clearly defined. Half of the total flow first goes to the upstream Taplek and Pokhariya subcommand areas. The other half is divided into 59 shares, with 55 going to Chherlung and 4 to Artunga, in that order. Thus, Chherlung gets 93.2% (55/59) and Artunga gets 6.8% (4/59) of the water downstream of Pokhariya. There are different rules for members for different times of year, and there are also restrictions on what the water can be used for (for instance, no farmer can grow pre-monsoon rice because of water scarcity). When continuous flow to field channels isn't possible because of a low water level in the main canal, the members use a rotation system in which each can take water for a length of time (in minutes) in proportion to their shares. A typical rotation cycle is 36 hours, although this can change depending on the situation. During water-scarce periods, such as in mid-April when all the farmers are ready to plant maize at once, the *chairman* of the main canal allocates water. He decides which requests are fulfilled and in what order based on what they consider to be a fair allocation considering total requests made, and what proportion of a farmer's fields will be irrigated. Overall, the work and water allocation rules establish a proportional equivalence between benefits and costs of being a member and are tailored to the specific conditions of this system (Principle 2). For example, when local wages have gone up because of recent labor shortages due to remittance-based employment, a falling birth rate and conflict driven rural to urban migration, the committee has discussed raising fines for missing labor days to be above the prevalent regional wage rate for that day.

The members have an annual meeting in mid-May, and typically also in April. This general assembly makes plans for annual maintenance that takes place soon after, elects a new chairman if needed, and revises the rules for operating the system if needed. While anyone can contest elections in theory, in practice it is a hereditary position. Disputes and conflicts among users and officials are common and are resolved at the annual meetings, or by the chairman if the conflict is less serious or requires faster resolution as needed (Principle 3 and 6). Association officers have a reduced labor burden during maintenance days in payment for their service.

Users monitor each other for compliance with both contributions and extraction rules along with the hired guards (*paale*), who monitor physical conditions. The organization charges a cash fine (Rs. 15) for those who miss work, and a range of fines from Rs. 5 to Rs. 50 for other infractions, depending on seriousness. When fines are not paid, the organization denies the person water, for instance by blocking the opening to their field channels. Other members also exert pressures for fines to be paid. These include social, physical, and psychological pressures calibrated to the infraction. For example, in Chherlung, the users repeated a version of the story of a user who refused to pay a fine that Martin and Yoder (1987) also detailed. He had his cooking pots confiscated by other members, who mortgaged them at a local store and threatened to sell them to pay the fine. He paid within two days. In the most extreme cases, which users considered to be administrative crimes (such as stealing money from the association), they would hand over the person to the local police. Overall, the punishments were calibrated to the seriousness of the infraction, appropriate exceptions were permitted, and there was strict oversight by individuals who were accountable to the members. Users also reported that it was very likely that infractions would be punished (Principles 4 and 5). Finally, national laws pertaining to irrigation governance permitted the users to devise their own rules for managing the resource and have consistently recognized these rules, despite changes in regime type. Users are also guaranteed long-term tenure rights to the water in accordance with these local rules (Principle 7).

Water was never abundant in the area, especially in the lower command areas, even after the canals were constructed. So, conflict over water has occasionally resulted in fights among irrigators, officials, and groups of upstream and downstream users. In 2013, water availability had declined in the tail-end service area of Artunga, a perpetually water-stressed area historically subject to wide fluctuations in water availability. There was some distrust and hostility between the WUA members from Artunga and the leadership because of this. This dispute was ongoing in 2013.

Aside from the present dispute with Artunga, the institutions devised for governing the use of water from this river are evidently adequate for resolving most conflicts, allocating water predictably, and ensuring stability in the command area. In 2013, all these institutional features were still present, and the Tallo Kulo System had survived myriad shocks. In fact, this system experienced all the shocks listed in Table 6, except for the installation of groundwater pumps. Formally, nothing had changed—the rules were all in place, and members were still committed to the organization and to achieving a fully functioning canal.

Underlying the institutions is a relatively high degree of social capital and mutual trust. The 130 members of the association have worked together in the past on a drinking water supply project and a road construction project. They are also involved in jointly managing their drinking water supply. They have been well known to each other for generations, and they are willing to assist each other without expectation of return. They also share the cultural and religious traditions of Dashain and Tihar that promote mutual cooperation. They largely believe each other's verbal promises. Users did not report any prominent communication problems due to religion, political affiliation, gender, or language. Although some own more shares than others, and this means that some receive much less water than others, the relatively poor within each subcommand area also received their water on time as promised. When people from outside the villages buy land there, they follow the rules, participate in maintenance, and are similarly punished as locally resident users.

Despite the water being tied to shares and not land, users report that members have not sold their water shares to urban areas or other users. Major disputes in the command areas are resolved by consulting elders, and their decisions are typically considered fair. There have been disputes with government agencies wanting to build a drinking water supply structure upstream on the Brangdi. In a show of unity, Tallo Kulo users protested and halted it. Overall, users conveyed a general antagonism toward government intervention in areas such as conflict resolution, although assistance for canal improvement projects was welcomed. Users reported that the two major challenges faced by the system are: the disagreements with users from the Artunga subcommand area, and the shortage of labor for maintenance due to out-migration of young males from the area in recent years.

Martin and Yoder (1983, 1988) and U. Pradhan (1990) have conducted thorough studies of the institutions used in Chherlung, with comparative studies also being done by Pradhan (1989) and Tang (1991). Together with the follow-up survey that I conducted in 2013, these observations confirm what was suspected from a collective action perspective: the institutions for governing the Tallo Kulo were clearly successful at enabling boundedly self-interested users to work together to achieve joint gain by enabling long-term, credible commitments in highly uncertain environments by preventing shirking, free riding, or other opportunistic behaviors. The institutions appeared to have been crafted to fit the local conditions precisely so as to enable collective action (Benjamin, Lam, and Ostrom, 1994; Lam, 1998; Shivakoti, 2002; Ostrom et al., 2011). The system also continues to embody the design principles. Tallo Kulo's institutions have continued to solve collective action problems successfully and resolve any conflicts along the way—the measure of this being the survival of the system. Furthermore, the ownership of private shares appears to give farmers a sense of ownership of their system, and to incentivize innovation and improvement (Pradhan, 1989), something with which systems with significant public investment have been reported to have difficulty (Frey, Villamayor-Tomas, and Theesfeld, 2016).

Perceived Unfairness in Tallo Kulo

Overall, the Tallo Kulo system has survived in challenging circumstances, and in the three subcommand areas that continue to receive water, the headworks and channels are in good condition, and the water is perceived by users to be timely, adequate, and reliable. However, the tail-end performance has declined. In 2013, users in Artunga reported that there hadn't been water in their stretch of canal for about two years, while a dispute with the main canal association went unresolved. Artunga users wanted to change their agreed-upon terms: they wanted to contribute only one laborer per share, not four. Around 2011, with the terms unchanged, Artunga farmers withdrew their labor contributions from maintenance of the main canal. As a result, the system was no longer irrigating as much land as it was designed to and that water availability upstream would have permitted. The Tallo Kulo had survived, but declined in performance.

Among members in Artunga, there was a shared sense in 2013 that the rules that their parents had agreed to in 1983 and that they had followed for three decades were no longer legitimate. Owning one share of water still required them to contribute four laborers during maintenance days, while all other shares required only one. As a result, they felt that their labor was devalued and that they were second-class shareholders and second-class members of the committee: contributing four laborers did not entitle them to four votes in the association, only one. With Taplek and Pokhariya not participating actively in governance, the main canal association was dominated by Chherlung users, who were already better off than Artunga users. With the requirement that Artunga users contribute four times the labor without proportionately higher voting power, they were kept at a disadvantage, and their power to push for changes through the general assembly was also thereby restricted. For Chherlung, their labor burden was reduced, and they had a source of reliable labor to help with the main canal.

During interviews,[4] Artunga users explained that it was now necessary, particularly after the recent Maoist *Kranti* (revolution) in the country, for the rules to treat everyone equally. It was difficult to understand, some reported, how such rules could be appropriate (*uchit*) to changed circumstances in a country that was being transformed by more egalitarian ideas. In 2008, the People's War had ended, the monarchy had been abolished, elections had been held, and the Maoist party became the largest party in the constituent assembly (220 of 575 seats), with the Chairman of the Maoist party elected prime minister with 29.28% of the popular vote.

Some reported that they did not understand the justification for the uneven arrangement in the first place. When the agreement was first reached in 1983, Chherlung users argued that Artunga users should contribute more because the existing users had already invested decades' worth of resources into the canal. It was only fair, they argued, that Artunga be required to repay this. They also argued that the water and the canal was their private property because their ancestors had constructed the canal without public funds. Current users in Artunga, however, reported a variety of contrary views: that the point of repayment had long ago been reached, that such an exploitative contract should not be binding on the next generation of users in Artunga, that the extension project to Artunga had also increased the water available to Chherlung through upstream investments by the Nepal government,[5] and that government investment had long ago turned the water and the canal into a public resource that should benefit all in the area.

Artunga was already disadvantaged in several ways prior to agreeing to these uneven terms. It was relatively remote from other command areas and major settlements. The farmers overall were poorer than in the other three subcommand areas. Artunga was also politically marginalized and historically neglected because it was in an area that was not contiguous with the rest of the district. The other three subcommand areas continued to be located in a different local political jurisdiction, so Artunga was outside of their politics as well. It is at the tail end of the system and is subject to fluctuations higher up because it received water last. It does not have a good alternative source of water; the

[4] Responses collected from individual and group interviews conducted on January 1, 2013, June 6, 2013, and January 12, 2018.

[5] One of the key factors sustaining the dispute was that the amount by which the flow was increased was never measured or recorded (Pradhan, 1990).

source that is available, the Bhulke spring, is low-quality and more saline. They are also new to organized irrigation because of this historic marginalization.

This physical remoteness meant that messages from the main canal association might not reach them in time. There were instances where they didn't know when different labor days were declared, or when emergency labor was requested on the main canal. In one incident in 1984, when they failed to show up for emergency work in time, they were fined. Artunga petitioned the district panchayat to intervene, and the Chief District Officer (CDO) helped broker a settlement in which the fine was reduced to Rs. 2,500 instead of the 4,100 that the canal association had imposed. The canal association was told they should only very rarely call an all-hands emergency (*jhara*) of the type that Artunga had missed, and that Artunga was required to hire someone from Chherlung to inform them of emergency canal maintenance work. They paid this person Rs. 10 per message conveyed.

The unwillingness of the main canal committee to change the rules, and the relative powerlessness of Artunga members in the governing association, hardened the perception over the years that the irrigation rules were designed to disadvantage them consistently. Even as early as 1990, field studies such as IWMI (1989) reported that Artunga was often in conflict with Chherlung over the timing of water delivery during the maize planting season. Although formally allocated shares, Artunga needed to determine when all farmers in Chherlung were done using water and then begin to use it (or risk a fine). Often, this meant that they took water long into the night. At times, they collected water into a pond at night and then irrigated from the pond the next day. In extreme cases, they had to suffer the indignity of begging for water from Thulo Kulo, another irrigation system in the area (Figure 9). Starting in 2011, after pressing their demands and refusing to contribute labor until the dispute was resolved, the association voted to stop water from flowing downstream to the Chherlung section of the canal.

Overall, the picture presented by users in Artunga suggested that they overwhelmingly perceived the current rules as unfair. Effectively, Artunga received less than 7% of the canal water that Chherlung received, even though it had the same command area, and they contributed four times more labor per share than the other users without corresponding voting power. Over time, this had the effect of further increasing the wealth gap between Artunga and the rest of the users. The rules were not perceived as legitimate; they were simple to understand, but their justification was difficult to accept. Artunga users were required to contribute their own labor for canal maintenance, but the proportion of costs to benefit they faced was far higher than what other users faced. Although they were members of the association, their voting power was so small as to be ineffective. These concerns weren't new, but they persisted for decades. The contrast with frequently changing national circumstances, it seemed, increased the significance of perceived unfairness until they stopped cooperating with the system in 2011. With water cut off, they had been completely deprived of water from the main canal for two years in 2013.

After this, Chherlung was completely responsible for providing labor for maintenance and operation, an increasingly challenging task. With a labor scarcity exacerbated by out-migration due to the People's War and subsequent opportunities in foreign countries other than India, many males had left the village and were absent for years. With this labor shortage growing, the labor contribution from Artunga became more acutely missed than usual. Four shares brought 16 people from Artunga, which is more than a quarter of the 59 workers available for the system during normal times. Furthermore, the rules for governing the canal allowed users to substitute money for labor. The better-off residents of Chherlung were more likely to pay rather than perform often grueling physical labor for nearly a month. By 2013, it had become difficult for the main canal association to find workers for maintenance.

Interviews revealed that it was clear to users in all four subcommand areas that the main canal was underperforming because of this dispute. This is consistent with the view that the perception of the rules for allocating labor as unfair had become the main obstacle to achieving a fully functioning canal, even though all the other prerequisites for successful collective action were present, and the group had already been successfully cooperating for nearly three decades.

Linking Fairness and Cooperation in Tallo Kulo

The connection between perceived unfairness and noncooperation is not automatic, as Tallo Kulo illustrates. At least some users perceived the governance institutions to be unfair in Artunga from the outset of the uneven agreement in 1983, but 28 years passed before the Artunga users stopped cooperating with the system in a significant way—that is, in a way that affected the functioning of the system. Indeed, Artunga users took the first recorded action against the existing arrangements around 2005, and had stopped raising the issue at general meetings nearly a decade before. This was despite the fact that a growing number of users in Artunga, particularly younger ones, were dissatisfied with what they saw as the backwardness of their arrangements compared to the promises of equality and welfare that successive national governments and political parties had espoused.

Hoping for a better outcome to conflicts with upstream users, Artunga consistently advocated for the involvement of state institutions in resolving irrigation disputes. This was repeatedly rejected by the main canal committee, although Artunga users were sometimes successful, as was the case when they missed an emergency workday in the 1984 example above. In every disagreement going back to the initial construction of the extension to Artunga, Chherlung users resisted, often successfully, the involvement of outside actors in resolving internal disputes.[6] Consequently, although there was a growing perception that the agreements were unfair, the users felt they could do nothing about it, that the state sanctioned it, or that it wasn't significant enough to do something about. As U. Pradhan notes, referring to the hierarchy of the two types of shareholders in the Tallo Kulo:

> Those, like in the Artunga group, who feel disadvantaged in this hierarchy have, at times, attempted to use the state as an ally in relocating positions in the hierarchy. Sometimes, these disadvantaged have even advocated that the state assume control and responsibilities of the irrigation system so that hierarchical arrangement is collapsed into a more egalitarian one. On the other hand, as we saw in Brangdhi Tallo Kulo, those in positions of power in the property hierarchy also were able to influence and rearrange the states actions so as to buttress the existing property structure, not alter it. (1990, p. 228)

When the People's War officially began in 1996, Tallo Kulo was relatively unaffected. Users continued to meet, and the canal continued to function, but the effects grew as the war spread throughout the Nepalese countryside. The relatively better-off users in Chherlung and further upstream were fearful, while a growing number of users in Artunga began professing sympathy with the rebels. Eventually, Maoist cadres sought shelter in homes around the command area. The chairman of the main canal WUA reported that rebels would force farmers to provide food and shelter, and that their permission was needed before calling their annual meetings, but they were not involved in the day-to-day functioning of the canal until about a decade later.

A major turning point came in 2005, when a contingent of the Maoist Army began to frequent the area around Artunga and used it as a base from which to launch nearby actions. Based on contemporary newspaper reports,[7] these actions included kidnapping hundreds of students at a time from schools in Palpa and "reeducating" them, attacks on district headquarters, threatening

---

[6] Indeed, the more powerful parties in Tallo Kulo resisted outside involvement every step of the way, starting from the extension of the Taplek canal.

[7] See, for instance, Magar (2004) for an English-language account that represents reports from that time.

functionaries from other parties and, crucially, becoming involved in local re-source governance. According to the Maoist party, they controlled 80% of the countryside in Nepal by mid-2006.

The functioning of the Water User's Association of Tallo Kulo was eventually disrupted. During the 2013 survey, users in Chherlung reported that the government was completely absent during the conflict and did not offer any help for maintenance and repair. It was not possible, according to the chairman, to continue canal management as they used to because of restrictions on movement and gatherings that the Maoists had imposed. Users noted that the Maoists would stay in the homes of villagers and compel them to provide food and shelter, and in some cases force them to leave their land altogether.

While users in Chherlung reported being forced by the Maoists to support them, users in Artunga were more likely to join the rebels. As long as the Maoists were there, the villagers' demands had the de facto backing of the Maoist Army. The unfair arrangements with Chherlung became a frequent discussion topic because of the importance of agriculture to Artunga residents, but even with the Maoist army present, not all users in Artunga were convinced that something should be done, and there were disagreements about the best path to take. Some perceived the current arrangements as fair in the name of adhering to precedent and prior agreements, as was the custom. Some learned from Maoist neighbors that the arrangements were "feudalistic" and therefore oppressive— a new reason to perceive it as unfair. Others perceived the arrangements as unfair, but did not feel that they were significant enough that changing them would alter their condition. Instead, they pointed to the need to use improved techniques and technologies to get more out of the water that they had. Others still perceived it as unfair and felt it was significant but also felt powerless under the weight of custom.

It is clear based on user responses that regular interactions with Maoist supporters in their village had an effect on their thinking. The Maoists convinced enough people to take action and again propose a renegotiation of labor allocation terms at the main canal meeting so that they would be treated equally. According to the chairman of the main association, the difference this time was that the Maoists threatened to kill him if he did not agree to make the Artunga shareholders equal by requiring only one laborer per share, just like everyone else.[8] According to the users in Artunga, the difference was that they felt emboldened to withdraw labor contributions in protest; additionally, being backed by the Maoists' threat of violence made them feel empowered to speak up against the customary rules. For approximately the next six years,

---

[8] "They would attend the meetings and tell me what to do and what not to do." Chairman of the Tallo Kulo main canal committee, interviewed June 2013.

Artunga irrigators enjoyed equal status with other members of their Water User's Association.

But the Artungas' equality did not last. By 2011, the Maoist party had split into two factions, one demanding a return to armed struggle and the other advocating working within the parliamentary system. The process of integrating the People's Liberation Army into the Nepal Army was underway, and a moderate Maoist leader would become Prime Minister—the second Maoist prime minister since 2008. Respondents reported that after the Maoists became less influential locally, the power in the irrigation association returned to the hands of Chherlung who, in turn, insisted on a return to their previous rule. They justified this in the name of respecting local culture, traditions, and norms, as well as restoring local sovereignty over their resource after a period of outside interference. Unable to return to an agreement that they had become convinced was patently unfair, farmers in Artunga withdrew their labor contributions instead. As punishment, the association voted to shut off their water.

Over the next two years, this led to the Chherlung-Artunga extension falling into disuse. This had more significant impacts on Artunga than Chherlung. It meant that Artunga farmers could no longer grow rice on some plots and had to reduce their irrigated lands. This led some farmers to reconsider agriculture as their primary livelihood. On the other hand, Chherlung suffered from a labor shortage, but its farmers also received significantly more water and had a shorter canal to maintain, meaning they could grow a wider range of crops and had nearly abundant water. The users in Artunga did not appear to blame these negative individual and comparative outcomes on their reluctance to agree to be bound by prior commitments, as the Chherlung users did. Instead, most respondents attributed the now-defunct canal, as well as their originally disadvantaged condition, to the committee's insistence on adopting an unfair system. For Chherlung farmers, sticking to a system that was modified by outsiders and that rejected local custom and tradition was itself unfair. Most of the members of the association shared the belief that meeting prior commitments was paramount to the continued survival of their system: it was essential that the rules for governing their canal be their own.

Overall, several factors connected the perception of unfairness to a withdrawal of cooperation in Tallo Kulo. The perception of fairness had to spread and broaden to include other considerations (such as "feudalism") before it was shared by most of the users. But this was not enough for them to reduce their cooperation despite their inconsistent success at trying to involve government agencies in resolving conflicts. There always seemed to be the hope that the next disagreement might involve the state differently, and the resulting agreement might be slightly less unfavorable to Artunga. There also wasn't agreement within Artunga about whether the perceived unfairness was more important than adhering to the local norm of respecting prior use rights by deferring to customary norms—norms that users in all four subcommand areas shared, and that could be traced back nearly three hundred years to a period before Nepal was a country (Regmi, 1976; Pradhan, 1990). The state, political parties, and a political movement all helped Artunga users to see their arrangements as unfair and realize that this arrangement had an important role in maintaining their uneven position in society. Finally, the Maoists succeeded in convincing them that it was significant enough to act and empowered them to withdraw their cooperation in protest.

Perceived Unfairness across Cases

Looking across cases, a similar relationship between perceived unfairness and performance holds: if collective action problems are critical to initial cooperation and remain important, avoiding the perception of unfairness can become essential to sustained cooperation. As we have seen in the case of Tallo Kulo, users need to come up with a set of rules that they guess will be perceived as fair in the future, and they are unlikely to get it right once and for all. But how significant is this to continued cooperation? Using the mapping from Table 20, it is possible to compare the significance of fairness-related factors to performance of these systems with the significance of other collective action problem-related variables, and it is possible to do so over time.

Figure 10 shows how perceptions of the fairness of these systems have changed. The biggest change occurred in whether some in the groups received considerably less water than they wanted, with nearly identical proportions going from yes to no and vice versa. The other aspects of perceived fairness appear to have stayed relatively the same across groups. There are two main exceptions: there has been a significant increase in the proportion (32%) of groups reporting that some users are consistently disadvantaged by the rules, and a significant decrease (22%) in the proportion of groups reporting that their rules are no longer legitimate, most likely because the rules have been updated.

Across cases, indicators of perceived fairness are more frequently (24 of 96) and significantly ($\alpha = 0.05$) associated with indicators of performance than the other collective action-focused variables examined so far (Table 40). This systematic pattern is not likely to be due to chance because one would expect between 4 and 5 by chance alone. Eight are associations of changes in these variables across time. Of the two aspects of performance (physical and perceived) there are more significant and more frequent associations of the fairness variables with the latter than the former. Three of eight of the fairness variables—legitimacy of the rules (*flegit*), substantially uneven work (*fevenwork*), and user contributions

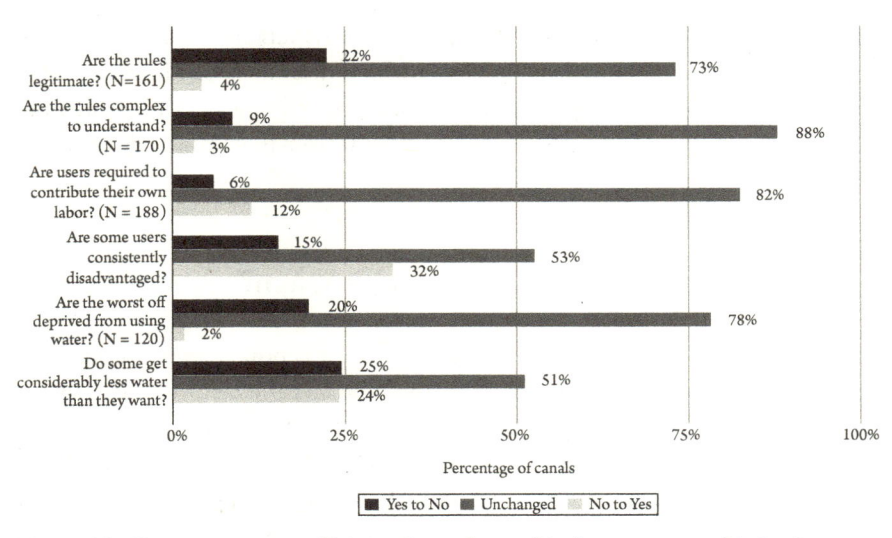

Figure 10 How perceptions of fairness have changed in farmer-managed irrigation systems in Nepal (1976–2013): changes in six aspects of perceived fairness within cases between the first and second surveys. Changes to each of the aspects are computed by subtracting their values in the two surveys. Two aspects of perceived fairness that did not show any significant associations with changes in performance variables are omitted. (These are: Are some users consistently advantaged? And do some have substantially more duties than others?)

of labor *(fselflabor)*—relate to the physical condition of the canal. These associations are both weak ($a = 0.05$) and infrequent (3 of 24 comparisons). This is consistent with the observation that it is difficult for a nonuser to know how much damage to a canal will noticeably affect its functioning for users. There are 21 (of 48) significant associations between these fairness variables and indicators of user-perceived performance. Of these, 6 are significant at the 0.001 level, 7 at the 0.01 level, and 8 at the 0.05 level.[9]

Compared to factors affecting collective action problems, the fairness variables (Figure 10) are more convincingly associated with performance and thereby with sustained cooperation. These have been discussed in the literature as norms of fairness, and are usually studied in lab settings due to the complexity of actual social interactions (Poteete, Janssen and Ostrom, 2010, pp. 224–225)

[9] The total number of observations for the cross-tabulations of fairness variables ranged from 35 to 214. This corresponds to a response rate of between 17.3% and 91.8%. Nevertheless, this variation in the usable sample does not impact our questions, as I use an exact test to compute the significance statistic. Furthermore, those variables that have the most missing values in the first round—substantially more duties for some *(fevenwork)* and some consistently advantaged *(fadvantage)*—show the fewest associations (one) across the three rounds. Discarding them would strengthen the results by raising the proportion of significant comparisons to 22 out of 72.

instead of in the field. Overall, these systems are remarkably robust to a wide range of external and internal changes, as the literature suggests. However, these results further suggest that perceptions of fairness, although not the only relevant factor, can be at least as significant as other factors to common governance outcomes.

What Is the Fairness Problem?

Pulling together all the observations made so far, it is now possible to devise a clearer working definition of the fairness problem and the factors connecting it to cooperation. The fairness problem consists of the obstacles to remaining fair in a situation of interdependent cooperation. In practice, the fairness problem can be understood as avoiding the perception of being too unfair. As illustrated by a long-running shared irrigation system, an interdependent situation is one in which each group member must rely on at least one other to achieve a desired outcome; they simply cannot do it alone. In all the examples in this book, the condition in which every farmer is doing their part to an adequate extent for the system to continue to function is a situation of interdependent cooperation. The cooperation between farmers is what enables the group to achieve the joint outcome—that is, a functional, well-maintained irrigation system that can provide adequate and reliable water to member-farmers. Without cooperation and without a third party taking over, the system would deteriorate. Fairness is but one of the myriad factors for farmers to consider when deciding whether to cooperate in an interdependent situation.

A simple type of fairness problem occurs at the point of starting to cooperate. Prior to cooperating for the first time, everyone's assessment of the fairness of proposed cooperation is necessarily based on their expectations. So, remaining fair in this initial, pre-cooperation state means that enough people expect that the arrangements will not take a form that they will perceive as unfair. This is the most rudimentary form of the fairness problem. This initial problem is solved straightforwardly through credible assurances that the cooperation will avoid unfairness, even though nobody knows for sure that this will be so, and even though nobody quite knows what they might come to perceive as unfair.[10]

As time passes, sustaining cooperation demands more than mutual assurances of fairness. The longer groups cooperate, the more information becomes available to them about the processes they have committed to and the outcomes that

---

[10] It is worth reiterating that I assume that these are voluntary arrangements, and that the individual cooperators have a choice not to cooperate. This means, for instance, that they are not forced to cooperate by a more powerful group of people.

result. At least some are likely to incorporate these experiences into assessments of how well the cooperative system has lived up to the initial promise of avoiding unfairness. Unequal outcomes are inevitable with this type of fixed rules. So over time, it becomes more likely that some will come to perceive the system as a whole—the rules, customs, traditions, intentions, their outcomes and so on—as not fair enough. After all, if it was the case that everyone got as much of the resource as they wanted when they wanted it, and only contributed as much labor as they wanted whenever it was convenient, institutions wouldn't be needed to regulate behavior in the first place. This points to a tendency for later perceptions of fairness of some cooperators to diverge from their earlier perception of the fairness of their arrangements. This divergence constantly changes the form of the fairness problem. In addition, it is difficult to predict when it will gain enough significance to affect their joint outcomes. This is because individuals might not act on perceived unfairness until provoked by some external factor such as a flood or political movement, which are unpredictable.

A clarification is necessary at this point. A less convoluted way to understand the observations presented so far seems to be that these farmers simply want to be treated fairly. While it may seem true in the abstract that farmers are seeking fairness, it mischaracterizes the situation of interdependent cooperation in a fundamental way. This is because farmers typically have difficulty defining fairness, and asking them what the concept means to them can be a dead end.[11] However, they appear much clearer about what isn't fair. So rather than try to define fairness, it can be more useful in practice to identify what clearly isn't fair, that is, what is patently unfair—although this, too, might change with time. Despite this, the *perception* of unfairness can be extremely difficult to articulate. Thus, it might be said of perceived unfairness that although we cannot say what it is, we know it when we experience it; it remains largely tacit. This is consistent with the observation that it is possible for individuals to detect unfair situations even when they cannot define what they think is fair. Avoiding unfair situations is the heart of the fairness problem, and detecting perceived unfairness is essential to a realistic assessment of the quality of cooperative institutions.

In light of the fairness problem, consider how groups of farmers work together over a long time period. When they share a resource that needs maintenance, they figure out how to maintain it, determine that it should be maintained and what will motivate enough of them to do their duties insofar as maintenance is concerned. But as they work together for many years (or many seasons), they also learn more about the arrangements that they are committed to. For example,

---

[11] There is no translation of the word "fairness" into Nepali, for instance.

they begin to see what difference it makes if they are assigned a role A, say, to cleaning long stretches of the canal, instead of role B, say inspecting the canal for damage. Both are physically demanding, but they make different demands on a farmer's time and body. Or in the case of Artunga, they learn that having to make disproportionate labor contributions can translate to a second-class status in society. As they encounter these differences, they are likely to develop opinions, thoughts or emotions about them. Eventually, fairness becomes another of the criteria by which they assess their rules—in addition to, for instance, whether the punishments are adequate to deter shirking. This illustrates how even though they may have considered fairness before, particularly when initiating cooperation, later considerations are substantially different. Furthermore, at least three familiar reasons complicate any attempt to avoid unfair situations: outcomes diverge from expectations, perceptions of fairness change, and every rule change has distributional consequences. Ultimately, the fairness problem doesn't have a straightforward solution, even after the conditions that are perceived as unfair have been enumerated.

It is also important to clarify why the fact that users initially agreed to the rules doesn't minimize the importance of the fairness problem. Initial commitment can be misleading from the perspective of perceived fairness. The enthusiasm associated with having access to a new resource that will transform farmer livelihoods—such as irrigated water—can obscure hesitations about the fairness of largely unknown, future outcomes. It is more likely, especially for already disadvantaged groups such as those in Artunga, that having access to the resource is transformative, that they will save any objections for after the possibility of receiving water, for example, is real (e.g., the canal extension has been completed). Respondents regularly reported that they did not object to the rules proposed prior to construction because they did not want to jeopardize the construction. So, although fairness matters at the start of cooperation, it is more likely to become a bigger problem later. Over time the same people who enthusiastically agreed to the rules may reduce their commitment to cooperation, having realized that the arrangements have turned out to be, or might become, unfair to them. Thus, the reason initial cooperation can be misleading is that groups are locked into a perpetual dynamic of guessing what might be fair in the future while crafting rules that will get the cooperators there. More precisely, the initial commitment binds them to a loop of anticipating what might come to be perceived as unfair and actively avoiding it and then avoiding the anticipated unfairness cause by the attempt. In fact, the initial agreement is what sets up this essential challenge contained in the fairness problem.

To complicate this further, our very perceptions of what is fair and what is not is malleable. While there may be a visceral element to it—for example, that we tend to avoid unfairness, as I assume here—there is also a healthy dose of learning and social influence that shape perceptions. As the interviews suggest, we also alter our views with experience. And at once we try to develop rules and patterns of behavior that will not diverge from what we might think of as fair. So based on these cases, I do not hesitate to venture that the central dilemma of co-operative arrangements is remaining fair. The point that makes remaining fair a problem is that the perception of fairness develops, and people become aware of it, primarily with experience.

It is clearer now how the argument presented in this book pertains, strictly, to why people stop cooperating. The thesis of this book can be stated as follows: individuals reduce their cooperation when they perceive the outcomes of the rules to be unfair. The inverse, that people cooperate only when outcomes are fair is not implied by this. However, that full cooperation over time is only secured when individuals do not perceive the institutions as unfair is the point. If the cooperation is perceived as unfair, then over a long enough time the group is more likely to experience challenging circumstances that will provoke decline by making the fairness problem too difficult for them to solve.

A Schematic Representation

Drawing on all 266 of the cases in this study, Figure 11 combines the key elements in a schematic diagram. Inside the rectangle are those variables primarily affecting the level of cooperation, and those outside primarily alter the nature and significance of the fairness problem itself.

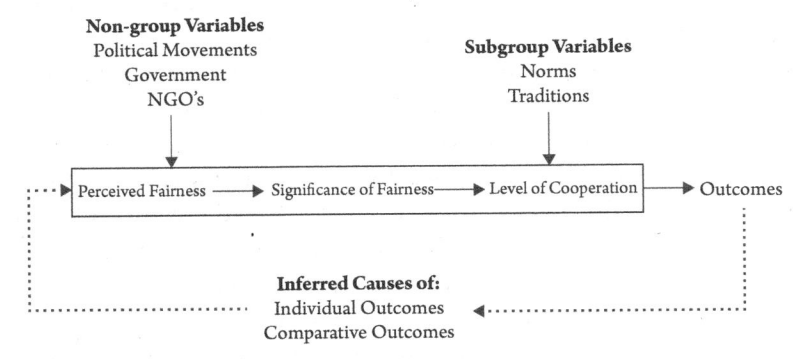

Figure 11 The contours of the fairness problem for a user already committed to a system: This schematic shows the relationship between the elements of the fairness problem and factors that affect it in the case of sustained cooperation. The rectangle contains "in the mind" variables for each individual, which can be affected by other variables. The arrows represent causal relationships. The model is animated by unfairness aversion.

In the figure, *Outcomes* refers to, at least, the expected result of cooperating. In the case of a well-functioning irrigation system this primary outcome every season is receiving adequate water in a timely manner. With every passing monsoon season, the amount of land that a person can irrigate, and therefore the crops they can grow, is determined by the amount of water they receive. So, the primary outcome—receiving water—grows over time to affect more of a person's life, such as what they can afford to buy, where their children can study, or their social status. Thus, over time the outcomes come to include these cumulative outcomes as well. Cumulative outcomes are the wider set of outcomes brought about by the primary outcome—the canal water received, in this example. In Artunga's case, outcomes initially referred only to the water that an individual received. Over decades, the consequences of receiving only that much water (and not more) in a comparatively less timely and less adequate way than those upstream became clearer. After decades, cumulative outcomes included overall social status and power in the user's association as well. In this way it is typically the case that the longer users cooperate, the larger the set of relevant outcomes.

Achieving joint outcomes also depends on the willingness of others in the group to cooperate, as well as some variables that are not under the control of the group or any individual in it. For example, climate patterns, war and natural disasters can all affect the qualities of water availability no matter the level of canal functioning. The primary variable that is largely in the hands of the individual is the level at which they will cooperate with the institutional arrangements that they are committed to.

The *level of cooperation* is a psychological, "in the mind, subjective" variable that cannot be directly measured (Ostrom, 1990, p. 38), but it is reflected in various ways. For instance, in these cases, a high level of cooperation is often associated with the attentive performance of work, and a low level with neglect of one's duties. The different qualities of work put forth by workers typically show up in the functioning of the system. So the level of cooperation of cooperators is apparent in the functioning of the system in cases like these. In these systems, it is impossible for everyone to be constantly monitored by a supervisor or guard while they perform their duties. Much of their work, in the absence of real-time supervision, is subject to their discretion. They may put in full effort, or not. Ultimately, only they can know how sincerely or wholeheartedly they are performing their work—qualities that indicate higher levels of cooperation. This is true of many shared resources that require maintenance to function, not just irrigation systems. The level of cooperation of an individual when pooled with the levels of cooperation of others in the group, leads to the output—a system that functions at various levels.

In the trajectory of cooperation between its initiation and breakdown, the level of cooperation is affected by a range of other considerations. One of these is the expected cost and benefit to oneself of continued cooperation, as may be considered when an individual first decides whether to commit or not. These are not shown here because this figure stylizes the continued cooperation situation in which fairness problems dominate these other considerations.

As in the case of Tallo Kulo, in this sustained, cooperation-type of situation, opportunities to reconsider one's commitment wholesale are scarce and atypical, whereas recalibration of one's level of cooperation is more frequent. For instance, recall that even when the water to them had been shut off, Artunga users were still members of the Water User's Association and still professed a commitment to their system. In their view, they had withdrawn cooperation with the aim of improving their shared system. This schematic diagram therefore represents a point in time in which the decision to calibrate one's level of cooperation—rather than start to cooperate or not—is the key decision faced by individuals.

The *perception of fairness* is the assessment of the unfairness of outcomes or processes, as described in earlier chapters. The *significance of fairness* indicates how willing an individual is to act on perceived unfairness. It represents how important perceived unfairness is to a person. These two variables capture the observation, such as in Artunga's case, that individuals might not act on perceived unfairness automatically, especially if they assess that it is relatively insignificant to them. Perceiving their system as unfair and also attaching a large enough significance to this perception are necessary conditions for them to act on it. Being significant is not sufficient for action, however, as we have seen. Sometimes acting on significant perceived unfairness depends on factors outside of an individual's control such as having the support of a powerful group.

Both the significance of fairness and the perception of fairness alter the level of cooperation. One may perceive the situation as unfair, but the individual may not alter their level of cooperation unless they regard fairness as significant to them or they feel confident that they can express their dissatisfaction. They may even calibrate their level of cooperation with regards to how unfair they perceive the situation to be, or how significant this perceived unfairness is to them. Similarly, one may hold fairness to be important but not as significant as other factors. All of these possibilities were illustrated by Artunga users after the Maoists became a common presence in their village, and they occur throughout the other 265 cases as well.

Other factors that affect the fairness problem branch out from each of these three internal ones. They include characteristics of the subgroup such as norms and traditions, nongroup variables such as political movements and the actions of government agencies, and the inferred causes of individual and comparative outcomes.

To retain focus on the mechanism of fairness, the wider range of factors that could conceivably influence the cumulative outcomes experienced by individuals are left out of the figure. These other factors have been discussed and illustrated at length, and I return to them shortly, so a brief reminder should suffice. Norms and traditions might define unfairness for individuals as well as discourage acting on one's own perceptions of unfairness of a system if it doesn't match the customary or prevalent norm. Political movements and government agencies have significant power to shape what individuals consider fair, how significant they consider unfairness, and to encourage and support the expression of perceptions of unfairness within a group. They can also provide the backing necessary for individuals to act on these perceptions. Both sets of variables— nongroup and subgroup—can influence what users attribute the results of cooperation to—both positive and negative.

The dotted arrow indicates the dynamic nature of the fairness problem in the form of a feedback loop of information. In this loop, outcomes are inputs to future behavior if they are inferred to result from past behavior or prior agreements. That is why they first pass through the *Inferred Causes*. This group of variables affects how and to what an individual attributes outcomes to. The outcomes that individuals might consider are the ones they experience (individual outcomes) as well as those that others do (comparative outcomes). The uneven distribution of outcomes across members in the group, a common type of feedback, is typically considered in assessing the fairness of arrangements. Part of this consideration is understanding why the distribution arose or inferring the causes of these comparative outcomes. This loop also illustrates how time is essential to understanding perceived fairness: it is only over time that the differential outcomes of a system of cooperation manifest themselves.

The tendency of human beings to act as though they are *unfairness-averse* animates this schematic. For individuals to continue cooperating, they must not perceive as too unfair the system as a whole, including rules, their enforcement, primary outcomes, and cumulative outcomes. If they do, they are likely to reduce their level of cooperation gradually or suddenly. As these cases indicate, continually updating the institutions so that they are perpetually perceived as fair enough can be a challenging problem for local groups. Cumulatively, the moving pieces of the fairness problem can make it too complex for individual irrigators to grapple with. These are: individual willingness to act on perceived unfairness (affected by the significance of fairness), changing perceptions of fairness, a range of factors affecting the level of cooperation, and the cumulative outcomes of the institutional arrangement. Nevertheless, it is important to note that some groups, as evidenced by low levels of perceived unfairness and high levels of performance, have successfully addressed the fairness problem.

Internal Factors Affecting the Nature of the Fairness Problem

Not all aspects of a cooperative situation are relevant to the perception of fairness. As I explained in Chapter 3, an individual assessment of how fair a situation is concerns the distribution among users of (1) contributions to the joint outcome, (2) joint gains, (3) qualification, and (4) exclusion of users from the system of cooperation, as well as (5) substantive outcomes resulting from the other aspects. Furthermore, an individual's overall fairness assessment can be thought of as multidimensional. Each dimension refers to either specific outcomes such as the distribution of water across space, or specific characteristics of the rules such as whether they are difficult to understand. As I emphasized in this chapter, because realized outcomes and actual processes naturally diverge somewhat from expectations, every system is likely to be perceived as unfair to an extent or by some. Those that exhibit unfairness to such an extent that it is recognizable even to those not in the group—that is, those that are patently unfair—can be thought of as cases where the fairness problem has been neglected or is beyond the ability of the group to address. These patently unfair systems are at risk of decline, if they are not declining already.

The perception of fairness is discursive, multidimensional, and powerful and involves both rules and outcomes. Many of its most significant aspects are left out in a single metric of inequality, or even a set of inequality metrics. Ultimately, it rests on the perception of these inequalities, which is purely subjective although not entirely individualistic. These features make it challenging to preempt and even more dangerous to cooperation to not try to do so. Indeed, the power of the fairness problem derives from this unpredictability. If it could be predicted, then institutional survival would be a matter of updating the rules to avoid or deal with predictions of what will be considered too unfair in the future.

Despite it being subjective, there are factors that affect perceived fairness. For instance, individuals in the group can shape each other's perception of the fairness of the system. They can also encourage or discourage each other from protesting unfair situations. One way to protest is for individuals to lessen, along with others, their level of cooperation with institutions. In normal times, this can manifest as work that is of a lesser quality or just passable, and in abnormal times, it can manifest as a lack of enthusiasm to do more than one is absolutely required to do. These actions are typically taken in a coordinated fashion. For example, a group of users might decide to react halfheartedly to infractions or rule-breaking during the monsoon season to exhibit a reduced level of cooperation. Since the rules of these systems are typically mutually enforced, this can implicitly weaken the functioning of the system.

Whether a perception of unfairness leads individuals in the group to act on it, such as by reducing their level of cooperation, depends on how significant perceived fairness is to the individuals. The significance of fairness can be thought of as an internal tolerance level for unfair situations that mediates unfairness aversion. This, too, can be affected by others inside or outside the group. The same perception of unfairness can lead to revolt in one situation, for instance when Maoist cadres encouraged users to act, and in another be considered an acceptable part of the agreement to cooperate, for instance when it is prescribed by customary norms. This significance of fairness determines how significant the fairness problem is to sustained cooperation. It is also affected by several factors outside the group.

External Factors Affecting the Significance of the Fairness Problem

Factors external to individuals can alter the significance of the fairness problem to sustained cooperation. These factors fall into two broad groups. The first group of factors alters how salient the fairness problem is to individual cooperators, and the second group alters the ability of groups to solve these problems. Each of the factors shown to affect the fairness problem in Figure 11 ultimately affects the decision whether or how much the individual will cooperate. The box represents the boundaries of the internal decision-making of the individual about their level of cooperation with the existing arrangements.

Inferred Causes, *Nongroup variables* and *Subgroup variables* all affect this internal dynamic from the outside. Of these, subgroup variables such as norms and traditions are the most obvious and well-studied, and the least obvious one is Inferred Causes. Inferred Causes refers to the attribution of observed outcomes to a cause—in this case, to the rules and how they were implemented. For the outcome of prior cooperation to affect future cooperation, the users must attribute it to the rules or some aspect of the system, such as a subgroup that is favored by the rules. In other words, they must blame the outcomes on the rules or the system in some way, in contrast to something completely outside the control of the individual or group such as a natural disaster. Attributing the cause of an unfair outcome to some aspect of the system or the group rather than to chance increases the odds that it will affect the individual's perception of system fairness (Shklar, 1990).

Individuals do not normally assess the fairness of their system continuously, or even at every point of action—such as when a farmer is embarking on their monitoring duties in the early morning, or diverting water to their fields late at night. These assessments are more typically made when provoked by unusual events. They can also be made in social settings such as in discussion with others. For instance, a Maoist re-education session in which they are taught the feudal roots of the current system is a frequent example, as is a visit to another irrigation system that prompts comparison with their own. Tallo Kulo members had, for instance, visited a system in the district of Sindhupalchok to see how it was running, which may have provoked a comparison. The assessment of how fair the system of cooperation has turned out to be concerns specific distributional aspects of the situation and not others. The challenges of fairness arise only gradually, and it seems thus unlikely that people will organize on their own to oppose a system they perceive as unfair.

As noted, the act of cooperation also does not imply that the system is perceived as fair by all cooperators. For instance, it is possible for users to notice a work gap and assess it to be unfair, but still not reduce their commitment to their institution. Anyone visiting the Tallo Kulo during the first decade after it was constructed would have likely been convinced that it was perceived by fair by all, even though Artunga users perceived the initial labor contribution agreement to be unfair. One way that users who perceive a situation as unfair are likely to express their dissatisfaction is to wait for unexpected situations that demand their extraordinary contribution. Consider the example above of downstream users of the DBA canal. Although they perceived the previous situation as unfair, they did not threaten to act on it until a disaster demanded extraordinary contributions from all users. In the same example, the downstream users also perceived the system as unfair, but did not act on it at all.

Mechanisms Linking Fairness to Sustained Cooperation

Consider some of the most prominent mechanisms that affect how significant the fairness problem is to cooperation, what its contours are, and how groups solve it. The mechanism of self-realization and motivation wherein an individual comes to recognize and act on perceived unfairness independently can sometimes be enough to solve the fairness problem, but it typically is not. This is because the local power structures are just that: powerful enough to impose severe punishment or to declare that the individual irrigators be shunned from local society. Some sort of external assistance or connection to outside agencies may more easily prompt action in these cases, and thereby provide opportunities to address the fairness problem.

External agents can provide additional opportunities to discuss fairness after the rules for cooperating have already been agreed upon. Before the users have begun to cooperate with the rules of an institution, they cannot know for certain what outcomes will result or how these outcomes will be distributed. This is particularly so with manmade resources, which are unproductive until users have made contributions such as cleaning the channels. Next, these opportunities to discuss or reflect on fairness can be unpredictable, and they also are more likely to occur the longer one is committed to a cooperative system. There are situations that are more likely to provoke these assessments such as discussions and community meetings, but it would mischaracterize the nature of these assessments—that is, perceived fairness—to assume that such meetings necessarily provide an opportunity for them to do so, or to assume that individuals act on perceived unfairness alone. For instance, it is common that fear of those in the community who are more powerful will silence dissenters and discourage dissent. Nevertheless, as earlier examples of Maoist reeducation campaigns have illustrated, these opportunities can be effective. In the case of these irrigation systems, the key outside actors are government agencies or agents, political parties, Maoist cadres, and NGOs. Together with self-realization, the mechanisms associated with these external actors affect the nature and significance of the fairness problem. I discuss each in turn in the context of these irrigation systems to further illustrate the relationships captured by the figure.

Government Proximity and NGOs

The "closeness" of a group to government can have a significant effect on the fairness problem. By closeness, I mean the nature of the relationship between a group and government agents such as irrigation officials or agricultural extension agents, as well as government departments. NGOs tend to be like government agencies in this regard and are often confused with government agencies by farmers. Both NGOs and government agencies provide technical, financial, and "capacity building" assistance to these groups. They also typically have longer-term relationships with them, being selected more often for assistance or project participation by NGOs. I will highlight three varieties of mechanisms involving government agencies and NGOs here.

Consider the example of the MS canal, a roughly 10km-long canal in Eastern Nepal that I visited with an agricultural extension agent in July 2014. Here, the canal was in disrepair because of an ongoing dispute: last season, a subgroup of users had refused to contribute to cleaning the canal. Consequently, it wasn't carrying any water and was clearly clogged with silt and weeds. The dominant view of the impasse shared by both government agents and the wealthier, better-off farmers was that poorer farmers became lazy after the system was awarded a grant to help with physical repairs two seasons ago. The WUA had used the money to repair the headworks of the system, which had been damaged by a flood. The new headworks required more work to maintain than before, but it was worth it in their view, as it provided about the same amount of water as before but was less prone to damage from increasingly frequent floods. Having received "help for free," as one farmer characterized it, they refused to put in the hard work to keep the canal going.

The view of the farmers shirking from their responsibilities, as agreed to many years before when they decided to continue using the canal, was different. A group of them privately shared the view that for many years, they had felt that the system was benefitting wealthier groups much more. However, they felt that was "just how it was," and that there were no grounds to protest or retaliate; after all, they were free to stop using the wealthy-farmer dominated canal. They had come to accept this as their lot, just a consequence of the agreement they were part of and into which their ancestors had entered.

Their perception of existing inequalities, the farmers reported, had changed after the government provided a grant two seasons ago. After receiving assistance from the government, the system no longer "just belonged to the wealthier users"; it was "all of ours." With this shift in understanding that the system also belonged to them, the users felt more confident asserting that they would not cooperate unless their concerns had been addressed, something that wealthier users continued to refuse discussion of at their meetings. More importantly, their sense of fairness had also changed. The users came to the view that they were part of a larger, national contract that ensures certain uniform treatment in terms of rules and outcomes to all citizens, not just bound to a local contract for using the irrigation system. In this case, they believed that the system, now belonging to everyone, promised to not treat some so badly for this reason. They compared that promise with what the local arrangements were giving them, and they realized the existing arrangements were unfair. In terms of the schematic diagram above, this case illustrates how due to the influence of a government agency, the perception of fairness changed, and the significance of fairness also changed so that users changed their level of cooperation. The level of cooperation is typically indicated by the quality of work, open dissent, or the raising of issues at meetings. Here, refusing to work was intended as a form of dissent.

In this way, when a government agency or NGO gives a group assistance in the form of money or resources for the canal, it can cement the view that the resource belongs to everyone in the group. This alone can be enough to induce people who perceive the system as unfair to no longer tolerate it because they are convinced that it also "belongs" to them, having been supported by the government or an outside group. This type of closeness to government agencies can encourage those who perceive unfairness to withdraw their cooperation. Whereas previously they were resigned to the existing power of some users locally, when they feel closer to the government they may feel more assured of a countervailing power and are more confident speaking out or acting out their perception of unfairness, whereas previously they had refrained. At the same time, the closeness can kill hope: in some systems, users viewed the continued failure of the government to act on their complaints of unfairness in their systems as implicit sanction of the unfair arrangements.

There is some suggestive evidence across cases that proximity to government agencies can alter the significance and nature of the fairness problem. Table 22 and Table 23 show the systems divided into two groups based on reported proximity to government agencies. In one group (Table 22) are those in which users remember having received government assistance at some point, and

Table 22 **Systems that are close to government [with government assistance, second round]. Association between indicators of fairness and performance, of institutions with memorable outside assistance (N = 184). Out of 28 possible relationships, 10 (35.7%) are significant at the 5% level and 8 (28.6%) at the 1% level. The values of the fairness variables are either yes or no. The values of the performance variables are poor, fair, and good. P-values are from Fisher's exact test.**

Indicators of Perceived Fairness	Observed physical condition		User perceived functioning	
	Canal	Head	Reliability	Adequacy
Do some parts get less water than they want?	0.004**	0.634	0.001**	0.000***
Are rules about who can be a user well defined?	0.349	0.1	0.204	0.007**
Are there users who consistently get less water?	0.003**	0.289	0.025*	0.027*
Is the water gap getting bigger?	0.374	0.808	0.279	0.112
Do rules give some groups a preferred season?	0.272	0.81	0.806	0.358
Do the rules give some groups unequal duties?	0.005**	0.317	0.787	0.155
Are the rules perceived as legitimate?	0.16	0.497	0.008**	0.001**

Note: $^*p<0.05$, $^{**}p<0.01$, $^{***}p<0.001$

Table 23 **Systems that are not close to government [without government assistance, second round]. Association between indicators of fairness and performance, of institutions without memorable outside assistance (N = 41). Out of 28 possible relationships, 4 (14.3%) are significant at the 5% level and 1 (3.6%) at the 1% level. The values of the fairness variables are either yes or no. The values of the performance variables are poor, fair, and good. P-values are from Fisher's exact test.**

Indicators of Perceived Fairness	Observed physical condition		User perceived functioning	
	Canal	Head	Reliability	Adequacy
Do some parts get less water than they want?	1	0.87	0.139	0.06
Are rules about who can be a user well defined?	0.54	0.921	0.075	0.368
Are there users who consistently get less water?	0.785	0.218	0.226	0.049*
Is the water gap getting bigger?	0.21	0.167	0.008**	0.011*
Do rules give some groups a preferred season?	0.909	0.227	0.794	0.052
Do the rules give some groups unequal duties?	0.028*	0.307	0.156	0.209
Are the rules perceived as legitimate?	0.501	0.066	0.020*	0.172

Note: *p<0.05, **p<0.01, ***p<0.001

in the other (Table 23) are those in which they don't. Note that nearly all the cases in the sample had received some form of government or donor assistance around the time that they were first studied, so it is not possible to compare the two groups in the first round. If, decades later, users did not remember any assistance whether initial or subsequent, this was attributed to the intervention not being memorable enough for users and an indication of distance from government agencies. Among those which reported being closer, there are more frequent associations between indicators of perceived fairness and performance than among the group which reported being further away. This is consistent with the observation that the relationship to external agents likely has a connection to fairness.

Political Movements

The influence of the armed Maoist Political Movement and their "re-education" programs, among other activities, illustrate how individuals can be actively taught not only what fairness is, but also the purported root causes of unfairness. This is one of the ways that political movements can change a user's perception of fairness, as well as the causes that they infer are responsible for unfairness. Across cases[12], 43.9% (93) reported that this movement and the nationwide conflict that it generated had a negative effect on the functioning of their systems (Table 24). The overall numbers convey a sense of the extent of influence of the movement, but can be misleading in the context of the fairness problem. For instance, while the effects on the canal might be perceived as negative, the underlying reason for those negative effects might be that some perceive these systems as unfair and sided with the Maoists, as the Tallo Kulo example illustrated. Even something like receiving less government help was seen by some as a positive effect. It meant less travel to district headquarters and that the users' association was less likely to be targeted by Maoists for being an extension of the state. In fact, users of one system refused to accept available government support as an adaptation that allowed them to continue to function. Fear also might not have been so severe as to have a negative effect on the systems

About a quarter of systems reported that the conflict obstructed the functions of their organization. This included preventing communication, banning meetings, destroying nearby banks, preventing gathering in large groups

Table 24 **Effects of the Maoist Conflict. This table shows the user-reported effects of the Maoist conflict on the functioning of user-governed irrigation systems (N = 212).**

Primary Effect	*Not Negative*	*Negative*	*Total*
None	106 (50.0%)	0	106 (50.0%)
Fear	5 (2.4%)	18 (8.5%)	23 (10.9%)
Less government help	2 (1.0%)	18 (8.5%)	20 (9.5%)
More government help	6 (2.8%)	0	6 (2.8%)
Obstructed functions	0	53 (25.0%)	53 (25.0%)
People fled	0	4 (1.9%)	4 (1.9%)
Totals	119 (56.1%)	93 (43.9%)	212 (100%)

[12] N = 212. This number includes the 202 systems that survived from the original sample, and an additional 10 systems that were added to the second round from districts not included in the original sample.

to maintain the system, occupying the areas around the headworks, and threatening visitors (or worse), preventing the water guards from doing their duties, and intimidating people into either fleeing or not being willing to occupy leadership positions in the association. The effects of leader selection on the success of commons governance are well documented (Kosfeld and Rustagi, 2015). In those systems where the primary effect was that people fled, their main difficulty was that so many people left the command area that the users no longer had enough labor to maintain the canal. Every system experienced multiple effects, never just one, and Table 24 shows only the primary effect.

The general environment was one of fear, but about 11% were able to continue functioning normally or in a slightly modified way. The sources of fear went beyond the risk of being caught in the crossfire of police stations and army outposts being attacked or Maoist bases being raided. Members and officers could face violent punishment if they were accused of corruption. In one instance, the chairman of the association was jailed by the police for being a Maoist; in another, the chairman was kidnapped by the Maoists. In another instance, Maoists killed the elder brother of the chairman, who then fled with all the records of the association. In another instance, Maoists planted a bomb that successfully killed the chairman.

In-depth user interviews reveal the importance of recognizing that the obstructions were not always directly because of the Maoists, nor was the fear. It was often fear of the security forces that also obstructed the functioning of these systems. This changed the demographics of the villages. As one respondent put it, "During conflict all the youths and many landlords were outside (of the village) so only old people and women were there to work on the canal and in farming. People above the age of 60 used to gather and work on the canal to maintain it." It also altered the traditionally hierarchical nature of societies, as another put it, "(during the conflict) Even little children used to threaten elder people and everyone was compelled to follow their orders. This included members of our association." This put pressure on the canal maintenance institutions, and forced a change in meeting practices. A respondent noted that in their system, "before, the irrigation committee met at night so that we could work during the day. During the conflict it was impossible for users to meet at night. Even if there were a light on in someone's house, a search team of the Nepal Army would arrive for interrogation. Every canal maintenance task was done during the day only after informing security. It was difficult to inform security time and again for the meeting so there were much fewer meetings during conflict." Another noted, "It was difficult to meet. Even when users were gathered for a local's funeral or Diwali (a major Hindu holiday), the Army came to interrogate us about the gathering. Users needed to explain to the Army what every gathering was about. Another time, when we were gathered for a funeral, a helicopter search team came above in the sky. All the people were "freaked out" at that time."[13]

Cumulatively, this made it difficult for the systems to continue functioning and for officials to do their jobs although most respondents ended on a hopeful note now that the conflict was largely over. In this vein, the following type of observation was typical across systems: "It was really hard for the leaders of the canal to occupy their posts. They had to answer to the Maoists for everything they did or said. Many times, the Chairman of our WUA was kidnapped, taken to the jungle, and threatened. Government aid was stopped. It was not easy to meet then as it is now. Even with these problems, however, users managed the canal with their own local resources. And above all, our unity helped us fight against these difficulties."

As these accounts suggest, some user groups adapted and continued to function, albeit at a reduced level of performance. Among the responses, the typical adaptations were to coordinate irrigation activities and association meetings with the rebels or the security forces, as shown in Table 25 above. This table is based on a small number of responses—23 out of 202—but is still indicative of the strategies. This is an instance where an unwillingness to talk about the effects of the Maoist conflict, let alone adaptations to it, may have reduced the response rate. Nevertheless, among the responses, the most common approach was to secure prior permission from the security forces. Some strategies were also rarer and quite striking. One system handed out identification cards that the Maoists and security forces were informed about the number of and could recognize. These were given to laborers who were on duty that day, noting that they

Table 25 **Adaptations to conflict. This table shows the most common adaptations that systems affected by the Maoist conflict reported to be effective in allowing them to continue functioning at an adequate level to keep the canal functional.**

Adaptations	Number of systems (%)
Get permission from Maoists and security forces	6 (26.1%)
Get permission from Maoists only	3 (13.0%)
Get permission from security forces only	8 (34.8%)
Other	6 (26.1%)
Total	23 (100.0%)

[13] The precise Nepali phrase he used was "Sabai jana freak out bhayo"—literally, everyone had a freak out (panic).

were working on essential irrigation activities only and not on political activities. Some systems moved all activities to the daytime, others rejected any form of official government recognition or assistance, some functioned through uncoordinated individual initiatives, and others mobilized the retired population to help with maintenance. Yet others communicated by passing messages secretly when committee members' children met each other at essential gatherings like weekly milk collection events or at the local shop.

Not all users participated in these adaptations, nor did maintenance always refer to maintenance of the entire canal. In several instances, a part of the user group had joined the Maoists or supported them and were intentionally left out of canal activities if they did not voluntary stay away. Respondents explained that users who joined the Maoists were always well known to them and typically perceived the system as unfair, had some prior grievance that was not addressed by the system, were greedy for a more powerful position in society or the committee, or just wanted more water than they were given.

Political Parties and Associational Groups

Users of these systems are not only members of the irrigation users' group, but they also typically belong to other groups such as their extended families (or clans), caste or ethnic groups, religious groups, and most importantly political parties. They may also belong to other local groups such as a forest users' association. All these groups can impact both in-the-mind and external variables affecting the fairness problem. I will focus on political parties here because they are the most general across these cases and because some of the mechanisms have appeared in earlier examples.

Some of the effects of political parties are like those of government agencies and the Maoist army above. More specifically, these parties are typically national and not restricted to the irrigation command area because this tends to cross political jurisdictions. These parties can differ greatly in the norms of fairness that they espouse. For example, the Communist Party of Nepal (UML) adhered to a class-based moral basis, the Nepali Congress Party (NC) appeared to adhere to a more liberal set of principles, and the National Democratic Party (RPP) adhered to a strictly conservative monarchist set of principles. A difference between these political parties and the Maoist Army is that their roles are more directly contested such as during the elections of the Water User's Association officers. It was common for users to refer to their system as run by one party or another, even though the most immediate answer from WUA officials was that their system was apolitical.

This was illustrated by a case in mid-western Nepal, the BM canal. This was a canal whose command area had land owned by national political figures, three of whom had come to be prominent ministers from different political parties after the transition to a constitutional monarchy in 1990. Each of these parties and individuals had a local following. It was often the case that irrigation disputes between those deputed to work on their lands could not be resolved by the local water user's association. One dispute, pertaining to who would receive water first after a new headworks was built using funds received from an irrigation improvement grant from the Ministry of Agriculture, was especially intractable for the local users. The local users reported that it had been referred to the Supreme Court. Its ruling was considered binding by participants, and in this way judges had assessed the fairness of the proposed rules. It should be noted that the ruling had not been implemented, perhaps in the hope that the next round of elections would change the balance of power nationally to give a different result.

In this way, these political parties and associational groups provided external forums and mechanisms for resolving local disputes that incorporate distributional issues. Users who belong to one party or another can actively seek out the dispute resolution possibilities of national organizations or state agencies such as courts. Similarly, those who belong to religious groups could bring their disputes before local religious heads, thereby bypassing the water user's association altogether. After reaching a resolution, they could subsequently attempt to influence the association's actions to enact it.

Self-Realization

This refers to the process by which users come to act on perceived unfairness largely on their own. It is very hard to identify and requires an uncommon degree of social independence, and is likely to be an unusual mode of coming to act on perceived fairness in these cases. Nevertheless, I include a discussion here for the sake of completeness. Through individual reflection and experience, a user may come to perceive that the outcomes of their arrangement are unfair. They do this either through discussion or isolated reflection. The perceived unfairness that they recognize is the seed of the fairness problem. Through self-realization, users might also come to recognize that this perceived unfairness is significant to them and therefore should be acted upon. It might then prompt action, typically of two types. One, they may make a comment during a public meeting that this gap should be addressed somehow. Two, if they should further infer that the gap is primarily caused by the rules, then upon reflection that the realized outcomes are unfair, the users might try to change the rules by proposing new ones at a meeting. The changes the group adopts would be decided according to the rules for changing the rules. In these cases, it would be mentioned at the next meeting of the WUA, proposed to the group, and if enough people appear to support it, brought up for a vote either of all present members or the officeholding members, or considered by an elder, depending on the mechanism that is used to make decisions in these systems.

This mechanism of perceiving unfairness, assessing it, and then deciding to take formal action at a meeting is the most individualistic and constrained by existing rules. It is for that reason the most compatible with the collective action-based approach to understanding cooperation in which fairness, to the extent that it matters to the individual, is reflected in collective action problems themselves. That is, these newly self-realized individuals set new, fairness-related conditions for cooperating; in this case, the condition would be that the rules be changed in accordance with their suggestion. But the mechanism of self-realization is likely to have been influenced at some point by external factors discussed previously.

The Fairness Problem during Political Transition

The period following 2008 was one of transition away from conflict to a new federal structure, which complicated the fairness problem further. In particular, the political wing of the Maoists went from heading a political movement to leading a mainstream political party that was forming an elected government. The Maoist Army was being absorbed under the command of the Nepal Army, or members were retiring as part of the peace process. There was also disagreement within the party about the viability of abandoning armed struggle. This growing split within the Maoist party provides a chance to distinguish the effects of political movements and the effects of political parties on the fairness problem.

The DBA[14] canal in Dang is particularly instructive because the Maoists were very influential there during the conflict, but once they shifted to an electoral stance, their local influence also shifted. Recall that DBA canal users were "reeducated" through regular meetings that they were forced to attend. During these reeducation programs, which involved song and dance, theater, debate, and discussions, the Maoist cadre repeatedly explained to farmer attendees the oppressive nature of Nepal's feudal system of land ownership, the wide-ranging implications for village life, and continuing class-based structures of oppression.

At least some of the DBA farmers were convinced that the continued exclusion of downstream farmers from receiving adequate water was due to systematic oppression by the upper classes—in their case, those belonging to higher castes (Chhetri and Brahmin). During these events, a group of attendees also

---

[14] Name withheld for anonymity.

resolved that their irrigation system was unfairly managed. Backed by the Maoist Army contingent that had settled in the heavily forested and inaccessible area where the headworks was also located, this group organized to overthrow their Water User's Association violently and set up a parallel water governance system with a "People's Irrigation Government." At the same time, some of the other attendees did not agree with the class-based explanation, while yet others agreed that class was the cause but disagreed about whether it was significant enough to resort to violence.

This example, however, is not straightforward and illustrates some of the complexities of the fairness problem. Not only can different users have different perceptions of fairness, but their willingness to act can also be affected by the power of these external groups. This new group of farmer-rebels attempted to take over the canal government at the next User's Association meeting. They did not allow the meeting to proceed on threat of violence. Instead, attendees were told to come to a different venue for a "People's Meeting." While the attendees did attend this parallel meeting, the actions of the rebel-irrigators were occurring at an unfavorable time when the Maoist party itself had begun to project a more benign, nonviolent image in order to broaden its electoral appeal in the upcoming national general elections that, as the head of government, its party president had been tasked with conducting. This overthrow of a local water user's group was publicly disowned by the party locally and labeled as driven by a breakaway "radical" Maoist party faction that did not want the elections to succeed. Ultimately, as the Maoists within the irrigation group became weaker in general, they failed to take over, so the system reverted to its usual governance structure.

However, the story did not end there. A large flood that subsequently destroyed part of the headworks provided a new opportunity for dissatisfied farmers to act, some of whom had become even more dissatisfied after attending the Maoist programs. Those downstream, with this unfavorable perception of the fairness of the system, a persistent belief that the unfairness was significant, and emboldened to act on this perception, broke off their branch of the system and created an alternative channel with its own governance structure. They diverted part of the source further upstream to bypass formerly upstream users. By doing so, they also rejected hundreds of years of custom that stated that those who build their intake first have full rights of access, and that subsequent users cannot build an intake upstream. Their argument was that the old system was unfair, and they did not want to return to it. Indeed, some households went further to distance themselves from what they saw as the oppressive feudal system of their earlier irrigation system and converted to Christianity, thereby stepping outside of the control of a mercilessly rigid caste hierarchy altogether. This lower branch came to be known by some locally as "Jesus's canal" (*Yeshu ko kulo*).

As to why the remaining upstream Maoists did not break away from the old canal, one explained that they were following the party's new analysis that these systems should be changed from the inside, just as the national party was using the elections to change the country. They had, in the end, come to subscribe to the view that the local rules for irrigation governance might possibly be adequate to address its perceived unfairness, so their response was not to reduce cooperation, but to increase it and participate more vigorously in existing processes to retain control.

Three Forms of the Fairness Problem

Generalizing across cases, the fairness problem is of three general types, each requiring a different approach. This typology is based on how deeply the fairness problem manifests, whether as differences between users in the use of language, favored norms, or accepted morals. More complex fairness problems can be a combination of all three. Recall that I use the term rule to denote a language statement that is expressed as either ignoring, forbidding, permitting or requiring an action. Rules are typically written down and backed by punishment, although they might not be. Norms are unwritten but commonly known rules without formal punishment (although there might be other punishments such as shunning). Morals are irreducible beliefs about right and wrong. These terms and the types of fairness problems described below are stylized to illustrate their differences, when in practice they can be hard to easily classify with closer study of individual instances.

The first type of fairness problem arises at the level of language and is the most common. Here, the problem is that individuals in the group disagree about how the rules should be expressed in language, in the belief that the rules are responsible for divergent outcomes. This is a linguistic problem (Poteete and Ostrom, 2004) in which the main obstacle that a group faces is agreeing on the language of the rules. They do not disagree about the justification or intention of the rules. Every linguistic expression only imperfectly reflects the intention of the one formulating it. So, two people who have the same morals and share norms may express the same intention differently in language. The simplest version of this type of fairness problem arises when group members share common morals and norms. More complex forms can arise when those differ. This is also the version of the fairness problem that appears initially before individuals start to cooperate. There is a general commitment to fairness and to achieving joint outcomes, but this has to be spelled out precisely in words. To the extent that they are concerned about fairness before cooperating, users argue for the adoption of rules that they favor. When they already share norms and morals, any disagreement about which rules to adopt is a result of language choice. For example, a group that shares a norm of reciprocity—that help from others (such as some water for irrigation when it is scarce) should be reciprocated—may have members that differ with respect how they expect it to be reciprocated, whether in kind (an equivalent amount of water later) or not (as roughly equivalent labor contributions later). They'd have to come up with a rule acceptable to those holding either form of the norm of reciprocity.

The second type of fairness problem arises from disagreement about the norms of acceptable behavior. Recall that norms are rule-like shared beliefs without formal punishment. When members of the group differ with respect to significant norms such as norms of participation or reciprocity, this can create difficult obstacles to continued cooperation. The solution to this problem in these systems is typically the assimilation of a minority group into a majority one, or the domination of one group over another. Even though users subscribe to different norms, these norms might derive from the same moral principles of right and wrong. For instance, it is possible in the earlier example that a set of users did not share this norm of reciprocity. Instead, suppose they held that material repayment constituted an insult because it reduced their relationship to a material give and take (not an uncommon belief in some localities). But, they believed that it was wrong to ignore the goodwill of others. The two groups of users—those for whom reciprocity was or wasn't the appropriate form of recognition—may have to decide what response to altruism was acceptable to the group (whether some form of material repayment or something else). However, when the disagreement stems from different moral beliefs, the problem is a version of the next type.

The third type of fairness problem arises from different moral principles held by people in the group. The difference in moral principles is not a difference in norms, but rather in more basic beliefs about what is right and wrong, which may be irreconcilable. Moral principles underlie norms and rules, so if there is a difference in morals, this can give rise to multiple fairness problems of the other two types. When these ideas are incompatible, this problem can be exceptionally challenging. In these systems, some of these incompatibilities are reflected in different beliefs held by those adhering to Maoism, holding orthodox religious beliefs, professing loyalty to the state, or motivated by more abstract ideas of equality or hierarchy.

For example, recall the ND canal at the end of Chapter 4. The orthodox Hindu belief held by some users that it is not right for lower castes, outcasts, and menstruating women to touch the main irrigation system at certain locations or times is a moral position. This is at odds with the belief held by other users that it is not right for anyone to be excluded from using their share of canal water. This disagreement might initially appear to be about the rules. For instance, whether to adopt a rule that says that customary rules governing the locality take precedence over the rules of the system. It could also appear as a disagreement about norms, for instance that any woman who touches the water at certain points in her menstrual cycle should be shunned from other village activities. But the actual disagreement would be a moral one. Another illustration appeared in the case of Tallo Kulo, where the two positions that prior agreements are paramount and the one that everyone must be treated equally were irreconcilable. Analytically, identifying this type of fairness problem requires a different vocabulary that can distinguish between norms as rules without punishment from normative beliefs about what is irreducibly right and wrong (i.e., morals).

Fairness Problems Can Grow in Complexity

To see how the fairness problem can grow more complex the longer people cooperate, consider individuals first deciding to cooperate. In long-running systems such as these, it is unlikely that any of the current members were those who made the transition from an independent to an interdependent situation. The individuals who originally agreed to the rules are most often no longer available. However, considering further the transition to a cooperative state can help to understand the evolution of the fairness problem from one of incomplete information to a moral one.

When individuals who have not cooperated to use and maintain this shared resource first commit themselves to a set of institutions for governing it, they are all equal in at least one sense: nobody has any experience with the proposed institutional rules. That is, they do not know how abstract rules will be implemented in practice in their specific instance. Even if the rules were copied from other groups, which is common, it is still new to their context, including the specifics of the resource, the individual members, their constraints, and their groups' characteristics. Given the nature of the transition from free, relatively independent farmers to imposing constraints on themselves and their descendants, they face significant uncertainty. True, these constraints promise greater gain—in this case, consistent irrigated water—that can transform their livelihoods. It is partly because of the profound improvement in water availability that individuals are less likely to ask critical questions about proposed rules, as few would want to jeopardize it.

The literature argues that in these constrained circumstances, limitations force some individuals to behave as though they are weighing the expected costs and benefits of cooperation using a form of utilitarian reasoning. Two of these limitations are particularly relevant to the problem of remaining fair. First, it is difficult to predict the effects the rules will have on their own future livelihoods.

Second, it is difficult to know how different or similar cumulative outcomes might be between group members. These two constraints were exemplified by the example of Mr. Darai, for whom the cumulative effects of water and labor allocation rules agreed upon decades earlier had such disproportionate effects on the life prospects of his children that he stopped cooperating with the group. He could not have predicted with certainty that his children would eventually be forced to go abroad looking for low-skilled work. Thus, for those considering the fairness of cooperative arrangements prior to first cooperating, much more is known about the statement and promise of the rules than either how they will be instantiated or their results in the future. Individuals who care about fairness commit to cooperative institutions based to a large extent on their best guess. At the same time, it is likely that weaker users agree to whatever is proposed to them out of a fear that they will get nothing.

Even in this original, individualistic position, fairness is a criterion that some individuals use to assess the proposed rules for cooperation. It is common that rules for allocating water or labor are regarded as unfair, although other rules may be also. For instance, current users of the GB canal recalled that one of the most contentious issues in their irrigation system is the rule that when water is scarce, those downstream are permitted to receive a certain share of water first before those upstream. They recounted a story of an elderly, educated farmer insisting that this was essential for the system to survive and refusing to eat until his demand was met and this rule adopted. No one could identify who this had been or where his land was, as these had passed out of local memory, but the moral of the story had not. When this rule was proposed, they reported, nearly all of the upstream users—wealthier, better-educated and more politically powerful—had opposed it on the grounds that it gave too much water to those downstream in proportion to how much land they owned and therefore needed to irrigate. That is, these upstream users perceived the rule as unfair. Farmers reported that this rule is still in dispute and is sometimes not implemented, an inconsistency that downstream users perceive as unfair. The downstream users argue, among other things, that there is no basis for not enforcing the agreed-upon rules strictly. This is a flipping of the usual script in the sense that it is typically the wealthier farmers arguing that rules should be strictly enforced.

Thus, initial commitments to cooperate are likely to be made with a healthy dose of belief in the future. For instance, the belief that a better future is possible through cooperating is indispensable for initiating cooperation. In these cases, they must believe that having access to irrigated water will be better for them than not, and they must believe that the group can use and maintain such a system together. Overall, when they lack adequate certainty about the future, individuals are left to trust each other that they will not be treated unfairly. In this initial situation, the problem of remaining fair is entirely that of devising rules that enough people in the group believe will be fair and to which they are willing to commit. This is largely the first and second type of fairness problem. When the group already has shared dominant norms of fairness, this problem becomes easier and becomes a mere question of the phrasing of the actual rules and not their spirit—the first fairness problem.

So how do they overcome this initial fairness problem? In the absence of force, unfairness-averse individuals are more likely to agree to cooperate after they come to believe that the rules will not turn out to be unfair. In this initial stage, personal assurances, particularly from elders or highly regarded community members, appear to be effective according to respondents across cases. These assurances pertain to both individual promises to abide by the rules (e.g., "Everyone else will abide by the rules if you do") and by the results of the institutions (e.g., "You won't be disadvantaged"). Evidently, in this original pre-cooperation position, the main obstacle to cooperation is a belief that others will not do their part, despite their promises. This is the central concern of collective action problems and of collective action-based frameworks for understanding successful cooperation. A second obstacle, as I have argued, is a belief that the institutions will not treat them unfairly, despite assurances. This is the central concern of fairness problems.

For these reasons, in this initial stage of coming to an agreement, people's behavior and concerns are likely to be adequately captured by the idea of collective action problems. People care about fairness, but fairness remains an abstract idea subjugated to the goal of having a functional resource. The fairness problem, in contrast, is still present but in embryonic form. The focus before joint gains are realized is naturally whether these gains can be achieved. As a farmer vigorously reminded me, "First we have to get the water. Then we can talk about other things (like who gets how much)."[15] Fairness remains a precondition for commitment for at least some individuals, but this precondition does not have as much teeth as it tends to develop later, after individuals have been cooperating for some time and they learn about their arrangements.

With this baseline agreement in place, however it was reached, the basic problem of cooperation begins to metamorphose into the fairness problem over time. Unlike collective action problems that can become easier to solve and overcome by devising institutions to structure interactions, the fairness problem typically grows in importance and difficulty over time. At the point of initiating cooperation, the individual cooperators may care about fairness, but they likely have only a hunch about the continued fairness of the arrangement they are entering. After experiencing the uneven fruits of cooperation, they have much more to argue about regarding fairness.

[15] User Interview, February 15, 2013.

Solving the Fairness Problem

Given this structure, it seems that fairness problems can only be temporarily addressed instead of being solved once and for all. It is true that I have previously enumerated the conditions that are perceived as unfair in these systems, but even with this list, avoiding these conditions is not straightforward. In order to solve the fairness problem once and for all, a group of irrigators would have to know to a significant degree of accuracy not only what arrangements will lead to what outcomes, but also how fair they will perceive them to be and when this perception will come to matter to their and others' commitment. The fairness problem is dynamic precisely because of the dynamic nature of its constituent elements: the significance of fairness, the perception of fairness, cumulative outcomes, inferred causes, and so forth, so "solving" the fairness problem is an iterative, continual process of discussion, trial, and error. A more attainable goal than solving unfairness, it seems from these cases, is to avoid being seen as too unfair for too long.

Consider the three key hurdles to remaining fair once and for all. The first hurdle is defining fairness: we often recognize unfairness, but have a difficult time defining what fairness is. It is only with time that some develop a tacit understanding of what offers a greater possibility of unfair outcomes coupled with a finer sense of what outcomes are patently unfair. Next, an individual's perception of what is fair and what is not may change with time, exposure to other ideas, and experience. This makes it difficult to predict what we may come to perceive as more or less fair. Finally, the actual outcomes that arise from a set of rules that govern behavior are complex and depend on factors beyond the rules themselves, or on rules that originate outside the community. This also makes predictions as to what rules will lead to what outcomes fundamentally inaccurate. Even if these individual problems of perception and prediction are adequately addressed, it is still difficult to predict when the perception of unfairness might alter an individual's decision to continue cooperating. Indeed, the extent to which fairness matters to each individual may also vary with time, so the response to unfairness may vary. For instance, as the earlier examples suggest, if I am tolerant of a degree of unfairness now, I may become less accepting later due to factors outside of my own control.

The dynamic nature of fairness proves difficult to detect in snapshots as prior studies have tried to do, but it becomes apparent when examples of sustained cooperation over decades are examined empirically, as done here. As individuals continue to work together, collective action problems remain important, but perceived fairness comes to be a significant factor affecting sustained cooperation, if not the most significant factor. Naturally, some groups can continuously address dynamic fairness problems, while others cannot. In cases of persistent unfairness, individuals reduce their level of cooperation. They may not immediately leave or stop cooperating, but it will take much less to get them to do so. The fairness problem could be considered "solved" for the time being when this type of attrition is no longer a danger to the continued functioning of the resource.

Short of a final solution, it is perhaps more accurate to say that fairness problems have been addressed when the system isn't too unfair—that is, it has avoided patent unfairness for a time. Despite the complexities of the fairness problem, some groups can address it by matching rules to what they think will be perceived as fair in the future. They are "solved" in this way through assurances, and eventually rules. These attempts to address the fairness problem can appear as changes in particular rules, especially those pertaining to the allocation of water or responsibility for contributing to maintenance. These rules are adapted and crafted, but there are limits to how much experimentation with the rules these groups can engage in, as too much experimentation risks being seen as arbitrary application of rules. Overall, engaging in the process of trying to cooperate fairly requires trust, but also builds trust and shared experience between cooperators.

Finally, because of unfairness aversion, it is necessary that the group address a form of the fairness problem before they begin cooperating. So, all successfully cooperating groups have addressed at least this rudimentary fairness problem. The continued existence of these cases shows that even complex fairness problems can be "solved"—as in, people can continue to cooperate even despite fundamental disagreement. In other words, even when users hold irreconcilably different moral beliefs, it is possible for the system to accommodate them in such a way that the system is never perceived as too unfair by its users. They can "solve" the fairness problem by the credible avoidance or satisfactory addressing of patent unfairness for a time.

Some Implications of the Fairness Problem

This reorienting of our understanding of successful cooperation to place the fairness problem in the center along with collective action problems is a small but significant change. It provides another way to understand long-enduring institutions and instances of cooperation. One old view is that these rules and institutions arise because of the need to solve collective action problems, and the resolution of distributional effects is implicit in the maintenance and creation of the rules. This is the collective action view. A second popular view is that the rules arise from conflict between groups of people, and that the rules reflect the current balance of power between these groups (Knight, 1992). Hence, survival is not a question of fairness, but rather of dominance (of groups and norms alike). As I have shown, the fairness view sees these situations as neither entirely collective action problems nor entirely situations of dominance and conflict. The rules might initially have come into being with these two motivations in mind. For instance, irrigation systems constructed in Nepal before 1990 are likely to have rules that embed customary hierarchies of power and dominance. Newer systems are more likely to be the result of participatory decision-making (although still likely to be influenced by older hierarchies). The new view suggests that even in these systems, the most significant factor influencing sustained cooperation in interdependent situations over time is an attempt to be fair, which is a difficult problem.

An understanding of sustained cooperation that incorporates a more realistic role for perceived fairness begins with understanding the fairness problem. As we have seen, individuals in a commitment to use and maintain a shared resource are more likely to reduce their commitment to their system if they perceive it as unfair. Remaining fair—or, more precisely, avoiding the perception of unfairness—is a necessary condition for sustained cooperation. These fairness-oriented reasons that people give for reducing their commitment to existing cooperative systems are obscured by focusing on collective action problems alone. Regarding sustained cooperation as a challenge of solving or avoiding collective action problems is to see it through the eyes of one particular type of person who fears being a sucker, while ignoring other types such as those who are unfairness-averse. However, it is not enough to add and rearrange variables into this old view in order to capture the fairness problem. To incorporate an adequate meaning of fairness into a collective action-based framework requires a different philosophical foundation than what is commonly used. The Ostromian framework, a prominent and well-known example, illustrates these limits and possibilities of subsuming fairness into collective action problems and therefore cooperation. This is shown most starkly by the fact that it does not anticipate the emergence of the fairness problem over time, or its significance to sustained cooperation.

Although this book concerns fairness and cooperation, the principal argument presented here pertains to why people stop cooperating. The thesis of this book is that individuals reduce their cooperation when they perceive the outcomes of the rules to be unfair. This does not imply the inverse—that people cooperate only when outcomes are fair—but rather that full cooperation over time is only secured when individuals do not perceive the institutions as unfair. Over a long enough time, institutions perceived as unfair are likely to experience challenging circumstances that will lead to decline. It is a necessary condition of survival that they address the fairness problem.

The Limits of Existing Models

Overall, the fairness problem highlights ways in which existing models of sustained cooperation in the use and maintenance of shared resources are limiting and limited. It makes plain the extent to which they focus on a special case where fairness is folded into collective action. They consequently focus on one type of fairness problem, the linguistic one. They focus on external factors, while perceptions are in the mind. They also lead one to de-emphasize norm heterogeneity, focusing attention instead on the rules for choosing rules. The existing approaches conflate fairness and cooperation. Ultimately, they give an incomplete picture over time because of the exclusive focus on collective action problems.

As people are shown to be unfairness-averse, the current collective-action-centered frameworks appear systematically inadequate for explaining their behavior. This forces us to reconsider how we study cooperative behavior and understand the continuation or breakdown of social contracts. Community self-governance institutions may have the advantage that if users perceive it as unfair, and if there are opportunities or impetus to react to that perceived unfairness, then there will be pressure on users to make it fair or face decline. In this way, if the conditions are right, then the community-based institutions (a form of small-scale social contract) may be self-correcting, and over a long enough period of time, there would be a natural selection for fair arrangements. That is, if one were to wait long enough, the surviving institutions would all be perceived as fair, and one would end up with myriad examples of fair social contracts that could never have been designed by outsiders. From a practical standpoint, this idea is difficult to make concrete. For instance, how long will it take for this sort of equilibrium to be reached? And what types of internal or external factors will exert selection pressure? It is possible that an unfair arrangement can persist for decades, as these cases show. Thus, instantiating this idea of evolutionary equilibrium with respect to time is difficult. In practice, it is unknown what conditions some would have to endure while they wait for their feedback to lead to a self-correction in the system that leads it to be fairer to them and their descendants. For that time, those who are subject to it will experience sometimes oppressive unfairness and feel powerless to object to it. This is an excessive burden to place on typically already disadvantaged and powerless communities. For state institutions that claim popular legitimacy, it would be systematically unjust.

Understanding the role of fairness in local cooperation requires expanding beyond neoclassical assumptions. The main animating assumption of neoclassical models of cooperation is that people are averse to shirking and free-riding, and that this aversion is central to solving collective action problems. The fairness problem shifts emphasis to the assumption that human beings are also averse to unfairness, which leads to a greater emphasis on the idea that individuals calibrate their level of commitment to an institution based on how fair they perceive it to be. This level of commitment may not be apparent in terms of whether users cooperate with existing institutions, but over time it becomes clearer as lessening commitment affects the quality of users' contributions.

These shifts allow for a reinterpretation of the well-known and well-studied cases of irrigation canals that are woven throughout the book in terms of perceived fairness. The cumulative effect of these shifts is to elevate the fairness problem to the level of collective action problems in terms of their influence on the possibilities and limits of sustained cooperation. It also provides a different way to understand the rules that such groups devise. Instead of seeing them as attempts to avoid collective action problems, they come to be seen also as attempts to grapple with the fairness problem. This helps to understand variations in fairness across cases of sustained cooperation over time. It also helps to explain regularities in the empirical findings that cannot be explained using the old understanding alone. Overall, the conditions that enable groups to solve collective action problems is joined by conditions that enable them to treat the fairness problem as worthy of study.

Thus, recognizing that perceived fairness eventually emerges as a problem between individuals working together over long periods of time has practical and theoretical implications. Conceptually, the challenges of solving the fairness problem come to shape cooperative local institutions alongside well-known collective action problems. This reorients how instances of successful cooperation are understood, starting with the unfairness aversion of individuals. At the same time, emphasizing the distinction between fairness and cooperation makes it easier to recognize that some instances of cooperation are perceived as fairer than others. The perceived fairness of these arrangements is a significant quality that affects the robustness of these institutions to change. In addition to facilitating an examination of instances of cooperation from the perspective of fairness, it encourages a further question about the conditions under which some cooperative arrangements are fairer than others.

Reconsidering Local Capacity to Self-Govern Fairly

That groups of locals may not be able to remain fair on their own has implications for how they are allowed to govern. This moves us away from assuming that locals are more likely than not to have the capacity to remain fair. These local arrangements are strongly shaped by power and history. The reach of custom on these systems is constrained to an extent by the fact that certain things are necessary for the system to be maintained. However, there can be many ways to distribute the responsibilities to and benefits of a functioning system. Locals may have the finest-grained ability to choose which one, but they are also prone to choosing unfair ones and then, over time, not being able to update these rules to escape their historical choices. They are prone to allow existing norms to play a central role, norms that may or may not have reasons other than age in their favor. This raises important questions about the extent to which local governance arrangements should be encouraged, or even permitted, to be in harmony with locally dominant customs and norms (Baland and Platteau, 1996).

The fairness problem raises significant questions of policy, particularly for those governments that have wholeheartedly embraced the idea of local self-governance of resources. The rationale that locals can effectively govern local resources leads to the further assumption that existing arrangements for doing so should be both acknowledged and officially recognized. Yet, if only some local groups can govern fairly, then state institutions concerned with fairness should exercise caution about being indifferent to how fair these arrangements are. The risk of state indifference to the fairness problem is inevitable if the idea persists that the very existence of these arrangements is a testament to their fairness.

Achieving short-term sustainability may not depend on being fair, but longer-term sustainability is a consequence. Even without this connection to sustainability, however, a policy of automatic official recognition of arrangements that even those subject to them perceive as unfair requires deliberation and justification. This does not imply that the state or its agents can solve complex collective action and fairness problems, nor does it settle the debate about what combination of local and nonlocal governance can best achieve this, but the fairness problem shifts the debate to explicit discussions of fairness irrespective of mode of governance. Considering the argument made here, it becomes important to examine the fairness of longstanding local institutions for the sake of both sustainability of the shared resources and justice itself. These findings also have implications for the local governance of traditional resources, particularly their maintenance, because it is in the performance of mundane day-to-day tasks of maintenance that perceptions of unfairness are likely to manifest in the form of neglect or lack of motivation.

For development planning, these findings suggest re-examining the role of the state in successful local resource governance. They also suggest prioritizing questions about whether local arrangements are capable of remaining fair. Recognizing the ability of these groups to solve collective action problems has re-balanced the focus of policy towards community governance or involvement from a previous focus on centralized state institutions. Policy based on this recognition has correspondingly reduced the role of the state and outside agencies.

Recognizing the fairness problem suggests a different emphasis, drawing attention to the question of whether there should be a greater role for these outsiders in matters of fairness. After all, communities alone may not be capable of remaining fair, although they can learn to cooperate on their own. Yet, we know far more about the conditions under which they can do the latter than the former. This suggests an agenda for future research that examines what locals can and cannot do with regards to avoiding patent unfairness. In light of the fairness problem, it becomes imperative to ask about the conditions under which "communities" should be permitted to govern their shared resources themselves. Considering the significance of the fairness problem, any answer would be wise to include the condition that they do so fairly.

It must be admitted that widespread local self-governance of shared resources has a good chance of resulting in a diversity of institutional rules for governing these resources fairly. This type of devolution is more likely to avoid the "pitfalls" of institutional monocropping that some have warned against (Evans, 2004). These locally crafted arrangements may even have a higher chance of survival and of reducing overt conflict in resource governance. However, there is a difference between order and fairness. Relying on community groups to deliver fairness likely implies upholding locally dominant ideas of fairness. There is much truth to the idea that locals would know best what fairness means to them, and that they would be highly motivated to devise their institutions accordingly. Yet there is likely to be a diversity of ideas about fairness in a given locality. In light of this diversity, the argument that locals know best leads to the assumption that the currently dominant local norms of fairness are dominant for good, even natural reasons. It follows that an argument that favors local self-governance for shared resources is naively hopeful that fairness and justice will arise as a matter of course through iteration. More attention must be directed to how these disagreements about how fundamentally irreconcilable moral positions are locally accommodated or addressed. This has implications for what the nature of state involvement in local resource governance arrangements should be.

In regions with histories in which some groups have dominated and exploited others, local customs might simply be dominant as the result of prior inequities and not the justice-oriented natural selection that advocates hope for. As Regmi (1976) explains, in the context of different types of customary land tenure in Nepal,

> Fiscal and tenurial concessions granted to cultivators of Jagera, Guthi, Jagir, and Kipat lands led to the emergence of Rakam tenure. Although Raikar was a reflection of the unlimited prerogative of an absolute government which identified landownership with sovereignty, its secondary forms were basically a response to the need to adapt the land system to different economic, political, social, religious, and administrative requirements. The Birta system thus helped to create a

feudalistic class that gave social and political support to the rulers; the Guthi system contributed to the satisfaction of religious propensities of both the rulers and the common people; and the Jagir and Rakam systems enabled the government to support an administrative structure without the use of much cash in a situation where an exchange economy had not yet fully developed. (p. 20)

Assuming customary norms are dominant because they are fair would be mistaken. As in many of the cases presented here, locally dominant ideas of fairness are just as likely to harbor stubborn ideas of racial superiority, ethnic originalism, religious dogma, and raw exploitation of the weak as to be the bulwarks of social change. In instances where local ideas of fairness demand unquestioning deference to customs, recognizing the right of locals to self-govern resources might perpetuate unfairness rather than curtail it. Here, the tendency towards granting greater local authority has a significant chance of legitimizing, in that locality and possibly beyond, the precise structures of oppression, exclusion, and discrimination that modern states claim to oppose. Analyzing whether and how these localities address the fairness problem is one systematic way to assess whether they can remain fair.

So, what sorts of relationships with government agencies can improve the chances that these arrangements will remain fair and performant? The intention of this question is not to reiterate the well-worn argument that the state should just enable users to do it themselves and no more. That makes too many narrow assumptions about the incapacities of state planners, the corruption of public agents, the ineffectiveness of state planning, the perverse nature of government intervention, and the predatory intentions of the state. The argument presented so far suggests that the question is more open than that. We know little about when locals can remain fair themselves. We know even less about the costs of their iterative approach that are borne by the already disadvantaged. So, the difficulty of addressing the fairness problem for local groups provides a stronger reason for continued government involvement. Most immediately, it suggests a reconsideration of unconditional "handover" policies in the case of irrigation systems.

Within the literature on commons governance institutions, recent work has called for recognizing the existence of a continuum of governance arrangements beyond the traditional three categories of Farmer, State and Joint management (Frey, Villamayor-Tomas, and Theesfeld, 2016). Indeed, of the 233 systems in the original data set, none are still managed purely by the farmers alone without any outside involvement. The broader decentralization literature also highlights a multitude of other factors and mechanisms that can impact the effectiveness of state institutions and agents (Mookherjee, 2015). It is beyond this text to summarize this literature, but some relevant examples follow. At the level of state institutions, the views of international donor agencies about the source of "failures" can direct states to favor some types of involvement over others (Mansuri and Rao, 2012); the quality of trust (or a "culture of distrust") between the state and local resource users can circumscribe the range of possible relationships (Baland and Platteau, 1996); users who own more land may have significantly more power over local governance decisions than others and therefore prove to be particularly effective interlocutors for state agents (Banerjee et al., 2001); existing clientelist relationships can shape state roles or be leveraged to alter local relationships (Bardhan and Mookherjee, 2020); and the size of the resource may demand greater state involvement at the outset (Somanathan, 2020).[16] At the level of the individual government agents, the level of discretion may shape their ground level interactions with locals (Lipsky, 2010); their training may critically shape agent–user relationships (Uphoff, 1992); and myriad local dynamics might render the precise nature of effective state involvement unique to local conditions (Tendler, 1997). Indeed, state agents—such as irrigation engineers or agricultural extension agents—might be the key to evoking local cooperation in some instances (Coman, 1911) through a range of interpersonal strategies and facilitation practices that can help to maintain the perception that the arrangements are—and continue to be—fair (Forester, 1999).

It is hopefully much clearer now that devolution of governing authority to local resource user groups should be far from unconditional. Indeed, if avoidance of patent fairness is a goal—whether for the sake sustainability or with the aim of treating all citizens fairly, or both—it might demand far greater oversight than currently imagined. Furthermore, it may be necessary for the nature and duration of state involvement to be conditional on the quality and persistence of perceived unfairness. Yet, it is also not clear what forms this involvement should take.

---

[16] It is worth noting here that perceived fairness may be a contributor to continued trust in governance institutions. I thank an anonymous reviewer for suggesting this.

Beyond Irrigation Systems and Physical Infrastructure

Retracing the Road to the Fairness Problem

The road from cooperation to fairness passed several milestones that offer clues for the road ahead. It started with the discovery that existing approaches are incomplete. Most predicted variables did not correspond to decline over time in paradigmatic cases. Next came the finding that individuals stopped cooperating for reasons of fairness. This was usefully captured by the seven common reasons for stopping cooperation in these cases of irrigation systems in Nepal. Third was the recognition that these reasons embodied different norms of fairness—norms that might not be compatible. Having made it that far, this road led further to the formulation of the fairness problem as one of remaining fair. The central point of the empirical investigation is that perceptions of fairness are dynamic, multidimensional and necessary for continued cooperation. Looking back at cooperation from the perspective of the fairness problem, it is now clear that perceived fairness is a key to better understanding how cooperation can be sustained. This key shift in perspective improved our understanding of why some irrigation systems continued while others declined, even though all of them exhibited the prerequisites for solving collective action problems. I have indicated in places at how this new perspective has implications beyond the example of irrigation systems in Nepal. In this chapter, I pull together the findings and implications to suggest how they apply to an understanding of cooperation over time in a more general sense.

In what follows, I trace some of the implications, limits, and possibilities of generalizing this fairness-centered understanding of sustained cooperation to settings beyond irrigation systems in Nepal. I begin by emphasizing the core insight of this book: cooperation and fairness are not the same thing. I then restate the key claim that perceived fairness affects the quality of cooperation, which

Beyond Collective Action Problems. Atul Pokharel, Oxford University Press. © Oxford University Press 2024.
DOI: 10.1093/oso/9780197755792.003.0006

then renders the institutions of cooperation receptive to changes. I recount how perceived fairness is a key to understanding better why some cooperative systems continue while others decline, even though all of them might exhibit the institutional prerequisites for solving collective action problems. I show how this approach can help assess the role of cooperation in the use and maintenance of shared resources. I explore what a fairness-centered understanding of cooperation means for our understanding of user-governed infrastructure as well as for future studies. I end by sketching some ways in which the search for fairness must be central to our understanding of sustained cooperation in physical and digital spaces.

Identifying the Fairness Problem

In one form or another, the fairness problem underlies successful cooperation over time. Furthermore, understanding the possibilities of sustaining cooperation requires seeing through cooperation to the fairness problems underlying it. This is a methodological insight as well as an analytical one, suggesting that a fairness-centered analytical framework is more appropriate for studying cooperation over time, where a collective action-centered framework might be more appropriate initially. Similarly, at this stage of the literature, empirical data most helpful for circumscribing fairness problems is more likely to arise from interviews or ethnographic work than from coded data. These problems can be easily missed if they are not explicitly and painstakingly reconstructed. Grasping the contours of this problem often requires interviewing the individual cooperators. For example, as done here, interviewing individuals about why they reduced their cooperation can be particularly effective for this purpose but need not be the only approach. Eventually, such interviews will lead to a finite set of dimensions along which perceptions of fairness can be characterized. They will also help to reveal the factors affecting their perceptions, impacting how significant they regard fairness to be and influencing how likely they are to act on perceived unfairness.

The fairness problem is likely to look different across cooperative systems and even within them at different times. This makes it even more important to understand the dynamics of individual cases. Among well-maintained systems of the same type—irrigation systems in these cases—some are perceived as fairer than others, and even the same system can be perceived as more or less fair at different times. A further reason for probing perceptions over time in addition to making measurements of parameters such as income is that the perception of fairness is not just indicated by an objective measurement of inequality in the distribution of resource gains (or contribution requirements). It is indicated also by how users perceive various types of inequalities that emerge in any cooperative arrangement over time. There might be seemingly excessive inequality in the distribution of water, for instance, but it might still be perceived as fair because it is considered proportional to the amount of land that each farmer seeks to irrigate.

Finally, the perception of unfairness might not affect cooperation at all in normal circumstances, making it very difficult to identify unfair systems passively. This is because the effect of perceived unfairness depends on how significant the individuals regard fairness to be as well as other factors that affect whether they act on it. Identifying unfair systems demands familiarity with the common reasons for unfairness in particular settings, as well as the specific perceptions of individual cooperators. It pulls the observer much further into the minds of respondents than current approaches suggest is necessary.

The fairness approach stands in contrast to a well-fortified edifice of research built over the last five decades on the assumptions that human reasoning shares a basic mathematical logic, and that we need only identify the variables that go into the algorithm to understand behavior. The fairness problem goes further and asks for understanding the dynamic evolution of the fairness logic expressed in some of these reasons over time, including the variables and their relationships. Getting deeper into the minds of others like farmers in developing countries seems like a fraught task. As a compromise, some have argued that it is better to assume a basic, universal rationality shared by all humans including farmers and analysts in order to avoid looking down on them (Boix, Stokes, and Bates, 2009). From the perspective of fairness, this move needs to go further. It is necessary to assume that unfairness aversion is shared by all to varying extents, in addition to a drive to do the best one can materially in a given situation. The fairness problem is critical for sustainability of user-managed resources in a rapidly changing world. Not attempting to empathize with individual cooperators to the extent that their perceptions of the fairness of their systems become legible is to risk conflating fairness and cooperation.

Fairness Is Important to but Different from Cooperation

It is easy to conflate cooperation and fairness in social phenomena. As I have shown, fairness and cooperation are intimately related but distinct. The fact that a group is exhibiting cooperative behavior such as maintaining their infrastructure or participating in public meetings does not mean that the cooperative system is perceived by enough of them as fair; nor can a system that is perceived as unfair by some users be relied on to automatically decline. These processes of decline unfold unevenly and unpredictably over time. I have argued that one can reliably assume that people behave as though they are unfairness-averse, but that acting on their aversion is affected by other factors. They might not complain out of fear of retaliation, or they might not attach much significance to their perceptions. They may believe instead that it is unfair but acceptable, for instance, because of their race's inferior social standing or in deference to customary gender roles. "This is how the world is,"[1] was not an uncommon refrain from interviewees.

An aversion to unfairness is the cause of the fairness problem, but there are many factors exacerbating or mitigating this problem as well. For instance, with increasing movement of people due to climate change, groups of cooperators are more likely to encounter members who adhere to different and possibly incompatible beliefs. Some of these differences may concern the meanings or relevance of the existing rules, while others may concern how to apply general rules to specific settings, and yet others may concern basic disagreements about right and wrong. Elaborating upon the commonly studied norms of behavior in these settings such as self-interest, reciprocity, and conditional cooperation can capture some of these problems. For instance, the process of adapting existing rules might be fruitfully studied as strategic interactions between self-interested coalitions of users culminating in a majority vote (Gardner, Walker, and Ostrom, 1994). However, as I have shown, significant disagreements about what is right and wrong more basic than these norms of behavior do exist. They can pose existential threats to the use and maintenance of user-governed infrastructure. Even for this reason alone and leaving aside the other less fundamental but still critical types of fairness problems, perceptions of fairness would be important to probe separately from the fact of cooperation.

Cooperation usually refers to a pattern of behavior and fairness to the quality of the results of that cooperation, or to the rules and processes used to facilitate it. Yet, in the context of social phenomena, it is often assumed that where there is cooperation, there is also fairness. Emphasizing their distinction can raise uncomfortable questions about the relationship between them. For instance, what is the relationship between fairness and cooperation? Are the conditions that foster cooperation adequate to encourage fairness? I have attempted to answer the first question here, and I hope this has opened the door to future work that can improve our understanding of the second one.

For the governance of shared resources, the distinction between fairness and cooperation implies that there can be unfair cooperation, as these irrigation systems have shown. Furthermore, institutions designed to encourage cooperative behavior could be effective at evoking cooperative behavior but also conserve

---

[1] The word used is *duniya*.

unfairness. This possibility is particularly relevant to those seeking social justice and sustainability through alternative cooperative arrangements and community governance. It bears repeating that even though unfair cooperation is less likely to persist over time than fair cooperation, there can be cooperation without fairness for prolonged periods of time. To avoid conflating the two requires looking beyond how groups can solve complex collective action problems to how they can cooperate in addressing fairness problems.

Fairness Elevates Existing Work on Collective Action

It might be feared that gazing beyond collective action problems diminishes the work done to date on cooperation and user self-governance by scholars such as Ostrom and many others. It is true that seen in the context of time, the current collective action-focused frameworks appear to be concerned with explaining a special case of cooperation—that is, one in which there is either a dominant set of norms or a set of norms that all group cooperators share. However, as I have illustrated, within these cases that have already been identified and thoroughly studied from the perspective of collective action are a smaller set of even more significant cases. These are cases in which the cooperators have figured out how to remain fair. All the cases that were previously analyzed as having successfully solved collective action problems would have also struggled with the fairness problem in one form or another. They would have done so in addition to the usual problems of finding the right rules and enabling a credible commitment to be made. Thus, some appear to have ways to address the fairness problem as well. They deserve further investigation using a fairness-based framework because they meet the prerequisites of a fairness-based analysis: that users have solved collective action problems and are already cooperating to achieve joint gains. The fairness-based approach developed here highlights how essential the large body of existing work is for understanding sustained cooperation.

What comes first in the use and maintenance of shared resources, fairness or cooperation? Putting together the pieces laid out so far, the answer is that it could be either. To see how, consider a group of people cooperating for the first time to use and maintain a shared resource. There are myriad problems they may need to solve in order to convince all to regulate their short-term behavior for long-term gains, and to overcome any hesitation about making contributions of labor and other resources now in the hope of achieving joint gains later. The fairness of the rules that are eventually proposed typically matters to whether individuals willingly agree to them, and therefore to whether they cooperate.

However, this seeming precedence of fairness is complicated by time. It is possible that some users perceive the rules as unfair but agree to them anyway. For them, cooperation comes first. For others who don't perceive the rules as unfair and therefore decide to cooperate, fairness seems to come first. Later, due to factors outside of their control, they might come to perceive the system as unfair, so at that time, it might appear that cooperation came first and fairness second.

The explanation presented here does not depart from the currently popular framework for analyzing these cases except in two minor ways. The first is to emphasize the centrality of fairness at the level of the individual. The second is to emphasize how the problem of remaining fair can be challenging and possibly intractable. While similar to the problems of collective action, the problem of fairness has a history of being difficult to grasp using a set of standard tools. These two modifications are made in the hope of updating a very useful framework to help with this. Thus, I have attempted to make the smallest and fewest modifications possible in order to enable this framework to explain the new data, so this work should be seen as complementing existing work rather than confronting or contradicting it. While it expands the usefulness of our current understanding, it also allows everything that currently uses the old version to continue to do so as long as it is explicitly stated.[2]

As the fairness-based analysis in this book shows, long-term sustainability is ultimately a consequence of remaining fair. Thus, solving collective action problems is not sufficient by itself for long-term sustainability, although it is necessary to do so. If a group does not address the fairness problem but does address collective action problems, it is less likely to continue to work together to achieve joint gains than if it did both. However, it is not clear that the same factors simultaneously improve the chances of doing both. There is likely to be overlap between these two problems, particularly in the initial period of cooperation, and over time the factors affecting these two types of problems are more likely to diverge. They will eventually appear as different challenges.

Fairness Problems Are Not Another Type of Collective Action Problem

It is important to reiterate that fairness problems are different from collective action problems. There are two common ways to define collective action problems.

---

[2] In software terms, this modification does not break user space.

In the most general sense, these are issues in terms of groups working together or collectively to achieve a joint outcome. There is also a more specific definition that is overwhelmingly used in the foundational literature on commons governance. This is that collective action problems are challenges that arise because humans fear "being a sucker" (Ostrom, 1990, p. 44). This is a feeling that one has been cheated or deceived—for example, if one commits to everybody taking less water than they could only to have someone take as much as they can. There are other problems in cooperation that do not arise from fear of being deceived, and humans have other tendencies as well. Fairness problems and unfairness aversion are cases in point. To see beyond collective action problems to fairness problems, it can help to distinguish the underlying fear of being a sucker from the equally basic aversion to unfairness or to being committed to unfair situations.

It is true that "being a sucker" could describe one who remains committed to a system of cooperation that is unfair to them, but that would lead to more confusion than clarity. In the literature, the phrase is already closely associated with the fear that others may not do their part in the collective endeavor even after committing to do so. This fear is understood to cause two immediate complications. First, it may prevent potential cooperators from cooperating, and second, it may lead cooperators to stop cooperating if someone is found to have cheated by free-riding, shirking, or otherwise acting opportunistically. All other collective action problems derive from these two root problems. Collective action problems are understood to stand in the way of achieving joint gains, ultimately, because of these two problems as well. One of the problems arises from a particular fear and the other from how one is expected to respond to the fear.[3] Thus, collective action problems can be mitigated in two corresponding ways. One way is to devise institutions to punish, monitor, and enable credible commitments.[4] A second way is to address the deep-rooted fear of "being a sucker" that cooperators are assumed to possess. That is, if noncheaters don't care so much whether others do their part, collective action

[3] The term "social dilemmas" is also used (Ostrom, 1990; Gardner, Walker, and Ostrom, 1994; Kollock, 1998). These are dilemmas that arise in social situations because of the combination of the particular situation and the characteristics of the people in the situation. The main reason they are difficult is partly because of "shirking, free riding and otherwise acting opportunistically" (Williamson, 2000) and also partly because of the way that others respond to those behaviors. There are two universal tendencies that are assumed to drive this process: first is the tendency to free ride, and next the tendency to react negatively to it. The cascade of retribution that leads to decline consists of action by one and reaction by others and then reaction again over and over.

[4] This solution is the focus of nearly all the literature.

problems become far less potent.[5] Unfairness aversion doesn't have the same implications or meanings.

Ultimately, fairness problems don't derive from a fear that others may not meet their commitments. As I have elaborated, they grow from an aversion to being committed to a situation that they perceive as unfair. Fairness problems typically don't stand in the way of achieving initial joint gains either. They come to matter later as the results of cooperation become apparent and affect later gains. This implies that fairness problems persist even after joint gains have been repeatedly achieved. That is, the fairness problem becomes prominent after people have already adequately addressed the fear of being deceived that stands in the way of initial cooperation. If the group had not overcome the fear that others would not do their part, they would likely not have achieved the joint gains from the shared resource in the first place, as they probably wouldn't have been able to act collectively to do so. It is only because they have solved collective action problems that they are able to work together, achieve joint gains, distribute them, see the differential outcomes across members in the group, and develop perceptions of fairness, and so it is only after they work together that fairness problems evolve into significant challenges. It is thus easier to look beyond collective action problems in cases where people have already successfully cooperated for some time.

How to Look beyond Collective Action Problems

To see past collective action problems in the context of cooperation, it is perhaps easiest to start from some key assumptions shared by a collective action-focused analysis of cooperation. With the assumptions clearly distinguished, the implications are easier to recognize. As I have discussed, one of the most significant assumptions is that the fear of being cheated is the dominant concern in cooperative situations. In a collective action-based analysis, this leads to the expectation that people occasionally free-riding by using more than they should, shirking by not contributing labor, or even acting opportunistically by stealing water at night can threaten the entire cooperative arrangement. This is because others are assumed to care primarily about not being cheated in this way. The key aspect of this assumption is not just that the feeling of being cheated is universal, and the aversion to it is universal, but also that these tendencies dominate human reason in cooperative settings.

---

[5] This is not as hypothetical a possibility as it seems. Benkler (2014), for instance, has observed that free and open-source software contributors care far less about shirking or free-riding by other contributors.

A collective action-based analysis is typically characterized by a focus on reducing opportunism and free-riding, and a consequent focus on the clarity of rules, the monitoring of behavior, and the qualities of punishment. The sanctity of the rules, the strictness of rule-following, and the undesirability of rule-breaking all take on great significance. The inherent ambiguity of rules, the wiggle room afforded by interpretation and discretionary enforcement, and the possible benefits (such as the expression of dissent) of rule-breaking become correspondingly less significant. In terms of fairness, the focus on rules largely limits one to recognizing procedural fairness to the detriment of outcome fairness. As noted earlier in the chapter, a way around this is to begin from other tendencies that human beings exhibit such as unfairness aversion.

The second assumption made in a collective action-based analysis that when recognized helps to see beyond collective action problems is that people are roughly robots with certain programmed behaviors (outputs). This implies that for the purposes of understanding obstacles to cooperation, there is no need to talk to users to understand their reasoning process, but rather to understand how they perceive costs and benefits (inputs). Once the inputs have been specified, the resulting behaviors are assumed to be automatic. It is perhaps obvious that this assumption narrows the focus of research to identifying the factors that alter the inputs—expected costs and benefits—for each individual.[6] So going beyond this level of investigation and interviewing individuals can help to see beyond this assumption and its implications.

One alternative to assuming that humans reason in this particular robot-like way is to recognize that they may have a variety of reasons for behaving as they do, some of which cannot be reduced to costs and benefits. For example, I have shown how irrigators' reasons for reducing their commitment to a cooperative arrangement might not be related to their reasons for having started to cooperate. That is, the reasons for behaving in a particular way or not may possess a certain asymmetry over time. Admitting an irreducible diversity of reason makes things more complex for the analyst, however. It directs the researcher to speak to individuals and to employ interview methods more widely to understand the reasons driving the behavior. Furthermore, it deprives the researcher of a convenient way to reduce human reason to a single unit of measurement (whether utility or something else). It takes the researcher back into the minds of the individuals and demands a far deeper and necessarily more subjective judgment of respondents' human condition.

---

[6] In this regard, there is little reason to believe that a fresh investigation using the same approach would lead to a different catalog of variables than what Ostrom's work has already meticulously documented.

Many of the factors that the collective action approach identifies as affecting the quality of cooperation derive directly from what behavioral tendencies individuals are assumed to exhibit. Thus, the starting assumptions about (1) what tendencies dominate the behavior of members of these cooperative arrangements and (2) what proportion of the group has what tendency can determine the eventual analysis of their cooperative system. It is already well established that individuals may be self-interested, greedy, or even other-regarding and reciprocating. To add to this list, I have added unfairness aversion. That is, they try to avoid or get out of situations that are perceived as unfair.

Understanding both the variety of behavioral tendencies and the varied interactions of diverse group members is one of the avenues suggested by existing scholarship for moving beyond limitations of collective action-based analyses. Reasserting a long-held understanding in the literature, Poteete et al. (2010, p. 177) noted that "people do not always behave like selfish rational actors." They observe that there are at least three types of "strategies" that participants tend to pursue in these settings. Based on these tendencies, there are three types of people: selfish rational, altruistic, and conditionally cooperative. Early work suggests that the presence of any selfishly rational person will tend to devolve the system into a downward spiral toward a situation in which collective action problems dominate (Poteete, Janssen, and Ostrom, 2010, p. 153). This lends some support to a focus on getting the rules right. However, rules made to deal with the vagaries of selfishly rational people can be detrimental to the altruistic tendencies of others subject to the rules. In particular, policies that are designed for self-interested citizens may undermine the "moral sentiments of others" (Bowles, 2008). The right rules in a given situation depends on the mix of behavioral tendencies present in the group.

Thus, looking beyond collective action problems is not difficult, but it is not clear that fairness problems will automatically become visible once that is done. In the main, whether or not individuals perceive these systems to be fair will only become clear over time, and that too in a dynamic way. This renders the fairness problem a particularly difficult factor affecting cooperative commitments because it can be challenging, if not impossible, to predict and therefore anticipate. It is an important qualification that the significance of the fairness problem depends strongly on how many people are unfairness-averse and how influential they are. I have argued that almost everyone is unfairness-averse because we all possess a sense of fairness that, like a sense of beauty, is variously developed. The evidence also appears consistent with this claim, at least in the case of irrigation systems in Nepal. The dominance of unfairness aversion cannot be taken for granted in all situations, however, as the growing body of evidence that people are of different normative "types" suggests.

This section clarifies how collective action problems derive from focusing on a particular type of person in these groups. When this focus changes to other types of people, the problems that one expects these groups to face and struggle with also necessarily change—that is, if these people are significantly different, as I have argued here. To briefly summarize the reasons presented so far for re-garding unfairness aversion as representing a significant difference: people are sensitive to perceived unfairness and although they might not tell you what fair-ness is, they can tell you when it is absent, and this aversion to unfairness is a primitive behavioral characteristic, like self-interest. If this is the case, the central problem of sustained cooperation over time is not collective action problems, but the fairness problem. A collective action-based framework may be appro-priate for understanding initial cooperation. However, a more appropriate framework for analyzing cooperation over time would be based on the fairness problem. This is because such a framework would be able to better identify and emphasize the growing significance over time of fairness-related factors in sus-tained cooperation.

Assessing Robustness of Cooperation Using Fairness

Had we taken these fairness factors into account when initially classifying the irrigation systems in the NIIS, we would likely have identified more of the sys-tems that subsequently declined. However, identifying which cooperative sys-tems have addressed the fairness problem can be challenging because, as I have reiterated in this chapter, unfair systems might not automatically decline, and systems exhibiting cooperation might not be fair. Many factors affect the robust-ness of cooperation—that is, the ability to continue to cooperate in the face of unusual shocks. Combining them into a robustness assessment entails a large de-gree of judgment on the part of the analyst. Notwithstanding these considerable practical challenges of interpreting what a fairness-based assessment reveals, all that is required to apply this framework is that users share a resource and commit to rules for some time. It applies most directly to irrigation situations that most resemble the current examples, but the implications reach beyond these cases to other cooperative systems as well.

An assessment of the unfairness of a cooperative system with regard to the seven dimensions identified earlier is an assessment of its susceptibility to ex-ternal shocks. Such an assessment falls short of precisely identifying which will actually experience these shocks and thus decline, but it is a starting point for further investigation. Robustness is negatively affected by perceptions of unfair-ness. Perceived fairness affects the quality of cooperation, which then renders the institutions of cooperation more or less robust to changes. When a system is perceived as unfair, it tends to be more susceptible to shocks and tends to be less well maintained. This is the basic mechanism through which unfairness affects robustness.

For reference, recall the discussion of the interaction of some of these groups such as in Artunga with the Maoist rebels. The latter's strategy can also be understood in these terms as altering the perceived fairness of these arrangements to instigate a decline. Rather than alter the functioning of the irrigation system, they altered the perception of fairness of the existing institution. They alerted users to current outcomes that they may not have been aware of, convinced users of possible future outcomes and thereby altered their assessment of how fair the rules would be over time, and finally also altered perceptions of fairness by emphasizing, altering, adding, or discounting some components of fairness. Thus, the same outcomes that had previously been assessed as fair could come to be assessed as unfair by the same people, which in fact came to pass. The users of Artunga eventually acted on perceived unfairness by withholding their labor.

Robustness is indicated especially clearly in how users regard two types of tasks: First, the mundane, asynchronous tasks that can't be fully supervised; and second, the extraordinary tasks that are not predefined, such as those needed for rebuilding after a disaster. The former tasks are the routine maintenance tasks that are needed to keep a system functional. The burden of doing them is usually pre-assigned to users and is rarely discussed save when they are not done properly or there is a problem. The latter tasks are unknown beforehand and arise due to new or altered conditions. It is not clear who should do them, or when or how. These types of unknown tasks create unforeseen burdens for users and sometimes demand extraordinary contributions. The burdens must be allocated on the spot at the time, and cannot be done beforehand.

These two types of tasks test the commitment of cooperators in different ways. Maintenance tasks aren't typically completed out of fear of being punished or out of the excitement of starting something new and promising; they are rarely exciting, rewarding or novel. They tend to be mundane, labor-intensive, and repetitive, and completing them well is typically unrecognized and unrewarded. Neglecting them occasionally can seem inconsequential to the return one receives from the joint outcome. Finally, it is typically infeasible to monitor the performance of all maintenance tasks. Maintenance tests the strength of individual commitments to predefined roles. In contrast, extraordinary tasks benefit from the urgency of having to be completed quickly. They are often of the "showstopper" type—that is, they immediately threaten the continued functioning of the resource. They can take unusual amounts of labor and other resources to complete, they can be exciting, and they are typically widely discussed and debated. They appear immediately significant, and completing

them can even be regarded as heroic. However, they tend to place disproportionate burdens on some users who are undercompensated in the name of the
public good. We saw this, for instance, in the case of BK canal's post-flood re-
construction, when certain poorer landowners were compelled to give up their
land for the building of a new canal diversion. These extraordinary tasks test
the strength of group commitments to continue working together. The unforeseen burdens that unforeseen circumstances impose become a litmus test of
how committed individual cooperators are, and in turn how fair the system is
perceived to be.

The quality of these commitments, thus tested by the dynamic context in which
they are made, affects the success of these cooperative arrangements. In this way,
individual commitments to the institutions of a cooperative system can be understood as effectively being commitments to the adequate performance of a range
of tasks, big and small, that are required to use and maintain the resource. These
agreements, particularly when voluntary, face myriad hurdles to success because
they depend on the continued commitment of those subject to them. A range of
internal and external factors affects these commitments and translates into the variable ability of these systems to survive and adapt. At the same time, a set of internal factors determines how likely a system is to survive exposure to these external
shocks.

Therefore, to get a fuller picture of how likely a system is to decline, one will need
to assess several aspects of the system and its context in addition to perceptions of
fairness. One of these additional aspects is the external relationships through which
individuals can feel themselves to be part of a larger social contract and therefore
may expect to be treated by their group in a way consistent with that. Another is
how significant users perceive unfairness to be. This can be affected, for example,
through education or awareness campaigns that teach users that the disparities they
notice should matter to them, or political movements as described at length.

These assessments must also weigh the power of those that perceive the system
as unfair for an understanding of how susceptible the system is to perceived unfairness. This may be a numerical power that is reflected in how many people
vote to express a perceived unfairness. In the case of voting, robustness is a
function of the proportion of people who are unfairness-averse and also perceive
the system as unfair, but the power may also be of a different form. It may derive
from the essential knowledge, skills, connections, or experience of a person or
group of people. This knowledge is typically unevenly distributed across group
members,[7] and could be passed on within a group or learned from experience.

---

[7] There are exceptions to this, as in the case of a Maoist commune's system in which every
member was required to perform every task, and therefore even specialized knowledge was more or
less evenly distributed.

It is also not easily found outside of the group. In the clearest instances, robustness is a direct consequence of how unfair this set of users perceives the system to be. There, the set of people are unfairness-averse and powerful enough that a reduction in their commitment systematically lessens the ability of the group to complete necessary tasks—both routine and extraordinary—because of the knowledge and expertise that they withhold from the group. This can be true, for instance, of those who typically perform routine maintenance tasks such as inspections and repair of cracks.

To summarize the process of applying this framework, recall the approach used in this book. The fairness approach proposed in this book starts with interviewing two types of users: (1) those who had reduced their commitment and possibly stopped their involvement, and (2) those who continued their commitment and had not stopped. Next, the key question for identifying the components of fairness was "Why did you stop or reduce your commitment?" After these are collected, one can look for patterns and commonalities across users.[8] One will still need to pay particular attention to those users and groups of users such as those who do physical labor or possess specialized knowledge, whose contributions are crucial to the resource's functioning. It is important to note here that this will require understanding the specific tasks that must be done to maintain the resource and identifying who is responsible for them. It will also require drawing attention to the relative power of these sets of people over time.

Finally, I caution the reader against comparing different cases to each other if possible and focusing instead on the comparison of the changes in perceived fairness of a specific system, as is done here. The reason for this is simply that, given the subjective and specific nature of the components of fairness as well as their assessment, there appears to be no basis—even if an aggregate score is computed—for comparing across systems. It would be a mistake to do so using an aggregated version of the components of fairness, such as might be readily provided by a principal component analysis or vector decomposition method, because the units of analysis are not clear. For instance, it is not clear how to numerically assess the change of a fairness component from "good" to "not good" in one case as compared to the same change in another. Indeed, it may be said that this difficulty prevents the aggregation of a sense of perceived fairness at the group level as well. This is certainly the case, and it therefore calls for using one's judgment in combining these components rather than relying on a standardized

---

[8] It may be possible, then, to aggregate the responses in some way across users in order to get an overall fairness score. However, this method can proceed—and might benefit from proceeding—without this sort of numerical aggregation because it might demand misleading assumptions for numerical convenience.

formula with predetermined weights. In other words, the weights themselves must be discussed and made explicit, just as the components have been. It is my hope that the art of judging how fair given arrangements are perceived to be can be learned and honed, just as any modeling exercise relies on a significant element of art and intuition gleaned from experience.

Perceived fairness thus takes us as far as identifying a significant point of failure for these systems and diagnosing it. However, perceived unfairness is not the only cause of decline. Changes that cause the institutions to be out of sync with changing conditions will pose a threat to continued survival of the system. The changes most directly relevant here are changing perceptions of fairness. The rules, aside from having to be crafted iteratively to match changing environmental conditions as well as the internal dynamics of the groups, must also match these changing perceptions of fairness. It can be said that just as the same outcome can be assessed as unfair by the same person over time, similarly, the rules must be changed and adapted to keep the negative effects of these changing perceptions at bay. While there will always be a gap between what is expected and what obtains, discontented users can be placated to some extent by rule changes that either promise to rectify the unfairness eventually or more immediately. Rule changes are unlikely to be enough, however, if outcomes diverge from what the rules promise. If the rule changes do not actually decrease the perceived unfairness of the institution, the group would simply be kicking the fairness problem down the road.

Fairness in the Time between Equilibria

Despite its potential for identifying the contours of the fairness problem, the central problem in the way of sustaining cooperation, it is not obvious how a fairness-centered analysis can inform policy. One might still expect that eventually, in rapidly changing environments, those that are perceived as unfair are less likely to survive because they are less robust. This provides some abstract justification for believing that an evolutionary process occurs, where after a long enough time only the "fittest" remain. The only thing that changes when using a fairness assessment is that in this instance, the fittest systems would be defined as those that are most fair. This type of evolutionary argument seems to suggest that if we wait long enough, systems in which fairness and cooperation do not co-occur would deteriorate and stop functioning. This logic is appealing if the goal is to construct a natural science-inspired framework to explain social phenomena (Ostrom, 1990), or to use agent-based techniques for modeling how cooperation evolves (Axelrod, 2006). As for norm diversity and incompatible norms, the evolutionary argument requires one to assume that some norms of fairness are superior to others in terms of conferring survival advantages on the group (Gintis and Bowles, 2011; Hilbe et al., 2018). This doesn't seem insurmountable: there are several contenders, and this is an active area of investigation. Thus, one might argue that there is very little need for greater involvement of state institutions in this naturally fairness-selecting evolutionary process.

For practical judgments in the realm of development policy and planning, this evolutionary characterization is problematic. It is not much help in addressing some key questions: How long does this dying out take? What is the fate of those who used the canal but now cannot because their system wasn't fit enough and declined? How long will users have to tolerate unfairness while they wait for their system to "die out"? Finally, for what length of time is it justifiable to subject users, usually already disadvantaged, to the searing injustices of unfair systems in the hope that the system will self-correct or die out? All of these questions probe the appropriateness of current policy advice regarding community-managed shared resources. This advice overwhelmingly suggests that, as a starting point, state institutions should unconditionally recognize all existing local arrangements as legitimate. Even for those seeking to ultimately delegate as much power as possible to local resource users in the name of sustainability, the possibility of persistent, unfair cooperation leads to questions about what can be done to encourage these arrangements to be both sustainable and fair.

"Equilibrium" is a metaphor that often guides current explanations of sustained cooperation, and is invoked in evolutionary explanations. This is a situation in which destabilizing and stabilizing forces are equally balanced. For example, the tendency of individuals to shirk and free ride and otherwise act opportunistically is balanced by the fear of punishment so that everyone works just as much as they need to, or their personal desires are also balanced by the group needs. In this equilibrium state, the rules are said to confer just the right punishments and rewards to keep enough people behaving as they should. Emergent unfairness, it is assumed, can be addressed in this rule-bound way. When there is a threat of destabilization such as people wanting different rules, a rule change is proposed. The proposed modification can be seen to affect each person differently. Hence, there are those who will benefit more and those who will benefit less from the proposed rules. Those who will benefit will form a coalition; those who will not will also form a coalition. There is then a voting process (or other collective choice process) to decide on the rule changes. Those whose demands are not met nevertheless still submit themselves to the new rules, and the system thus adapts. Implicit in this is that all the users are committed to the process and the rules (Ostrom, 2005).

However, nothing explicitly rules out that these rule-bound processes might lead to unfair equilibria. This can happen, for instance, when the wealthy keep the rules in their favor through force. This evolutionary process of decline that occurs when the systems are perceived as unfair is expected to erase these bad equilibria over time. This would lead to an equilibrium of sorts in which the system no longer exists, and questions of unfairness become moot. That is, the resource might be exhausted or deplete before institutions become fair (Brander and Taylor, 1998; Diamond, 2005). But that is the long-term view, and we do not know how long unfair systems might run. Timeless theory need not nor can it address how long it will take for unfairness to be corrected, and what factors might affect the time that it takes for this evolutionary selection to kick in. For policy and implementation, this question of time is paramount. Will such institutions decline in a single season, several seasons, or a generation? After all, the systems are in a peculiarly worrisome condition: they are perceived as unfair, and they cannot be altered to be fairer by the users who perceive it as unfair. Depending on how long is considered to be too long, a wider range of policy options beyond automatically conferring legitimacy on existing local groups may need to be considered. Local groups can indeed self-organize, but until the conditions under which they can do so fairly are better understood, absolving state institutions of the power and responsibility to unilaterally challenge questionable agreements in the name of fairness seems counterproductive.

How This Applies More Broadly to Policy and Other Settings

Policy options should be informed by lessons derived from existing systems that have addressed the fairness problems successfully. These systems have achieved constraint of the divergence between observed outcomes and perceptions of fairness to an extent acceptable to cooperators. It has long been known that these systems show that groups of users can devise institutions and govern shared resources over long periods of time. In light of the fairness problem, some also show that in the midst of changing circumstances, complex relationships with outside entities and situations, heterogeneous norms and other forms of diversity, they can somehow continue to be perceived as fair. But how do they do it?

As of this writing, it is more common to regard instances of cooperation around shared resources as primarily illustrating that users can come up with the right rules to keep a system going. Combined with a rational-choice-based approach, this leads one to conclude that what the rules do is align incentives to make cooperation rational. However, a fairness-based analysis reveals a different set of lessons concerning how users adapt to factors that are of utmost importance to our present and future: the complex processes involved in remaining fair over decades. The factors previously associated with initial cooperation will likely need to be reconsidered for, as I have shown, fairness and cooperation are different things despite their close connection. Therefore, it is urgent to recognize how these systems have attempted to address the fairness problem. I summarize next two lessons that go against currently popular features of development policy. One concerns reconsidering the role of the state in resource governance policy, and the other suggests paying greater attention to maintenance of shared resources than to their creation.

Reconsidering the State's Role in Local Sustainability

The logic that underlies recommendations that local arrangements should be recognized by state institutions is based on the idea that institutional diversity across cases is generally favorable (Evans, 2004). That some of these cooperative systems are perceived as fairer than others can be considered a type of diversity that is a part of the process of eventually achieving fairness. This variation could be also seen as contributing to a natural process of selection by avoiding institutional monocropping. There are, after all, no panaceas to resource governance, and it is a dynamic process with a multitude of factors that underlies these mechanisms (Meinzen-Dick, 2007). The argument continues that the locals are likely to know best what the specific conditions are, and that this fact provides strong arguments against non-local involvement. Furthermore, external state agents and agencies are likely to be incompetent at best (Ostrom, 1990), and their primary role should therefore be conflict resolution at a distance (Mansbridge, 2014). Accepting a generally passive role for the state is a form of recognition of the legitimacy and ability of these local arrangements to self-govern, as well as an admission that locals are likely to know best.

Typically, diversity in local arrangements might not be concerning and might even be desirable, but the fact that some arrangements may be unfair for prolonged periods—not just the outcomes, but the processes themselves—gives pause. The first question is whether the state should discriminate between these types (fair and unfair) at the point of recognizing their legitimacy and after. The second question is what policies are available if it does. Should some be selectively recognized based on their ability to remain fair? Should the option of returning to state control be retained for those that persistently remain unfair? In other words, should the state be ready to take back from local groups what it handed over to them? Or should this local sovereignty be constrained, or made conditional on fairness? All of these questions go against the recommendation that the external state should unconditionally recognize the local right to organize. Yet, as we see, the right to organize does not translate automatically into fair arrangements. It might over time, if one believes the evolutionary argument, but during that time many will be subject to unfair situations. Is this necessary?

Local self-governance cannot be entrusted with consistently remaining fair, even though these groups might do so at times. The perspective of fairness suggests taking a more balanced view of the local possibilities for achieving long-term sustainability that is also fair. At the same time, local arrangements can be pockets of refuge for fairness when the state is unfair or sites of revolt when the state is oppressive. But they can also be the last holdouts of unfairness and some of the worst forms of minority or racial oppression precisely because of the state's reluctance or inability to look inside them (Ambedkar, 2014; Vaid, 2014; Basu, Sarkar-Roy, and Majumder, 2016; Vyas, Hathi, and Gupta, 2022). Their preservation is enabled by policy that conflates cooperation and fairness. This does not mean automatically returning complete control of local resources to state institutions, but it also does not mean automatic autonomy for local organizations.

There is a range of state involvement possible between total local control and total state control and this is an area that deserves greater attention. For example, if there are common patterns of unfairness across irrigation systems, the state can facilitate the assessment of fairness across systems. It can also attempt to change the external conditions so that those who perceive their systems as unfair are more powerful. Furthermore, trained government planners can facilitate fairness discussions and guide groups to finding alternative arrangements that might be perceived as fairer but still acceptable to all parties (Coman, 1911; Forester, 1999; Islam and Susskind, 2013).

The danger of too much intervention is that the systems might decline because the involvement is unsuccessful or incompetent. But the alternative was always either that these unfair systems eventually decline, or they continue in an unfair state. If the existing arrangements are exploitative, the state should see the consequences of inaction as worse than decline through well-intended interventions. Without action, the state risks subjecting people to unfairness for decades, only to face a likely collapse of their livelihoods in the end when the resource collapses. Waiting too long for unfair systems to self-correct can be unjust. The locals typically have local knowledge, disaggregated and contextual, and the state has access to aggregate knowledge and information across cases. Both are relevant in the context of fairness, as I have shown. Thus, intervention can be justified, although what forms are effective is an empirical question.

Recall that in prior studies such as those of Lam (1998) and Joshi (2000), the performance of these self-governed canals was compared to the performance of canals managed by government agencies. The canals were classified as either completely government-managed and were called Agency-Managed Irrigation Systems (AMIS), or jointly managed with government agencies, called Jointly

Managed Irrigation Systems (JMIS). The third possibility was farmer managed (FMIS). "Managed" refers to who makes the institution's rules–farmers, a government agency, or both. This resulted in conclusions that Farmer-Managed Systems were superior to Agency-Managed ones (Cole, 2012). The distinction between these three types relied on the extent to which farmers or a government agency decided who could use the canal, how the water was allocated, and how it was to be managed in general. It is no longer possible to make this comparison between agency- and farmer-managed systems using this data set, since most of the canals in the sample have been formally handed over to local institutions, and they now exhibit a complex set of relationships with state institutions.[9]

Yet a closer look at the resilience of those that were government-managed then versus those that were completely self-governed shows that nearly all of those that have stopped functioning were of the "Farmer-Managed" type in the first study. In contrast, only one of those that were managed in cooperation with government agencies has stopped functioning. It should be noted that 18 of the 20 agency-managed systems in the original sample were subsequently "turned over" to farmers under policies seeking greater local resource management. Taken at face value, this seems to go against the basic claim that decreased government involvement improves resilience. Indeed, farmer-managed systems had a higher failure rate (17%) than the sample as a whole. This suggests that the more the government was involved then, the greater the chance of survival now, despite being handed over to local users in the meantime. These findings do not shed much light on why this is so. More recently some have proposed a continuum of forms of government involvement in an attempt to capture these mixed forms (Frey, Villamayor-Tomas, and Theesfeld, 2016). These are promising avenues for examining state involvement in governing shared resources in terms of fairness as well.

Reconsidering Infrastructure Maintenance

The fairness approach strongly suggests that the focus of resource governance policy should be on maintenance. Several of the prerequisites that give rise to the fairness problem appear in the maintenance of shared resources more

---

[9] This raises a concern about the extent to which policy-relevant studies change what they study. To the extent that they do, the study itself must be considered part of the eventual intervention. This places limits on direct reproducibility of findings. In the cases here, the predictions of earlier studies were used to make policies to "hand over" canals to user management. These policies changed the management of canals in such a way that the original prediction can no longer be tested using the same sample at a later time.

readily than in their creation. This implies that fairness comes to matter most to maintenance, and therefore, maintenance and not construction should receive greater policy attention. The current fairness-based approach is also most applicable to the former. Indeed, sustained cooperation is the hallmark of successful maintenance. Planning, discussing, and constructing are unusual events in the life of a shared resource compared to the tasks of maintenance. Furthermore, the specific tasks of maintenance of the shared resource are usually different than those in the early stages. Maintenance typically requires routine tasks, typically distinctly different from the novel tasks of design and construction.

When the resource is new or newly proposed, there tends to be greater excitement arising from the promise of what it might provide. When a new irrigation canal is being built, or an old one extended, those who previously had to rely on rain-fed agriculture might now have a more reliable source of water. This promise was felt by farmers in Artunga, for instance, when the extension from Chherlung was proposed. At such junctures, some may even feel obligated to contribute, as illustrated by the example of one small farmer using the BK canal after it had been damaged and rerouted. The only new feasible route, according to other farmers, would reduce his relatively small cultivable plot by a third. He wanted the community to consult a government engineer about alternative solutions, but ultimately, he could not resist the pressure from the wider community and agreed to the proposal. He knew that he would bring tremendous hardship on his family for generations by being shunned by the wider community if he objected.

Maintenance typically requires routine tasks, not the novel activities of designing and constructing something new. The canal must be inspected regularly, cleaned, and repaired. These are repetitive, time-intensive tasks that rarely involve solving new problems or building new structures. These mundane tasks can't sustain the initial excitement of building something new. Instead, they are familiar and possibly even onerous. In this respect, it was often reported that maintenance is hard, particularly for younger farmers. By the time maintenance tasks come to be paramount, users will typically have acquired information about the outcomes of prior cooperation. Their exposure to uneven outcomes may even have informed their sense of unfairness. Hence, when deciding whether to continue to cooperate to maintain a resource, the perceptions of fairness that affect their continued commitment may include the outcomes as well as the rules—one of the features captured by the fairness problem.

Motivation to perform mundane maintenance tasks may falter through sheer repetitiveness, seeming insignificance, and the effects of not doing the tasks being invisible. Thus, when motivation might be lacking and self-benefit calculation vague (because the effects are marginal), commitment is what ties people to maintenance. The quality of the work that one does is determined by the strength of this commitment. In those moments when there is nobody around and one is questioning why one is doing this—particularly when neglect or doing something else is a distinct possibility, and particularly when the only thing that is penalized is whether something has been done and not the quality of the work—motivation may be lacking. Any measure of quality of the work may be invisible or undetectable because the task itself is so mundane. For example, what does it mean that one has inspected a canal for potential blockages better than another? Nevertheless, commitment alters the quality of this work, and perceived fairness alters commitment.

It takes time, normally, for a commitment of this sort to be broken. A commitment carries with it an inertia: once in a commitment, one will tend to preserve this commitment. One internalizes what the "right thing" is to do (Sen, 1977). This difference is what distinguishes a commitment from a simple strategic move. These irrigators have made a commitment to abide by their working rules, which are a mix of custom, norms, tradition, heuristics, and written and unwritten rules. Thus, they will tend to work on the canal unless there is a reason not to. Rethinking whether to not do one's duty is not a frequent occurrence, certainly not before every instance that one must do it. At the same time, how well to do it, whether to do extra, or neglect it in small ways can vary, perhaps even unconsciously. Perceived unfairness may have this demotivating effect on the completion of maintenance tasks that depend on commitment more than excitement or promise. Although one does the job, one may do it better at some times than others. Over time, the canal can deteriorate even when people appear to be doing their duty if it is perceived as unfair. In this way, the quality of maintenance work is impacted by perceived fairness, an impact that is less prolonged in the early life of shared infrastructure.

Cases of community infrastructure maintenance meet several necessary conditions that the fairness framework identifies as indicating the prominence of the fairness problem to be applied to particular cases. This strongly implies that it is the cooperation needed to successfully maintain a shared system over time that is likely to be affected by perceived unfairness. First, individuals must have some discretion in the carrying out of their work. This work must have, either individually or collectively, some effect on the performance of the shared resource. The individuals must submit their overall discretion and decision-making to the rules in place. In other words, akin to Hobbes' description of the preconditions of order, individuals will have given up some of their individual desires or impetuses to the dictates of the rules. This means that at times they will be required to do things that they may not at that time agree to, or even see the value of. However, because of their commitment, they must do it.

It is likely that user commitment to maintenance will be affected consciously or otherwise by the perception of fairness of the outcomes of the rules. The outcomes are cumulative outcomes, and so the resource must generate cumulative outcomes. That is, the thing to be distributed must eventually have visible and noticeable differences in outcomes if distributed differently to each member of the group. In this situation, some will get more and others less. Finally, they must have worked together for decades so that there are high levels of familiarity with each other and also what we might call "social capital" at some point in the past. That is, the preconditions for cooperation were met at some point, and might continue to be or might not. Mutual monitoring, although a shared characteristic of these systems, is not a required condition for the framework explained here. This argument would apply to situations in which monitoring is done by someone else who is hired, or even when the monitoring is done by some external authority. The only condition is that the one monitoring cannot see the work of the individual in the finest detail. In other words, differences in effort or quality only show up over time, and that too in the functioning of the resource in such a way that it is not easily traceable back to the person or persons who neglected their duties.

There are many commons resources outside of shared infrastructure that might be amenable to the fairness-based analysis developed here, although they would have different characteristics in terms of the actual physical properties among other differences. Forests, air, lakes, fisheries and groundwater are all types of resources that a collective action approach has been successfully used to examine. In the Ostromian approach, all resources can be classified in two dimensions—subtractability (the extent to which one person using it means another cannot) and difficulty of exclusion (how easy it is to prevent someone from using it). Those that have high subtractability and high difficulty of exclusion are called common pool resources and fall within the scope of the framework to analyze while others do not (Ostrom, 2010). For example, it is difficult to prevent a person from breathing a particular volume of clean air (it is difficult to exclude someone), just as their breathing it necessarily implies that another cannot (the resource is highly subtractable). As I have discussed previously, this classification scheme is derived by asking what is paramount to one whose reasoning is dominated by the fear of being taken advantage of. The fairness-oriented framework developed here is based on a different type of person, that is, one whose animating tendency is aversion to unfair situations. So in the first place, it is not clear whether subtractability and excludability are the most relevant dimensions of shared resources. And in the second, it is not yet clear what the most relevant dimensions are. Thus, the extent to which the fairness approach developed here could apply to the broader set of resources without modification will require significant future work.

Fairness in Digital Infrastructure

An area where community maintenance is proving to be particularly important is a particular type of community-managed software that is used in the digital infrastructure of modern society. Through the pervasive use of this type of open-source software, we are building our digital future on the faith that communities can maintain infrastructure voluntarily. The infrastructure is digital, and the community usually interacts online. In comparison to communities that use and maintain shared physical resources, we know much less about digital communities—so little, in fact, that we are still at the stage of understanding which of our insights from the physical realm might apply to this new world. We do know, however, that there are clear parallels between the condition of shared digital and physical infrastructure, and this presents a possibility of understanding both better through comparison. As attempts to develop and generate community spread widely online, the familiar question of how to sustain community involvement in use and upkeep once again assumes importance.

It might seem that a discussion of software on the Internet is out of place in a book about farmer-managed irrigation systems in Nepal. However, these two types of shared infrastructure are remarkably similar from the perspective of the users sustaining cooperation, even though their physical forms are dramatically different (Morell, 2014). Open-source software is computer code that is voluntarily maintained by a group of users, and whose quality depends on continued cooperation among them. Without regular maintenance, it deteriorates and becomes unreliable if not dangerous for people to use. In fact, terms such as "upstream" and "downstream" are commonly used to describe the interdependence of different users in open-source projects, just like in irrigation systems (English and Schweik, 2007). The largely similar situations faced by users cooperating to share these two types of infrastructure draws attention to avenues and obstacles to generalizing findings from one to the other.

Applying the fairness approach to open-source software promises to help identify pieces of critical digital infrastructure that might be vulnerable because of perceived unfairness. This is analogous to the argument in this book that had we considered aspects of perceived fairness in the past, we may have been better able to judge which irrigation systems in Nepal would have deteriorated. The difference is also one of scale. A group of irrigation system users that is not identified as needing assistance with the fairness problem has a much smaller impact than a misidentified group of contributors to an open-source software project that is used in millions of web servers. Consider an example.

Heartbleed was the name given to a bug found in a piece of cryptography software in 2014.[10] The offending code was contained in software called OpenSSL, which was widely used on the Internet for protecting private information transmitted online. By some estimates, nearly 17% of all servers using the SSL encryption protocol were affected (about half a million servers), and many more client computers (Netcraft, 2014).[11] This includes banking passwords, email passwords, Social Security numbers in the United States, credit card information, or anything else transmitted with confidence that it was secure. Because of Heartbleed, it was possible for anyone to see this information if the browser had relied on OpenSSL—which it most likely did. In other words, any data transmitted "securely" before April 8, 2014 and after February 1, 2012 (such as by trusting the "https" or the lock icon shown by your browser) when the bug was introduced may no longer be private. The startling feature of this bug was that it revealed not only the information being sent, but also the secret digital key the computer used and reused to secure other information. For 18 months, the keys to the castle were widely available because of lapses in how a critical piece of software infrastructure was maintained. The implications were alarming.

OpenSSL belongs to a large set of open-source software commonly used for critical applications that is maintained by a group of typically unpaid volunteers. They depend on it and share it freely so that others can improve and build on it. There are hundreds of other examples of such free and open-source software that is used in critical applications beyond security and the maintenance of which is typically taken for granted (Harrison and Herr, 2016). All of them likely have bugs that have not yet been discovered. Although this all-volunteer model of software maintenance is being augmented with private firms paying their software engineers to contribute to some projects, it is still common for groups of unpaid volunteers to be tasked with maintaining critical software. The community of users reports problems in open-source software, fixes them, and makes the fixes available to other users a way that resembles the irrigation systems in this book. Their continued cooperation is essential to the reliable functioning of the software, and the quality of this cooperation is likely to depend on how fair they perceive it to be.

Open-source software can be usefully viewed as a commons resource that is similar to the shared irrigation systems in this book in important ways (English and Schweik, 2007; Schweik and English, 2012; Frischmann, Madison, and Strandburg, 2014). Software deteriorates through a process called bit rot, just

---

[10] CVE-2014-0160 in the Common Vulnerabilities and Exposures database. More information can also be found at https://heartbleed.com.

[11] There are other software libraries that implement the SSL protocol.

as physical canals do. Lack of maintenance leads to further deterioration in both the physical infrastructure and the institutional infrastructure for managing it (Ostrom, 1990, 2005; Frischmann, Madison and Strandburg, 2014). Just as fairness is important for the maintenance of shared physical infrastructure commons such as irrigation systems (Frey and Rusch, 2014), it is also likely to be a reason that users participate less in maintenance and governance activities of digital infrastructure of this type, opening the door to more bugs like Heartbleed. As we increasingly rely on such software, important parts of our future will continue to be built on the social phenomenon of sustained, voluntary cooperation around shared resources.

Thus, it will be increasingly important to understand the evolution of the fairness problem and its relationship to maintenance in these digital contexts as well as physical ones. For instance, there were other bugs in OpenSSL that had been discovered and fixed by developers after release. There are numerous others that were fixed before the software was released. Indeed, bugs are common in software, and in the case of open-source software, their discovery and removal is an indication of the quality of maintenance. From a collective action perspective, the developers had clearly figured out how to solve collective action problems to use and maintain the shared resource that was OpenSSL by fixing bugs, one of the most common metrics for assessing quality of cooperation in open-source projects (Schweik and English, 2012). From this perspective, the Heartbleed bug was one of many introduced unintentionally by a "quite trivial" coding error, according to Dr. Seggelmann, the developer whose code contribution introduced it (Grubb, 2014). It was also missed by a code reviewer. Nevertheless, according to noted security scholar Bruce Schneier, the impacts were "catastrophic." He continues, "On the scale of 1 to 10, this is an 11" (Schneier, 2014).

A collective action assessment would likely have raised no flags because the software was regularly updated, bugs had been promptly fixed after release, and others quashed beforehand, all indications of good-quality cooperation. However, although there isn't enough information to attribute the Heartbleed bug to the perceptions of unfairness of the contributors, assessing the project from a fairness perspective would have highlighted at least one area of concern. If asked, the developers would likely have admitted that as the project grew, a few users were doing a disproportionate amount of the maintenance work while others were disproportionately gaining from it.

Although few knew it, at the time the Heartbleed bug was discovered, there were only two full-time programmers working on the project. This, despite it being a piece of software that about 500,000 Internet servers used to secure communications (Perlroth, 2014). Dr. Seggelmann would later report that he had submitted many other fixes to the software that day and in the past, so he wasn't new to the task. Finally, maintenance of the OpenSSL codebase, about

300,000 lines of code, required highly specialized knowledge and many eyes auditing it. Indeed, many other users of the software were likely just as capable of contributing to the project. For example, the engineers at Google and at the Finnish security firm who discovered the bug as well as the security engineers at the major firms relying on the software to conduct their business would all have been qualified users. It did not appear that they or their firms were contributing in proportion to their gains from using the software. Indeed, disproportionate labor contributions by some users and disproportionate gains by other users are aspects of fairness that characterize the project.[12] While there is no evidence that this fact affected the contributors, it is possible that it dissuaded many others from participating altogether, or led some others to stop doing so. It is also an aspect that the fairness approach would have identified, even in the current form, which is not adapted to digital contexts.

A Challenge to Social Science

The recognition that perceived unfairness eventually emerges as a problem between individuals working together over long periods of time has practical and theoretical implications. Conceptually, the challenge of solving the fairness problem, along with collective action problems, comes to shape cooperative local institutions. This reorients how instances of successful cooperation are understood, starting with individuals' aversion to unfairness. At the same time, emphasizing the distinction between fairness and cooperation makes it easier to recognize that some systems of cooperation are perceived as fairer than others, and their perceived fairness significantly affects their robustness to change. The examination of instances of cooperation from the perspective of fairness raises a further question about the conditions under which some cooperative arrangements are fairer than others.

The fairness approach therefore takes away emphasis on external circumstances to refocus on the many reasons (not simply benefit) that people might or might not work together. "Emptying" the rationality principle by assuming everyone reasoned in the same way (Ostrom, 1990, p. 38) may have been prudent at a time when there seemed to be few alternatives to understanding human reasoning. However, the time may have come to heed the multitude of reasons that individuals and groups give for their actions, desires, and aspirations. Rational choice's valiant effort emphasizes the useless complexity of trying to model situations without seeking to grasp how people understand their situations and

---

[12] This would be addressed to a certain extent after Heartbleed, when the OpenSSL project received large donations to do its work better.

their actions (Ostrom, 2005). Trying to explain the observations presented here makes rational choice arguments unwieldy and complex, undercutting a major reason for using it: parsimony and simplicity. However, a consideration of influences on fairness and how it may be perceived, while not as elegant as early understandings based on rational choice, is less unwieldy. As I have shown, it is also a more promising as a way to understand why institutions survive or decline over time. Future research will need to focus on types of fairness across cases and time as well as the conditions under which these arrangements are fair.

In addition to its main findings, this research has attempted to re-introduce the idea of revisiting old, well-established topics in the social sciences. While it has been customary to take established explanations as the final word on their respective empirical cases, it may be fruitful in the sense of generating more findings to revisit them. Even if the conclusions are found to still hold, this will be a significant service to the endeavor of learning about social phenomena. At the very least, one will have contributed another set of observations that can be used to study the dynamics of the phenomena of interest. Repeating earlier studies is one way to approach the task of verifying earlier results, and given the advances in technology since the early studies, replication should be less costly than was the case here.

While the focus has recently been on refining research designs to be more thorough, the scientific mindset can never take evidence as final. Indeed, more than any research design, the ability to reproduce the findings of others plays a significant role in scientific enquiry. This is a challenge to social science because it is tempting for those working on limited research budgets to think that finding out something "new" by directing one's research focus to areas and ideas that have not yet been studied is more promising. Documenting one's choices and research findings carefully with a reader in mind can also seem like an unnecessary investment when nobody is going to use it to do the study again.

This is especially true in light of the possibility that research that is well done is likely to come to conclusions that hold up to scrutiny of this sort, and to be robust in that sense. Thus, for a scholar seeking something new, the confirmation of the old can be a disappointment. The point, however, is that social research can always be done better, or at least done differently in ways that might not be anticipated when first done. Without the means to relate new methods and data to old ones, the possibility of reliable findings is lessened. Finding reasons to revisit established cases and established conclusions is a challenge to social science; however, it is one that should not be dismissed out of hand if we are to stand on rigorous foundations.

For the purposes of making policy and informing planning, recognizing that perceived fairness is central to cooperation is still lacking in important ways. Obtaining a general-purpose framework to guide action will require much more painstaking qualitative fieldwork to identify elements of perceptions of unfairness in different settings. Precisely because fairness is different from cooperation, and the fairness problem is different from collective action problems, fieldwork will have to focus explicitly on the fairness aspects of these systems to make progress in this direction. As I have shown, studies focusing on collective action problems tend to miss significant aspects of the fairness problem. Furthermore, data sets constructed without the explicit intention of probing fairness-related factors and those that only look at a point in time are likely to miss the fairness problem. New data sets will need to probe fairness explicitly, while the usefulness of existing ones will need to be assessed. The framework of fairness problems laid out in this book is intended to guide this growth, but it will need to be tested independently by others. Nevertheless, these shortcomings do not detract from the implications for how we view cases of successful cooperation in the use and maintenance of shared resources.

As an empirical attempt to understand what fairness might mean, how it might come to relate to sustained cooperation, and how to conceptualize this point, the fairness approach to cooperation is a small elaboration that interfaces with a far broader and longer-running research agenda and framework. In relation to the mass of work using collective action-focused approaches to cooperation, this work is an attempt to revive and elaborate upon a set of variables that were already identified as important to the framework, but it has done so using a different study design than has been possible before and by including interviews to develop a more general understanding of the mechanisms through which these variables may come to affect performance. Focusing on these variables of fairness, though, has suggested changing a basic element of the collective action-centered framework: the main animating principle behind sustained cooperation. Instead of assuming that sucker-aversion is the main driver, human beings act as though they are unfairness-averse. Seen in terms of this new behavioral trait, the rest of the framework also looks different because instead of solving collective action problems alone, groups seem to be grappling with the fairness problem.

More succinctly, the argument presented here is that perceived fairness affects the quality of cooperation. This renders the institutions of cooperation more or less robust to changes. Over time, this fairness problem becomes more significant than collective action problems, and hence, not only must the search for fairness be central to theories of sustained cooperation, but the proper approach to analyzing sustained cooperation must adapt to recognize fairness problems better. Recall that upon commencing this argument, I set out to solve two problems. The first is *how* to systematically document changes to local self-governance institutions. This I did by analyzing cases over time. The second is to explain *why* some of these institutions decline while others adapt. The answer hinged on the reasons that people who were already committed reduced their commitment. This then set the stage for understanding what it takes to sustain cooperation even in challenging circumstances and over long periods of time. It was in the course of this study that perceived fairness emerged as a central part of the solution.

The cooperative mode of social and economic organization—popularly associated with the sharing economy, free and open-source software, public-private partnerships, local self-governance of the commons, alternative currencies, land trusts, and so on—has often felt like a welcome corrective to the failed planning of the past. In the popular imagination, these alternative ideas enthusiastically bring together all the words that we associate with a new and more just society—sharing, cooperation, voluntarism, collective benefit, and the commons. Where the competitive mode emphasized narrow self-interest and a prioritizing of short-term over long-term benefits, the new mode is associated with its opposite. These cooperative ideas promise a varying mix of a collective or social benefit, a taste of voluntary cooperation, and possibly new institutions that make emphasizing long-term interests easier.

The main question to be asked of these cooperative alternatives is: does the emergence of cooperation make considerations of justice and fairness secondary? Even if so, then there are strong reasons of fairness for understanding how to evoke and sustain cooperation. I have offered arguments here that should induce some caution: fairness and cooperation are not the same thing. Indeed, the relationship between fairness and cooperation is not as simple as it might seem, as it is possible and even likely that cooperative arrangements will be perceived as unfair by the participants.

The commons approach taken by Ostrom and others is one way to understand why and how groups of individuals cooperate over long periods of time in the use and maintenance of shared resources. It is the most widely used in analyzing shared digital infrastructure as well (Benkler, 2014). This form of governance embodies all that is held to be good about alternative governance approaches. By assuming that individuals are reasoning in a way that is least likely to lead to cooperation on its own, it is a hopeful story that shows that even in such cases it is still possible. It is widely used and well-known.

The Ostromian framework takes on a difficult problem in showing how even those least likely to cooperate could conceivably do so, while simplifying another problem. In particular, it assumes that these individuals will continue to cooperate as long as it is profitable to do so, and they will stop when it ceases to be profitable. That is, they respond to incentives, and if the incentives are aligned, they will continue to cooperate. In contrast, unfairness-averse individuals behave and reason as though they are concerned with a less clear concept: fairness. This concept is not initially that important, but it gradually becomes more so over time. It moves motivation beyond incentives alone and into a realm of comparison and perception. The complexity introduced by recognizing diverse human tendencies may not be insurmountable, as the many cases that continue to function well and are perceived as fair illustrate. But how the fairness problem is solved, what features contribute to this, and whether this can be done by locals themselves remains to be adequately understood.

As I have shown, the central problem is not just fitting the rules to the incentives of each farmer and the physical features of the resource, but also a third factor. The rules must constantly adapt to changing perceptions of fairness and to emerging effects of previous commitments. The question that I raise here is whether we can expect locals to solve this problem on their own. This is not to imply that some sort of outside authority will always be able to solve the problem, but only that it may be asking too much for locals to be able to do this alone. As we see from well-functioning canals that are run by oppressive rules and arrangements, it is possible for these to be unfair but still survive and function very well. In the long run, these will decline and disappear. But in that meantime, people will be subject to injustice and unfairness. The decline may simply be too slow from the perspective of justice.

The Road Ahead

The next generation of work on sustainability will have to address questions of fairness sooner rather than later. As we move to digital realms that so far have been idyllic, with largely homogeneous participants maintaining digital infrastructure, the question of fairness will need to be addressed lest it emerge when we are least prepared. If we look at the users of open-source software and the contributors, we already see a numerical mismatch. True, it is not clear what fairness means, whether a sense of fairness can be demanded of voluntary associations, or even whether "outsiders" have any say in voluntary agreements. But these objections sound familiar. Before this work, it was precisely these arguments that made it seem that a serious inquiry into the fairness of seemingly successful cooperative arrangements was unnecessary. If these 269 farmer-managed irrigation systems are any guide, then over time, although it is difficult to know how, fairness will come to matter.

If we seek to understand why local resource management arrangements that possess the features of successful cooperation appear to deviate from expected patterns, it is necessary to rule out perceived unfairness as the reason. The key distinction that generates this analysis is between the decision faced by one who has never cooperated, and one who is in a cooperative arrangement. Most importantly, the conception of fairness that users have after having cooperated for some time concerns outcomes to a greater extent than it does initially. Although it can appear to be a "soft" concept, perceived fairness is a prominent reason that individual cooperators give for stopping or reducing their cooperation, even when other conditions are met. It is perhaps because it is difficult to define once and for all that fairness gets its power: it uncompromisingly compels research to focus on better understanding the myriad perceptions of fairness and how these perceptions affect behavior.

Studies of collective action and fairness are separately built into the foundations of many fields, from philosophy to computer science to development. Our knowledge centers overwhelmingly on why people cooperate, not necessarily on why they continue to do so over long periods of time. I have elaborated a way to think about sustained cooperation over decades, based on a follow-up of cases that laid the original foundation, 16 to 37 years later. Both of these contributions signal the next steps: namely, thinking about collective action over time based on rigorous longitudinal studies, and theorizing the conditions under which collective action can be sustainable and just.

Human history is full of examples of continuously maintained shared infrastructure. This history holds an important lesson: eventually perceived fairness matters to sustained cooperation. Clear and strict property rights crafted and enforced by groups and reflecting locally dominant norms are not enough to sustain cooperation, despite the insistence of a long line of advocates (Ostrom and Cole, 2010; Cole, 2012). All these systems have well-defined property rights, yet only the fair ones are sustainable. The order enforced by strong property rights is not the same as the fairness sought by those who are subject to them. Getting the incentives right is also incomplete. Furthermore, fairness problems are not likely to be solved in the same ways as collective action problems. Therefore, over time, sustainability is a consequence of fairness and not the other way around.

Appendix 1

METHODS

This study became possible through a unique set of circumstances. In the Spring of 2012, two months before her death, Elinor Ostrom provided gave me a copy of the famous NIIS database and coding forms. These cases of successful farmer management had come to be highly regarded through their influence on her thinking, as she recounted also in her Nobel Prize speech. The database itself was poorly documented and therefore relatively inaccessible, but corresponded to the coding forms. In the first phase, I used these coding forms to reconstruct the original data set. During this "archaeological" phase, I also interviewed several of the individuals who had been involved in coding cases for it and designing it. Because it was a meta-analysis, I was also able to track down the original accounts. I was confident that I had reconstructed the dataset when I was able to reproduce some results of earlier studies. Including preliminary visits, the fieldwork for this study was conducted between March 2011 and November 2013.

In the second phase, I created a new survey instrument based on the original coding forms. This second survey contained all of the questions from the first one plus several questions about the intervening years (such as the armed conflict). With the assistance of 18 enumerators, I then replicated the original study using this questionnaire. Most significantly, the enumerators recorded the conversations that took place while they were administering the instrument. This provided approximately 1,200 hours of supplementary qualitative material.

The second round was then entered into a database, checked for errors and then combined with the first one. The combined panel dataset, with only the variables that have been used in the accompanying analysis is publicly available. The final analysis was conducted in Stata SE (version 12).

Sampling

This study is a direct replication of an earlier study by Elinor Ostrom and her team of irrigation canals in Nepal, with an additional sample and new data sources (interviews). Figure 12 illustrates the "spilled panel" design. Overall, this study had several iterative stages of data collection and analysis. They resulted in two observations each for 233 irrigation systems separated by between 16 and 37 years, one observation each for 39 systems, recorded interviews with 827 respondents, and detailed case studies of two canals. Figure 13 shows the sampling procedure.

The survey portion of this study is in the form of a longitudinal data set of 509 variables per case at two time periods. Over this time period, the canals experienced multiple changes due to changes that occurred in Nepal.

The research began with a set of field visits to irrigation systems in Nepal, without knowledge of whether they had been studied before nor not. During this preliminary stage, I visited twelve villages in six districts: Morang, Sindhupalchok, Kathmandu, Chitwan, Kailali, and Rolpa. Nepal has 75 districts. On the visits to Sindhupalchok, I accompanied individuals who had conducted the studies on which the NIIS was based. On the visits to Kailali,

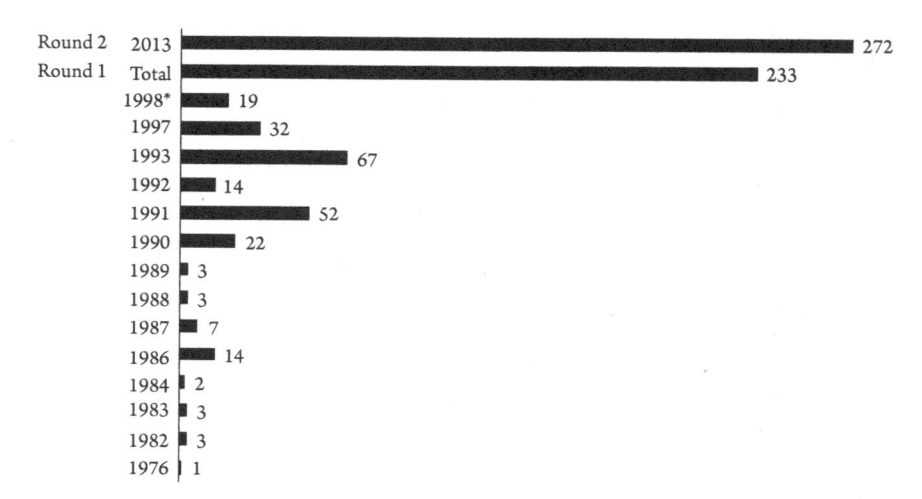

Figure 12 **Sample by years of fieldwork and round:** The black bars indicate how many cases were studied in each year listed. The elements of the "Spilled Panel" consist of two rounds of data collection, and 39 additional cases in the second round. The data collected in 2013 is Round 2, and the Round 1 refers to that collected between 16 and 37 years ago. The cases from 1998 are revisits to 19 in the first round. They are treated as part of the first round.

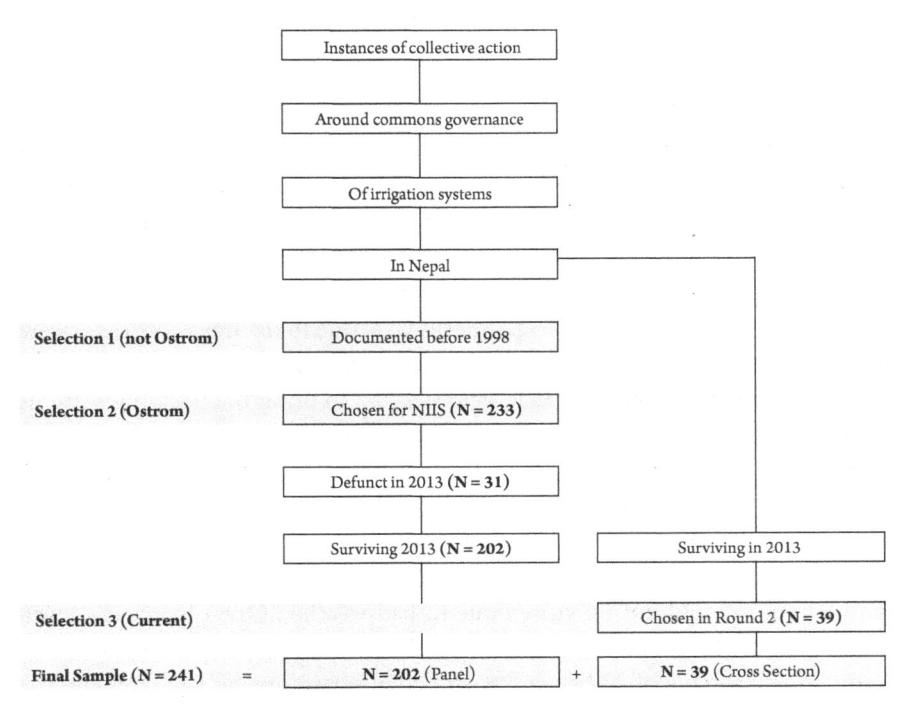

Figure 13 Years and stages of selection that resulted in the final data set.

I was accompanied by the secretary of an NGO which had worked in the district for several years. In Morang, I made the visits with an Agricultural Extension Officer of the Department of Agriculture, Government of Nepal. In Chitwan, I was guided by a professor who knew of the NIIS, but hadn't taken direct part in its creation or maintenance. And in Rolpa, I was guided by members of the Maoist Party who lived and worked in the area where the People's War originated. Through these preliminary field visits, I found that the canals were facing complex situations, in consonance with the changes the country as a whole had experienced.

After sharing the initial observations with Elinor Ostrom, I was granted access to the NIIS database. I reconstructed the history of the database as described above and began a re-analysis of the original NIIS data. This stage consisted of phone and in-person interviews with many of those involved in creating the NIIS, and those who had authored the papers and reports from which the cases were drawn.

Based on the preliminary visits, initial analysis of the NIIS data, and a re-construction of the history of the NIIS project, I designed a survey instrument. My survey contained all of the questions from the first survey, with additional questions based on the data collected during my preliminary field visits. The additional questions were primarily about the effects of the decade-long conflict, and contained several open ended questions particularly about the effects of the conflict.

The second stage consisted of revisiting each of the 233 cases and administering the new survey instrument while simultaneously recording all of the interviews with willing respondents. Using this data, I was able to observe patterns that needed further investigation. The primary reason for additional fieldwork was that I could not rule out that these patterns were due to the way these cases were initially selected, as I describe in greater detail below. To do this, I then added an additional sample of 39 cases that were selected in order to check the patterns that had begun to appear in the analysis of the two visits. The original goal was to reach all the remaining 45 administrative districts that had not made it into the NIIS. However, the summer of 2013 saw an extremely heavy monsoon leading to unusually severe floods and landslides. Because of these conditions, canals in these six districts—Baglung, Dailekh, Myagdi, Mustang, Manang, and Humla—could not be visited due to bad weather. One canal was chosen from each of the remaining 39 unsampled districts based on convenience. This resulted in a sample of 272 canals, with two observations for each canal in the original sample. I also added an additional set of questions to the survey at this stage because I wanted to probe further certain patterns that had already started to emerge. The additional 39 cases were chosen by the enumerators by going to the district headquarters and asking about well-functioning irrigation canals in the area. They then chose one and surveyed it. Thus, it was somewhat arbitrary but likely oversampled from those that were accessible.

The third stage consisted of another round of survey work for the added sample, again to collect data and record interviews. After cross checking the initial findings with this added set of cases, I selected two cases to examine in greater depth based on geographical variation and how accessible they were to me. One was located in the district of Tanahun, and the other in the district of Dang. The final stage consisted of ethnographic-type fieldwork of these two cases over two months in order to gain insight into the day to day functioning of the canals over an extended period of time. When I lived in each of these locations, I focused on observing user discussions, their relationships with government agencies, political parties, and each other. The overall spilled panel design allowed for systematic observation of why some institutions for sustained cooperation survived, and continued to perform well while others declined in the face of myriad changes that they experienced between the first and second visits.

Table 26 **Sampling by District: Of Nepal's 75 districts, the original NIIS contained systems from 30. The addition includes an additional 39 of the remaining 45. Six could not be visited due to extreme weather in the summer of 2013.**

District	Sampled	District	Sampled	District	Sampled
Achham	8	Ilam	1	Panchthar	1
Arghakhanchi	1	Jajarkot	1	Parbat	1
Baglung	0	Jhapa	1	Parsa	1
Baitadi	1	Jumla	1	Pyuthan	2
Bajhang	1	Kailali	7	Ramechhap	1
Bajura	1	Kalikot	1	Rasuwa	1
Banke	1	Kanchanpur	1	Rautahat	1
Bara	3	Kapilbastu	7	Rolpa	1
Bardiya	1	Kaski	10	Rukum	1
Bhaktapur	1	Kathmandu	1	Rupandehi	4
Bhojpur	1	Kavre	4	Salyan	1
Chitawan	66	Khotang	1	Sankhuwasabha	1
Dadeldhura	1	Lalitpur	2	Saptari	2
Dailekh	1	Lamjung	4	Sarlahi	3
Dang	28	Mahottari	1	Sindhuli	1
Darchaula	1	Makwanpur	5	Sindhupalchok	19
Dhading	13	Manang	0	Siraha	1
Dhankuta	1	Morang	1	Solukhumbu	1
Dhanusa	3	Mugu	1	Sunsari	1
Dolakha	1	Mustang	0	Surkhet	1
Dolpa	1	Myagdi	0	Syangja	4
Doti	1	Nawalparasi	6	Tanahu	6
Gorkha	6	Nuwakot	5	Taplejung	1
Gulmi	1	Okhaldhunga	1	Terhathum	1
Humla	0	Palpa	3	Udayapur	1

Protocols

All enumerators were trained for two to three weeks before administering the survey instrument. Each enumeration team consisted of two members. All of the enumerators had college educations and at least one member of each team was a civil engineer. All audio was recorded while administering the survey, unless permission was denied by respondents. No identifying information was recorded in the audio. Each instrument was filled out based on multiple responses and therefore these responses could not be traced to individual respondents. I trained the enumerators to inspect the canals and classify any damage they saw, as well as the level of water and the amount of siltation.

For each irrigation system in the original database, the enumerators used the location and village name from the original survey to find it. If they could locate the canal but not the village, they chose the village closest to the head and made note of it. If the village had split since the first survey, they chose the one closest to the head and made note of it. If two villages had combined, they made note of it. If the canal had split, they chose the village that was using the named water source for irrigation. They walked the length of the canal to inspect damage, and to examine the headworks. Where the physical infrastructure was not recognizable because, for instance, a road had been built on top of it, the canal's location was verified by interviewing those in the area.

The unit of analysis is the group of users. The members are the primary respondents. The respondents were chosen as follows: For each canal, identify the same set of users in the village if noted in the survey. Otherwise, treat the group of current users as the group of respondents. From this group, choose at least 3 respondents, such that one is a poorer user. A poorer user is one who appears to have fewer assets and smaller landholdings. Choose one who appears to be knowledgeable about the canal, and choose one who was the first to speak to them. Speak to more users if further information is required. In case of canals that no longer exist, look for older users who had lived there continuously. Among them, find former users. Choose one as the primary respondent. Overall, if you receive multiple conflicting answers to a question, try to resolve it by speaking to more users. Use reasoned judgment and instinct when aggregating the answers.

Thus, enumerators interviewed at least three users: the first user that was willing to answer questions, one who was regarded as being knowledgeable about the canal, and a poorer looking user based on their material condition (house, appearance, size of land). Enumerators aggregated subjective responses as follows: any occurrence of a poor assessment resulted in an aggregate of poor, and for the others, whether satisfactory or good was more frequent across respondents determined the coding. Enumerators then returned to Kathmandu and entered the data using a custom web-based form (using mysql and php).

Interview Coding

Interviews were coded by the author. There were approximately 1,200 hours of audio in total. Because of the volume and cost these interviews were not transcribed or translated. Instead they were coded by the author based on notes taken while listening to them. An interview with each individual was marked as containing comparative statements for stopping or reducing cooperation with existing institutions. These comparisons were collected across interviews and grouped by similarity of comparison. This led to eight categories of reasons for reducing or stopping cooperation. The interviews were retroactively assigned these category labels, and each one had at least two. Interviews were conducted in a group setting or individually.

Table 27 **Breakdown of Interview Types**

Type of Interview	Total Participants	Percent
Individual Interviews	585	70.74%
Group Interviews	242	29.26%
Total Individuals	827	100%

Table 28 **Characteristics of Group Interviews**

Characteristics	Participants
Max Size	16
Min Size	3
Mean Size	8
Std. Dev. Size	4
Total Group Interviews	30

Table 29 **Gender Characteristics of Individual Interviewees**

Characteristics	Participants
Male	468
Female	92
Unknown	25
Total	585

Table 30 **Whether or not participants had an official position in the Water User's Association**

Characteristics	Participants
Officers	163
Not Officers	395
Unknown	27
Total	585

Variable List

The following variables were used in this analysis. The variable names in the final column are referred to in the main text. Note that differences between rounds in the values of a particular variable are calculated by subtracting the second round value from the first round one. These change variables are coded Less, More, and Same. Their prefix is the same as below, but their suffix is "change" instead of the round number, for example, *gtrustchange*.

Summary Statistics

Data Quality and Assumptions

Because this study depends on an earlier study, several aspects of the data have to be addressed. This section has the necessary assumptions that had to be made in order to construct the study. Many of these assumptions become necessary because this is an independent and direct replication. I had no relationship with Ostrom's team when they did the study, and I did not do this follow-up under their influence. The primary difference between the two rounds of data collection is that the baseline was derived by coding extant case studies while the follow-up was through direct application of a survey to users.

Precision

Because the variables in this data set contain subjective assessments, the precision cannot be ensured across rounds. However, no measurements are involved.

Assumption: Problems of precision do not significantly alter the results across cases.

Table 31 **variables used in the dataset variable names are suffixed with 1, 2, or "change" depending on the round, unless they were only asked in one round. * represents the names of other variables that are evident from their position in the list**

#	Question	Type	Values	Name
1	Is the canal still in use?	Reported and Observed	Yes; No	survived
2	Please state the year in which fieldwork was completed.	Calculated	Positive Integer	duration
3	How is the adequacy of water? (Pugne gari aaune)	Reported and Observed	Good; Satisfactory; Poor	padeq
4	How is the reliability of water? (Bharpardo)	Reported and Observed		prel
5	How well maintained is the headworks?	Observed		phead
6	How well maintained is the canal?	Observed		pcanal
7	What are the causes of deterioration in the canal?	Reported	Neglect; Disaster; Conflict; Natural	canalcause
8	What are the causes of deterioration in the headworks?	Reported		headcause
9	Do takers share cultural practices that promote cooperation?	Reported	Yes; No	ccocult
10	Have they worked together on other activities in the past?	Reported		ccoact
11	How easy to believe verbal promises?	Reported	Difficult; Somewhat Easy; Easy	gtrust
12	Income difference between wealthiest and poorest users?	Reported	Low; Moderate; High	fecogap
13	Is there a difference between users with respect to Gender?	Reported and Observed	Yes; No	hgender
14	Is there a difference between users with respect to Ethnicity?	Reported and Observed	Yes; No	hethnic
15	Is there a difference between users with respect to Caste?	Reported and Observed	Yes; No	hcaste

(continued)

Table 31 **Continued**

#	Question	Type	Values	Name
16	Is there a difference between users with respect to Religion?	Reported and Observed	Yes; No	hreligion
17	Is there a difference between users with respect to Language?	Reported and Observed	Yes; No	hlanguage
18	Is there a difference between users' Political Party?	Reported and Observed	Yes; No	hparty
19	Has any private agency, government or donor given assistance?	Reported	Yes; No	massist
20	Are the rules perceived as legitimate?	Reported	Yes; No	flegit
21	Are there any who have been consistently disadvantaged?	Reported	Yes; No	fdisadv
22	Do some get considerably less water than they want?	Reported	Yes; No	fspace
23	Have the relatively worse off been deprived of water?	Reported	Yes; No	fworsedeprived
24	Are the rules complex?	Reported	Yes; No	fcomplexrules
25	Are some assigned substantially more duties than others?	Reported	Yes; No	fevenwork
26	Do users contribute their own labor?	Reported	Yes; No	fselflabor
27	Do the rules give consistent advantage to some users?	Reported	Yes; No	fadvantage
28	Was this canal added to the sample in the second round?	Assigned	Yes; No	added
29	How many shocks did this canal experience?	Calculated	Positive Integer	numchanges
30	What is the length of the shared parts of the canal (in km)	Reported and Observed	Grouped by range	mlength
31	Percentage spending significant time not on agricultural?	Reported	<0; 10 –25; > 25	msubnot

Table 32 **Summary statistics. This table shows the summary statistics grouped by Round. Round 1 refers to the original NIIS dataset, Round 2 to the new dataset. Changes refers to the difference in the values of each variable between the two rounds, calculated by subtracting the value in the first round from the second, in some cases after a transformation. See supplementary materials for further details on their encoding. Except for length, which has a straightforward interpretation, 0 indicates no change, -1 indicates a decrease and a +1 an increase. This does not contain the 39 added systems. msubnot is coded as 1 (less than 10%), 2 (10 to 25%) and 3 (more than 25%)}**

	Round 1						Round 2						Changes					
	n	*mean*	*sd*	*min*	*max*	*rr*	*n*	*mean*	*sd*	*min*	*max*	*rr*	*n*	*mean*	*sd*	*min*	*max*	*rr*
Pct in non Ag occupations (msubnot)	187	1.27	0.51	1	3	80.26	192	1.83	0.85	1	3	95.05	161	0.60	0.88	−1	2	79.70
Length of Canal in 100m (mlength)	173	6.18	3.24	1	11	74.25	173	6.18	3.24	1	11	85.64	173	6.18	3.24	1	11	85.64
Received External Assistance (massist)	220	1.00	0.07	0	1	94.42	194	0.80	0.40	0	1	96.04	191	0.19	0.41	−1	1	94.55
Perceived Adequacy (padeq)	220	0.43	0.50	0	1	94.42	188	1.18	0.74	0	2	93.07	183	−0.04	0.68	−1	1	90.59
Perceived Reliability (prel)	220	0.77	0.42	0	1	94.42	187	1.16	0.80	0	2	92.57	167	−0.32	0.65	−1	1	82.67
Condition of the canal (pcanal)	212	1.14	0.43	0	2	90.99	194	0.92	0.67	0	2	96.04	185	−0.18	0.67	−1	1	91.58
Condition of the headworks (phead)	211	1.18	0.42	0	2	90.56	194	0.97	0.79	0	2	96.04	185	−0.17	0.80	−1	1	91.58
Income gap within group (fecogap)	213	0.93	0.73	0	2	91.42	188	0.94	0.61	0	2	93.07	180	−0.02	0.76	−1	1	89.11
Caste Heterogeneity (hcaste)	215	0.81	0.39	0	1	92.27	194	0.88	0.32	0	1	96.04	186	0.09	0.50	−1	1	92.08
Ethnic Heterogeneity (hethnic)	219	0.72	0.45	0	1	93.99	194	0.86	0.35	0	1	96.04	190	0.17	0.57	−1	1	94.06
Gender Heterogeneity (hgender)	206	0.65	0.48	0	1	88.41	194	0.91	0.29	0	1	96.04	179	0.26	0.59	−1	1	88.61
Language Heterogeneity (hlanguage)	216	0.51	0.50	0	1	92.70	194	0.63	0.48	0	1	96.04	187	0.17	0.71	−1	1	92.57

(continued)

Table 32 **Continued**

	Round 1						Round 2						Changes					
	n	*mean*	*sd*	*min*	*max*	*rr*	*n*	*mean*	*sd*	*min*	*max*	*rr*	*n*	*mean*	*sd*	*min*	*max*	*rr*
Political Heterogeneity (hparty)	71	0.97	0.17	0	1	30.47	194	0.92	0.28	0	1	96.04	52	-0.15	0.36	-1	0	25.74
Religious Heterogeneity (hreligion)	215	0.37	0.48	0	1	92.27	194	0.77	0.42	0	1	96.04	186	0.43	0.62	-1	1	92.08
Prior noncultural activities (ccoact)	199	0.32	0.47	0	1	85.41	194	0.97	0.16	0	1	96.04	169	0.62	0.50	-1	1	83.66
Prior cultural activities (ccocult)	199	0.26	0.44	0	1	85.41	194	0.76	0.43	0	1	96.04	169	0.51	0.56	-1	1	83.66
Easy to believe promises (gtrust)	218	1.49	0.62	0	2	93.56	194	1.43	0.66	0	2	96.04	187	-0.07	0.71	-1	1	92.57
Rules are legitimate (flegit)	189	0.91	0.29	0	1	81.12	194	1.54	0.78	0	2	96.04	161	-0.18	0.49	-1	1	79.70
Rules are complex (fcomplexrules)	195	0.09	0.28	0	1	83.69	194	0.05	0.21	0	1	96.04	170	-0.06	0.34	-1	1	84.16
Substantially more duties for some (fevenwork)	56	0.16	0.37	0	1	24.03	194	0.27	0.44	0	1	96.04	50	0.10	0.51	-1	1	24.75
Users contribute own labor (fselflabor)	218	0.87	0.34	0	1	93.56	194	0.92	0.27	0	1	96.04	188	0.06	0.42	-1	1	93.07
Some consistently advantaged (fadvantage)	49	0.20	0.41	0	1	21.03	194	0.40	0.49	0	1	96.04	45	0.20	0.73	-1	1	22.28
Some consistently disadvantaged (fdisadv)	209	0.27	0.44	0	1	89.70	194	0.44	0.50	0	1	96.04	179	0.14	0.67	-1	1	88.61
Poor are excluded (fworsedeprived)	136	0.18	0.39	0	1	58.37	194	0.02	0.12	0	1	96.04	120	-0.18	0.43	-1	1	59.41
Some get considerably less water (fspace)	195	0.52	0.50	0	1	83.69	194	0.56	0.50	0	1	96.04	166	-0.01	0.70	-1	1	82.18

Note: sd = Standard Deviation; n = nonmissing responses; rr = resulting response rate

Bias

The follow-up study favors sampling groups close to the headworks/intake. This results in oversampling better functioning areas with generally less variability and better functioning. However, assessments are compared at the tail end so this mitigates this bias to an extent. **Assumption:** Comparing responses at the tail end mitigates biases over the dataset.

Representativeness

The sample is not known to represent any population. Within each village, the sampling of respondents is not as comprehensive as some of the studies on which the prior dataset was based. No effort was made to get a representative sampling of users as it was not clear how this sampling would have had to been done. The responses cannot be guaranteed to be representative of the responses of the set of users. Also, earlier users could not be identified in all cases and may not have been alive. We do not know who was spoken to in the baseline because this was not recorded. In some instances, users noted that they remembered participating in a similar survey. But this was not reliable as these canals likely have been studied multiple times since then. **Assumption:** Assuming common knowledge and symmetric information between users (as Ostrom did) and selecting three or more users from each location provides adequate representativeness of user perceptions across cases.

Comparability

The variable encoding, when subjective, cannot be guaranteed to be comparable across two rounds. For example, adequacy (which depends on the respondent) and physical condition (which depends on the enumerator). **Assumption:** These assessments are comparable across rounds.

Some variable values are collapsed from trinary to binary in order to be directly comparable across rounds. This comparability cannot be assured. Also, when there is a choice for collapsing (odd to even number of categories for instance), this can affect the result. **Assumption:** Results will be robust to alternative collapsing across cases.

Completeness

The follow-up sample is complete compared to the baseline. All questions asked in Round 1 were also asked in Round 2. Some canals could not be found.

When respondents (former users) were available to explain, they verified what happened. When not, it could be that we failed to locate it. This can only be the case with 31 or less of the canals. **Assumption:** Those that could not be located and where we could not find respondents were no longer in use.

Sensitivity

We cannot assess the sensitivity of enumerator assessments. The sensitivity of the sample is addressed by Fisher's exact test. The training of enumerators also lessens this variability across enumerators. **Assumption:** The results of enumerator assessments are not significantly sensitive to the enumerator across cases.

Appendix 2

EXPANDED RESULTS

In this section, I collect all the tables and other analyses that were referred to in the main text but could not be included for reasons of readability. Although this section could be read through from beginning to end, much as the endnotes of a text can be, it is more advisable for reasons of clarity and context that it be used to follow along with the arguments in the main text.

Table 33 **The number of user-reported changes experienced by surviving canals. The table shows then number of canals (n) that experienced a certain number of external changes (x). It is apparent that most of the canals faced multiple changes in their external conditions. (N = 194, μ_x = 4.4, σ_x = 0.96). 8 were missing.**

Number of changes (numchanges)	Number of canals (n)	% of canals (%)
1	1	0.5
2	3	1.5
3	28	14.5
4	69	35.6
5	74	38.1
6	17	8.8
7	2	1.0

Table 34 **User-reported causes of physical deterioration in surviving canals: Row percentages are in parentheses. (N = 202)**

	Conflict	Disaster	Natural*	Neglect	Total
Head deterioration (headcause)	1 (0.8)	43 (33.9)	67 (52.8)	16 (12.6)	127
Canal deterioration (canalcause)	0 (0.0)	48 (30.2)	94 (59.1)	17 (10.7)	159

No deterioration = 19; * Normal wear and tear which users expect to repair.

Table 35 **Sampling and assistance. Being in the original study does not relate to having received some form of assistance from government or other sources after initial construction. (N = 233)**

In the original study? (added) Received outside assistance? (massist2)	Yes	No	Total
No	31	8	39
Yes	163	31	194
Total	194	39	233

Fisher's Exact Test = 0.391

Table 36 **Canal performance (2013): The table shows how users perceived the functioning of their canal coded as Good, Satisfactory and Poor. Row percentages are in parentheses. (N = 202)**

	Good	Satisfactory	Poor	Total
Perceived Adequacy (padeq2)	71 (37.8)	79 (42.0)	38 (20.2)	188
Perceived Reliability (prel2)	76 (40.6)	64 (34.2)	47 (25.1)	187
Physical condition of headworks (phead2)	58 (29.9)	73 (37.6)	63 (32.5)	194
Physical condition of the canal (pcanal2)	36 (18.6)	107 (55.2)	51 (26.3)	194

Table 37 **Changes in canal performance (1976–2013) This table shows changes in canal performance within cases between the first and second surveys. Changes to physical condition are computed by subtracting the two survey assessments (each coded as Good, Satisfactory or Poor) and then collapsing them into a binary classification. User perceptions are collapsed to binary before comparison. Row percentages are in parentheses. (N = 202)**

	Better	*Same*	*Worse*	*Total*
Physical condition of the canal (pcanalchange)	28 (15.1)	95 (51.4)	62 (33.5)	185
Physical condition of the headworks (pheadchange)	45 (24.3)	63 (34.1)	77 (4 1.6)	185
User perceived adequacy (padeqchange)	39 (21.3)	98 (53.6)	46 (25.1)	183
User perceived reliability (prelchange)	17 (10.2)	80 (47.9)	70 (41.9)	167

Table 38 **Performance by number of external shocks (2013) This table shows the significance of the relationship between the aspects of canal performance and the number of external shocks (numshocks) that the canal was reported to have experienced since the first observation. p-values are computed using Fisher's Exact Test. (N = 202)**

	p
Physical condition of headworks (phead2)	0.992
Physical condition of canal (pcanal2)	0.402
Perceived Adequacy (padeq2)	0.182
Perceived Reliability (prel2)	0.148

Table 39 **Fairness and Performance Association between indicators of fairness and performance. The values of the performance variables are poor, fair and good. Δ% can be interpreted analogous to magnitude and direction of this association. It represents the change in the column variable when the value of the row variable changes. For trivariate ordinal variables (e.g. physical condition), the change is the difference between the lowest two categories (e.g. fair and poor). P-values are from Fisher's Exact Test. For changes, Pearson's r shows the direction of the relationship, and the magnitude does not have a clear interpretation.**

	Round 1 (N=233)			Round 2 (N=202)			Changes (N=202)		
	Δ%	p	n	Δ%	p	n	r	p	n
Rules are legitimate (flegit)									
Condition of the canal	−12.11	0.127	178	10.97	0.479	194	0.1	0.642	154
Condition of the headworks	8.74	0.575	178	2.14	0.245	194	0.24	0.045*	154
Perceived Adequacy	10.86	0.451	186	−11.55	0.466	188	0.01	0.862	154
Perceived Reliability	−4.84	0.768	186	6.72	0.165	187	−0.07	0.74	142
Rules are complex (fcomplexrules)									
Condition of the canal	−6.69	0.825	185	−7.81	0.904	194	−0.06	0.645	163
Condition of the headworks	8.45	0.579	184	15.25	0.524	194	−0.05	0.716	163
Perceived Adequacy	−42.12	0.001***	192	30.36	0.267	188	−0.2	0.004**	162
Perceived Reliability	−26.49	0.029*	192	35.89	0.174	187	−0.15	0.285	149

Substantially more duties for some (fevenwork)									
Condition of the canal	−6.64	1	50	−9.59	0.023*	194	−0.15	0.727	44
Condition of the headworks	0.34	1	50	−6.69	0.361	194	−0.28	0.25	45
Perceived Adequacy	0.56	1	53	12.41	0.326	188	−0.04	0.583	46
Perceived Reliability	−33.61	0.104	53	6.98	0.72	187	−0.05	0.389	41
Users contribute own labor (fselflabor)									
Condition of the canal	−1.1	1	207	−1.56	0.578	194	−0.16	0.259	181
Condition of the headworks	5.37	0.749	206	−10.95	0.526	194	0.03	0.037*	181
Perceived Adequacy	37.14	0.000***	214	−2.43	0.883	188	0.13	0.038*	178
Perceived Reliability	27.61	0.003**	214	−6.55	0.584	187	0.12	0.003**	162
Some consistently advantaged (fadvantage)									
Condition of the canal	−10.36	0.775	43	−7.45	0.302	194	0.23	0.82	39
Condition of the headworks	0.74	1	42	−4.98	0.392	194	0.11	0.767	39
Perceived Adequacy	−10.21	0.701	46	4.22	0.763	188	−0.04	0.186	41
Perceived Reliability	−42.35	0.042*	46	−13.06	0.203	187	−0.29	0.058	35

(*continued*)

Table 39 **Continued**

	Round 1 (N=233)			Round 2 (N=202)			Changes (N=202)		
	Δ%	p	n	Δ%	p	n	r	p	n
Some consistently disadvantaged (fdisadv)									
Condition of the canal	5.49	0.615	202	−6.18	0.404	194	−0.08	0.599	175
Condition of the headworks	10.03	0.227	200	−1.49	0.098	194	−0.03	0.99	174
Perceived Adequacy	−41.01	0.000***	208	−19.4	0.024*	188	−0.27	0.003**	173
Perceived Reliability	−32.38	0.000***	208	−10.71	0.035*	187	−0.21	0.07	158
Poor are excluded (fworsedeprived)									
Condition of the canal	−0.47	0.904	132	−18.85	0.588	194	0.1	0.343	117
Condition of the headworks	5.36	0.681	131	−30.37	0.777	194	0.05	0.899	117
Perceived Adequacy	−24.14	0.040*	136	−38.38	0.23	188	−0.19	0.169	117
Perceived Reliability	−31.28	0.002**	136	−7.43	0.617	187	−0.23	0.015*	108
Some get considerably less water than they want (fspace)									
Condition of the canal	−2.83	0.605	185	−10.53	0.065	194	−0.13	0.445	159
Condition of the headworks	−7.77	0.402	186	−0.6	0.759	194	−0.08	0.807	161
Perceived Adequacy	−32.64	0.000***	191	−27.3	0.001***	188	−0.16	0.113	157
Perceived Reliability	−17.84	0.001**	191	−23.47	0.003**	187	−0.23	0.045*	142

Note: *p <0.05, **p<0.01, ***p<0.001

Table 40 Group Heterogeneity and Performance Association between group variables and performance. The values of the performance variables are poor, fair and good. Δ% can be interpreted analogous to magnitude and direction of this association. It represents the change in the column variable when the value of the row variable changes. For trivariate ordinal variables (e.g., physical condition), the change is the difference between the lowest two categories (e.g., fair and poor). P-values are from Fisher's Exact Test. For changes, Pearson's r shows the direction of the relationship, and the magnitude does not have a clear interpretation.

	Round 1 (N=233)			Round 2 (N=202)			Changes (N=202)		
	Δ%	p	N	Δ%	p	N	r	p	N
Income gap between wealthiest and poorest (fecogap)									
Condition of the canal	−3.09	0.806	203	5.88	0.095.	188	0.05	0.972	173
Condition of the headworks	−16.33	0.053.	202	7.96	0.756	188	0	0.43	173
Perceived Adequacy	−19.21	0.055.	209	−2.97	0.099.	183	−0.12	0.129	171
Perceived Reliability	−7.55	0.528	209	10.08	0.105	182	−0.01	0.203	157
Caste Heterogeneity (hcaste)									
Condition of the canal	0.88	0.276	205	−28.27	0.006**	194	−0.02	0.318	179
Condition of the headworks	−2.25	0.091.	204	−10.48	0.106	194	0.03	0.143	179
Perceived Adequacy	6.63	0.48	212	18.26	0.222	188	0.13	0.07.	177
Perceived Reliability	−0.87	1	212	16.6	0.255	187	0.07	0.255	162
Ethnic Heterogeneity (hethnic)									
Condition of the canal	−0.56	0.267	209	−17.17	0.047*	194	−0.08	0.611	183
Condition of the headworks	−3.36	0.217	208	−3.99	0.246	194	0.08	0.443	183
Perceived Adequacy	19.84	0.01**	215	12.58	0.378	188	0.16	0.035*	180
Perceived Reliability	13.62	0.041*	215	17.2	0.194	187	0.12	0.488	164

(continued)

Table 40 **Continued**

	Round 1 (N=233)			Round 2 (N=202)			Changes (N=202)		
	Δ%	p	N	Δ%	p	N	r	p	N
Gender Heterogeneity (hgender)									
Condition of the canal	2.9	0.591	196	−10.16	0.521	194	−0.03	0.071.	170
Condition of the headworks	11.54	0.082.	195	−3.79	0.624	194	0.06	0.319	170
Perceived Adequacy	−8.03	0.294	202	−7.39	0.775	188	−0.09	0.315	167
Perceived Reliability	−11.07	0.075.	202	−4.21	1	187	−0.08	0.16	151
Language Heterogeneity (hlanguage)									
Condition of the canal	0.97	0.598	206	−8.5	0.361	194	−0.16	0.236	180
Condition of the headworks	−0.18	0.948	205	9.39	0.37	194	0	0.438	180
Perceived Adequacy	10.5	0.13	212	−0.17	0.887	188	0.02	0.668	177
Perceived Reliability	4.18	0.507	212	1.93	0.933	187	0.05	0.597	162
Political Heterogeneity (hparty)									
Condition of the canal	13.64	1	68	−7.02	0.69	194	0.1	0.675	50
Condition of the headworks	9.09	1	67	−8.29	0.449	194	−0.07	0.255	50
Perceived Adequacy	−33.33	1	71	0.29	0.881	188	−0.03	0.673	52
Perceived Reliability	−11.59	1	71	−3.4	1	187	0.01	1	47
Religious Heterogeneity (hreligion)									
Condition of the canal	−4.81	0.075.	205	−16.35	0.047*	194	−0.1	0.543	179
Condition of the headworks	−1.64	0.563	204	−7.37	0.532	194	−0.03	0.908	179
Perceived Adequacy	−2.89	0.773	212	5.83	0.661	188	0.03	0.855	177
Perceived Reliability	−6.71	0.299	212	6.7	0.753	187	0.01	0.774	162

REFERENCES

Chapter 1

Agrawal, A. (2001) "Common Property Institutions and Sustainable Governance of Resources," *World Development*, 29(10), pp. 1649–1672. Available at: https://doi.org/10.1016/S0305-750X(01)00063-8.

Aligica, P.D. and Tarko, V. (2012) "Polycentricity: From Polanyi to Ostrom, and Beyond," *Governance*, 25(2), pp. 237–262. Available at: https://doi.org/10.1111/j.1468-0491.2011.01550.x.

Axelrod, R.M. (2006) *The Evolution of Cooperation*. Rev. ed. New York: Basic Books.

Baldwin, E. et al. (2016) "Polycentric Governance and Irrigation Reform in Kenya," *Governance*, 29(2), pp. 207–225. Available at: https://doi.org/10.1111/gove.12160.

Blomquist, W. et al. (1994) "Regularities from the Field and Possible Explanations," in *Rules, Games, and Common-Pool Resource*. Ann Arbor: University of Michigan Press, pp. 301–318.

Chambers, R. (1988) *Managing Canal Irrigation: Practical Analysis from South Asia*. New York: Cambridge University Press.

Cole, D.H. and McGinnis, M.D. (2014) *Elinor Ostrom and the Bloomington School of Political Economy: Polycentricity in Public Administration and Political Science*. Lexington Books.

Cole, D.H. and McGinnis, M.D. (2017) *Elinor Ostrom and the Bloomington School of Political Economy: A Framework for Policy Analysis*. Lanham, MD: Lexington Books.

Coman, K. (1911) "Some Unsettled Problems of Irrigation," *The American Economic Review*, 1(1), pp. 1–19.

Congleton, R.D. (2014) "The Contractarian Constitutional Political Economy of James Buchanan," *Constitutional Political Economy*, 25(1), pp. 39–67. Available at: https://doi.org/10.1007/s10602-013-9151-x.

Cox, M., Arnold, G. and Tomás, S.V. (2010) "A Review of Design Principles for Community-based Natural Resource Management," *Ecology and Society*, 15(4). Available at: https://www.jstor.org/stable/26268233.

Elster, J. (ed.) (1985) *Ulysses and the Sirens: Studies in Rationality and Irrationality*. Revised ed. edition. Cambridge: Cambridge University Press.

Fehr, E. and Fischbacher, U. (2003) "The Nature of Human Altruism," *Nature*, 425(6960), pp. 785–791. Available at: https://doi.org/10.1038/nature02043.

Fehr, E. and Schmidt, K.M. (1999) "A Theory of Fairness, Competition, and Cooperation," *The Quarterly Journal of Economics*, 114(3), pp. 817–868. Available at: https://doi.org/10.1162/003355399556151.

Frey, U. (2020) *Sustainable Governance of Natural Resources: Uncovering Success Patterns with Machine Learning*. Oxford: Oxford University Press.

Gardner, R., Walker, J. and Ostrom, E. (1994) *Rules, Games, and Common-Pool Resources*. Ann Arbor: University of Michigan Press.

Gintis, H. et al. (2003) "Explaining Altruistic Behavior in Humans," *Evolution and Human Behavior*, 24(3), pp. 153–172. Available at: https://doi.org/10.1016/S1090-5138(02)00157-5.

Gintis, H. et al. (2005) *Moral Sentiments and Material Interests: The Foundations of Cooperation in Economic Life*. Cambridge, MA: MIT Press. Available at: http://ebookcentral.proquest.com/lib/nyulibrary-ebooks/detail.action?docID=3338575.

Gintis, H. and Bowles, S. (2011) *A Cooperative Species: Human Reciprocity and Its Evolution*. Princeton, NJ: Princeton University Press.

Hardin, G. (1968) "The Tragedy of the Commons," *Science*, 162(3859), pp. 1243–1248. Available at: https://doi.org/10.1126/science.162.3859.1243.

Hobbes, T. (1996) *Leviathan*. Rev. student ed. Edited by R. Tuck. Cambridge: Cambridge University Press.

Kahneman, D., Knetsch, J.L. and Thaler, R. (1986) "Fairness as a Constraint on Profit Seeking: Entitlements in the Market," *The American Economic Review*, 76(4), pp. 728–741.

Kara, S. (2014) *Bonded Labor: Tackling the System of Slavery in South Asia*. Illustrated edition. New York: Columbia University Press.

Lam, W.F. (1998) *Governing Irrigation Systems in Nepal: Institutions, Infrastructure, and Collective Action*. Oakland, CA: ICS Press.

Levi, M. (1989) *Of Rule and Revenue*. Berkeley, California: University of California Press.

Locke, R.M. (2001) "Building Trust," *Annual Meetings of the American Political Science Association*. San Francisco, CA: Hilton Towers, Available at: http://web.mit.edu/clawson/www/poli sci/research/locke/building_trust.pdf.

Mansbridge, J. (2014) "The Role of the State in Governing the Commons," *Environmental Science & Policy*, 36, pp. 8–10. Available at: https://doi.org/10.1016/j.envsci.2013.07.006.

McGinnis, M.D. (1999a) *Polycentric Governance and Development: Readings from the Workshop in Political Theory and Policy Analysis*. Ann Arbor, MI: University of Michigan Press.

McGinnis, M.D. (1999b) *Polycentricity and Local Public Economies: Readings from the Workshop in Political Theory and Policy Analysis*. Ann Arbor, MI: University of Michigan Press.

McGinnis, M.D. (2011) "An Introduction to IAD and the Language of the Ostrom Workshop: A Simple Guide to a Complex Framework," *Policy Studies Journal*, 39(1), pp. 169–183. Available at: https://doi.org/10.1111/j.1541-0072.2010.00401.x.

McGinnis, M.D. and Ostrom, E. (2012) "Reflections on Vincent Ostrom, Public Administration, and Polycentricity," *Public Administration Review*, 72(1), pp. 15–25. Available at: https://doi.org/10.1111/j.1540-6210.2011.02488.x.

Meinzen-Dick, R. (2007) "Beyond Panaceas in Water Institutions," *Proceedings of the National Academy of Sciences of the United States of America*, 104(39), pp. 15200–15205. Available at: https://doi.org/10.1073/pnas.0702296104.

Nagel, T. (1959) "Hobbes's Concept of Obligation," *The Philosophical Review*, 68(1), pp. 68–83. Available at: https://doi.org/10.2307/2182547.

Nash, J. (1951) "Non-Cooperative Games," *The Annals of Mathematics*, 54(2), p. 286. Available at: https://doi.org/10.2307/1969529.

Nobel Media AB (2014) *Nobel Prize Lecture, Elinor Ostrom*. Available at: http://www.nobelprize.org/mediaplayer/index.php?id=1223.

Olson, M. (1965) *The Logic of Collective Action; Public Goods and the Theory of Groups*. Cambridge, MA: Harvard University Press.

Ostrom, E. (1990) *Governing the Commons: The Evolution of Institutions for Collective Action*. Cambridge; New York: Cambridge University Press.

Ostrom, E. (2005) *Understanding Institutional Diversity*. Princeton, NJ: Princeton University Press (Princeton paperbacks).

Ostrom, E. (2007) "A Diagnostic Approach for Going beyond Panaceas," *Proceedings of the National Academy of Sciences*, 104(39), pp. 15181–15187. Available at: https://doi.org/10.1073/pnas.0702288104.

Ostrom, E. (2010) "Beyond Markets and States: Polycentric Governance of Complex Economic Systems. Prize Lecture, December 8, 2009," *American Economic Review*, 100(3), pp. 641–72.

Ostrom, E. et al. (2011) *Improving Irrigation in Asia: Sustainable Performance of an Innovative Intervention in Nepal*. Northampton, MA: Edward Elgar Pub.

Ostrom, E. and Cox, and M. (2010) "Moving beyond Panaceas: A Multitiered Diagnostic Approach for Social-Ecological Analysis," *Environmental Conservation*, 37(4), pp. 451–63.

Ostrom, E., Ingram, G.K. and Hong, Y.-H. (2009) "Design Principles of Robust Property Rights Institutions: What Have We Learned?" in *Property Rights and Land Policies*. Cambridge, MA: Lincoln Institute of Land Policy. Available at: https://www.lincolninst.edu/pubs/2076 _Design-Principles-of-Robust-Property-Rights-Institutions-What-Have-We-Learned.

Ostrom, E. and Walker, J. (eds.) (2003) *Trust and reciprocity: interdisciplinary lessons from experimental research*. New York: Russell Sage Foundation.

Ostrom, V., Tiebout, C.M. and Warren, R. (1961) "The Organization of Government in Metropolitan Areas: A Theoretical Inquiry," *American Political Science Review*, 55(4), pp. 831–842. Available at: https://doi.org/10.1017/S0003055400125973.

Poteete, A.R., Janssen, M. and Ostrom, E. (2010) *Working Together: Collective Action, the Commons, and Multiple Methods in Practice*. Princeton, NJ: Princeton University Press.

Ribot, J.C., Agrawal, A. and Larson, A.M. (2006) "Recentralizing While Decentralizing: How National Governments Reappropriate Forest Resources," *World Development*, 34(11), pp. 1864–1886. Available at: https://doi.org/10.1016/j.worlddev.2005.11.020.

Roemer, J.E. (2019) *How We Cooperate: A Theory of Kantian Optimization*. Illustrated edition. New Haven, CT: Yale University Press.

Scheve, K. and Stasavage, D. (2017) *Taxing the Rich: A History of Fiscal Fairness in the United States and Europe*. Reprint edition. Princeton, NJ: Princeton University Press.

Sen, A.K. (1977) "Rational Fools: A Critique of the Behavioral Foundations of Economic Theory," *Philosophy & Public Affairs*, 6(4), pp. 317–344.

Sen, A.K. (1993) "Positional Objectivity," *Philosophy & Public Affairs*, 22(2), pp. 126–145.

Thiel, A., Blomquist, W.A. and Garrick, D.E. (eds.) (2019) *Governing Complexity: Analyzing and Applying Polycentricity*. Cambridge: Cambridge University Press. Available at: https://doi.org/10.1017/9781108325721.

Tyler, T. and Blader, S. (2013) *Cooperation in Groups: Procedural Justice, Social Identity, and Behavioral Engagement*. Boca Raton, FL: Psychology Press.

Uphoff, N.T. (1991) *Managing Irrigation: Analyzing and Improving the Performance of Bureaucracies*. New Delhi: Sage Publications.

Uphoff, N.T. (1992) *Learning from Gal Oya: Possibilities for Participatory Development and Post-Newtonian Social Science*. Ithaca, NY: Cornell University Press.

Wade, R. (1979) "The social response to irrigation: An Indian case study," *Journal of Development Studies*, 16(1), pp. 3–26. Available at: https://doi.org/10.1080/00220387908421741.

Wade, R. (1988) "The Management of Irrigation Systems: How to Evoke Trust and Avoid Prisoner's Dilemma," *World Development*, 16(4), pp. 489–500. Available at: https://doi.org/10.1016/0305-750X(88)90199-4.

Williamson, O.E. (1975) *Markets and Hierarchies, Analysis and Antitrust Implications: A Study in the Economics of Internal Organization*. New York: Free Press.

Chapter 2

Agresti, A. (2012) *Categorical Data Analysis*. 3rd ed. Hoboken, NJ: Wiley.

Arrow, K.J. (1974) *The Limits of Organization*. 1st ed. New York: Norton.

Baland, J.-M., Bardhan, P.K. and Bowles, S. (2007) *Inequality, Cooperation, and Environmental Sustainability*. Princeton, NJ: Princeton University Press.

Baland, J.-M. and Platteau, J.-P. (1999) "The Ambiguous Impact of Inequality on Local Resource Management," *World Development*, 27(5), pp. 773–788. Available at: https://doi.org/10.1016/S0305-750X(99)00026-1.

Bardhan, P. and Dayton-Johnson, J. (2002) "Unequal Irrigators: Heterogeneity and Commons Management in Large-Scale Multivariate Research," in E. Ostrom (ed.) *The Drama of the*

Commons. Washington, DC: National Academy Press, pp. 87–112. Available at: http://site.ebrary.com/id/10032451.

Bardhan, P. and Mookherjee, D. (2020) "Clientelistic Politics and Economic Development: An Overview," in Jean-Marie Baland, François Bourguignon, Jean-Philippe Platteau, and Thierry Verdier (eds.) *The Handbook of Economic Development and Institutions*. Princeton, NJ: Princeton University Press, pp. 84–102. Available at: https://doi.org/10.1515/9780691192017-004.

Bastakoti, R., Shivakoti, G. and Lebel, L. (2010) "Local Irrigation Management Institutions Mediate Changes Driven by External Policy and Market Pressures in Nepal and Thailand," *Environmental Management*, 46(3), pp. 411–423. Available at: https://doi.org/10.1007/s00 267-010-9544-9.

Freedman, D. and Lane, D. (1983) "A Nonstochastic Interpretation of Reported Significance Levels," *Journal of Business & Economic Statistics*, 1(4), pp. 292–298. Available at: https://doi.org/10.2307/1391660.

Frey, U. (2020) *Sustainable Governance of Natural Resources: Uncovering Success Patterns with Machine Learning*. Oxford: Oxford University Press.

Frey, U.J. and Rusch, H. (2014) "Modeling Ecological Success of Common Pool Resource Systems Using Large Datasets," *World Development*, 59, pp. 93–103. Available at: https://doi.org/10.1016/j.worlddev.2014.01.034.

Gardner, R., Walker, J. and Ostrom, E. (1994) *Rules, Games, and Common-Pool Resources*. Ann Arbor: University of Michigan Press.

Hayek, F.A. (1945) "The Use of Knowledge in Society," *The American Economic Review*, 35(4), pp. 519–530. Available at: https://doi.org/10.2307/1809376.

Hosmer Jr., D.W., Lemeshow, S. and Sturdivant, R.X. (2013) *Applied Logistic Regression*. Hoboken, NJ: John Wiley & Sons.

Lam, W.F. (1998) *Governing Irrigation Systems in Nepal: Institutions, Infrastructure, and Collective Action*. Oakland, CA: ICS Press.

Locke, R.M. (2001) "Building Trust," in *Annual Meetings of the American Political Science Association*. San Francisco, CA: Hilton Towers, Available at: http://web.mit.edu/clawson/www/polisci/research/locke/building_trust.pdf.

Lejano, Raul P. (2023) *Caring, Empathy, and the Commons: A Relational Theory of Collective Action*. Cambridge: Cambridge University Press.

Mahoney, J. and Thelen, K.A. (eds.) (2010) *Explaining Institutional Change: Ambiguity, Agency, and Power*. Cambridge: Cambridge University Press.

Meinzen-Dick, R. (2007) "Beyond Panaceas in Water Institutions," *Proceedings of the National Academy of Sciences of the United States of America*, 104(39), pp. 15200–15205. Available at: https://doi.org/10.1073/pnas.0702296104.

Ostrom, E. (1990) *Governing the Commons: The Evolution of Institutions for Collective Action*. Cambridge: Cambridge University Press.

Ostrom, E. (2005) *Understanding Institutional Diversity*. Princeton, NJ: Princeton University Press.

Ostrom, E. (2007) "A Diagnostic Approach for Going beyond Panaceas," *Proceedings of the National Academy of Sciences*, 104(39), pp. 15181–15187. Available at: https://doi.org/10.1073/pnas.0702288104.

Ostrom, E. (2010) "Beyond Markets and States: Polycentric Governance of Complex Economic Systems. Prize Lecture, December 8, 2009," *American Economic Review*, 100(3), pp. 641–672.

Ostrom, E. (2011) "Reflections on 'Some Unsettled Problems of Irrigation,'" *American Economic Review*, 101(1), pp. 49–63. Available at: https://doi.org/10.1257/aer.101.1.49.

Ostrom, E., Janssen, M. A., and Anderies, J. M. (2007) "Going beyond Panaceas," in *Proceedings of the National Academy of Science*, 104(39), pp. 15176–15178. https://doi.org/10.1073/pnas.0701886104

Ostrom, E. and Walker, J. (eds) (2003) *Trust and Reciprocity: Interdisciplinary Lessons from Experimental Research*. New York: Russell Sage Foundation.

Ostrom, E., Walker, J. and Gardner, R. (1992) "Covenants with and without a Sword: Self-Governance Is Possible," *American Political Science Review*, 86(02), pp. 404–417. Available at: https://doi.org/10.2307/1964229.

Poteete, A.R., Janssen, M. and Ostrom, E. (2010) *Working Together: Collective Action, the Commons, and Multiple Methods in Practice*. Princeton, NJ: Princeton University Press.

Powers, D.A. (1999) *Statistical Methods for Categorical Data Analysis*. 1 edition. San Diego: Emerald Group Publishing Limited.

Rawls, J. (1972) *A Theory of Justice*. Oxford: Clarendon Press.

Simon, H.A. and Simon, P.A. (1962) "Trial and Error Search in Solving Difficult Problems: Evidence from the Game of Chess," *Behavioral Science*, 7(4), pp. 425–429. Available at: https://doi.org/10.1002/bs.3830070402.

Varughese, G. and Ostrom, E. (2001) "The Contested Role of Heterogeneity in Collective Action: Some Evidence from Community Forestry in Nepal," *World Development*, 29(5), pp. 747–765. Available at: https://doi.org/10.1016/S0305-750X(01)00012-2.

Williamson, O.E. (2000) "The New Institutional Economics: Taking Stock, Looking Ahead," *Journal of Economic Literature*, 38(3), pp. 595–613. Available at: https://doi.org/10.1257/jel.38.3.595.

Chapter 3

Aligica, P.D. and Tarko, V. (2013) "Co-Production, Polycentricity, and Value Heterogeneity: The Ostroms' Public Choice Institutionalism Revisited," *American Political Science Review*, 107(4), pp. 726–741. Available at: https://doi.org/10.1017/S0003055413000427.

Becker, G.S. (1968) "Crime and Punishment: An Economic Approach," *Journal of Political Economy*, 76(2), pp. 169–217.

Bicchieri, C. (2005) *The Grammar of Society: The Nature and Dynamics of Social Norms*. Cambridge: Cambridge University Press. Available at: https://doi.org/10.1017/CBO9780511616037.

Cole, D.H. and McGinnis, M.D. (2014) *Elinor Ostrom and the Bloomington School of Political Economy: Polycentricity in Public Administration and Political Science*. Lanham, MD: Lexington Books.

Elster, J. (1989) *The Cement of Society: A Study of Social Order*. New York: Cambridge University Press.

Epstein, G. *et al.* (2021) "Drivers of Compliance Monitoring in Forest Commons," *Nature Sustainability*, 4(5), pp. 450–456. Available at: https://doi.org/10.1038/s41893-020-00673-4.

FAO (1985) *Irrigation Water Management Training Manual*. Rome: Food and Agriculture Organization.

Gardner, R., Walker, J. and Ostrom, E. (1994) *Rules, Games, and Common-Pool Resources*. Ann Arbor: University of Michigan Press.

Hirschman, A.O. (1967) *Development Projects Observed*. Washington D.C.: Brookings Institution Press.

Levi, M. (1989) *Of Rule and Revenue*. Berkeley, CA: University of California Press.

Ostrom, E. (1990) *Governing the Commons: The Evolution of Institutions for Collective Action*. Cambridge: Cambridge University Press.

Ostrom, E. (2000) "Collective Action and the Evolution of Social Norms," *Journal of Economic Perspectives*, 14(3), pp. 137–158. Available at: https://doi.org/10.1257/jep.14.3.137.

Ostrom, E. (2005) *Understanding Institutional Diversity*. Princeton, NJ: Princeton University Press.

Ostrom, E., Ingram, G.K. and Hong, Y.-H. (2009) "Design Principles of Robust Property Rights Institutions: What Have We Learned?" in *Property Rights and Land Policies*. Cambridge, Mass.: Lincoln Institute of Land Policy. Available at: https://www.lincolninst.edu/pubs/2076_Design-Principles-of-Robust-Property-Rights-Institutions-What-Have-We-Learned.

Poteete, A.R., Janssen, M. and Ostrom, E. (2010) *Working Together: Collective Action, the Commons, and Multiple Methods in Practice*. Princeton, NJ: Princeton University Press.

Scott, J.C. (2008) *Weapons of the Weak: Everyday Forms of Peasant Resistance*. New Haven, CT: Yale University Press.

Uphoff, N.T. (1991) *Managing Irrigation: Analyzing and Improving the Performance of Bureaucracies*. New Delhi: Sage Publications.

Williamson, O.E. (1975) *Markets and Hierarchies, Analysis and Antitrust Implications: A Study in the Economics of Internal Organization*. New York: Free Press.

Chapter 4

Aligica, P.D. and Tarko, V. (2013) "Co-Production, Polycentricity, and Value Heterogeneity: The Ostroms' Public Choice Institutionalism Revisited," *American Political Science Review*, 107(4), pp. 726–741. Available at: https://doi.org/10.1017/S0003055413000427.

Aumann, R.J. (1976) "Agreeing to Disagree," *The Annals of Statistics*, 4(6), pp. 1236–1239.

Axelrod, R. (1986) "An Evolutionary Approach to Norms," *American Political Science Review*, 80(4), pp. 1095–1111. Available at: https://doi.org/10.1017/S0003055400185016.

Becker, G.S. (1968) "Crime and Punishment: An Economic Approach," *Journal of Political Economy*, 76(2), pp. 169–217.

Bicchieri, C. (2005) *The Grammar of Society: The Nature and Dynamics of Social Norms*. Cambridge: Cambridge University Press.

Bicchieri, C. (2016) *Norms in the Wild: How to Diagnose, Measure, and Change Social Norms*. 1st edition. New York, NY: Oxford University Press.

Binmore, K. and Shaked, A. (2010) "Experimental Economics: Where Next?," *Journal of Economic Behavior & Organization*, 73(1), pp. 87–100.

Brennan, G. and Buchanan, J.M. (1986) *The Reason of Rules: Constitutional Political Economy*. Cambridge: Cambridge University Press.

Buchanan, J.M. (1965) "An Economic Theory of Clubs," *Economica*, 32(125), pp. 1–14. Available at: https://doi.org/10.2307/2552442.

Buchanan, J.M. (1987) *Economics: Between Predictive Science and Moral Philosophy*. College Station, TX: Texas A & M University Press.

Cole, D.H. (2015) "Advantages of a Polycentric Approach to Climate Change Policy," *Nature Climate Change*, 5(2), pp. 114–118. Available at: https://doi.org/10.1038/nclimate2490.

Colin F. Camerer (2011) *Behavioral Game Theory: Experiments in Strategic Interaction*. Princeton, NJ: Princeton University Press. Available at: http://proxy.library.nyu.edu/login?url= https://ebookcentral.proquest.com/lib/nyulibrary-ebooks/detail.action?docID=765287.

Congleton, R.D. (2014) "The Contractarian Constitutional Political Economy of James Buchanan," *Constitutional Political Economy*, 25(1), pp. 39–67. Available at: https://doi.org/10.1007/s10602-013-9151-x.

Cooper, D.J. and Kagel, J.H. (2016) "Other-Regarding Preferences: A Selective Survey of Experimental Results," in J. H. Kagel and A. E. Roth (eds.) *The Handbook of Experimental Economics*, Volume 2. Princeton, NJ: Princeton University Press, pp. 217–289.

Cox, M., Arnold, G. and Tomás, S.V. (2010) "A Review of Design Principles for Community-Based Natural Resource Management," *Ecology and Society*, 15(4). Available at: https://www.jstor.org/stable/26268233.

Dimick, M., Rueda, D. and Stegmueller, D. (2018) "Models of Other-Regarding Preferences, Inequality, and Redistribution," *Annual Review of Political Science*, 21(1), pp. 441–460. Available at: https://doi.org/10.1146/annurev-polisci-091515-030034.

Fehr, E. and Fischbacher, U. (2002) "Why Social Preferences Matter: The Impact of Non-Selfish Motives on Competition, Cooperation and Incentives," *The Economic Journal*, 112(478), pp. C1–C33.

Fehr, E. and Fischbacher, U. (2003) "The nature of human altruism," *Nature*, 425(6960), pp. 785–791. Available at: https://doi.org/10.1038/nature02043.

Fehr, E. and Leibbrandt, A. (2011) "A field study on cooperativeness and impatience in the Tragedy of the Commons," *Journal of Public Economics*, 95(9–10), pp. 1144–1155. Available at: https://doi.org/10.1016/j.jpubeco.2011.05.013.

Fehr, E. and Schmidt, K.M. (1999) "A Theory of Fairness, Competition, and Cooperation," *The Quarterly Journal of Economics*, 114(3), pp. 817–868. Available at: https://doi.org/10.1162/003355399556151.

Friend, C. (no date) "Social Contract Theory," *Internet Encyclopedia of Philosophy* [Preprint]. Available at: https://iep.utm.edu/soc-cont/.

Gauthier, D. (1987) *Morals by Agreement*. Clarendon Press.

Gauthier, D. (2007) "Why Contractarianism?" in R. Shafer-Landau (ed.) *Ethical Theory: An Anthology*. New York: John Wiley & Sons, pp. 620–630.

Gintis, H. et al. (2003) "Explaining Altruistic Behavior in Humans," *Evolution and Human Behavior*, 24(3), pp. 153–172. Available at: https://doi.org/10.1016/S1090-5138(02)00157-5.

Gintis, H. and Bowles, S. (2011) *A Cooperative Species: Human Reciprocity and Its Evolution*. Princeton, NJ: Princeton University Press.

Hardin, G. (1968) "The Tragedy of the Commons," *Science*, 162(3859), pp. 1243–1248. Available at: https://doi.org/10.1126/science.162.3859.1243.

Harsanyi, J.C. (1976) *Essays on Ethics, Social Behavior, and Scientific Explanation*. Dordrecht: Springer Netherlands. Available at: http://proxy.library.nyu.edu/login?url=http://link.springer.com/10.1007/978-94-010-9327-9.

Hilbe, C. et al. (2018) "Evolution of Cooperation in Stochastic Games," *Nature*, 559(7713), pp. 246–249. Available at: https://doi.org/10.1038/s41586-018-0277-x.

Hobbes, T. (1996) *Leviathan*. Rev. student ed. Edited by R. Tuck. Cambridge: Cambridge University Press.

Locke, J. (1988) *Locke: Two Treatises of Government Student Edition*. Cambridge: Cambridge University Press.

Malthouse, E., Pilgrim, C., Sgroi, D., and Hills, T.T. (2023) "When Fairness is Not Enough: The Disproportionate Contributions of the Poor in a Collective Action Problem." *Journal of Experimental Psychology: General*. Advance online publication. https://doi.org/10.1037/xge0001455

Ostrom, E. (1986) "An Agenda for the Study of Institutions," *Public Choice*, 48(1), pp. 3–25. Available at: https://doi.org/10.1007/BF00239556.

Ostrom, E. (1990) *Governing the Commons: The Evolution of Institutions for Collective Action*. Cambridge: Cambridge University Press.

Ostrom, E. (1998) "A Behavioral Approach to the Rational Choice Theory of Collective Action: Presidential Address, American Political Science Association, 1997," *The American Political Science Review*, 92(1), pp. 1–22. Available at: https://doi.org/10.2307/2585925.

Ostrom, Elinor (2000) "Collective Action and the Evolution of Social Norms," *Journal of Economic Perspectives*, 14(3), pp. 137–158. Available at: https://doi.org/10.1257/jep.14.3.137.

Ostrom, E. (2000) "Collective Action and the Evolution of Social Norms," *Journal of Economic Perspectives*, 14, pp. 137–158.

Ostrom, E. (2005) *Understanding Institutional Diversity*. Princeton, NJ: Princeton University Press.

Ostrom, E. (2007) "Collective Action Theory," in C. Boix and S. C. Stokes (eds.) *The Oxford Handbook of Comparative Politics*. New York: Oxford University Press, pp. 186–210.

Ostrom, E. (2010a) "Analyzing Collective Action," *Agricultural Economics*, 41, pp. 155–166.

Ostrom, E. (2010b) "Beyond Markets and States: Polycentric Governance of Complex Economic Systems. Prize Lecture, December 8, 2009," *American Economic Review*, 100(3), pp. 641–672.

Ostrom, E., Ingram, G.K. and Hong, Y.-H. (2009) "Design Principles of Robust Property Rights Institutions: What Have We Learned?" in *Property Rights and Land Policies*. Cambridge, MA: Lincoln Institute of Land Policy. Available at: https://www.lincolninst.edu/pubs/2076_Design-Principles-of-Robust-Property-Rights-Institutions-What-Have-We-Learned.

Ostrom, V., Tiebout, C.M. and Warren, R. (1961) "The Organization of Government in Metropolitan Areas: A Theoretical Inquiry," *American Political Science Review*, 55(4), pp. 831–842. Available at: https://doi.org/10.1017/S0003055400125973.

Platteau, J.-P. (2000) *Institutions, Social Norms, and Economic Development*. Boca Raton, FL: Psychology Press.

Poteete, A.R., Janssen, M. and Ostrom, E. (2010) *Working Together: Collective Action, the Commons, and Multiple Methods in Practice*. Princeton, NJ: Princeton University Press.

Rawls, J. (1958) "Justice as Fairness," *The Philosophical Review*, 67(2), pp. 164–194. Available at: https://doi.org/10.2307/2182612.

Rawls, J. (2005) *Political Liberalism: Expanded Edition*. New York, NY: Columbia University Press.

Rawls, J. (2008) *Lectures on the History of Political Philosophy*. Cambridge, MA: Belknap Press.

Rousseau, J.-J. (1968) *The Social Contract*. London, England: Penguin.

Scanlon, T.M. (1982) "Contractualism and Utilitarianism," in A. Sen and B. Williams (eds.) *Utilitarianism and Beyond*. Cambridge: Cambridge University Press, pp. 103–128. Available at: https://doi.org/10.1017/CBO9780511611964.007.

Scanlon, T.M. (2000) *What We Owe to Each Other*. Revised edition. Cambridge, MA: Belknap Press: An Imprint of Harvard University Press.

Sen, A.K. (2009) *The Idea of Justice*. Cambridge, MA: Belknap Press of Harvard University Press.

Sigmund, K. (2012) "Moral Assessment in Indirect Reciprocity," *Journal of Theoretical Biology*, 299(5), pp. 25–30. Available at: https://doi.org/10.1016/j.jtbi.2011.03.024.

Skyrms, B. (2004) *The Stag Hunt and the Evolution of Social Structure*. Cambridge, UK: Cambridge University Press.

Skyrms, B. (2014) *Social Dynamics*. Oxford, UK: Oxford University Press.

Southwood, N. (2014) *Contractualism and the Foundations of Morality*. Reprint edition. Oxford: Oxford University Press.

Thaler, R.H. and Sunstein, C.R. (2008) *Nudge: Improving Decisions about Health, Wealth, and Happiness*. New Haven, CT: Yale University Press.

Thiel, A. and Moser, C. (2019) "Foundational Aspects of Polycentric Governance: Overarching Rules, Social-Problem Characteristics, and Heterogeneity," in A. Thiel, D.E. Garrick, and W.A. Blomquist (eds.) *Governing Complexity: Analyzing and Applying Polycentricity*. Cambridge: Cambridge University Press, pp. 65–90. Available at: https://doi.org/10.1017/9781108325721.004.

Tricomi, E. *et al.* (2010) "Neural Evidence for Inequality-Averse Social Preferences," *Nature*, 463(7284), pp. 1089–1091. Available at: https://doi.org/10.1038/nature08785.

Williamson, O.E. (1975) *Markets and Hierarchies, Analysis and Antitrust Implications: A Study in the Economics of Internal Organization*. New York: Free Press.

Chapter 5

Adhikari, A. (2014) *The Bullet and the Ballot Box: The Story of Nepal's Maoist Revolution*. New York: Verso.

Baland, J.-M. and Platteau, J.-P. (1996) *Halting Degradation of Natural Resources: Is There a Role for Rural Communities?* Rome, Italy: Food & Agriculture Org.

Banerjee, A., Mookherjee, D., Munshi, K., and Ray, D. (2001) "Inequality, Control Rights, and Rent Seeking: Sugar Cooperatives in Maharashtra," *Journal of Political Economy*, 109(1), pp. 138–190. Available at: https://doi.org/10.1086/318600.

Bardhan, P. and Mookherjee, D. (2020) "Clientelistic Politics and Economic Development: An Overview," in Jean-Marie Baland, François Bourguignon, Jean-Philippe Platteau, and Thierry Verdier (eds.) *The Handbook of Economic Development and Institutions*. Princeton, NJ: Princeton University Press, pp. 84–102. Available at: https://doi.org/10.1515/9780691192017-004.

Benjamin, P., Lam, W.F. and Ostrom, E. (1994) *Institutions, Incentives, and Irrigation in Nepal*. Washington, D.C.: USAID.

Coman, K. (1911) "Some Unsettled Problems of Irrigation," *The American Economic Review*, 1(1), pp. 1–19.

Evans, P. (2004) "Development as Institutional Change: The Pitfalls of Monocropping and the Potentials of Deliberation," *Studies in Comparative International Development*, 38(4), pp. 30–52. Available at: https://doi.org/10.1007/BF02686327.

Forester, J. (1999) *The Deliberative Practitioner: Encouraging Participatory Planning Processes*. Cambridge, MA: MIT Press.

Frey, U.J., Villamayor-Tomas, S. and Theesfeld, I. (2016) "A Continuum of Governance Regimes: A New Perspective on Co-Management in Irrigation Systems," *Environmental Science & Policy*, 66(C), pp. 73–81.

IWMI (1989) *Report on Training Cum Observation on Rapid Appraisal Methods and Water Users Association Activities*. International Irrigation Management Institute. Available at: https://cgspace.cgiar.org/handle/10568/36357.

Knight, J. (1992) *Institutions and Social Conflict*. Cambridge: Cambridge University Press.

Kosfeld, M. and Rustagi, D. (2015) "Leader Punishment and Cooperation in Groups: Experimental Field Evidence from Commons Management in Ethiopia," *American Economic Review*, 105(2), pp. 747–783. Available at: https://doi.org/10.1257/aer.20120700.

Lam, W.F. (1998) *Governing Irrigation Systems in Nepal: Institutions, Infrastructure, and Collective Action*. Oakland, CA: ICS Press.

Lipsky, M. (2010) *Street-Level Bureaucracy: Dilemmas of the Individual in Public Services*. New York: Russell Sage Foundation.

Magar, J.B.P. (2004) "Forced Indoctrination—Nepali Times," *The Nepali Times*, 17 September. Available at: http://archive.nepalitimes.com/news.php?id=2229.

Mansuri, G. and Rao, V. (2012) *Localizing Development: Does Participation Work?* World Bank Publications.

Martin, E.D. and Yoder, R. (1987) "Organizational Structure for Resource Mobilization in Hill Irrigation Systems," in *Irrigation Management in Nepal: Research Papers from a National Seminar*. *National Seminar on Irrigation Management in Nepal (1988)*, Kathmandu Nepal: International Irrigation Management Institute, pp. 85–102.

Martin, E.D. and Yoder, R. (1988) "A Comparative Description of Two Farmer-Managed Irrigation Systems in Nepal," *Irrigation and Drainage Systems*, 2(2), pp. 147–172. Available at: https://doi.org/10.1007/BF01102924.

Martin, E.G. and Yoder, R. (1983) "The Chherlung Thulo Kulo: A Case Study of a Farmer-Managed Irrigation System," in *Water Management in Nepal: Proceedings of the Seminar on Water Management Issues, July 31–Aug 2, 1983*. Kathmandu, Nepal: Ministry of Agriculture, pp. 203–217.

Mookherjee, D. (2015) "Political Decentralization," *Annual Review of Economics*, 7(1), pp. 231–249. Available at: https://doi.org/10.1146/annurev-economics-080614-115527.

Ostrom, E. (1990) *Governing the Commons: The Evolution of Institutions for Collective Action*. Cambridge: Cambridge University Press.

Ostrom, E. (2010) "Beyond Markets and States: Polycentric Governance of Complex Economic Systems. Prize Lecture, December 8, 2009," *American Economic Review*, 100(3), pp. 641–72.

Ostrom, E. et al. (2011) *Improving Irrigation in Asia: Sustainable Performance of an Innovative Intervention in Nepal*. Northampton, MA: Edward Elgar Pub.

Ostrom, E., Ingram, G.K. and Hong, Y.-H. (2009) "Design Principles of Robust Property Rights Institutions: What Have We Learned?," in Gregory K. Ingram and Yu-Hung Hong (eds.) *Property Rights and Land Policies*. Cambridge, MA: Lincoln Institute of Land Policy. Available at: https://www.lincolninst.edu/pubs/2076_Design-Principles-of-Robust-Property-Rights-Institutions-What-Have-We-Learned.

Poteete, A.R., Janssen, M. and Ostrom, E. (2010) *Working Together: Collective Action, the Commons, and Multiple Methods in Practice*. Princeton, NJ: Princeton University Press.

Poteete, A.R. and Ostrom, E. (2004) "Heterogeneity, Group Size and Collective Action: The Role of Institutions in Forest Management," *Development and Change*, 35(3), pp. 435–461. Available at: https://doi.org/10.1111/j.1467-7660.2004.00360.x.

Pradhan, P. (1989) *Patterns of Irrigation Organization in Nepal: A Comparative Study of 21 Farmer-Managed Irrigation Systems*. Colombo, Sri Lanka: International Irrigation Management Institute (Country paper—Nepal, no. 1).

Pradhan, U. (1990) *Property Rights and State Intervention in Hill Irrigation Systems in Nepal*. Ithaca, NY: Cornell University Press. Available at: http://hdl.handle.net/10535/5584.

Regmi, M.C. (1976) *Landownership in Nepal*. Berkeley, CA: University of California Press. Available at: https://www.degruyter.com/document/doi/10.1525/9780520331839/html.

Shivakoti, G. (2002) *Improving Irrigation Governance and Management in Nepal*. Oakland, CA: ICS Press.

Shklar, J.N. (1990) *The Faces of Injustice, The Faces of Injustice*. New Haven, CT: Yale University Press. Available at: https://www.degruyter.com/document/doi/10.12987/9780300161496/html.

Somanathan, E. (2020) "Institutions, the Environment, and Development," in Jean-Marie Baland, François Bourguignon, Jean-Philippe Platteau, and Thierry Verdier (eds.) *The Handbook Of*

Economic Development and Institutions. Princeton, NJ: Princeton University Press, pp. 733–750. Available at: https://doi.org/10.1515/9780691192017-022.

Tang, S.Y. (1991) "Institutional Arrangements and the Management of Common-Pool Resources," *Public Administration Review*, 51(1), pp. 42–51. Available at: https://doi.org/10.2307/976635.

Tendler, J. (1997) *Good Government in the Tropics.* Baltimore: Johns Hopkins University Press.

Uphoff, N.T. (1992) *Learning from Gal Oya: Possibilities for Participatory Development and Post-Newtonian Social Science.* Ithaca, NY: Cornell University Press.

Chapter 6

Ambedkar, B.R. (2014) *Annihilation of Caste: The Annotated Critical Edition.* London: Verso Books.

Axelrod, R.M. (2006) *The Evolution of Cooperation.* Rev. ed. New York: Basic Books.

Basu, A., Sarkar-Roy, N. and Majumder, P.P. (2016) "Genomic Reconstruction of the History of Extant Populations of India Reveals Five Distinct Ancestral Components and a Complex Structure," *Proceedings of the National Academy of Sciences*, 113(6), pp. 1594–1599. Available at: https://doi.org/10.1073/pnas.1513197113.

Benkler, Y. (2014) "Between Spanish Huertas and the Open Road: A Tale of Two Commons," in Brett M. Frischmann, Michael J. Madison, and Katherine J. Strandburg (eds.) *Governing Knowledge Commons.* New York: Oxford University Press, pp. 69–98.

Boix, C., Stokes, S.C. and Bates, R.H. (eds) (2009) "From Case Studies to Social Science: A Strategy for Political Research," in *The Oxford Handbook of Comparative Politics.* Oxford: Oxford University Press, pp. 172–185.

Bowles, S. (2008) "Policies Designed for Self-Interested Citizens May Undermine 'The Moral Sentiments': Evidence from Economic Experiments," *Science*, 320(5883), pp. 1605–1609. Available at: https://doi.org/10.1126/science.1152110.

Brander, J.A. and Taylor, M.S. (1998) "The Simple Economics of Easter Island: A Ricardo-Malthus Model of Renewable Resource Use," *The American Economic Review*, 88(1), pp. 119–138.

Cole, D.H. (2012) *Property in Land and Other Resources.* Cambridge, MA: Lincoln Institute of Land Policy.

Coman, K. (1911) "Some Unsettled Problems of Irrigation," *The American Economic Review*, 1(1), pp. 1–19.

Diamond, J.M. (2005) *Collapse: How Societies Choose to Fail Or Succeed.* New York: Penguin.

English, R. and Schweik, C.M. (2007) "Identifying Success and Tragedy of FLOSS Commons: A Preliminary Classification of Sourceforge.net Projects," in *First International Workshop on Emerging Trends in FLOSS Research and Development, 2007. FLOSS '07*, pp. 11–11. Available at: https://doi.org/10.1109/FLOSS.2007.9.

Evans, P. (2004) "Development as Institutional Change: The Pitfalls of Monocropping and the Potentials of Deliberation," *Studies in Comparative International Development*, 38(4), pp. 30–52. Available at: https://doi.org/10.1007/BF02686327.

Forester, J. (1999) *The Deliberative Practitioner: Encouraging Participatory Planning Processes.* Cambridge, MA: MIT Press.

Frey, U.J., Rusch, H. (2014) "Modeling Ecological Success of Common Pool Resource Systems Using Large Datasets," *World Development*, 59, pp. 93–103.

Frey, U.J., Villamayor-Tomas, S. and Theesfeld, I. (2016) "A Continuum of Governance Regimes: A New Perspective on Co-Management in Irrigation Systems," *Environmental Science & Policy*, 66(C), pp. 73–81.

Frischmann, B.M., Madison, M.J. and Strandburg, K.J. (2014) *Governing Knowledge Commons.* Oxford: Oxford University Press.

Gardner, R., Walker, J. and Ostrom, E. (1994) *Rules, Games, and Common-Pool Resources.* Ann Arbor, MI: University of Michigan Press.

Gintis, H. and Bowles, S. (2011) *A Cooperative Species: Human Reciprocity and Its Evolution.* Princeton, NJ: Princeton University Press.

Grubb, B. (2014) "Man Who Introduced Serious 'Heartbleed' security flaw denies he inserted it deliberately," *The Sydney Morning Herald.* Available at: https://www.smh.com.au/technol

ogy/man-who-introduced-serious-heartbleed-security-flaw-denies-he-inserted-it-deliberat ely-20140410-zqta1.html.

Harrison, R. and Herr, T. (2016) *Cyber Insecurity: Navigating the Perils of the Next Information Age.* Lanham, MD: Rowman & Littlefield.

Hilbe, C. et al. (2018) "Evolution of Cooperation in Stochastic Games," *Nature*, 559(7713), pp. 246–249. Available at: https://doi.org/10.1038/s41586-018-0277-x.

Islam, S. and Susskind, L. (2013) *Water Diplomacy: A Negotiated Approach to Managing Complex Water Networks.* New York, NY: Routledge.

Joshi, N.N. et al. (2000) "Institutional Opportunities and Constraints in the Performance of Farmer-Managed Irrigation Systems in Nepal," *Asia-Pacific Journal of Rural Development*, 10(2), pp. 67–92.

Kollock, P. (1998) "Social Dilemmas: The Anatomy of Cooperation," *Annual Review of Sociology*, 24(1), pp. 183–214. Available at: https://doi.org/10.1146/annurev.soc.24.1.183.

Lam, W.F. (1998) *Governing Irrigation Systems in Nepal: Institutions, Infrastructure, and Collective Action.* Oakland, CA: ICS Press.

Mansbridge, J. (2014) "The Role of the State in Governing the Commons," *Environmental Science & Policy*, 36, pp. 8–10. Available at: https://doi.org/10.1016/j.envsci.2013.07.006.

Meinzen-Dick, R. (2007) "Beyond Panaceas in Water Institutions," *Proceedings of the National Academy of Sciences of the United States of America*, 104(39), pp. 15200–15205. Available at: https://doi.org/10.1073/pnas.0702296104.

Morell, M.F. (2014) "Governance of Online Creation Communities for the Building of Digital Commons: Viewed through the Framework of Institutional Analysis and Development," in B.M. Frischmann, M.J. Madison, and K.J. Strandburg (eds.) *Governing Knowledge Commons.* Oxford: Oxford University Press, pp. 281–312.

Netcraft (2014) "Half a Million Widely Trusted Websites Vulnerable to Heartbleed Bug," *Netcraft News.* Available at: https://news.netcraft.com/archives/2014/04/08/half-a-million-wid ely-trusted-websites-vulnerable-to-heartbleed-bug.html.

Ostrom, E. (1990) *Governing the Commons: The Evolution of Institutions for Collective Action.* New York: Cambridge University Press.

Ostrom, E. (2005) *Understanding Institutional Diversity.* Princeton, NJ: Princeton University Press.

Ostrom, E. (2010) "Beyond Markets and States: Polycentric Governance of Complex Economic Systems. Prize Lecture, December 8, 2009," *American Economic Review*, 100(3), pp. 641–72.

Ostrom, E. and Cole, D.H. (2010) *The Variety of Property Systems and Rights in Natural Resources: An Introduction.* Cambridge, MA: Lincoln Land Institute of Policy.

Perlroth, N. (2014) "Heartbleed Highlights a Contradiction in the Web," *The New York Times*, April 19. Available at: https://www.nytimes.com/2014/04/19/technology/heartbleed-hig hlights-a-contradiction-in-the-web.html.

Poteete, A.R., Janssen, M. and Ostrom, E. (2010) *Working Together: Collective Action, the Commons, and Multiple Methods in Practice.* Princeton, NJ: Princeton University Press.

Schneier, B. (2014) "Heartbleed," *Schneier on Security*, April 9. Available at: https://www.schneier. com/blog/archives/2014/04/heartbleed.html.

Schweik, C.M. and English, R.C. (2012) *Internet Success: A Study of Open-Source Software Commons.* Cambridge, MA: MIT Press.

Sen, A.K. (1977) "Rational Fools: A Critique of the Behavioral Foundations of Economic Theory," *Philosophy & Public Affairs*, 6(4), pp. 317–344.

Vaid, D. (2014) "Caste in Contemporary India: Flexibility and Persistence," *Annual Review of Sociology*, 40(1), pp. 391–410. Available at: https://doi.org/10.1146/annurev-soc-071913-043303.

Vyas, S., Hathi, P. and Gupta, A. (2022) "Social Disadvantage, Economic Inequality, and Life Expectancy in Nine Indian States," *Proceedings of the National Academy of Sciences*, 119(10), p. e2109226119. Available at: https://doi.org/10.1073/pnas.2109226119.

Williamson, O.E. (2000) "The New Institutional Economics: Taking Stock, Looking Ahead," *Journal of Economic Literature*, 38(3), pp. 595–613. Available at: https://doi.org/10.1257/jel.38.3.595.

INDEX